Water Management in Medieval India

मध्यकालीन भारत में जल प्रबंधन

Water Management in Medieval India

मध्यकालीन भारत में जल प्रबंधन

Editor

Dr. Vinay Shrivastava

Originals

(an imprint of Low Price Publications)

Delhi

First Published 2012

ISBN 13: 978-81-8454-113-7
ISBN 10: 81-8454-113-9

Published by

Originals

(an imprint of Low Price Publications)
A-6, Second Floor, Nimri Commercial Centre,
Ashok Vihar Phase-IV, Delhi 110052 (INDIA)
tel.: +91.11.27302453 fax.: +91.11.4706 1936
e-mail: info@Lppindia.com url: www.Lppindia.com

Printed at
D K Fine Art Press Private Limited
Delhi

Contents

Editor's Note

The Water resources and Water Management has played an important role for the development of human civilization on the earth. Water is the main basis for development since antiquity. These are some basic and important sources of Water Management & Water Works for the study of Water Works in different regions of India.

The alternative absence and abundance of water is crucial to Indian life, and the stepwells and stepped ponds generated by the use water are especially imaginative. These two major buildings types have quite different qualities. As distinctive these buildings are they are also among the least known or visited monuments in India. Many elaborate Water Works are in small towns and villages far from any international tourist destination. They can be found with in palace compounds and religious establishments, although their use is not limited to one religious group or any single social level; neither are they meant for individual pleasure. They are for communal use-in India, people gather together around water.

Stepped ponds are most often used for ritual bathing related to temple worship or mosque ceremonies, while stepwells-important as sources for the water needed in daily life provided pleasurable retreats from the heart and dust of the subcontinent. They are among the greatest examples of ecologically sensitive architecture in any country. No matter how pleasurable the buildings are, it is the function of their space that is most important. The study of these structures therefore involves discussions of social, religious, historical and architectural contexts.

For twelve hundred years stepwells and step ponds-elaborate water buildings with stairs-have been integral to life in western India. These underground buildings, usually from three to nine stories deep, became community centers, as passages into the subterranean; they were invested with religious meanings. An estimated three thousands of them were built between the seventh and the mid nineteenth centuries A.D.

while various water structures such as tanks, cisterns, paved stairways along rivers(Ghats) and cylindrical wells are found elsewhere in India, stepwells and step ponds are indigenous to the semi-arid region of Gujarat and Rajasthan. These buildings are the visible architecture that mark entry to the invisible landscape of underground water throughout the region, providing life and sustenance to towns and villages. The well has thus determined life to an extraordinary degree, and the link between underground water and surface life is as rich, colourful, and textured as India itself.

Stepwells and stepped ponds also had secular uses, they survived the long and turbulent transition to Muslim rule, from the early eight century to the eleventh, relatively unharmed. The Muslims destroyed some temples and shrines-though not the number with which they are blamed-but began to their beloved hamams, or bath houses, as sites for ceremony and pleasure. The Muslims modified Hindu construction methods and architecture and stepwell ornament changed to reflect Islam's social mores and aesthetic sensibilities. The stepwell show transformed, may be the most elegant and graceful example of architecture ever built in western India. In Rajasthan the Mughals innovative use of water buildings as pleasure quarters-enlivened with textiles, flowers, lights and perfumes-spread to stepped ponds by the sixteenth century. And in 1800s the merchants of Shekhawati, a part of Rajasthan north to Jaipur, produced stunning painted wells. India's use of passive water collecting systems, which was born in ancient times and continued unbroken through the middle ages, changed under British rule in the nineteenth century; the British had both a distance for water buildings as water sources and a love of them as architecture. The book concludes with a discussion of India's attitude towards water, stepwells and preservation during medieval period. The vigor, spontaneity and imagination of Indian life continue to reinvent these disintegrating buildings as sacred and aesthetically powerful places.

India is sorely lacking in medieval buildings owing to a combination of social and structural factors, water buildings-while never the most prominent structures in their time -may be the most numerous buildings of the medieval period to survive. In this they provide a welcome measuring line for architecture and are not just survivors, but superior achievements of Indian architecture, with their own voice.

In the arid region of western India, nothing is more sacred than water-indeed, it defines the lives, myths and rituals of its people. Preserving the water of the monsoons has been the Preserving the water of the monsoons has been the challenge of five hundred years, and the magnificent stone cisterns known as stepwells or stepped ponds have been the vessels for capturing and conserving the areas precious rains. There lattice like walls, carved columns, decorated towers, and intricate sculpture call out their exceptional architecture, while their very presence tells much about the regions ecology and history. From the fifth to nineteenth century, stepwells were an integral part of western Indian communities as sites for drinking, washing, and bathing, as well as for colourful festivals and sacred rituals.

The rulers of Medieval Malwa , Rajasthan, Gujarat and other states of India have take care of their states very well. They have independent and powerful rulers. Their ideals were based on the ritual policies and religious granthas, such as Vedas, Puranas, Manusmriti, Sukraniti, Arthashastra, etc. are the special noticed. Arthashastra has clearly mentioned about the internal and foreign policies of the state and the duties of the king towards the people of the state and Water Management. Sukraniti has clearly mentioned that the King has taken care of Water Management and availabilities of Water bodies in his capital and state. The development of the state, Agriculture and people life has been depended on the water resources. The Mandan has accepted and recognized that the construction of water resources is very pious and noble work of Punyavans like Vishnu Dharmottar. He said that the water has protected the life of the animals and human beings. It has clearly mentioned that the king and the people of the state have to construct the water bodies and water resources for the social welfare of the society.

Originally, the religious feelings has inspired for the construction of the process of water resources, on the other hand the water resources have compulsorily required in the state for drinking water, agriculture irrigation and the economic development. Therefore, in the medieval period many rulers of Malwa, Rajasthan and Gujarat have constructed the number of water resources in many places. They have taken keen interest for the development of water resources in their areas. The rulers of Malwa, Rajasthan and Gujarat have inspired to their Jagirdars, Samantas and Rayyats to construct the wells, stepwells, kup, tanks and reservoirs in their region for the economic development of the state.

In Medieval Malwa the Muslim rulers have also made the wonderful efforts for the Water Management. The residue of extensive and scientific water resources like huge bawdies, reservoirs, cisterns etc. is present in different places of Malwa. According to Vakiyat-E-Mushtaqi, Nasir-Ud-Din Khilji has constructed the palaces, Hauz and Ahukhana in different places of Malwa. In Kaliyadeh Palace Ujjain, the beautiful reservoirs were constructed with excellent engineering and architect.

In the regional folk songs of central &western India the construction of stepwells were supposed to religious work. The people who have constructed the stepwells and wells they were appreciated in the society. Many virads (folk songs) have written in the local language for their appreciation, for example-Kan ne Khudayo kuon, un kan ne bandhai bawdi. This type of virads were used to sing in the villages by the people.

In Central India, specially Malwa, there are two main techniques of rain water harvesting storage of rain water on surface for further use. Recharge to ground water the storage of rain water on surface is a traditional techniques, and structures used were under-ground tanks, ponds, check, dams, weirs etc. rooftop collection of rain water diversion and collection of run off into dry tanks. Artificial recharge is the process by which the ground water reservoir is augmented at a rate exceeding that under natural conditions of replenishment. Sustainability of drinking water sources has become one of the major issues of army and royal drinking water supply sector, since rain water harvesting and artificial recharge can play a major role in providing sustainability to drinking water sources.

An attempt has been made in this book to discuss some aspects of tools and techniques and the structure of different water bodies and its role in progress of human life. Water Management Techniques, Tools and construction of water buildings etc. gave impetus to irrigation development in Malwa and other parts of India. The book is an outcome of the ideas exchanged at the National Research Seminar on History. The topic of the seminar was –**Water Management in Medieval India and** its Historical importance; organized by the Department of History, S.V. Govt. Post Graduate College, Neemuch (M.P.), with the financial support from U.G.C., C.R.O. Bhopal. Water Management in medieval India traces on their current use, preservation, and place in Indian communities the fascinating history of stepwells and other water bodies from their Hindu Origins to their second flowering Muslim rule and eventual decline. It also reflects on their current use, preservation, and place in Indian communities.

Dr. Vinay Shrivastava
Editor

Tradition and Technology of Step-Wells: Special reference to Udaipur City

K.P. Singh and Ritu Sharma

Stepwells are generally typical of regions which extremely hot, dry and long lasting summers where ground water is often the only available source of water during the hot seasons (Hegewald 2002: 167.)

Tradition and technology of constructing wells as a source of fresh water have been in use in the Indian sub-continent from the Harappan times, which is from 2500 BCE onwards (Mate 1998: 99). Dholavira, an important site of Indus valley civilization have several reservoirs to collect rain water; similar evidences come from Mohenjodaro and Harappa (Joshi, J. P. 2008: 121), (Bhadani and Singh 2007). The tradition of stepwell architecture is indigenous to India, but was adopted and refined by the Muslim rulers who constructed stepwell in north-western India, particularly during the 14th and 15th century. Most of the stepwells date from a period between the 12th and the 17th century (Hegewald 2002: 156).

Perhaps the most amazing aspect of traditional water management system is its longevity. Many *naulas, bawaris* and *kunds* still in use are hundreds of years old. Clearly the traditional water management system has a high degree of sustainability. Urban water supply was a comparatively late phenomenon. Cities of ancient India were generally located along the banks of perennial rivers, natural springs, or depressions where water gets accumulated during the monsoon (Singh and Kharakwal 2010). In Mewar, the Udai sagar dyke located 10 km east of the city of Udaipur, was constructed in 1550 CE by Maharana Udai Singh. Later two dams Jana Sagar or Bari Talab (8 km north of Udaipur) and Rajsamand (located 60 km north of Udaipur) were built in 1676 and 1678 CE by Maharana Raj Singh. Jai Samand or Debar Lake (one of the largest dams) was constructed between 1685-87 CE by Maharana Jai Singh, so the period between 1550 CE to 1680 CE should be characterized as the golden period in the history of Mewar in this context. Most of the stepwells of Udaipur are also built in the same period. For this hydraulic engineering in Mewar during this period, Maharan Raj Singh is also known as 'Hydraulic Man'.

The concept of stepwells is known from inscriptions to date back as far as 423 AD, and it may even have its genesis from the time of Indus Valley civilization. However, most stepwells appear to have flourished during the 8th to 18th centuries. They were an essential rain harvesting, groundwater recharge and storage system. Stepwells also express an aesthetic sense of Indian and are examples of what water, art and architecture meant for simple folk. The stepwells of Rajasthan have different decorative designs and symbolize the refined taste of the people of the time. They also reflect the deep rooted religious attachment and faith in this type of water system (Misra 2009: 21).

The stepwell is an unique construction of a well with steps either on one side, two, three or on all the four sides leading to the water surface (Savalia 2009: 88). These steps provide direct access to people who descend the steps to reach the water of the well (Hegwald 2002: 155). Single-faced stepwell is also known as Nanda *Baori,* two-faced is Bhadra *Baori*, three-faced is Jaya *Baori* (Rohit Kumar 2008: 399) and four-faced is known as Vijaya *Baori* (Hegwald 2002: 160). Stepped construction of a well is known as *Vapi* (in Sanskrit) (Savlia 2009: 88) and *Vapya* (Prasad 1998: 71). There are at least fifteen different names for stepwells. In Gujarat, they are commonly known as *Vav* or *Bav*, where as in Rajasthan they are usually known as *Baori* or *Kund* (Cox 2008: 14). The main function of stepwells is to supply water, but because stepwells frequently have galleries built along the long corridor of steps and around the storage basins, integrating stone benches with sloping backrests into their design, they are also used as cool retreats from the summer heat by villagers and travellers (Hegwald 2002: 155). Moreover in Rajasthan and Gujarat the stepwell was converted into an architectural monument of great beauty. It combined the utilitarian aspect with pleasure resort (Mate 1998: 102).

Some famous and unique stepwells of Udaipur are Trimukhi *Baori*, Bedvas *ki Baori*, Sarvrituvilas *ki Baori*, Sunderbav, Bhuvana *ki Baori* and Naulakha *Baori*. It is noteworthy that some stepwells have inscriptions which throw light on the technical aspects as well as on the management and construction of stepwells. Rulers, Jagirdars, Officers and even common man build them.

Sarvrituvilas *ki Baori* – Rajprasasti tells us that in the south east of Udaipur both this stepwell and Sarvrituvilas palace were built by Maharana Raj Singh in 17th century (Shyamaldas. 1986: 381-83). This stepwell was a source of water supply for the city.

Bedvas *ki Baori* – It was built in village Bedvas, 8 km from Udaipur. Inscription of this stepwell tells that the stepwell was built by Fateh Chand Bhatnagar, a minister of Maharana Raj Singh, on 26 April 1669 CE. Bedvas *ki Baori* is also known as Nanda *Baori* due to its single-face (Ojha 2008: 122).

Naulakha *Baori* – This stepwell was built in 1667 CE at Gulab bagh. According to its name number 9 is important in its construction. On the flight of nine steps a small corridor is there. Both sides of steps have space for 9 icons in which sculptures of Ganesh and Bhairav made up of white marble are situated (Menariya 1973: sarg-13, shalok-28-30).

Trimukhi *Baori* – This stepwell is located at a distance of 9 km to the city of Udaipur. Inscription of this stepwell tells us that this stepwell was built by Ramrasde, queen of Maharana Raj Singh, on January 1676 CE at Debari village (Vyas 1988: 223). This stepwell has steps on three sides and on fourth side a pillar *Mandap.* There is also space of icons on both sides of steps (Shrimali, 2000). The construction work was completed under the supervision of Lal Porvad and Dhaibhai Satidas. The main sculptor was Nathu Gaur. Rs. 24000 spent on its construction (Ranawat 2000: 93). This three-faced stepwell is also known as Jaya *Baori*.

Debari *Baori* – This stepwell is situated on medieval period outer (eastern) fortification wall of Udaipur city. This is built by Maharana Raj Singh in 1659 CE. (Ranawat 2000: 142)

Karnvav – In 17th century, Karnvav was built by Maharana Karan singh near Sarvrituvilas (Shyamaldas 1986: 443).

Sunderbav – This stepwell was built by Khavasan Sunder in 1616 CE. Sunderbav is located in the village Paida at a distance of 4 km from Udaipur (Shyamaldas 1986: 436). This stepwell is an unique example of stepwell architecture. On the flight of 10 steps a small pavilion come and after 20 step, have a roofed corridor with two marble arches on decorated pillars. Shiv temple called Sandeshwar Mahadev is also built near this stepwell (Purohit 1930: 108).

Bhuwana *ki Baori* – Maharana Raj Singh donate some land in village Bhuwana, to Govindram Vyas (son of Vyas Balbhadra) when the construction of Sunderbav was completed. On this land Varatan Lali

Brahmani (mother of Govind Ram) built a stepwell named Bhuwana *ki Baori*. This stepwell is also known as Lali Brahmani *ki Baori* (Shyamaldas 1986: 436, 578). Inscription of site has indication of all information.

Gujarat Dhai-bhai Rupa built a stepwell, temple of Rupnarayanji, a small garden and a *sarai* on February 5, 1762. The construction of another stepwell was started on April 3, 1767 in the village Saleda by Champubai (mother-in-law of Dhai bhai). The construction work was completed on May 14, 1769 with a cost of Rs. 7000 (Shyamaldas 1986: 73).

These stepwell were useful for storing water, so that it could be utilized in summer when the water scarcity was very common. The stepwell was a combination of a utilitarian device and a pleasure resort as they provided water and cool resting places to travellers and their animals. Stepwell are one of the best examples of vernacular architecture of water bodies. The construction of these stepwells also reflect a number of influences natural geographical features, types of soil, rainfall, ground water level, distinctive style of the respective regions, nature of the patronage under which they were commissioned and their religious significance.

Due to growing urbanization, pollution and life threatening health hazards, the state authorities introduced a system of tap water supply and stepwell have become victim of disuse and disintegration (Singh, K.P. 2010). Stepwell have lost their inherent function of water supply and storage. They are in broken down condition due to negligence. We cannot ignore the fact that they are the mute witness of our ancient tradition of stepwell building. With proper repair and care stepwell can be included in the places of tourist attraction of Udaipur.

Conclusion – This is, in short, the history of our glorious stepwell tradition of water harvesting by the village community, individuals and erstwhile state. Harvesting of water and its management was an integral part of our native culture and community life. But at present the Stepwells have lost their inherent function of water supply and storage. They are in broken down condition due to negligence. We cannot ignore the fact that they are the mute witness of our ancient tradition of stepwell building. With proper repair and care stepwell can be included in the places of tourist attraction of Udaipur. We should protect and expend the tradition and technology of this old water harvesting which is very much beneficial for all.

Bibliography

Bhadani, B. L. and K. P. Singh 2007. *History of Water Management in India from 1000 BCE to 1800 CE*. Deccan College, Pune. (Meeting on History of Science and Technology).

Cox, Richard 2008. *'Stepwell' subterranean Architecture, Stepwells in Western India*. Torfaen: Lantarnam qranye Arts Centre.

Hegewald, Julia. A. B. 2002. *Water Architecture in South Asia: A Study of types, Development and Meaning*. Leiden: Koninklijke Bri l nv.

Joshi, J. P. 2007. *Harappan Technology*. New Delhi: Infinity Foundation and Rupa Publication.

Mate, M. S. 1998. *Water Management and Hydraulic Technology in India (1500 BC to 1800 BC)*. Delhi: B. R. Publishing corp.

Menariya, Motilal 1973. *Rajprasasthi Mahakavyam*. Udaipur: Rajasthan Vidhyapeeth.

Misra, S. K. 2009. Power of Creativity. In *special Issue: Heritage of Water Management*. (Eds. Mao Chiba and Bhanu Neupane). Noida/ New Delhi: L. B. associates (Pvt.) Ltd and UNESCO-New Delhi team.

Ojha, Priyadarshi 2008. *A study of water management in Mewar in 17th & 18th century*. (Ph.D. thesis). Udaipur: MLSU.

Prasad, E. V. R. 1997-98. Ancient Indian Hydrology in Modern Context. In *Sri Ventateswar University Oriental Journal*. Vol. 30-31 : 69-80.

Purohit, Devnath 1930. *Udaipur Darshan*. Udaipur.

Ranawat, Ishwar Singh 2000. *A critical study of water resources of Mewar*. (Ph. D. thesis). Udaipur: MLSU.

Savalia, Ramjibhai 2009. *Steps of Indology*. Ahmedabad: B.N. Institute of Learning & Research.

Shrimali, Govind 2000. *Rajasthan Ke Abhilakh*, 2 vols, Jodhpur: Maharaja Man Singh Pustak Prakash.

Singh, K. P. (2010). Ethnoarchaeological Survey of South Rajasthan: Udaipur, Banswara and Dungar districts. *In proceeding of Rajasthan History Congress*. (Seminar held at Jodhpur). Vol. XXV. Pp. 31-38

Singh, K. P. and Jeewan Singh Kharakwal 2010. Kumbhalgarh and its Structures. *In Forts of India*. Pp. 111-121.

Singh, Rohit Kumar (ed.) 2008, *Rajasthan Sujas*. Jaipur: Rajasthan Jansampark Vibhag.

Shyamaldas. 1986. *Vir Vinod.* Delhi. Motilal Banarasidas (Reprinted).

Vyas, Rajshekhar 1988. *Art & Architecture of Mewar.* Jaipur: Rajasthan Prakashan.

The Eco System of Water Buildings

Dr. Asha Shrivastava

There is a lot of variations in water Eco system. This may be from small, artificial, temporary hallow up to ocean. There is a lot of variations in the environment and animals of water eco system. According to the nature of water there is two types of water eco system.

1. Fresh Water Eco System
2. Sea Eco System

Fresh water Eco System is made in salt free water. The river and springs are the illusion of flowing water eco system, sea eco system while the lake and tanks are the illusion of stopped water eco system is made in the salty water.

Pond or tank is one of the best illusion of fresh water eco system. There is a one difference between ponds and lake. Tanks are shallow and small in size, while the lake is extensive area. The water of huge tanks has stable like the water of lake.

There are two types of tanks-

1. *Temporary tanks* and
2. *Permanent tanks*.

1. Temporary Tanks-

These tanks are filled with water in the rain and dried in the summer. The eco system of these tanks has stable like fields.

2. Permanent Tanks-

These thanks have always filled with water throughout the year. These tanks are connected with the rives, lakes and dams

The Chart (Tree) of Aquatic ECQ System

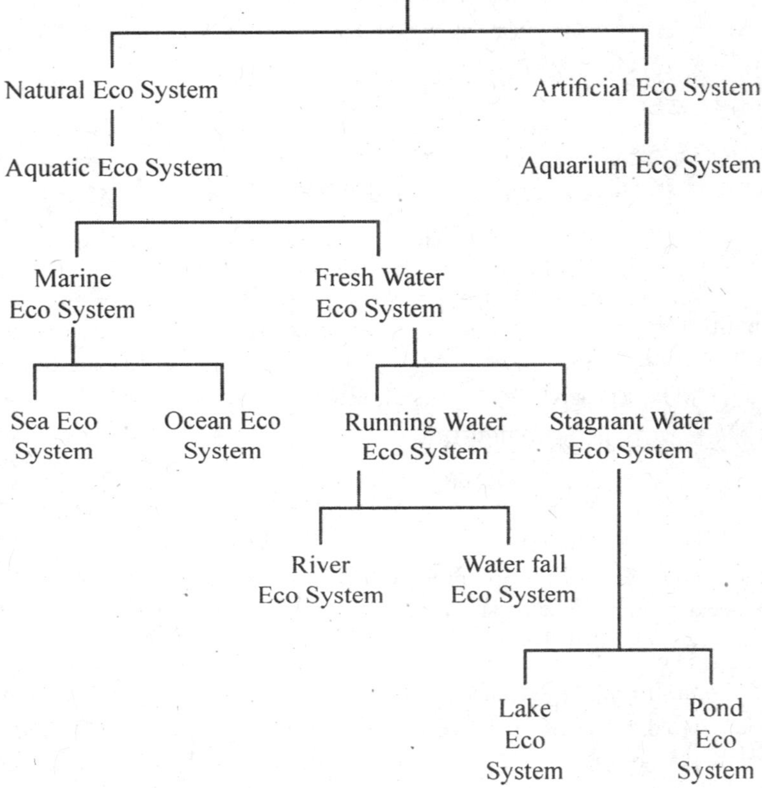

As long as the sun and moon endure, may this well remain for the nourishment of insects, birds, plants and animals.[1] Hindus animals, especially if they figure in their myths and there are numerous creatures to be nourished by a well. Some water animals make their way to step well when the monsoon fuses the dusty line between land and water, but most are put in the water by Hindus who think well should have living being. They bring a fine tortoise or a fish to a well to gain merit. Further blessing come from scattering grain on the roof, the parapet and in the water, thus beginning a cycle of life, Turtles eat the flower garlands thrown in the water, frogs eat the insects and there is some creature to eat every organic things that drops or is blown into the well. Although Indians will not deliberately hare a living things, they used to discourage excessive colonizing by routinely cleaning nests and plants from the well surfaces.[2]

The scientific pointed of view. "Eco system is the basic unit of ecology in which biotic community and abiotic environment by influencing each other maintain the functional mobility of system by flow of energy and chemical substances interactions.

Eco system is composed of two components Abiotic component and Biotic components.

All water system like, natural and man-made water system are the self regulating and complete unit of fresh water eco system. All water system has following components-

Abiotic Components-

In all water system many inorganic elements and oxygen. CO_2 and other gases are found in dissolved form in water. Various nutrient elements are also found in soil. The green plants of the lake, talab and well obtain energy from sun. After death of plants and animals, the supply of abiotic components in the water continously goes from their decomposition.

Biotic components include producers, consumers and decomposers.

Producers, the include chlorophyll, containing macrophytes, such as chara, hydulla vallisneria, algae, volvox etc. found in the different water sources. They synthesize organic food material in the presence of sunlight with the help of carbon dioxide and water through photosynthesis.

Consumers, they include hetrotrophic animals primary consumers is water sources. Water various small insects, crustaceans and their larvae are present which eat leaves of aquatic plants and algae. Besides arthopods, some molluse and some small fishes also eat producers. From the nutrition point of view all primary consumers are herbivores.

Secondary consumers eat herbivores. They include some aquatic insect such as frog and fishes and tertiary consumers are some large fishes found in lake and talab. Decomposers, like various bacteria and fungi are present in water and soil of the lake, talab and other water sources which sources which decompose the rotten organic substances of produces and the consumers into substances, hence they are called decomposed substances again return into the water from where they are consumed by producers.[3]

The well ecosystem protects animals whose predators can not negotiate the ladges. An occasional crocodile gets in one of the large 'sarovars' or tanks. Because the crocodile is the vehicle of mother goddess. She is welcome in theory. Therefor, the number of water monsters, stepwells.[4]

Water rich step wells, shaded from wind and sun are a niche out of the merciless heat. The wells have drinking trough for grazing animals and camels and people fill their basins as an act of merit lifting up more water them their own beasts need. Animals life is so integrated into the building. In a step well and other water sources animals found every where on the stone surface and in the water. Often camouflaged in the dark of among the reflections.[5]

The concern for eco system since age nature worship and the conservation ethics have been in inseparable part of India thought and traditions traces go back to ancient civilisation of India. When people used to nature the philosophy of the oneness of life. The Indian tradition has always taught that, human land is a part of nature and one should look upon all creation with the eyes of a love and respect.

Hindus love animals in their wells they also love plants. When moist dirt and the sun connect, the step well is like a walled garden. The mating of water and a stone container provides rich nutrients for plants roots. The deeper the step well the less the sun works its way past pavilions and the less the well acts as a solar collector. At the some time the shade prevents excessive evaporation. The higher parts of wells are gradually eroded by wind, salt crystallization and human forces, while animals and plants operate from inside until eventually the ground is again level.[6]

So lona as the water in the step well/well was kept fresh nothing could be cooler during the heat of the day in early summer than these rock-hewn chambers and doubtless they were often occupied for an hour or two during season of recreation

Among waters' properties that helped it stay was its ability to throw off particles as temperature charged its density cool water on the surface of wells shrinks while warm water under neath expands and rises. The cool water falls into the warm water below. This cause a current that sweeps downward any particles held in suspension in the water. It is this steady downward current that clears the pond so that the still cold water is cleaned and the bottom of the pond is seen to be covered with a film of mud lying as lightly as dust.

Water also has a remarkable ability to absorb wasters absorb transform them into useful substances. Some of this self purification is entirely mechanical. The motion of a pool stirs up debris into particles that either settle to the bottom or are diluted to harmlessness by incoming fresh water. In additions does it absorbs oxygen from the air from and from water weeds that release it during the process of photosynthesis.

The dissolved oxygen may act on organic waste directly by oxidation in effect "burning" it chemically so that nothing remains except carbon dioxide water and a little ash. More often the oxygen operates indirectly by sustaining harmless bacteria and other organic wastes.

References

1. Dada harir step well, Ahmedabad, Jutta, Jain Neubauer, ''The step wells of Gujrat in Art Historical Perspective New Delhi, Abhinav Publications 1981, appendix 2

2. Living Morna, ''step of water: page 151

3. Vyas S.K., Biology, pp.-20.6, 21.6, 22.6

4. Brodsky joseph, "water mark" page 101

5. Livingston Morna, "step of water: page 151

6. Livingston Morna, "step of water: page 155

7. Burgess James, "Muhammadan Architecture in Gujrat" New imperial series 23, Western India, Vol 6, page 47

8. Dorothy Hartley, "Water in England" page 41

9. Savitri V. Kumar, "The Puranic Lore of holy Water places"

Water Management in Shilpashastra

Dr. Pushpa Dullar and Dr. Gayatri Tandon

We can see the vastu shastra architectural reference in ancient texts as an elaboration on the different Yantra construction as well as their process and working functions.

Vari Yantras: Water Machines

1. **Pata-Yantra**: for the purpose of watering the plants of a garden
2. **Ucchraya- Samapata –Yantra**
3. **Patasamocchraya Yantra**
4. **Ucchraya Yantra-** modern pipe lines fixed in a tank or well of the modern boring having their prototype of these.

It may be noted that shilpa shastra makes two broad classifications of vari yantras. Pleasure-giving (**Kridartha**) and purposeful (**Karya Sidhyartha**). The second category is illustrated in the pata yantra and second in the three following Ucchraya, Patasamoccharava and Ucchraya Yantra. All the above four tabulated vari yantras result in the manipulation of the movement of water. In the first, it is the downwards flow from an overhead tank in the second, release of water at the higher level from tanks placed at the equal level; in the third, is a contrivance using bored columns for letting down water from a height and then taking it up through columns placed aslant; and lastly in the fourth, water from a well or a canal on the ground is sent up by a device.

Two other yantras falling in the category of vari –yantras are first the wooden –elephant drinking water placed in a vessel, any amount of it, and neither the intake nor the water taken in, is perceivable. The other one is the underground conduit is based on the samucchraya principle of circulation of water on the same level. Here water is brought to a tank from a distance source. The future important types of yantras not so far included in the above classification through covered by the Vari- Yantra and swing Machines are respectively the Dharagrha and the dolagrha.

Dharagrha

Five Varieties of the Dharagrhas are-

1. Dharagrha
2. Pravarsana
3. Pranala
4. Jalamagna
5. Nandyavarta

Dharagrha is a shower bower in a garden. It was very popular medieval times both in the east and west and formed essential constituent of vast palace equipment.

Regarding heir construction the shilpa shastra lays down that firstly they are to be in the proximity of big reservoir; secondly, they should occupy a site with beautiful surrounding and thirdly, pipes have to be prepared double and treble the height and other requirement of the fountain. Again the pipes are said to be able to carry water from pores and smooth inside.

The text gives an impression that they were the characteristic of the age and were high super structures with several stories and the water mechanism attached to them for jala–krida in connection with the amorous sports of the kings and their queens, the most talked of in the kavyas "Bharavi", "magha", and other early poets. These dharagrhas were the most beautiful baths well furnished, well decorated and were the finest of flooring and plaster and were specimens of pillar architecture here not only showers, ucchraya-yantras were lead on, but a good many paintings of elephant couples. Doll women's, pouring out shores form the breast and navels etc. were also to be seen the text is full of such beautiful and poetic description, a brief notice is called for.

In the wood work of these structures, carved pillars, platforms, projections, windows, cornices etc. fine and fragrant timber e.g. Devdaroo, sandal, sala are to be used. The many fold motifs of decorations as already pointed out are female figures and models of birds, animals like monkeys many fold forms with gaping mouths, nagas, and kinneras etc., dancing peacocks kalpavrksas, creepers, and cuckoos, bees and swans. The main pine is to be lead in the center of the fountain with its exterior made charming to the top of it is fitted the mechanism for taking up water, scattering and throwing it in a varieties of ways. The king's seat is right in the centre and he enjoys the bath and the play of water both the text in emphatic that these dharagars are not fit to be used by the ordinary run of man they are only for the kings.

More specific description of the four types of the dharagar now follows.

The main speciality of the first there parvasana, the shower, is that it pours down water strong figures of three four or seven man should be set up with carved tubes the whole mechanism is fitted with water which is poured out in different ways by these figures "bhoja calls this shower house the pseudo- cloud Anukarnam ekam jalamucam. Somadeva suri's commentator gives it the name the kritrima maghmandria. A boon in summer and a feast to the eyes. Kalida's reference to the yantra dhara has already been noted but when he says in the meghaduta nesyanti tvam surayuvatayo yantra dhara – girihatvam, that the celestial damsels on the Himalayas would scratch the cloud with there bangles and convert it into a yantra dhara griha, he seems to know the name of this type called after the cloud.

The next variety called pranala is two storied with a single pillar of four, eight or sixteen built like a pushpaka vimana with decorative design. At the centre bellow is a water tank with a big lotus, its pericarp fashioned as the seat of the king around are female figures looking at the lotus, when the over head tank is filled and closed water is poured by the figures on the king sitting on a lotus kings.

The third JalaMagna is a chamber under water, the idea being that of the submarine abode of Varune or naga raja. A square chamber is built at the bottom of a big and deep water reservoir the approach to it being through a subterranean passage. A continuous flow of the water above keeps the chamber completely cool and the whole reservoir is full of mechanical lotuses, fishes, birds etc. when resting in this chamber alone or in private company, the king can be seen only by select personal friends and urgent visitors like other princes or ambassadors.

The last type, nandyavarta, has, in mid tank, a big flower like structure, all around the central floral design in mid water are placed low walls in swastika designs, providing a sufficient screen.

As well as a passage, the purpose being to permit playing in the water the game of the hide and seek.

References

1. Dr. D.N. Shukla: Royal Arts- Yantras and Citras; Publishers Vastuvanmaya-Prakasna- sala; first edition; pg 43-47
2. Sammelan Patrika- Kala Visheshank
3. Dr. D. N. Shukla: Bhartiya Vastu Shastra; 1978
4. Aprajit Vastushastra- Varanasi; 1920

Tools and Techniques of Water Management in Medieval Malwa

Dr. Vinay Shrivastava

In the era of Mohanjodaro and Harappa like the local dock yard and the common bathing construction of the Indus valley civilization have been found as the earliest water management technique. After Indus valley we find many sources of water management depicted in different text. [Shukraniltisar, Mayamot and Manser, etc.

In the 11th century a lot of historical and cultural text on human civilization has been written which is important aesthetically as well as socially. Samrangnasutradhar, Vishnu Dharmotarpuran as well as Aparajit pracha talk about the process as well as different colour aspect have specified Raj prasad has refereed to the bathing pool, ponds and other water bodies like Varigraha, Dharagraha in this text. Administrative and domestic establishment have been also elaborated on.

In the later periods these water planning develop into the Deeg palace Goverdhan' s cenotaph of Surajmal and pinjor garden.

These mechanisms also lead to water conservation as it kept the water in flow. Literature is a mirror reflection of the society hence any text can be taken as an ask of ideal inspiration and definitions of that era. So Samrangansutradhar is an important paradigm developed in medieval period on the important aspect of water management.[1]

As the number of crops cultivated by the plough-using Indian peasant grew in ancient times, with two major harvests within the year over most of India achieved as early as 1500 BC. Irrigation become an increasingly important element of agriculture technology. Central India and the peninsula are eminently suitable for reservoirs created by embankments thrown across gorges or narrow outlets in hilly and undulating terrain. In the millennium 600-1500 India became one of the great zones of tank irrigation. Ruins of the great reservoirs of king Bhoja in central India.[2] [11th century]

The grand dam in Bhojpur was built under the great king Bhoj in the half of the 11th century. This dam situated between two large hills. Raja Bhoj was the great parmar king of Dhar[3] [Malwa].

Much of India's irrigation was and still is derived from tapping underground water through wells. Oxen were used to draw up leathern buckets by a rope over the pulley wheel. In order to give continuous flow people made use of the 'noria' the 'araghatta' of ancients texts.[4]

A 'noria'[5] is the scientists's term for a vertical wheel that has water containers on its rim. Set up over a sheet of water its rim containers pick up water as these go down into the water and them come up with a rotation of the wheel. When they pass the top of the wheel and descend they empty themselves pouring their water into channels prepared alongside.

In India the first definite appearance of the 'noria' is in an early version of the 'panchatantra' [300 AD] where a man is said to have operated an 'araghatta' literally meaning a wheel with earthen pots [ghatta] tied to [the ends of] it spokes [ara]. Which words occurs in Buddhaghoshs [5th century]. This water lifting mechanism obtained much greater ability to lift water from greater depth when the pots were transferred from the spokes or rim to a rope chain or ' pot-garland'[6] [Malwa]. The earliest allusion to this 'pot-garland' occurs in 'yashodharman's' Mandsor inscription of AD 532. Two contemporary inscriptions found on two type stone pillars of victory set up by king 'Yashodharman' of unknown origin near mandsour one of them is dated in Malwa year [532-22] AD The dated on records the construction of a large well by one Daksha, whose brother Dharmadosa was the minister of Yashodharman[7]

['Noria'- The Arabic terms for the surface wheel is 'naura' which has been anglicised as noria. In Persian it is called 'dulab'. The noria or dulab operates an open water surface. Such as rivers, tanks or lakes. It has pitchers or pottery vessels fixed on the rim of the wheel. It was turned by the hand of man and revoled horizontally]

In 'Babarnama' Babar writes the different modes of water lift in India. According to Babur 1524-30 "The kharif crop ripens of itself owing to the rains of the rainy season and strong still, the rabi crops can grow too without rain. The trees of one or two years growth are watered by bringing up water either through the [persian] wheel [charkh] or by the leathern water bucket, In many region of India they irrigate by means of the wheel. They make circles [halqa] out of two long ropes, equal to the depth of the wheel. They tie up pieces of wood each attached to both the ropes with earthen jarstied to each piece of wood. This double rope to which the well. At the other end of the axle of this wheel, another wheel is placed whose axle is set up right. When the ox rotates this wheel its cogs [parra], engaging with the cogs [parra] of the second wheel is turn rotates that wheel which carries the pots. Where the water pours out, a cistern is provided and water is then taken from that cistern in every direction as disired.[8]

Secondly he writes a water bucket Many people used water with a bucket. This involves much labour and is also a dirty method. They fix on the side of the well a pole of wood with two branches on top. Between the two branches they set a pully and over that pulley they put a long rope [arghamchi], to which is tied a large bucket [dalv]. One end of this rope is tied to the ox. One man is required to drive the ox and one person is required to pour out the water from the bucket. Every time the ox walking away from the well, pulls up the bucket, the rope upon its return and being dragged along the track of the ox and getting soiled with its urine and dung falls again into the well.

Some cultivated fields, when watering is required women and men irrigate by drawing up water by earthen jars.[10]

In many records find in Malwa where used many modes of water lift like pot-garland [persian wheel], water bucket ['chadas' leather water bucket] pulley set on two wooden pole, kachach wells [large holes in ground] etc. in irrigation.[11]

Painting of Akbar's time show that the gears were formed by wooden pags joining two horizontal circular boards, the pegs being so spaced as to mesh with pege jutting out from the rim of a vertical wheel placed on the same axle as the gearing Well-Wheel carried the chain of pots. This kind of gearing is known technically as 'pindrum' or 'Lantern' gearting.[12]

The arrival in India of this sophisticated apparatus from the Mediterranean and Iraq.

Persian wheel so as to enable it to lift water to reach a height much above the level of the oxen. This was done by making the drawbar rotate a long vertical axle, at the top of which was put the horizontal wheel, whose pegs meshed with the cogs of a vertical wheel, which by being set on the same axle in turn rotated the well-wheel carrying the chain of pot's. Such a device for raising water to a height is referred to by Abu'l Fazl and illustrated in two painting from Akbar's time.

The Malwa agriculture has always depended on various sources of water both natural and artificial for its irrigational requirements viz-rain, wells, river, tanks, canals, etc. The construction of water-works and the technological changes that took place in the traditional irrigation system in India during the Malwa parmara king and sultanate hitherto neglected, need a scientific study. The relevant evidence available in the contemporary Indian and Persian works through the construction of water works and the changes that irrigation technology and water refining technology underwent from time to time. In particular the setting up of the Persian wheel on wells and the construction of large artificial canals provide clues to the introduction of certain mechanical devices in the irrigation system employed during the period under review.[13]

Dams, lakes and water reservoirs were some of the important means of irrigation in Malwa at 11th century. The artificial lake at Bhojpur [near Bhopal] commissioned by king Bhoj in the middle of the 11th century covered 250 sq. miles.[14]

West of Bhojpur once lay a vast lake, but nothing remains except the ruins of the magnificent old dams by which its water were contained. The site was chosen with great skill, as a natural wall of hills enclosed the whole area except for two gaps, 100 yards and 500 yards in width respectively. These were closed by gigantic earthen dams. Faced on both sides with enormous blocks of sandstone, many being 4 feet long, 3 feet broad and 2.5 feet thick, set without mortar. The smaller dam is 44 feet high and 300 feet Thick at the base the larger dam 24 feet high with a flat top 100 feet. broad. These embankments held up an expanse of water of about 250 square miles. This great work is ascribed to king Bhoj.[15] but it may possible be of an earlier date.

The lake was destroyed by Hoshang Shah of Malwa [1405-34], who cut through the lesser dam and thus either intentionally or in a fit of destructive passion, added an enormous area of the highest fertility to his possessions. According to Gond legend, it took an army of them three month to cut through the dam and the lake took three years to empty, while its bed was not habitable for thirty years afterwards.[16] The climate of Malwa is said to have been considerable altered by the removal of this waste sheet of water.[17]

An important aspect of Indian agriculture is artificial irrigation to supplement the natural bounty of the monsoons. The principal means employed for this purpose has been the construction of well, tanks and canals. In Malwa, wells must have provided the chief source of irrigation. Number of artificial devices were used to lift water from well. Pulleys were employed over wells for this purpose. Another device worked on the lever principal. In the region of all Malwa there was the wooden 'arhat' or 'rahat'[18] called by the English the 'Persian wheel' with the chain of pots and pin drums gearing. Persian wheel in a number of village in Malwa. Around Agra and further east & west the 'chadas'[19] or the leather bucket lifted out of water by yoked oxen, pulling a rope thrown over a pulley was most common in agriculture area or field.

On other techniques in which uses of heavy wood piller of tree, and small hardest and clay make a kacha Bandha on river then growing the label of water and make a temporary canal uses, water for irrigation. This type of temporary canal called 'saran'

In his general account of Malwa and Mewar agriculture is artificial irrigation to supplement the natural bounty of the monsoons. In Malwa and Mewar, wells and 'Deekli' [local language], ' kotumbi' and 'Bundha' must have provided the chief source of irrigation. Around western India the 'chadas' or the ' leathern bucket' lifted out of water by yoked oxen pulling a rope thrown over a pulley was most common. 'Rahat' was very uncommon and very less example found in Malwa irrigation.

In Malwa wells must have provided the chief source of irrigation. Most of the wells were 'kachcha' that is made without use of masonry. These necessarily had to be dug afresh every year.

In Malwa out of a very large number of water tank's recorded in all region and many ruins of 'Wooden Rahat' also found in this regions.[20]

It seems clear from a reading of Abul-Fazl's account of the various provinces in the A in that he has found it superfluous to say any thing about the role of irrigation of the crops depended mostly upon rainfall and only partly on wells.[21]

Some cultivated fields when watering is required women and men irrigate by drawing up water by other techniques like 'kutumba' and 'Odi' [abat]. These techniques found in Malwa and Mewar.

In 'kutumba' long hollow tree like 'kajui' and other any long Nal tree one side attached on height and second terminal attached in agriculture area then water moving up to down.

The greater part of the Hindustan country is situated on level land Many though its towns and cultivated lands are it nowhere has 'running waters.' Rivers and in some towns, it is practicable to convert water by digging channels this is not done. For not places standing waters are its running-water even where as for some doing it there may be several reasons. One being that water is not at all necessity in cultivating crops and orchards. Autumn crops grow by the downpour of the rains themselves and strange, it that spring crops grow even when no rain falls.[22]

On the other hand a notable aspect of technology of technological progress in India was its dependence on state support. Without the support of a technologically inclined nobility, without grants from the royal treasuries, many of the technological developments that took place in the field of water management, construction and metallurgy simply would not have taken place. Progress is astronomy also benefited from active state support.

The need for accurate prediction of the monsoons spurred development in Malwa, Rajasthan and Gujrat step wells were built deep into the ground astronomy while the intense heat of the summer led to innovations in architecture. In something descending as much as a hundred feet. Mathura and Ujjain to facilitate advances in the astronomical science. Manually operated cooling devices were also invented. The samarangana sutradhara and Arthashastra mentions the vari yantra.[23] (probably a revolving water spray for cooling the air.)

In addition to a chapter on town planning and samaragana-sutradhara also included chapters on mechanical engineering, soil teshing, orientation of buildings, the selection of building material, architectural styles and the vertical and horizontal components of buildings.

The samarangana sutradhara also discribe machine and mechanical devices such as chirning chronometers (putrika-nadiprabodhana) and in his 'yuktikalptar' Raja Bhoj also warned ship builders about using iron along the bottom of the vessels for this would render them vulnerable to magnetic rocks at sea.[24]

Rain water harvesting

Rain water is a clean, expensive and readily available source of water. Even in desert areas substantial amounts of rain water are being collected stored and used for a variety of purpose.

Large scale rain water harvesting in when a river is dammed and the stored water is then used for irrigation and domestic uses. Small scale rain water harvesting in when a property owner.

In Malwa many examples of roof water harvesting find in Madhu. The monument of 'Jaahaj Mahal' and Rani Rupmati Mahal are the great example of Rain water harvesting. Asirgarh fort and 'khundi Bhandara' of Bharahanpur, are also the great example of Rain water harvesting.

Water was not just for agriculture, irrigation, occupation and domestic needs. Since water generally held importance in ritualistic practices, structures like tanks, reservoirs, wells, step wells, temple, tanks etc. were invariable accompaniments to religious complexes, temples and sacred groves etc. Besides this, the royalty and aristocracy (along side with endowing public reservoirs, wells and step wells etc. and providing state patronage to large irrigation works, " bunds' and embankment etc.) combined water bodies their palaces and gardens. Thus there developed a vast range of water related architectural features-both religious and secular with regional and sub regional styles.

Example of water related architecture in Malwa include from a steps built on the banks of rivers, reservoirs and dams or ghats, which form a characteristic feature at various pilgrimages sites and religious enclosures, wells, royal pleasures pavilions fronting or situated on rivers and lakes and ornamental pools and water gardens attached to palaces. Other types of water related architecture include deep stepped basins, village tanks and wells which served as communities and hunting pavilions used by royalty and aristocracy at water holes frequented by animals.

Alongside this since the palaces and forts of the rulers and their feudatories incorporated water bodies to meet drinking water needs as well as for aesthetic and weather-conditioning purpose, elaborate systems of transporting water within palaces and forts and of fountains and water channels that ran through chambers and gardens were devised (In the context of Malwa for example, Baj Bahadur and rani Roopmati Mahal, Jahaj Mahal, Kaliadah Mahal at Ujjain, Shahi Hammam at Madu Burhanpur, Asirgarh fort, Mahal Gulara and Ahukhana at Burhanpur, Reva kund at Mandu etc.

The terms bain and baoli are of Indian origin and refer to what is called 'step-well'. The sultan and the governors evinced interest is the construction of these wells if cities, towns and along the high ways. Ibn Battuta refers to a number of step-wells that he found in different part of north India. He also informs us that Maliks and amirs posted in the provinces tried to outwit one another in building bains and the road for the benefit of travellers. He gives a detailed description of step well in the territorial unit of Malwa.[25]

The epigraphic sources also yield interesting information this regards. For instance the inscription found in Balibagarh in the Damoh district of Madhya Bharat dated 1328 AD sheds interesting light on the religious policy of sultan Muhamad bin Tughlaq and his officers towards the

Hindus. Its records the construction of a cow temple along with a step well inside a garden by the order of the sultan.[26]

The fifteenth century inscription noticed in the step-wells show the continuation of old traditions by the regional etc. Moreover they were made parts of endowments made for the benefit of the people.

The survey of the traces of the 15th century step wells in Malwa show that they were multistoried of the numerous baoli found in and around chanderi, ex. Battisi Baoli insription records show the well was built in AH 890 (1485AD) in the region by Ghyath shah khalji of Madhu.[27]

Likewise a new phase started in the architecture of step well built in Malwa. It also contains rooms built all around with chisel dressed stones and time mortar.

The construction of water works and the technological changes that took place in the traditional irrigation system in India during the Delhi sultanate hitherto neglected, need a scientific study. The relevant evidence available in the contemporary Arabic and Persian works, thorough brief and laconic, sheds interesting light on the engineering skill that went into the construction of water works and the changes that irrigation technology underwent from time to time, in particular, the setting up of the Persian wheel on well and construction of large artificial canals provide clues to the introduction of certain mechanical devices in the irrigation system employed during the period under review. It also gives an insight into regional disparities the lives and conditions of peasants in different territorial units under the rules of sultan. In fact the diffusion of advanced irrigation technology in a region brought about prosperity and also helped the growth of material culture.

Rain water harvesting is enjoying a renaissances of sorts in the world but in traces its history to biblical times. Extensive rain water harvesting apparatus existed 4000 years ago in the Palestine and Greece. In ancient Rome, residences were built with individual cisterns and paved courtyards to capture rain water to augment water from city's aqueducts in Baluchistan and kutch impounded rain water and used for irrigation dams.

Artificial recharge to ground water is a process by which the ground water reservoir is augmented at a rete exceeding that obtaining under natural conditions or replenishment any man made scheme of facility that adds water to aquifer may be considered to be an artificial recharge system.

In Malwa there are two main techniques of rain water harvesting storage of rain water on surface for future use. Recharge to ground water the storage of rain water on surface is a traditional techniques and structures used were underground tanks, ponds, check, dams, weirs, etc.[28]

Dug wells-Existing dug wells may be utilised as recharge structure and water should pass through filter media before putting into dug well.

Rooftop collection of rain water diversion and collection of run off into dry tanks. Artificial recharge is the process by which the ground water reservoir is augmented at a rate exceeding that under that under natural conditions of replenishment. Sustainability of drinking water sources has become one of the major issues of army and royal drinking water supply sector. Since rain water harvesting and artificial recharge can play a major role in providing sustainability to drinking water sources.

References

1. Aparajit Vastushastra- Varanasi; 1920

2. HABIB IRFAN, ''Medieval India-the study of a civilization" page-72, pub-Oxford university press National book trust of India. New Delhi, 2008

3. Chaturvedi kranti, "Madhya pradesh ki jal Sanrakshah ki parampara" p-10

4. HABIB IRFAN, "Medieval India- the study of a civilization" page-13, pub-Oxford University press National book trust of India, New Delhi,2008

5. HABIB IRFAN, "Technology in Medieval India" 650-1750 page-09, pub-Aligarh historian society, Tulika books, New Delhi,2008

6. HABIB IRFAN, "Technology in Medieval India" page-10

7. Vishnuvardhana. (Mandsour GaZetter) page-23

8. HABIB IRFAN, "Tools and Technology in Medieval India" page-27,28

9. HABIB IRFAN, "Technology in Medieval India" page-28, pub-Aligarh historian Society, Tulika books New Delhi,2008

10. HABIB IRFAN, page 28 Technology in Medieval India 650-1750 and Kosambi, D.D. "An Introduction to the study of Indian history",page,121

11. See in Field Work

12. HABIB IRFAN " Technology in Medieval India" page-13

13. See in Field Work

14. Ganguly D.C. parmar Rajvanse ka Itihass page-181

15. Ganguly D.C. parmar Rajvanse ka Itihass page-181

16. WWW. theindiatravel. com/favourites/exotic_places

17. bhojpur.html

18. 'Rahat'- (A hindi equivalent of the persion wheel) Babur refers to the perison wheel being in India as 'Charkh' page-486

19. According to Babur-water lifting through 'Charas' (leather bucket) was also a common method of irrgations.

20. See in field Work under Major Research Project (UGC) New Delhi, of Dr. Vinay Shrivastava.

21. Abul Fazal's-A-In-I-Akabari, (Eng. trans-H.Blockman Vol-II) pub, LPP, New Delhi page 209-210

22. Babur-nama, '(Eng. trans- Beveridge)' vol-II, pub-Lpp, New Delhi, p-486

23. Dr. D.N.Shukla; Royal Arts-Yantras and Citras; publishers Vastuvanmaya-prakasna-sala; first edition; pp43-47

24. Sanskrit-a) Samarangana-Sutradhara

b) Rasanama-Rasa-Raja-Maranka (Bhoja)

c) Yaktikalptaru

25. Ibn Battuta, Travells in Asia and Africa, (trans;ated A.H. Gibb), pub Lpp, New Delhi.p220,226

26. Annual report of the Archeological department Gwalior state for year 1924-25, V. Samvat 1981 page-5

27. Annual report of the Archaeological department Gwalior state for yeaar 1924-25, V. Samvat 1981 page-5

28. I.H. Soddiqui-journal of Economic and social history of the orient, Vol XXIX 'Water Works and irrigation system in india during premughal times'

The Techniques of Water Harvesting: With Reference to the 'Vavs' of Gujarat

Dr. Meghna Sharma

Water existence[1] and harvesting[2] has been a special concern since 3rd millennium B.C, stone rubble dams[3], reservoirs,[4] irrigation systems,[5] use of floodwaters,[6] building of anicuts,[7] construction of artificial lakes.[8] have been significant from the viewpoint of water harvesting.

The utility of water[9] in yajurveda[10] is as follows:

- Those works/activities by which we consume the water available on earth.
- Activities in which is included, the construction of artificial water-bodies like dams, water ponds, bawadies[11] etc. also mention that i.e activities by which water content is managed.

Baoris or *bers, the* community wells in Rajasthan, were built by *Banjaras* (mobile trading communities) for their drinking water needs. They can hold water for a long time because of almost negligible water evaporation.

Stepwell locations often suggested the way in which they would be used. When a stepwell was located within or at the edge of a village, it was mainly used for utilitarian purposes and as a cool place for social gatherings. When stepwells were located outside the village, on trade routes[12] they were often frequented as resting places. Many important stepwells are located on the major military and trade routes[13,14] from Patan in the north to the sea coast of Saurashtra. When stepwells were used exclusively for irrigation, a sluice was constructed at the rim to receive the lifted water and lead it to a trough or pond, from where it ran through a drainage system and was channelled into the fields. A major reason for the breakdown of this traditional system is the pressure of centralisation and agricultural intensification.[15]

Talking about the religious significance of these water reservoirs, women gathered to appease the Jal-deva (water deity) in order to be blessed with a boon of fertility. They propitiate the gods with offerings like milk, grain and rice, young mothers with new born babies come for the thanks giving, besides praying for the longevity of the child.[16] The water god is requested to give darshan.[17]

The Technology of Water Harvesting: Special Reference, 'Vavs'

Rainwater, runoff and the floodwaters from rivers were all harvested. Water harvesting systems were located in the open to capture, in the path of a stream or its runoff, beside rivers to catch the flood waters. The forts witnessed fierce battles and were often under siege for months. During such times, there had to be enough water inside the fort.[18] The only solution was their elaborate water harvesting system. Chittorgarh fort[19] has 'Gaumukh' reservoir, Kumbhalgarh[20] has 12 bawadis. Internal fort, Katargarh[21] also has a big pond and several Bawadis. Similarly Ghosundi Bawadi[22] was constructed by Rani Shringar Devi Marwar, the daughter of king Jodha and Queen of Maharana Raimal. Mehrangarh fort[23] also harvested run-off water.

Gujarat is home to hundreds of step wells scattered throughout the state. In fact constructing a well was held to be a pious deed that absolved ones' sin and certainly it earned more merit than mere sacrifices.[24] In India, the science of construction of VAV i.e. Step-well has been developed to such an extent that, it is never available in any other country of the world. The construction of such step-well is found in Gujarat from tenth century upto the end of eighteenth century, in huge amplitude.

The construction of stepwells, in Gujarat, date from four periods[25]:

- Pre-Solanki Period (8th to 11th century),
- Solanki Period (11th to 12th century),
- Vaghela Period (mid-13th to end-14th century),
- Sultanate period (mid 13th to the end of 15th century)

Vavs were built in the South Western region of Gujarat, in the late 6th and 7th centuries. The grandest period of the stepwell construction spanned from 11th to 16th century, the most extravagant of which is the Rani ki Vav, at Patan in Gujarat.[26]

Different Kinds of Step Wells[27]:

1. A step well with a diameter of **0.75** mtr and **one exit** is called **"Nanda"; e.g. Matar Bhawani Vav** situated in **Ahmedabad.**

2. A step-well with a diameter of 1.5 mtr. and two exits, is called **"Bhadra"; e.g. Dadahari Vav.**
3. A step-well with a diameter of **2.75 mtr.** and three exits, is called **"Jaya";** e.g. In **Adalaja Vav in Gandhi nagar District.**
4. A step-well with four exits, is called **"Vijaya",**
5. A step well which is 32 mtr. Long and 4 mtr. Wide and 3, 5 mtr. High, is called **"Dirghika"** well. Some times a reservoir having a length equaling 300 Nos. of arrows is also called the **Dirghika.**
6. The step well in which inner part is broader than the upper part, is called **"Bolari Vav".**
7. **The** step well which is always found full of water and never gets dried up in any time, is called a **"Jivati Vav".)**

Sculptures and inscriptions in stepwells demonstrate their importance to the traditional social and cultural lives of people.

Some Prominent Vavs of Gujarat Constructed in Medieval Times:

Step-wells of Gujarat rank in first category for their construction throughout our country.

The historical, cultural and social status of some prominent Vavs of Gujarat[28] is given below:

* Three old step wells are situated in the present town of Vadhvan, of Saurashtra. The first is known as Madhavav, second is known as Gangavav, and third is known as Lakhavav. According to a stone inscription found in Madhavav, it can be presumed that, the construction was undertaken during the terminal period of the Vaghela rulers. This Madhavav has 2 storeys and is constructed in stone masonry. As the Nagar Brahmin whose name was Madhav, have constructed this Vav, it is known as Madhavav. This Madhav Brahmin was a minister of King Karanghelo.

* **Bhadrakhali Vav of Umreth** : **Minaldevi,** the **mother of kind Jaysingh Siddhraj** had got constructed this seven storeyed Vav (near Bhadrakhali temple in Umreth town) which is very famous for its superior type of Art and technique of construction. This Vav is also therefore called as Minaldevi Vav but generally is known as **Bhadrakhali Vav.**

* Vav situated in Adalaj[29] of Gandhinagar District : Built by Queen Rudabai[30] in 1499, it provided a cool and secluded retreat during the hot summer, Sultan Begara in his quest for expansion had subdued Dandai Desh and killed the Vaghela king, Veer Singh. He sent forth his

matrimonial proposal to Rudabai Devi who begged for time in order to complete the vav in memory of her dead husband. The Sultan agreed but he never knew that the queen would drag the work for twenty long years. Still it remained incomplete as evident from the missing canopy. The Sultan renewed his request for marriage and the queen responded by plunging herself from the balcony of the well and thus met her watery death. In other words it became a jal samadhi and thus she sacrificed herself to save her honour and also to appease the jal devi, who would be responsible for the perpetual flow of water.[31] This Vav is having ornamental construction of superior quality[32] It has three entrances. According to archeology, it falls in the category of "Jaya" pattern of step well.[33(a)]

On entering in this Vav of Adalaj, we find *Mandap* having its sides 7 mts. long. An octagonal dome was also constructed on this *Mandap* but the dome is not found at present. The pillars which are constructed along the way to go down in the *Vav*, are of superior workmanship.[33(b)(c)] We find elephant type shaped inscriptions, below the galleries.

* Rani Vav[34] situated in the North Eastern side of present Patan City, Ranivav has the peak of the construction technique of step wells. On account of its grandeur of wide area and ornamental varieties and beautiful construction technique found in all its seven storeys,[35] This Vav is known as Queen of all step wells of Gujarat in the western part of the country- It is, therefore, known as Rani-Vav. It was constructed by Uadayamati, the queen of the King Bhimdev Solanki in the year 1050 A.D. It is said that, during the course of excavation from this Vav, a beautiful idol of the queen Uadayamati was found which is at present preserved as a national monument and is being protected accordingly. This Vav is stretched in west and east direction in a length of 28 mts. approximately and its construction is of "Khajurao" pattern, but there are no romantic idols found as found in "Khajurah."[36], very good idols of God Vishnu and Shiv are also found from the excavation work of this step well. The size of the Rani Ki Vav is so huge that the tourists appear to be ants climbing an anthill.[37]

Modhera Vav[38] of was constructed by Rajamata Udaymati near the Sun temple of Modhera, **Gebalalsha** Vav,[39] **Sevasi Vav**[40] are other such constructions. During the Mohammedan rule in Gujarat , the step-well of village **Vadthal**[41] near Kathlal town was assuming great importance. The construction of this step-well was undertaken in 15th century and the stone inscriptions of the birds which were eating snakes, frogs, scorpions, fish etc. staying in the step-well, is depicted very vividly.

The inscriptions of human beings found in this step well are also worth noting. The step-well situated in the village tank of Mahudha village was also possessing Mohmedan architecture. Similarly, Vav of **Varsola** village also was of the same type. A contemporary step-well of these two step-wells of Khanbhali has been constructed by following Hindu architecture. The Vav - Sudha situated in the village limits of Shiholadi near town Vaso was constructed in lime masonry is well known for its inscription work throughout Charotar area. There are so many step wells in Khera District. However, only few are beautiful like Vanjara Vav of village Ode. In short, the Vavs of Gujarat are in other words inscriptive ornaments which happen to be a valuable property for bringing social good wishes.

Mata Bhavani Vav[42] in Asarva, on the outskirts of Ahmedabad is another step well assigned to the Chalukiyan period and dedicated to Amba-Bhavani. Noted for its religious significance rather than its architectural appeal, the well has some pre-medieval carvings and sculptors can be admired on the parapets that house the canopied roofs, niches and friezes.

Dada Harir ki Vav[43], of Asarva, brings us to the early sixteenth century reign of Sultan Mehmud Begarah (1458-1511) - the most outspoken among the Gujarat sultans. Bai Harir Sultani was the superintendent of the royal harem and she had planned the Vav[44], her mausoleum is adjacent to the Vav. Inscriptions in Sanskrit and Persian tell us about the cost of construction, which was 3,29,000 Mahmudis (gold coin) of the Begara era.

References

1. (a) Yajurveda, Chapter 15, Shloka 4

   (b) Vedshrami, Pt; Vedic Sampada, p. 381

2. http://cpreec.org/pubbook-traditional.htm,

3. 3rd millennium B.C---Dams built of stone rubble were found in Baluchistan and Kutch

4. (3000 – 1500 B.C- Indus - Sarasvati Civilization had several reservoirs to collect rainwater runoff. Each house had an individual well)

5. *(a)* (321 – 291 B.C- Archeological evidence for dams, lakes and irrigation systems in the time of Chandragupta Maurya's rule,

(b) 3rd Century B.C- Kautilya's **Arthasastra mentions irrigation** using water harvesting systems, 12th Century A.D-- Rajatarangini by Kalhana describes a well- maintained irrigation system in Kashmir)

6. 1st Century B.C- Sringaverapura near Allahabad had a sophisticated water harvesting system using the floodwaters of the Ganges)
7. 2nd Century A.D- Grand Anicut or Kallanai built by Karikala Chola across the river Cauvery to divert water for irrigation is still functional)
8. 11th Century A.D- King Bhoja of Bhopal built the largest artificial lake (65,000 acres, in India fed by streams and springs)
9. (a) Yajurveda; Chapter 4, Shloka 3

   (b) Vedshrami, Pt.; Vedic Sampada, p. 377

   (c) Jaisingh; Pracheen Bharat Mein Naag Tatha Jal Puja, p. 41
10. Yajurveda; Chapter 16, mantra 38
11. Many stories are constructed in them (bawadies) and during summers 'rehat' and 'chadas' run upon them. By this, the water which is driven out and again felt inside the bawadi makes the surrounding environment , cool, like coolers/AC do, in present times; Ranawat; Dr. Ishwar Singh, Rajasthan ke Jal Sansadhan, p. 44)
12. Sharma, Dr. G. N. Sharma; Rajasthan ka Itihaas, p. 494),
13. One such significant trade route, from Mewar to Gujarat was, Delwara-Eklingji-Ahar-Udaipur-Bagad-Gujarat. Ref---Somani Ramvallabh; History of Mewar; p. 90)
14. Another being Udaipur to Gogunda, Ajmer via Mandal and Gogunda to Udaipur, Ahmedabad via Edar. Akbarnama, Part-3, pp. 57, 272-73, 275
15. www.rainwaterharvesting.org/rural/traditional1.htm
16. (http://www.tsiindia.com/gujarat/tourist-attractions-gujarat/forts-monuments/rani-udaymati.htm)
17. (a) Yajurveda; Chapter 4, Shloka 3

    (b) Vedshrami, Pt.; Vedic Sampada, p. 377

    (c) Jaisingh; Pracheen Bharat Mein Naag Tatha Jal Puja, p. 41
18. Article 'Water management in the forts' on the NET, website: http://www.gobartimes.org/20061231/history_you.htm

19. see slide/picture 5

20. Kumbhalgarh Prashasti, Shloka 135. Paper Presented by Dr. Ishwarsingh Ranawat 'Maharana Kumbha Kaleen Suraksha Vyavastha ke Pramukh Pahlu' (Kumbha Smarika, 1998-99; p. 69)

21. Menaria, Dr. Purshottamlal, 'Aparajeya Durg Kumbhalgarh; (Kumbha Smarika, 1994)

22. (a) Ghosundi Rock Edict; Vaisakh Sudi 3, Wednessday Samvat 1561 (17th April, 1504 A.D)

    (b) Journal of Asiatic Society of Bengal, Part-56, pp.79-82.

    (c) Ojha; Jodhpur Rajya ka Itihaas, part-I, p. 251.)

23. Picture downloaded (http://www.gobartimes.org/20061231/history_you.htm) on water management in the forts. Slide/picture 6

24. http://www.indiasite.com/gujarat/stepwellsofgujarat.html

25. www.dancewithshadows.com/vavs_stepwell_gujarat.asp)

26. ibid.

27. Excerpts from 'Rajvallabh', of the medieval architect Mandan, available on (http://www.supportnarmadadam.org/water-civilization-mr-gandhi1.htm)

28. An article presented upon 'Water and Civilisation' by M.R. Gandhi Retired Chief Engineer Narmada, Water Resources and Water Supply Department. Government of Gujarat, Gandhinagar, on http://www.supportnarmadadam.org/water-civilization-mr-gandhi1.htm

29. The total length of this Vav is 80 mts. Adalaj Well is richly carved. Every pillar and wall surface is covered with leaves and flowers, birds and fishes and friezes of ornamental designs. http://travel.buzzintown.com/ahmedabad/id--407.html

30. http://www.tsiindia.com/gujarat/tourist-attractions-gujarat/forts-monuments/rani-udaymati.html)

31. see slide/picture 7

32. see slide/picture 8

33. (a) see slide /picture 9, 10

    (b) see slide /picture 11

    (c) see slide / picture 12

34. http://www.indiasite.com/gujarat/stepwellsofgujarat.html

35. see slide/picture 13

36. see slide/picture 14

37. http://www.gujaratorbit.com/archeology-in-gujarat/rani-ki-vav/rani-ki- vav.html)

38. http://www.tsiindia.com/gujarat/tourist-attractions-gujarat/forts-monuments/rani-udaymati.html)

39. Situated at a distance of 1-2 furlong on the west side of Pavagadh village, is three storied whose construction was started in 11th century and was completed in 17th century.

40. Situated in the village Sevasi of Baroda Taluka, it was constructed during the time of Mohmedan Emperor Mohammed Begada. On each side of the main entrance gate, the statue of two tigers are found inscribed and similarly that of an elephant is found in the right side. The gate has very good arches and there is a circular dome over it.)

41. (a) The tour details expressed by a tourist and my friend Harpreet Kaur on www.dancewithshadows.com/vavs_stepwell_gujarat.asp)

    (b) see slide/picture 17

42. An article presented upon 'Water and Civilisation' by M.R. Gandhi Retired Chief Engineer Narmada, Water Resources and Water Supply Department. Government of Gujarat, Gandhinagar, on http://www.supportnarmadadam.org/water-civilization-mr-gandhi1.htm

43. ibid

44. see slide/picture 18

Conservation Study of Medieval Hydraulic Heritage structures of Delhi

Dr. Aman Kumar Singh

The oldest existing *tal* of Delhi is Anangtal near Qutub Minar, built in the tenth century A.D, during the reign of Rajput Tomar dynasty. This *tal* was used to collect and store rainwater. Medieval architecture of Delhi is fusion of indigenous styles of architecture of India and that of Muslim Arabia, Trans- Oxiana, Iran, Afghanistan, Egypt, Northern Africa, and the countries of South Western Europe. Some of the fundamental forms of Iranian architecture, like the pointed and trefoil arches, the transverse vault, the octagonal form of dome and vault are found in medieval architecture of Delhi and one of its integral parts is hydraulic structures. The first hydraulic structure in Delhi is *Gandhak ki baoli* near Qutb Minar, followed by *Hauz-i-Shamshi, Rajo ki ben baoli in* Mehrauli and a reservoir in Hauz Khas. The largest numbers of hydraulic structures in Delhi were constructed in the period of Tughlaq Dynasty, especially during the time of Firoz Shah Tughlaq. In Red fort, there are two hydraulic structures named on season like Sawan and Bhado. A large number of functional hydraulic structures in the Sultanate period were constructed by Firoz Shah Tughlaq while many Mughal period hydraulic structures were used for decorative as well as functional purposes. This paper intended to explore the functional aspect of the structures for preservation, promotion and presentation.

<u>Gandhak ki Baoli:</u>

The *baoli* is located at about 100 meters south of Adham Khan's tomb in Mehrauli village. It was built during the reign of Emperor Illtutmish, the founder of the Slave Dynasty. It is the first step well in Delhi. It is one of the largest step-wells or *baolis* in and around Mehrauli. The *baoli* is known as Gandhak ki Baoli because of the smell of its water like *gandhak*.

<u>Hauz Shamsi:</u>

This structure was constructed by Illtutmish in 1230th century A.D for the purpose of water storage reservoir or tank. There is a pavilion on the west side which was originally in the middle of the tank. One mythological story of Islam says that it contains hoof print of the horse ridden by the prophet. According to a popular legend, in Illtutmish's dream, Prophet Muhammad directed him to build a reservoir at a particular site for the construction of a water tank. Since drinking water supply was acute in the newly founded capital of Illtumish, a tank was dug at the location indicated in the dream, which resulted in water jetting out from a spring source. It was, thereafter, named as Hauz-i-Shamsi, and Khawaja, the saint who divined it, came to be known as Hazrat Qutbuddin Bakhtiar Kaki.

Hauz-i-Shamsi originally covered an area of 2 hectares (4.9 acres). The domed pavilion constructed by Illtumish to mark the hoof mark of Muhammad's horse located in the middle of the tank is a double storied structure constructed of red sandstone supported on twelve columns. It could have been approached only by a boat at that time but now it is reached through a foot bridge. The original stone, on which the hoof mark of the horse of Muhammad was imprinted, could be seen at this pavilion. It has since been removed but replaced by a new one. In view of its religious significance, the water stored in the tank was considered sacred. Many famous emperors and saints have been buried on the periphery of the reservoir. Over the years, the area has been shrinking in size due to encroachment and siltation. The pavilion is in sad state of preservation.

Jharna:

A *jharna* or water fall emanating from the Hauz-i-Shamsi is located close to the Jahaz Mahal. It is identified as a significant water structure that had been developed by Nawab Ghaziuddin around 1700 AD as a pleasure garden during the Mughal rule. An underground pipe (still visible in ruins) supplied the runoff to the *jharna* from Hauz-i–Shamshi. This was in addition to an open channel close by that carried the overflow of the tank to Tughlaqabad fort to enhance the drinking water supply. The *jharna* structure was built in three parts. The first part consisted of the reservoir or the tank, the second part was the water fall and the last part consisted of the fountains.

Jahaz Mahal:

Jahaz Mahal (in Urdu Language '*Jahaz*' means "Ship" and '*Mahal*' means "Palace", the "Ship Palace"), is located next to Hauz-i-Shamsi. It was so named, since its reflection (illusion) in the surrounding reservoir looked like a ship floating on a lake. It is inferred to have been built during the Lodi Dynasty (1452-1526 AD) as a pleasure resort or a *sarai* or an inn. One reason for building the Jahaz Mahal retreat was to provide transit accommodation as a *sarai* to the large number of pilgrims from Afghanistan, Arabia, Iran, Iraq, Morocco and Turkey who came to Delhi to visit the many Muslim shrines. Another version is that it was built as a retreat for the emperors, (Akbar Shah II and Bahadur Shah II and their families, during the summer months, away from the heat and dust of Delhi).

Hauz Khas Tank:

Hauz-i-Alai, a large reservoir constructed by Ala-ud-din Khilji (1296-1316 AD) to supply water to second city Siri. It went dry soon after the death of Ala-ud-din Khilji in 1316 AD. It was again rebuilt by Firoz Shah Tughlaq 50 years later. It is spread over seventy acres of land surrounded by forest and supplied water for resident of Delhi at that time. The hydraulic structure *jheel* was constructed near Tughlaqabad Fort built by Sultan Ghiyas-ud-din Tughlaq in 1325 AD also remains dry throughout the season. Now, an Air Force residential complex has come up in its place.

Boali at Firoz Shah Kotla:

The baoli is located in the center of the garden of Firoz Shah Kotla. The large circular *baoli* has subterranean apartments. It has a large underground drain towards its eastern side. Like all other *baolis*, this *baoli* also served as a cool retreat in summer and was used by persons of royal lineage.

Rajon ki ben *baoli*:

The *baoli* was constructed for *rai mistri* (masons) during the reign of Sikander Lodhi. So it is known as Rajon ki Baoli. It is one of the beautiful *baoli*s in Delhi and has four stories. The fourth storey has internal rooms with arched gateway. Generally, the water level comes up to the third storey. This *baoli* has two functions— one is resting place in summer and the other is the use of its water. It has been built up with Delhi Quartzite. It has pointed arches and slopping *chhajjas.* The *baoli* is in good state of preservation.

Khari Boali:

It was during Mughal Emperor Shah Jahan's reign that the *khari baoli*, with b*aoli* was constructed. Khari Baoli etymologically means the well having salty water (*khari* meaning salty and *baoli* means step well), thus it was salty water stepwell used for animals and for bathing. It was constructed along with a fortified gateway Lahori Gate of the city of Shahjahanabad. However, today there is no trace of either the Baoli or the gateway here, which now lies buried under the main road of the market.

Ugrasen ki Baoli or Agrsen ki Baoli:

The *baoli* located near Connaught Place on Hailey Road. The *baoli* was constructed by king Agrsen. It is a four storied structure with fine carving in well area. It is in good state of preservation.

So, large numbers of hydraulic structures of medieval period exist in Delhi which require rejuvenation to solve the water scarcity in Delhi. It will also lead to face lifting of heritage structures as well as Delhi's image.

Bibliography

1. Verma Urmilla, *"Delhi: A Tale of Seven Cities"*, Swati Books, New Delhi, 2001.
2. Sharma, Y.D., *"Delhi and its Neighbourhood"*, Archaeological Survey of India, New Delhi, 2001(Reprint).
3. Singh, B.P. and Pavan Kumar Verma, *"The Millennium Book on New Delhi"*, Oxford University Press, New Delhi, 2001.
4. Carr, Stephen, *"Archaeological and Monumental Remains of Delhi"*, Aryan Books International, New Delhi, 2002 (Reprint).
5. Dube, D.N. and Jaya Ramanathan, *"Delhi: The City of Monuments"*, Timeless Books, New Delhi, 1997.
6. Kaul, H.K., *"Historic Delhi: An Anthology"*, Oxford University Press, New York, 1998.
7. Frykenberg, F.Y. (Ed.), "Delhi Omnibus", Oxford University Press, New Delhi, 2002.
8. Irving, R.G., "Indian Summer: Lutyens, Baker and Imperial Delhi, Oxford University Press, London, 1981.
9. Kaye, M.M. (Ed.), "The Golden Calm", Viking Press, New York, 1980.
10. Khosla, Romi (Ed.), " Idea of Delhi", Marg, Mumbai, 2005.

मालवा एवं पश्चिमी राजस्थान की जल-अनुपूरक विधियाँ

डॉ. श्याम सुन्दर निगम

भारत के विभिन्न क्षेत्रों में जल-प्रबंधन का आधार उस क्षेत्र की प्राकृतिक सरंचना, जलवायु की स्थिति, मानवीय आवश्यकता एवं जल-स्रोतों की उपलब्धि आदि रहे हैं। सामान्यतया जल-आपूर्ति के साधन नदियाँ, नाले, नहरें, तडाग, कुण्ड, कूप, चौपड़े, वापियाँ आदि माने जाते है, इन पर पर्याप्त चर्चा हुई और उनका ऐतिहासिक, पारंपरिक, पुरातत्त्वीय, तकनीकी, प्रशासनिक एवं आंचलिक दृष्टि से विवेचन भी होता रहा है। ऐसा होते हुए मालवा एवं निकटवर्ती क्षेत्रों में विद्यमान रही अंतर्जलीय व्यवस्था की चर्चा लगभग नगण्य ही रही है। प्रस्तुत पत्र इस व्यवस्था, उसके बहुविध स्वरूप, उसकी आवश्यकता एवं उपादेयता पर प्रकाश डालने का एक विनम्र प्रयास है।

जल-अनुपूरक व्यवस्था के दो स्थूल विभेद रहे हैं-

(अ) ग्रामीण ओड़ियाँ एवं

(ब) नगरीय जल-अनुपूरण

इन पर चर्चा की जाना अन्यथा न होगा-

(अ) ग्रामीण ओड़ियाँ - ग्रामीण अंचलों में 'ओड़ी' के रूप में जल अनुपूरण व्यवस्था अस्तित्व में रही। 'ओडी' शब्द संस्कृत के 'अवली' या प्राकृत के 'अवड़ी' शब्द का मालवी रूपांतर हो सकता है। इस पद्धति द्वारा जल-युक्त क्षेत्र से जल-विहीन या कम जल वाले क्षेत्र तक कृत्रिम साधनों द्वारा जल आपूरण किया जाता है। यह जल-सम्प्रेषण या तो लघु कुल्याओं या अंतर्वती नहरों द्वारा किया जाता था। स्वतंत्रता पूर्व तक मालवा व निकटवर्ती क्षेत्रों के अनेक ग्राम-परिसरों में यह व्यवस्थ देखी जा सकती थी। जल की सदाबहार आपूर्ति, निर्माण-कार्य में मितव्ययता एवं सरलता तथा स्थानीय तकनीकों की विद्यमानता इस पद्धति के लोकप्रियता के प्रमुख कारण रहे। आज जल-स्रोतों के सूखने, सिंचाई के साधनों के यांत्रिकीकरण, आंतरिक जल-स्तर

के कई फीट नीचे उतर जाने, वर्षा की अनिश्चितता आदि कारणों से जहाँ एक ओर तड़ागों, कुओं, बावड़ियों आदि पर भारी सकंट मंडरा रहा है, वहीं नदियों व नालों की दिन-प्रतिदिन बढ़ती प्रवाहहीनता एवं शुष्कता ने इस संकट को और भी गहरा कर दिया है। ऐसी स्थिति में जब जल-आपूर्ति के ये प्राकृतिक साधन ही दम तोड़ रहे हैं तो जल-ग्रहण करने वाली ओड़ियाँ बड़ी तेजी से निष्प्रभावी होकर अतीत के गर्त में समा चुकी हैं और समा रही हैं।

उक्त पृष्ठभूमि में ओड़ी व्यवस्था की आवश्यकता एवं स्वरूप की चर्चा की जाना अन्यथा न होगा।

आवश्यकता - ओड़ी निर्माण का लक्ष्य स्थानीय जल-पूर्ति एवं जल-प्रबंधन को अनौपचारिक रूप से ग्रामीण तकनीक द्वारा संतुलित करना है। यह संतुलन कृषि-भूमि की सिंचाई, पशुओं के लिये पेय-जल का प्रबंधन, सनई के डंठलों के सन-त्वक् निकालने, आधिक्य वाले जल-संग्रह से कमी वाले संग्रहों तक जल-पहुँचाने, स्थानीय रूप से अतिरिक्त जल-संग्रह करने, कुल्या-मार्गों पर वृक्षारोपण करने आदि के काम में आता था। निश्चित है, पथरीली, पठारी या डूंगर वाले इलाकों में यह पद्धति कतई उपयोगी सिद्ध नहीं होती। यह उन स्थानों के लिये अधिक मुफीद सिद्ध होती रही, जो काली या दुमट मिट्टी वाली समतल भूमि पर स्थित हो और जो जल आदान-प्रदान करने वाले स्थलों से अति निकट हों।

ओड़ियों का स्वरूप - ओड़ियों के कई प्रकार होते थे। इनका संक्षिप्त विवेचन इस प्रकार है-

(१) झांझा ओड़ी - यदि खेत या बगीचे की कुछ दूरी पर नदी या नाला बहता हो और उसका जल सिंचाई के लिये पास लाना हो तो एक झरननुमा खाई खोद कर नदी या नाले का जल लाकर कच्चे कुएं में डाल लिया जाता है। जिस पर बने नाले से सिंचाई हो जाती है। कच्चे कुएं विभिन्न आयामों और आकारों के होते हैं और स्थानीय भाषा में झांझा कहलाते हैं। इस ओड़ी को झांझा ओड़ी कहते है।

(२) ढंकनी - कई बार ऐसी ओड़ी मार्ग या पगडंडी पर आ जाती है। ऐसी स्थिति में कुल्या को बड़े पत्थरों से ढांक दिया जाता है ताकि वे दिखाई न दें और आने-जाने का मार्ग अबाध चलता रहे। ढंकी होने पर ओड़ी ढंकनी कहलाती है। शेष स्थिति झांझा ओड़ी की तरह ही होती है।

(३) बहुली - कुछ स्थानों पर कृषक सम्मिलित रूप से बहुली ओड़ी का निर्माण करते रहे हैं। वे अपने अकेले खेतों के पास सिंचाई हेतु कुएनुमा ओड़ी खोद लेते हैं। फिर

एक ही नहर से नदी या खाल से पानी लाकर फिर उससे अपनी-अपनी ओड़ियों को जलपूरित कर लेते हैं।

(४) जनावर ओड़ी - यह ओड़ी किसी एक विशाल ताल के निकट एक लघु तलैया के रूप में होती थी; बड़े ताल से यह सटी हुई अपना पृथक् अस्तित्व रखती थी और पानी कम होने या सूखने की स्थिति में बड़े ताल से पतली किंतु नियंत्रित नहरों से इसके जल की पूर्ति की जाती थी। ओड़ी का निर्माण विशेषकर ग्रामीण पशुओं के लिये उन के लिये पेयजल, उनके स्नान या महिष आदि की बैठको के निमित्त होता था।

(५) ईटाली ओड़ी - ऐसी ओड़ियाँ किसी नदी, नाले या तालाब से निःसृत करके बनाई जाती थीं। इन स्रोतों का जल एक तलैयानुमा ओड़ी में एकत्रित कर लिया जाता था। इस जल में निकटवर्ती मिट्टी को सांध कर ईंटें या कवेलू बनाये जाते थे। इस कारण इन्हें ईंटाली संज्ञा दी जाती थी।

(ब) नगरीय अंतःपूरण - अंतर्जलीय विधि के कुछ रूप मध्यकालीन नगरों एवं किलों में भी कुछ भिन्न रूप में दिखाई देते हैं। ग्रामीण विधियों से ये इस रूप में भिन्न हैं कि प्रारंभ में वे प्राकृतिक रूप में रही होंगी किंतु नगरों एवं किलों के विकास के साथ-साथ इन्हें ईंटों या प्रस्तर-शिलाओं से मंडित कर स्थायी रूप दो कारणों से दिया गया-

(१) सुरक्षा की दृष्टि से (२) उपभोग की दृष्टि से

इन पर संक्षेप में विचार समीचीन होगा-

(१) कोटल - प्रारंभ में यह एक परिखानुमा ओड़ी थी जो नगरकोट के इर्द-गिर्द बनी परिखाओं को जल से पूरित करती थीं। नदी तट पर जो नगर होते थे, उनकी सुरक्षा के लिये प्राकार निर्मित होते थे। इन प्राकारों से सटी हुई परिखाएँ होतीं थीं जिनमें हिंसक घड़ियाल या ऐसे ही जल-जीव घूमते रहते थे। ये परिखाएँ काफी गहरी होती थी, जब नदी में बाढ़ होती थी, तो विशाल कुल्याओं से परिखाओं में वर्ष भर के लिये जल-पूरित कर दिया जाता था। नदी एवं परिखाओं के बीच एक विशाल गहरे कूपनुमा ओड़ी होती थी जो परिखाओं में जल कम होने पर उसकी पूर्ति करती थी। कोट से सटी होने से ऐसी ओड़ी कोटल कहलाती थीं। लगभग सत्तर वर्ष पूर्व तक शिप्रातट पर स्थित काल भैरव के मंदिर के सामने जो विशाल परिखाएँ हैं, वे भी ऐसा ओड़ियों से जुड़ी थीं।

(२) झरन ओड़ी - ऐसी ओड़ियाँ सैनिक गढ़ियों, सामंतीय या राजकीय किलों आदि में उन स्थानों पर होती थीं, जहाँ पर पर्वतीय सोते होते थे। ये गढ़ियों या किलों में

जल-आपूर्ति के अत्यंत उपयोगी स्रोत होती थीं। इसकी उपयोगिता की दृष्टि से इसके निर्झरण पर गोमुख या सिंहमुख बना दिये जाते थे जिनमें से निरंतर पानी प्रवाहित होता रहता था। कई बार उच्च पर्वत-श्रेणी के तड़ाग का जल भी गुप्त नालिकाओं के माध्यम से इन स्थानों पर पहुँचाया जाता था। इस प्रकार ये ओड़ियाँ या तो नैसर्गिक होती थीं या मानव-निर्मित। मानव-निर्मित ओड़ियों के मूल स्रोत एवं नालिकाओं को सुरक्षा कारणों से अत्यंत गोपनीय रखा जाता था। मार्ग में या स्रोत स्थान को सुरक्षित करने की दृष्टि से ओड़ी को पक्के कुण्ड का सुरक्षित रूप दे दिया जाता था। कई बार अतिरिक्त जल-कुण्ड नालियों द्वारा प्रवाहित होकर गुप्त मार्ग से किले में स्थित त्रिस्तरीय ओड़ी में पहुँचा दिया जाता था। तीनों स्तरों के मध्य विभाजक दीवारें होती थीं। दो दीवारों के मध्य सीढ़ियाँ बनी होती थीं। प्रथम स्तर सबसे ऊपरी भाग में होता था। इससे पेयजल की आपूर्ति होती थी। उससे नीचे के दूसरे स्तर पर घाट बना होता था। जहाँ महिलाएँ स्नान करतीं या कपड़े धोती थीं। उससे नीचे तीसरा स्तर पर सीढ़ियों की बजाय ढालू किंतु खुरदरा संकरा रास्ता होता था जहाँ पर हाथी, अश्व या अन्य पालतू पशुओं को पानी पिलाया जाता था। प्रत्येक स्तर अपना पृथक् किंतु अपारदर्शी अस्तित्व रखता था। चूंकि जल सतत प्रवाहमान होता था, इसलिये प्रदूषण की संभावना नगण्य ही होती थी। तीसरे स्तर से जल निःसृत होकर किले का बाहर एक परिखा या नाले का रूप ले लेता था। यह झरण ओड़ी विभिन्न किलों में विभिन्न नाम से जानी जाती रही है। इसके कुछ अच्छे उदाहरण बुरहानपुर, आमेर या गागरोन में देखे जा सकते हैं। ऐसी अंतर्वर्ती कुल्याओं को पेयजल के अतिरिक्त हरमों और अंतः पुरों में स्नानादि के निमित्त निर्मित किया जाता था। ठंडे पानी की कुल्याएँ ईंटों या पकी मिट्टी की बनाई जाती थीं। ठंडे पानी को गरम करने के लिये बहाव के नीचे एकाधिक जगहों पर लकड़ियाँ जला कर पानी को गरम कर लिया जाता है। फिर जिसकों जितना गरम जल चाहिए, वह उसे उपकुल्याओं के माध्यम से अपने हौज में डाल कर स्नान कर सकता था।

इस प्रकार ये ओड़ियाँ विभिन्न नाम-रूपों में मालवांचल एवं निकटवत्री कई अंचलों में विद्यमान होती रहीं और सिंचाई, पशु-जगत्, आदि के निमित्त जन-जन के उपयोग में आती रहीं।'

मेवाड़ में जल प्रबन्धन ठिकाना पारसोली के सन्दर्भ में

डॉ. गिरीश नाथ माथुर

रियासतकालीन मेवाड़ में राजधानी के लिये सामरिक, व्यापारिक एवं पानी की पर्याप्त उपलब्धता आदि महत्त्वपूर्ण बिन्दुओं को ध्यान में रखकर स्थल चयनित किये गये। वहीं प्रशासनिक दृष्टि से बनाये गये ठिकानों के स्थल चयन करते समय भी ठिकानेदारों ने उक्त बिन्दुओं का पर्याप्त ध्यान रखा। इन बिन्दुओं में जल की उपलब्धता को सर्वाधिक महत्त्व दिया गया। मेवाड़ के प्रथम श्रेणी के ठिकाने पारसोली[1] के सन्दर्भ में जल प्रबन्धन के सन्दर्भ में जल प्रबन्धन अध्ययन यहाँ प्रस्तुत है।

सामरिक दृष्टि से ठिकाना पारसोली सुरक्षित स्थान पर बनाया गया। इसे पहाडों के मध्य बसाया गया। यह मेवाड़ की प्राचीन राजधानी से २२ मील की दूरी पर स्थित था।

पारसोली क्षेत्र में वार्षिक वर्षा का औसत २० से ४५ इंच रहता था।

पारसोली में बहने वाली नदियाँ

पारसोली में पाँच नदियों का बहाव क्षेत्र रहा है। **प्रथम बेड़च नदी** यह नदी चित्तौड़ दुर्ग की ओर से बहती हुई पारसोली क्षेत्र में ही बहने वाली बनास नदी में मिलती थी। इसमें वर्ष भर पानी रहता था।

दूसरी नदी बनास यह नदी पारसोली के गाँव दोवनी के पास से होकर निकलती थी। **तीसरी नदी रूपारेल** यह नदी मध्य प्रदेश में इन्दौर के कस्बे नंदवास के पास दक्षिण की ओर से बहती हुई ठिकाना पारसोली के नजदीक से बहती हुई पारसोली स्थित दो पहाड़ों के नकवासों के मध्य होकर पारसोली में उत्तरी क्षेत्र के गाँव रावपुरा के पास बेड़च नदी में मिल जाती थी।

चौथी नदी गोमती यह नदी गोमती क्षेत्र में पारसोली के दक्षिण में बहती हुई पारसोली ठिकाने में सम्मिलित होती थी।

पाँचवी नदी ओराई यह नदी पारसोली के दक्षिण की तरफ से बहती हुई गाँव बड़ीपार के पास होकर पारसोली पश्चिमी क्षेत्र के गाँव लुहारिया के पास बेड़च नदी में सम्मिलित होती थी।

उक्त पाँचों नदियों का पानी कृषि के लिये उपयोग में लिया जाता था। विशेषकर पारसोली के ऊपरी क्षेत्र के गाँवों की कृषि भूमि को सिंचित करने में ये नदियाँ बहुत सहायक थीं। क्योंकि पाँच में से प्रथम तीन नदियाँ पारसोली के ऊपरी क्षेत्र में ही बहती थी और उनमें वर्ष भर पानी रहता था।[२]

पारसोली के तालाब

पारसोली ठिकाने में पाँचों नदियों के बहाव क्षेत्र से काफी दूर स्थित कृषि भूमि की सिंचाई एवं दिन प्रतिदिन जलीय आवश्यकता की पूर्ति हेतु ठिकानेदार ने तालाब व बांध के निर्माण करवाये। पारसोली ठिकाने में चार तालाब व एक बांध का उल्लेख मिलता है।

प्रथम तालाब गाँव इठावा में, दूसरा तालाब गाँव दुगार में, तीसरा तालाब राव लक्ष्मण सिंह ने गाँव नाहरगढ़ में एवं चौथा तालाब (१८७७-८८) में राव रतनसिंह ने बनवाया। चार तालाबों के अतिरिक्त गाँव गल्यावड़ी में बहते हुए एक नाले पर १८९० ई. में एक बांध बनवाया गया।[३]

ठिकाना पारसोली में पीने के लिये एवं सिंचाई हेतु कुओं की व्यवस्था

ठिकाना पारसोली में जहाँ नदी एवं तालाबों से सिंचाई संभव नहीं थी वहाँ पानी के लिए बड़ी संख्या में कुए खुदवाये गये। उन कुओं में बरसाती पानी के अतिरिक्त नदियों के पानी की शीर आती थी जिसमें उनमें **वर्ष** पर्यंत पानी रहता था।

जागीरी क्षेत्र में कुए

ठिकाना पारसोली के सामंतों ने भी समय-समय पर अपने जागीरदारों के क्षेत्र में आवश्यकतानुसार कुओं का निर्माण करवाया। तद्नुसार सोनगरा चौहान की जागीर में २ कुए, चुण्ड़ावत सिसोदिया की जागीर में २ कुए, ब्राह्मण दवे सनावड़ की जागीर में २ कुए, कनीकजादे पुजावत चौहान की जागीर में १ कुआ, गूजर धाबाई हुण की जागीर में १ कुआ, बन्दूक साज उस्ता मुसलमान की जागीर में १ कुआ, कपड़दार दरजी की जागीर में १ कुआ, नाई खवास की जागीर में एक कुआ, सनावड़ पुरोहित की जागीर में १ कुआ, भाई रज सींगोत ड़ाहरी की जागीर में १ कुए की व्यवस्था थी। यों ठिकाना पारसोली के जागीरदारों के पास कुल १४ कुए थे।

एक कुए से औसत ७५ बीघा भूमि में सिंचाई होती थी।

ठिकाने के गाँवों में कुऐं

ठिकाने के गाँवों में सिंचाई हेतु भी कुओं की व्यवस्था थी। इसके लिए दौलतपुरा गाँव में १ कुआ, गाँव इठावा में १ कुआ व गाँव मुरलेये में २ कुओं की व्यवस्था थी। इस प्रकार ठिकाने के गाँवों में कुल चार कुए थे।

पारसोली में भू मालिकों के पास कुऐं

पारसोली में छोटी जोत के भू-स्वामियों के लिये १ कुए की व्यवस्था थी। यहाँ कुल ऐसे बीस व्यक्ति थे व उनके पास कुल मिलाकर ६२ बीघा औषि भूमि थी।

पारसोली ठिकाने में सिंचाई हेतु साझे में कुओं की व्यवस्था

ठिक़ाना पारसोली में जहाँ कृषि भूमि के मुकाबले कुओं की संख्या कम थी वहाँ भू स्वामियों को कुओं का उपयोग साझे में करने की व्यवस्था की गई। तद्नुसार मीणा की जमीन, देवलच मीणा व नाहरगढ़ के मीणों के बीच ३ कुओं की व्यवस्था की गई। गाँव हमीरपुर के मीणों, गाँव दुगार के मीणों के बीच एक कुआ, गाँव इठावा के मोणों एवं गाँव ड़ेकड़ी खेड़ा के मीणों के एवं गाँव गल्यावड़ी के भीलों की औषि भूमि की सिंचाई हेतु दो कुओं की व्यवस्था की गई।[४]

ठिकाना पारसोली में मंदिरों के रखरखाव हेतु ठिकाने की ओर से प्रदत्त भूमि पर कुओं की व्यवस्था–

ठिक़ाना पारसोली में मंदिरों के रखरखाव व सेवापूजा की व्यवस्था हेतु समय-समय पर वहाँ के सामंत द्वारा जो भूमि प्रदान की गई वहाँ जल के लिए कुए की व्यवस्था भी की गई। यथा ठिकाना पारसोली में चत्राभुज की भूमि पर एक कुआ, चत्राभुज जी के लिए प्रदत्त गाँव गल्यावड़ी की भूमि पर एक कुआ, गाँव गल्यावड़ी में श्री ठाकुर जी के मंदिर हेतु दो कुए, गाँव देवलच स्थित ठाकुर जी के मंदिर हेतु एक कुआ, गाँव मोतीपुरा उर्फ गुलेसरी श्री ठाकुर जी के एक कुआ, गाँव बख्यास श्री ठाकुर जी के एक कुआ, गाँव चावंड़या ठाकुर जी के दो कुए, गाँव दोवनी के ठाकुर जी के एक कुआ, गाँव ड़ेकड़ी खेड़ा श्री ठाकुर जी के दो कुए, कस्बा गड़बोर श्री चत्राभुज के गाँव लुबारूया में एक कुआ, ठिकाने पारसोली सीव विलास के लिये एक कुआ एवं गाँव इठावा में शंकर (शिव) के लिये एक कुए की व्यवस्था थी। इसी तरह गाँव बख्यास में शिव मंदिर हेतु एक कुआ, गाँव देवलच देवजी के मंदिर के लिये एक कुआ, गाँव सारण उर्फ माधुपुर देवजी के मंदिर के लिये एक कुआ, श्री शंकर भगवान मंदिर हेतु

एक कुआ, देवजी के मंदिर हेतु एक कुआ एवं गाँव गल्यावड़ी देवजी के मंदिर हेतु एक कुए की व्यवस्था की गई।

ब्राह्मणों को पुण्यार्थ दी गई भूमि पर कुऐं

ठिकाना पारसोली में ठिकाने की ओर से ब्राह्मणों को पुण्यार्थ दी गई भूमि जो औषि योग्य होती थी, उसकी सिंचाई हेतु भी कुए खुदवाये जाते थे। यथा सनावड़ बड़वा की जमीन हेतु एक कुआ, पण्ड्या की भूमि हेतु एक कुआ, गाँव नाहरगढ़ में जोसी के एक कुआ, गाँव चौसाला में एक कुआ, गाँव मोतीपुरा उर्फ गुलेसरी में एक कुआ, गाँव माधोपुर उर्फ सारण में दो कुए, गाँव दुगार में एक कुआ, गाँव लुवार्या में एक कुआ, गाँव सोभागपुरा उर्फ चांवड़या में तीन कुए, गाँव गल्यावड़ी में १४ कुए, गाँव गल्यावड़ी में जोगी भोलानाथ के मठ हेतु दी गई भूमि के लिये पाँच कुओं की व्यवस्था थी। यों पुण्यार्थ दी गई भूमि पर कुल ३८ कुए थे।५

ठिकाना पारसोली क्षेत्र में नदी, तालाब व कुओं की पर्याप्त संख्या के कारण यहाँ वर्ष भर जल की कमी नहीं रहती थी। इस क्षेत्र में जमीन में २० से ६० फुट नीचे पानी उपलब्ध हो जाता था।

जल की उपलब्धता के कारण ही सियालु व उन्हालु दोनों ही फसलों में अनाज के अतिरिक्त भी आवश्यक फसल (उपज) होती थी।

खरीफ (स्यालु) में मक्का, ज्वार, तिल, कपास, उड़द, मूँग, चवला, सण, कुलथ, कोदु, मोठ, अंबावड़ी अर्थात मड़ेली, कांगणी, फेवड़ों, मलीचो, सांवों, माल, सिंगाड़ा, अड़क, साल, राजगीर कुदी, मिर्च, तम्बाकू आदि।

रबी (उन्हालु) में गेहूँ, जव, चना, मसूर, बटला, अफीम, गन्ना (सांठा), धणिया, लहसुण, कांदा (प्याज), मेथी, राई, रजका, अलस, सरसों एवं राई आदि।

जल की उपलब्धता के कारण ही पारसोली के जंगल में स्वास्थ्य के लिए उपयोगी फल वाले एवं इमारती लकड़ी देने वाले वृक्ष बहुतायत में थे। यहाँ प्राप्त होने वाले वृक्षों में आम, बड़, पीपल, महुआ, जामुन, नीम, इमली, बोरसली, आसापाला, सहतुत, सेमला, कचनार, कोड़िया, आकोल, टीमरू, आंवला, बहेड़ा, किरमाला, बील, धामन, सालर, गुरजण, खिरणी, लुणीचा, हलधा, कुलम्ब, धोकड़े, खेजड़े, हिगोरण, खैर, घटबोर, झाड़ी बोर, खरेटी, गंगेरण, कठाज, सीयाली, फरागंड़ी, सेलपी, खांखरा, कांटयोधो, बिन्दी, चितावल, सारी, नीसोत, पेमली बोर, बड़बोर, घरल, लेसवा झींजा, गुंदी, खड़े, सरस्यों, रेण, जामुन, गुराड़, बंम्बुल, खजूर, सांगरी, कोटबड़ी, बकाण, सुरजणों, बांस, सीसम, उमर, कचुंबर, रोइस, कदम, केर एवं बेकल आदि।

ठिकाना पारसोली में जनसंख्या के अनुपात में पर्याप्त जल संसाधन की उपलब्धता ने वहाँ के जनजीवन को खुशहाल बनाये रखा। २६ फरवरी १८९१ ईस्वी की जनगणना के अनुसार यहाँ की जनसंख्या : ८४७६ थी। जो उपलब्ध संसाधनों की तुलना में कम थी। अवश्य यहाँ के अतिरिक्त उत्पादन बड़े कस्बों व नगरों की मांग की पूर्ति करते होंगे।

निष्कर्ष रूप में यह कहना उचित रहेगा कि मानव बस्ती बसाने से पूर्व जल की उपलब्धता को प्राथमिकता देनी चाहिये एवं ज्यों ज्यों जनसंख्या वृद्धि हो तब जल संसाधन भी उसी अनुपात में बढ़ा लेने चाहिए। ठिकाना पारसोली उसका उदाहरण है।

सन्दर्भ सूची

१. 'पारसोली के सरदार बेदले के स्वामी रामचन्द्र चौहान के छोटे पुत्रा केसरी सिंह के वंशज हैं और 'राव' उनकी उपाधि है।

केसरी सिंह पर बड़ी कृपा होने के कारण महाराणा राजसिंह (१६५२-८०) ने उसे प्रथम श्रेणी का सरदार बनाया।'

ओझा गौरीशंकर हीराचन्द; उदयपुर राज्य का इतिहास भाग २, पृष्ठ ६१६-२१.

२. ठिकाना पारसोली इतिहास स्वस्थान ठिकाने पारसोली, जागीर मुल्क मेवाड़ पृष्ठ २०८-६.

उद्धृत चौहार प्रकाश सम्पादक डॉ राणावत प्रताप शोध प्रतिष्ठान, भूपाल नोबल्स संस्थान उदयपुर प्रथम संस्करण २००१.

३. मुहम्मद अलीमुद्दीन, इतिहास स्वस्थान ठिकाने पारसोली, जागीर मुल्क मेवाड़, पृष्ठ ४७१. प्रताप शोध प्रतिष्ठान उदयपुर.

४. मुहम्मद अलीमुद्दीन; इतिहास स्वस्थान ठिकाने पारसोली, जागीर मुल्क मेवाड़, पृष्ठ ४६० एवं ४६३ प्रताप शोध प्रतिष्ठान, उदयपुर.

५. मुहम्मद अलीमुद्दीन; इतिहास स्वस्थान ठिकाने पारसोली. जागीर मुल्क मेवाड़, पृ. ४६३-४६६, प्रताप शोध प्रतिष्ठान, उदयपुर.

६. मुहम्मद अलीमुद्दीन; इतिहास संस्थान ठिकाने पारसोली. जागीर मुल्क मेवाड़, पृ. ४७२, ४७३, ४८६ एवं ४८७

मनासा-रामपुरा अंचल की मध्यकालीन ऐतिहासिक जल संसाधन बावड़ियाँ : उनका प्रबंधन एवं उपयोगिता

डॉ. पूरन सहगल

मनासा-रामपुरा अंचल, नीमच जिले की एक तहसील है। यहाँ मध्यकाल में भीलों की सत्ता और फिर मेवाड़ से निष्कासित चन्द्रावतों की सत्ता रही। चन्द्रावतों का सीधा सम्बन्ध मेवाड़ के सीसोदिया वंश से है। इसी क्रम में यहाँ मेवाड़ के भाग ोज माधौसिंह कछावा का भी अधिकार रहा। फिर चन्द्रावत और आखिर मे इन्दौर के होल्करों का आधिपत्य रहा।

रामपुरा दुर्ग अरावली की तलहटी में स्थित है। इस अंचल की मुख्य नदियाँ चम्बल, शिवना, रेतम, ईडर अंसर, गुंजाली आदि है जो वर्षाकाल के पश्चात खाली हो जाती हैं। इनका पानी बहकर एक नदी से दूसरी नदी में होता हुआ बहकर चम्बल में मिलता है। चम्बल पर गाँधी सागर बाँध बनने के कारण चम्बल के अंचल-पथ में पानी बना रहता है। वर्ष का औसत इस अंचल में २५-३६ इंच है।

जलाशयों में यहाँ गाँव गाँव बावड़ियाँ और छोटे-छोटे मगरों तक में ताल तलैयाँ मौजूद हैं। कुँए तो खूब हैं। लोक में एक दोहा प्रसिद्ध है।

गाँव-गाँव में बावड़ियाँ, खेड़े-खेड़े ताल।
कुँवा खुद्र्या है मोकरा, मालवदेस खुसाल।।

मालवा का यह दशपुर अंचल जल संसाधनों में प्राचीन काल से ही सम्पन्न रहा है। इसीलिए कबीर ने अपनी मालव यात्रा में कहा था। "मालवमाटी गहन गम्भीर, पग-पग रोटी डग-डग नीर।"

पीपल्या रावजी की बावड़ियों में सबसे महत्वपूर्ण है 'ननवाणा बावड़ी' इस बावड़ी का निर्माण पालिवाल दुर्गादास ननवाणा ने तत्कालीन चन्द्रावत ठिकानेदार हाथीराम

चन्द्रावत के आदेश से करवाया था। पालीवाल समाज मूल रूप से जोधपुर का है। बावड़ियों के वास्तुशिल्य में यह समाज प्रवीण माना जाता था।

श्वेत चूनाश्म शिलाओं से निर्मित यह बावड़ी संवत् १५८२ विक्रमी संवत् वैशाखसुदी को अस्तित्व में आई। इसका निर्माण गंगोज के निमित्त करवाया गया था। इसमें ६५ सीढ़ियाँ है। बावड़ी पश्चिम मुखी है पूर्व में चड़स चलाकर पानी निकालने का थाला बना है। यहाँ से कृषि सिंचाई की जाती थी। पाँच मंजिल पंक्तियों वाली यह बावड़ी मध्यकालीन युग की प्रतिनिधि बावड़ी है। सुन्दर मेहराब और राजपूत शैली की यह बावड़ी पीपल्या सिकान, तहसील मनासा की सुन्दर बावड़ियों में से एक है। इसकी २७ वीं सीढ़ी पर अभिलेख खुदा है।[1]

रावली कुंडबावड़ी - रावली कुंडबावड़ी का निर्माण राजा बाग जी के आदेश से गाजध ार नियांसी संतराम जी तथा उसके पुत्रा जग्गा गोत्रा बमड़ोद सतराम जी तथा उसके पुत्रा जग्गा गोत्रा बमड़ोद निवासी रामपुरा ने संवत् १७८६ विक्रमी माघ सुदी ५ वसंत पंचमी गुरुवार को मंदिर व कुंडबावड़ी का काम पूरा किया।[2]

मंदिर में मूर्ति की स्थापना मंदिर निर्माण से पूर्व चन्द्रपीठिका पर की जा चुकी थी। मूर्ति संवत् १७८५ वि. अषाढ़ सुदी ११ को स्थापित की जा चुकी थी। इसका कारण मूहूर्त की शुभगणना थी।[3] बावड़ी का निर्माण पूर्व में ही हो चुका था। वह निर्माण रोककर पहले मंदिरों का निर्माण किया गयी फिर बावड़ी व मंदिरों को पूर्णता दी गई। १७वीं शाताब्दी की यह बावड़ी-मंदिर पीपल्या रावजी की सर्वाधिक मनोहर और नक्काशीदार बावड़ी है। पाँच मंजिली पंक्तियों वाली तथा सुन्दर सुविधा जनक सीढ़ियों वाली यह बावड़ी शक्तावत ठिकाने की शोभा है। यहाँ पर कार्तिक पूर्णिमा पर कन्याओं द्वारा टाटियाँ तिराने का मांगलिक कार्य किया जाता था। आज भी यहा बावड़ी पूर्णतः सुरक्षित है। ननवाणा बावड़ी जहाँ पूरे गाँव की जल आपूर्ति तथा कृषि सिंचन में उपयोगी है वहीं यह कुंडबावड़ी मांगलिक कार्यों व स्नानादि के लिए महत्वपूण् र्ा जल संसाधन है।

गुवा की बावड़ियाँ - यह बावड़ी श्मशानघाट के निकट गुवा (गोचर) में स्थित है १२ फुट व २४ फुट की चौड़ाई वाली यह बावड़ी। पूर्व दिशा में सीढ़ियाँ २७ सीढ़ियों में बाद चौक। यह १५ वीं शताब्दी की निर्मित है।

छोटी कुंड बावड़ी - अरन्या गाँव मार्ग पर स्थित यह बावड़ी १६वीं शताब्दी की है। पशुचरों व राहगीरों के लिए यह सुलभ सीढ़ियों एवं बाहर खेल (पानी हौज) के कारण महत्वपूर्ण बावड़ी है। एक समय यह एक जंगल क्षेत्र था।

गोपावत बावड़ी - कूप नगर के मध्य यह जल संसाधन पेयजल प्रदाय का आज भी एक सुलभ साधन है। विद्युत पम्प द्वारा जल प्रदाय किया जाता है। इसका निर्माण १६वीं शताब्दी का है।

तेलिया बावड़ी - सत्यनारायण बावड़ी, महादेव बावड़ी, बाबाजी की बावड़ी, राजबावड़ी, ये बावड़ियाँ १५वीं-१६वीं शताब्दी के मध्य की बावड़ियाँ है। इनक प्रबंधन व्यक्तिगत स्तर पर होता है। इनसे कृषि सिंचन एवं जल प्रदाय हो रहा है।

ढाँतोली गढ़ की बावड़ी - अरावली पठार पर स्थित दांतोली गढ़ में यह बावड़ी १५वीं शताब्दी की है। इसका पानी सदैव बना रहता है। गढ़ के भीतरवासियों के लिए जल प्रदाय की यह एक महत्वपूर्ण बावड़ी थी। आज गढ़ नहीं है किन्तु बावड़ी हैं।

भाटखेड़ी की बावड़ियाँ - ननवाणा पालिवालों की बावड़ी। यह बावड़ी रामद्वारा के निकट स्थित है। पीपल्या राव के पालीवाल परिवार ने यह बावड़ो बनवाई थो। यह पालिवालों की कृषि भूमि थी। उस भूमि की सिंचाई एवं नगर (गाँव) के जलप्रदाय का यह महत्वपूर्ण संसाधन माना जाता है।

कायस्थों की बावड़ी - यह बावड़ी १५वीं शताब्दी की है। रावजी पीपल्या के कायस्थ परिवारों ने इसका निर्माण करवाया था। इसका जल राजपरिवार के लिए तथा कायस्थ परिवारों के लिए उपयोग होता था। आज विद्युत पम्प द्वारा ठिकाने में इस बवड़ी से जल प्रदाय किया जा रहा है।

सतियों की बावड़ी - यह सतियों की बावड़ी है। लोक में भ्रमवश इसे "हत्यारी बावडी" कहा जाने लगा है। मालवी में 'स' से 'ह' हो जाता है। इसका मूल उच्चारण 'सत्याँ री बावड़ी' है। यहाँ सतियाँ हुई थी। इस कारण इसका नाम सत्यों की बावड़ी हुआ। महादेव बावड़ी, सतियों की बावड़ी और कायस्थों की बावड़ी का निर्माण तथा गुवा (चरनोई की) बावड़ी का निर्माण १५वीं शताब्दी का है। इन्हें शक्तावत ठिकानेदारों से पूर्व चन्द्रावत ठिकानेदारों ने चरनोई में पशुओं व चरवाहों तथा 'वाट बटाऊ' (राहगीरों) की जल सुविधा के लिए बनवाया था बाद में इनका गहरीकरण व मरम्मत शक्तावत ठिकानेदारों ने करवाई। ऐसा लोकमत है। इनके निर्माण शिल्प को देखते हुए रामपुरा की बावड़ियों से मिलता है।[४]

पड़दां की बावड़ियाँ - पड़दाँ गाँव, जिसे पूर्व में 'लोहपट्टण' कहा जाता रहा है। मनासा तहसील से ८ किलोमीटर अरावली पठार की तलहटी में स्थित है। यहाँ की खदानों से कच्चा लोहा निकाला जाता था। जिसे यहीं गलाकर उससे कृषि औजार और हथियार बनाए जाते थे।

पड़दाँ में १५ बावड़ियाँ प्रमुख हैं। इनका निर्माण यहाँ के होल्कर राज्य द्वारा पदस्थ अधिकारियों एवं सेठ-साहूकारों ने जनकल्याण एवं कृषि सिंचाई के लिए करवाया था।

(१) सांड बावड़ी, (२) गंगा बावड़ी, (३) हाजी की बावड़ी (पटवारी बावड़ी), (४) खतारियों की बावड़ी (प्राचीन तालाब के निकट), (५) दादा साहब की बावड़ी, (८) पुरोहितों की बावड़ी, (७) पटेलों की बावड़ी, (८) रंगावतों की बावड़ी (बोहरों के कब्रिस्तान के निकट), (६) सेठजी की बावड़ी, (१०) बाजार की बावड़ी, (११) बाबा साहब की बावड़ी, (१२) खत्रियों के समाज की बावड़ी, (१३) खोड़ियांर की बावड़ी (तालाब के निकट), (१४) शहरियों की बावड़ी, (१५) तैय्यब जी की बावड़ी (बोहरा कब्रिस्तान के निकट)।

पड़दाँ की सभी बावड़ियाँ चूनाश्म शिलाओं से बनी हैं। सभी बावड़ियाँ पेयजल व्यवस्था एवं कृषि सिंचन के लिए उपयोगी हैं। बाजार की बावड़ी को बंद कर दिया गया है। शेष सभी बावड़ियाँ सुरक्षित हैं।[५] इनका प्रबंधन व्यक्तिगत रूप से बावड़ी के मालिक करते हैं। जो सार्वजनिक हैं उनका प्रबंधन पंचायत द्वारा होता है। गाँव के जल प्रबंधन के लिए इनका उपयोग होता है।

ढण्ढेड़ी की बावड़ियाँ - ढण्ढेरी गाँव मनासा-रामपुरा मार्ग पर ५ किलोमीटर दूरी पर स्थित है। यहाँ चारभुजा का विशाल मंदिर है तथा एक बहुत बड़ा तालाब भी है। जो आज कृषि भूमि में बदल गया है। ढण्ढेड़ी में दो बावड़ियाँ हैं जिसे मनासा के साहुकारों ने लोक कल्याण हेतु बनवाया था।

झंवरों की बावड़ी - १५वीं शताब्दी की यह सात मंजिली बावड़ी है। इसका प्रवेश मंदिर की ओर से (दक्षिण) है। पानी की खेल (हौज) बनी है। पशुओं और राहगीरों के जल पीने के लिए यह बावड़ी झंवर परिवार से बनवाई थी।६

समदानियों की बावड़ी - झंवरों की बावड़ी से दाहिनी ओर यह बावड़ी बनी है। इसका निर्माण मनासा के समदानी परिवार ने करवाया था। झंवरों की बावड़ी व समदानियों की बावड़ी दोनों का निर्माण परिवार की वरिष्ठ 'दादियों' ने करवाया था।६ठ

मनासा से २५ किलोमीटर दूर आंतरी माता जी में चन्द्रावत कालीन दो बावड़ियाँ बनी हैं। यह गाँव चन्द्रावतों का ठिकाना रहा है। चित्तौड़ से निष्कासित होने के बाद सबसे पहले चन्द्रावत यही आकर मुकामी हुए। यहीं अपनी कुलदेवी की स्थापना की।

माता जी की बावड़ी - यह बावड़ी संवत् १४१३ वि. में राव सज्जन सिंह ने बनवाई। रेतम नदी के किनारे स्थित माता के मंदिर की मरम्मत करवाई व यह बावड़ी बनवाई। इस पर एक लाख सत्तावन हजार रुपये खर्च हुए। जनश्रम की खूब हुआ।

छप्पन भैरव की बावड़ी - इस बावड़ी का निर्माण सहसमतल जी ने १४७६ में जनकल्याण के लिए करवाया। बाद में यह बावड़ी खण्डहर हो गई तब १७वीं शताब्दी में वहाँ के साहूकारों व जन भागीदारी से इसकी मरम्मत व गहरी करण किया गया। १८५६ के अकाल में इस बावड़ी को फिर से सुधारा गया। तब यह बाबड़ी गाँव व आसपास के पशुओं व मनुष्यों के लिए जल सुलभता का साधन बनी। आज इससे कृषि सिंचन किया जा रहा है।

मनासा की बावड़ियाँ - मनासा नगर में आठ बावड़ियाँ हैं।

आबा जी की बावड़ी - यह बावड़ी वर्तमान लक्ष्मीबाई मार्ग स्थित हनुमान-महादेव मंदिर के पीछे आबा जी के क्षेत्र में बनी है। यह बावड़ी आबाजी परिवार ने अपनी औषि सिंचन, पशुओं व मनुष्यों को जल सुविधा हेतु बनवाई थी। यह बावड़ी तो आज भी है किन्तु इसे ऊपर से बंद कर दिया गया है।

ननवाणों की बावड़ी - इस बावड़ी का निर्माण पीपल्या राव जी वाले पालिवाल (ननवाण ा) परिवार ने करवाया था। इसी अंचल में उनकी जागीर की विस्तृत भूमि थी। कृषि सिंचन एवं जन कल्याण हेतु बनी यह चूनाश्म शिलाओं से बनी बावड़ी मनासा जी सर्व सुन्दर बावड़ियों में से सर्वश्रेष्ठ थी। आज भी यह बावड़ी तो मौजूद है किन्तु उपेक्षा के कारण व प्रबंधन के अभाव में इसका कोई उपयोग नहीं है।

हाजी की बावड़ी - मंत्रियों की बावड़ी, चार भुजा बावड़ी, नृसिंह मंदिर बावड़ी ये तीनों बावड़ियाँ आज भी मौजूद हैं। इनका निर्माण मंदिरों के जल प्रदाय के लिए विशेष रूप से होता था। नृसिंह मंदिर पूर्व में नागाओं का अखाड़ा था। उन्हीं ने यह मत बावड़ी बनवाई थी। इनका वास्तुशिल्प देखकर आभास होता है कि, ये सभी बावड़ियाँ एक ही भाँति की बनी हैं। लगभग १५-१६वीं शताब्दी की ये बावड़ियाँ किसी समय मनासा के जल-प्रदाय का महत्वपूर्ण स्रोत रहीं। मंत्रियों की बावड़ी से आज कृषि सिंचन हो रहा है। मनासा में किसी भी ठिकानेदार की स्वतंत्रा सत्ता नहीं रही यह साहुकारों और भील मीणों का नगर रहा। यहाँ के जल स्रोत जितने भी हैं वे सभी साहुकारों द्वारा निजी व्यय से धर्मार्थ बनवाए गए हैं।७

फूलपुरा की बावड़ी - यह बावड़ी रामपुरा-मनासा नगर के मध्य मुख्य सड़क पर स्थित हैं यह अत्यंत सुंदर बावड़ी है। उत्तर में सीढ़ियाँ बनी हैं। प्रत्येक सीढ़ी पर एक

चौक बना है। ऐसे चार चौक बने हैं। प्रत्येक मंजिल में बारादरी बनी है। यह बावड़ी १६वीं शताब्दी की इस पूरे अंचल में सर्वाधिक सुन्दर बावड़ी है। चार चौक और चार बारादरियों वाली यह सात मंजिली बावड़ी सड़क के किनारे होने से आकर्षण का केन्द्र हैं। इस बावड़ी का निर्माण रामपुरा के एक जैन साहुकार ने धर्मार्थ जनकल्याण के लिए करवाया था। बावड़ी के चारों कोनों पर सुन्दर मेहराबदार छत्रियाँ। उत्तर में बनी नक्काशीदार तथा मेहराबदार विशाल बारादरी। चौड़ी पक्की पाल। भीतर प्रत्येक ऋतु के लिए समशीतोष्ण वातावरण। भीतर की बारादरियों पर किसी समय भजन कीर्तन तथा नृत्यगान की महफिलें सजा करती थीं। वनभोज तो इन बारादरियों में सदा सर्वदा होता ही रहता था। बावड़ी से पानी निकालने के लिए पश्चिम में थाला बना है। इससे पशुओं के लिए 'खेल' (पानी भरने का हौज) भरा जाता था। कृषि सिंचन तथा पेयजल के लिए भी इसका उपयोग होता था। आज भी इसमें जल की कमी नहीं है।

यहाँ पर प्राचीन हनुमान मंदिर और आधुनिक शनि मंदिर बना है। श्रद्धालुओं का जमघट यहाँ तीर्थ की भाँति बना रहता है। इस बावड़ी का निर्माण भी चूनाश्म शिलाओं की सुन्दर घड़ाई से किया गया है। इसके निर्माण की प्रेरणा रामपुरा में स्थित शाह पातु की बावड़ी से मिली।

रामपुरा की बावड़ियाँ - रामपुरा दुर्ग के किलाकोट के भीतर एवं बाहर दस पक्की व सुन्दर बावड़ियाँ निर्मित हैं। ये सभी बावड़ियाँ चौदहवीं शताब्दी से लगाकर सोलहवीं शताब्दी के मध्य निर्मित हुईं। इनका प्रबंधन कुछ काल तक राज परिवार द्वारा किया जाता रहा। बीच में कुछ काल तक उपेक्षित रहा। आज इनमें से अधिकतर बावड़ियों का प्रबंधन रामपुरा नगर पंचायत द्वारा किया जा रहा है।

पातुशाह की बावड़ी - रामपुरा किलाकोट में स्थित बावड़ियों में यह बावड़ी सबसे सुन्दर बावड़ी है। इसका निर्माण हुशंगशाह गौरी के वजीर 'पातौशाह' ने १५वीं शताब्दी में करवाया था। बावड़ी के निकट अभिलेख स्तंभ के अनुसार संवत् १४६८ वि. तिथि वैशाख सुदी पूर्णिमा को पूर्ण कर उद्यापन किया गया। पातौशाह ने इसे ध ार्मार्थ बनवाया।९-१०

प्रत्येक ११ सीढ़ियों के दोनों ओर सुन्दर गोखड़े बने हैं। जहाँ पर बैठकर स्नान करने के बाद पूजा अर्चना की जाती थी। सीढ़ियों के बाद एक सुन्दर मेहराबदार द्व ार है। बारादरी की छवि अत्यंत मनोहर है। रामपुरा में उपलब्ध बावड़ियों में यह सर्वाधिक सुन्दर एवं जलपूरित बावड़ी हैं नगर पंचायत द्वारा विद्युत पम्प लगाकर नगर में जलप्रदाय किया जाता है। उत्तरी कोने पर एक 'धर्म स्तंभ' गढ़ा है। जिसमें गोदान के पश्चात गाय बाँध दी जाती थी। जिसे पुजारी खोल लेता था। गुप्त गोदान की यह

अद्भुत मिसाल थी। पातीशाह रामपुरा का जैनकुल का साहुकार था। अपनी जन्मभूमि के हित में उसने यह बावड़ी बनवाई। इसी बावड़ी की प्रेरणा से फूलपुरा की बावड़ी का निर्माण हुआ।

रामपुरा की बावड़ियाँ में दूसरी प्राचीन बावड़ी चौपड़ा बावड़ो है। यह श्रीपुरा मोहल्ला में स्थित है। यहाँ पहले सिद्धों का मठ था। भैरव मंदिर के निकट इस बावड़ी का निर्माण सिद्धों ने १५वीं शताब्दी में करवाया था। पूर्व में कृषि सिंचाई होती रही। आजकल नगर पंचायत द्वारा विद्युत पम्प द्वारा नगर की पेयजल व्यवस्था की जातो है।

राव दुर्गभान की बावड़ियाँ दुर्गभान ने गद्दी पर बैठते ही जब महलों को नवीनीकरण करवाया तभी महलों के भीतर दो बावड़ियाँ भी बनवाईं। इनके निर्नाण में २०७०६८ कलदार रुपये व्यय हुए।

धनराज की बावड़ी - यह बावड़ी नगर कोट के बाहर बनी है। १५वीं शताब्दी की यह बावड़ी धनराज नामक साहुकार ने गोचर भूमि में बनवाई थी। कृषि भूमि सिंचन तथा पशुओं के पानी की सुविधा इसके निर्माण का उद्देश्य था।[११]

सास की बावड़ी - इस बावड़ी का निर्माण चन्द्रावत राव अमर सिंह की हाड़ी रानी राठोड़नी जी जोधपुरी जी ने करवाया था। इसमें ११ सीढ़ियों पर एक चौक है। ऐसे तीन चौक बने हैं पूर्व में सीढ़ियाँ हैं। तीन सुन्दर बारादरियाँ बनी हैं। यह बावड़ी गोचर में जल प्रदाय के लिए बनी थी। इसके निर्माण में २३५६७८ रुपये खर्च हुए।[१२]

बहू की बावड़ी - यह बावड़ी चन्द्रभान जी की रानी राठौड़जी को बीकानेर वालों ने बनवाई थी। यह सास की बावड़ी से पूर्व में निकट ही स्थित है। बीच में (दोनों वाड़ियों के) महादेव का मंदिर बना है। इसका उद्देश्य भी चरागाह में जल व्यवस्था था। इसके निर्माण में २ लाख पच्चीस हजार नौ सौ अट्ठावन रुपये कलदार खर्चा आया।[१३]

हरिश्चन्द की बावड़ी - यह चार मंजिली सीढ़ियों वाली अत्यंत सुन्दर बावड़ी है। इसका निर्माण १४वीं शताब्दी उत्तरार्द्ध में करवाया गया। इस पर खुदे स्तम्भ आलेख के आधार पर इसका निर्माण सं. १४७८ वि. माघ सुदी पंचमी के दिन उद्यापन किया गया। इससे कृषि सिंचाई भी होती है। पंडा बावड़ी और शिव मंदिर बावड़ियाँ चन्द्रावत हंसराज ने गोचर भूमि में जागीरें निकाल कर अपने कुल पुरोहित विलास जी पंडा तथा महादेव मंदिर की पूजा अर्चना हेतु सुगत पुरोहित को दान में दी थी। इन बावड़ियों पर कुल मिलाकर तीन लाख बहत्तर हजार छह नौ छप्पन रुपये तथा महामंदिर पर २ लाख रुपये सिल्यासी हजार कलदार खर्च आए थे। भव्य किन्तु शिव मंदिर दर्शनीय है।[१४]

आज भी हमारे मध्यकालीन जलसंसाधन कायम हैं। उनका प्रबंधन यदि ठीक से किया जाए तो पानी का जो अभाव हम भोग रहे हैं वह समाप्त हो जाए। इस सत्य को मनासा-रामपुरा के लोगों ने समझा है और अपने गौरवशाली जल संसाधनों को पुनर्जीवित करने में तत्पर हुए हैं। हमें अपने इन ऐतिहासिक जल संसाधनों से प्रेरणा लेना चाहिए।

आलेख के संदर्भ आधार

१. डॉ. विनय श्रीवास्तव, मालवा के प्रमुख ऐतिहासिक दुर्ग

२. डॉ. पूरन सहगल लोहपट्टाण पड़दाँ

३. इतिहास चंद्रावतान सिसोदिया वंशस्व. किशन लाल फरक्या कामदार भाटखेड़ी जागीर, सुरक्षित-मालवा लोक संस्कृति अनुष्ठान मनासा

४. पाटनामा - चन्द्रावत वंश

५. इन्दौर स्टेट का गजेटियर

६. मंदसौर गजेटियर

७. चारण की बेटी, डॉ. पूरन सहगल

८. व्यक्तिगत सर्वेक्षण एवं ग्रामवासियों से प्राप्त जानकारी

सन्दर्भ सूची

१. बावड़ी की २७वीं सीढ़ी पर खुदे अभिलेख में उपरोक्त संवत् तथ तिथि का वर्णन है.

२. सत्य नारायण मंदिर की ६टी सीढ़ी के दाहिने व बाएँ स्तंभ पर खुदे शिलालेख.

३. कुंडबावड़ी के चन्द्रपीठ का अभिलेख।

४. शक्तावतों के (पीपल्या रावजी के) रेकार्ड में जो जानकारी मिलती है वह निर्माण की नहीं रखरखाव (प्रबंधन) की है। किसी समय यह समूची भूमि चरागाह थी। आज औषि हो रही है। ये बावड़ियाँ औषि सिंचन के उपयोग में आ रही हैं।

५. लोहपट्टण पड़दाँ डॉ पूरन सहगल पृष्ठ ३१-३२ एवं चारण की बेटी डॉ पूरन सहगल.

६. । ६ ठ ऐसा इन घरानों की बेटियों से ज्ञात हुआ। अपने-अपने स्व. पतियों की स्मृति में ये बावड़ियाँ बनवाई थी। दोनों बावड़ियों पर अभिलेख स्तंभ लगे थे जो अब टूट कर भवन निर्माण में लगाय जाते हैं।

७. बावड़ियों पर लगे स्तम्भ आलेखों से यह स्पष्ट होता है कि, इन बावड़ियों का निर्माण निजि स्तर पर ही किया गया था। आबाजी की बावड़ी.

८. बावड़ी के दक्षिणी कोने पर लगा अभिलेख स्तंभ तथा बावड़ी की १२वीं सीढ़ी पर खुदा अभिलेख.

६. बावड़ी के दक्षिणी कोने में स्थित स्तंभ अभिलेख एवं भीतर चौवीस्वीं सीढ़ी पर खुदा संवत १४४५ वि. तिथि पूर्णिमा वैशाख.

१०.व्यक्तिगत सर्वेक्षण द्वारा

११.उपरोक्त

१२.-१३. हालात चन्द्रावतान सीसोद वंश-किशन लाल फरक्या कामदार माटखेड़ी ठिकाना की हस्तलिखित पोथी.

१४.दोनों मंदिरों पर अभिलेख स्तंभों पर यह विवरण खुदा है। आज इन्हें ठीक से पढ़ पाना कठिन है। दोनों बावड़ियाँ एक जैसी हैं।

ओरछा राज्य का विशाल जल संग्रहण क्षेत्र समुद्रसागर

डॉ. संजय स्वर्णकार

विशाल जलाशयों के निर्माण की परंपरा इस देश में प्राचीनकाल से मौजूद रही है। हड़प्पा सभ्यता में भौतिक रूप से जलाशय की उपलब्धता[1] तथा वैदिक एवं प्राचीन साहित्य में जलाशयों के निर्माण की तकनीकी का वर्णन इस तथ्य की पुष्टि करता है। इसी क्रम में मौर्यकाल में अपनी नीति कुशलता तथा प्रबंध के लिये विख्यात मनीषी कौटिल्य अपने ग्रंथ अर्थशास्त्र में अच्छे प्रशासक के लिये यह परामर्श देते हुए कहते है कि - भूमि की सिंचाई के लिये एक राजा को चाहिये कि नदियों पर बड़े-बड़े बॉंध बनवायें अथवा वर्षा ऋतु के जल को ही बड़े-बड़े जलाशयों में भरवा दें।[2] बुंदेलखंड की विषम भौगोलिक परिस्थितियों में इस क्षेत्र के शासकों ने प्राचीनकाल से जल-संरक्षण के विभिन्न उपायों को अपनाया था। उन्होंने इस हेतु कुएँ खुदवाये, बावड़ियॉं बनवायी, जलाशय निर्मित कराये, झीलें बनवाई तथा नहरें निकलवाई। चंदेल शासकों ने अपने राज्य क्षेत्र में लगभग ६२५ छोटे-बड़े जलाशयों का निर्माण करवाया था, जिसमें से केवल ४२१ जलाशय ही अभी अस्तित्व में हैं।[3] इनमें से भी केवल १२५ जलाशय सिंचाई के कार्य में लिये जा रहे है। चदेल राजाओं के पश्चात् बुंदेला राजाओं ने इस क्षेत्र पर अपना आधिपत्य स्थापित किया तथा अपने राज्य में जल-संरक्षण एवं जल प्रबंधन में रूचि प्रदर्शित की। इसके तहत् उन्होंने पुराने जलाशयों का जीर्णोद्धार कराया तथा कई जलाशयों का निर्माण भी कराया। मढ़वा राजगढ़ के समीप बीरसागर, गढ़कुढ़ार में सिंह सागर, नदनवारा में समुद्रसागर, अड़जार गॉंव में सुजानसागर, विंदपुरा में यज्ञसागर तथा धर्मसागर, ग्वालसागर, टीकमगढ़ में महेंद्रसागर एवं सुधासागर आदि विशाल जलाशयों का निर्माण ओरछा राज्य के विभिन्न शासकों ने कराया थां।[4]

समुद्रसागर की भौगोलिक स्थिति

समुद्रसागर टीकमगढ़ जिले का सबसे बड़ा जलाशय हैं। इसके नाम से ही स्पष्ट होता है कि यह अत्यन्त विशाल जलाशय होगा। वस्तुतः यह एक बड़ी झील के समान

प्रतीत होता है। नदनवारा के जलाशय को सिंधुसागर के नाम से भी जाना जाता है।[५] समुद्रसागर टीकमगढ़ जिले की जतारा तहसील के एक छोटे से गॉव नदनवारा मे स्थित है तथा इसकी भौगोलिक स्थिति २५°२' उत्तरी अक्षांश तथा ७८°५२' पूर्वी देशांतर के मध्य है।[६] नदनवारा गॉव की स्थापना दाँगियों द्वारा की गई थी, यही कारण है कि इस गॉव में तथा आस-पास गॉवों में दाँगियों का वर्चस्व है। यह गॉव तहसील मुख्यालय जतारा के पश्चिमी दिशा में लगभग ३५ किमी. दूरी पर स्थित हैं। नदनवारा गॉव का कुल क्षेत्रफल ५०८ हेक्टेअर है, जिसमें से समुद्रसागर का फैलाव लगभग २२५ हेक्टेअर हैं।[७] वर्ष २००१ की जनगणना के अनुसार यहां की अनुमानित जनसंख्या २५०० है। बरगी नदी की घाटी में निर्मित समुद्रसागर के दो ओर ऊँची-ऊँची पहाड़ियाँ है। इसमें से रतनगॉव की पहाड़ी ३८५.५६ मीटर ऊँची है। इन पहाड़ियों में क्वार्टज प्रचुर मात्रा में पाया जाता है।[८]

समुद्रसागर का ऐतिहासिक परिचय

बुँदेला शासकों द्वारा जिन क्षेत्रों पर शासन किया गया था, उनमें विशाल जल स्रोतों का अभाव था। ओरछा राज्य के पश्चिमी-उत्तर भाग में बेतवा घाटी स्थित थी। बेतवा घाटी के अंतर्गत् जामुनी नदी के आसपास का क्षेत्र अधिक समतल एवं मिट्टी की दृष्टि से समृद्ध है। ग्रेनाइट युक्त जलोढ़ मिट्टी ललितपुर क्षेत्र से बहते हुए जामुनी घाटी मे फैली हुई है, जो कृषि के लिये अधिक उपयुक्त है।[९] ओरछा राज्य में बुँदेला शासकों द्वारा जिन बड़े तालाबों का निर्माण करवाया था - उनमें बीरसागर गॉव स्थित बीरसागर, बिंदपुरा गॉव स्थित यज्ञसागर, नदनवारा स्थित समुद्रसागर, अड़जार गॉव स्थित सुजानसागर, जेरान स्थित जेरान ताल, पृथ्वीपुर स्थित राधासागर, गढ़कुढ़ार स्थित सिंहसागर, टीकमगढ़ स्थित महेंद्रसागर एवं सुधासागर, बम्हौरी स्थित बम्हौरी ताल, लिधौरा स्थित लिधौरा ताल तथा धर्मसागर, पद्मसागर एवं ग्वालसागर आदि प्रमुख है।[१०]

ओरछा राज्य के बुँदेला राजवंश के महान शासक बीरसिंहजूदेव बुँदेला (१६०५-१६२७) ने वास्तुकला एवं प्राकृतिक सौंदर्यता के प्रति अपने प्रेम को प्रदर्शित करते हुए कई इमारतों का निर्माण कराया था। बीरसिंह बुँदेला वीर योद्धा होने के साथ-साथ धर्म प्रेमी भी थे और इसीकारण मथुरा से वाराणसी तक कई बार भ्रमण किया एवं इन तीर्थयात्राओं के दौरान ही कई धार्मिक एवं सार्वजनिक भवनों, जलाशयों एवं कुओं का निर्माण कराया। बीरसिंह बुँदेला ने एक ही शुभ मुहूर्त (माघ सुदी ५ संवत् १६७५ - दिसंबर, १६१८) में जिन ५२ वास्तुओं का शिलान्यास किया था।[११] इन वास्तुाओं मे उन्होंने अपने राज्य के निवासियों की सुविधा के लिये जल संग्रहण

का उद्देश्य पूर्ण करने के लिये चार विशाल जलाशयों का निर्माण कराय, जिन्में से तीन का नामकरण स्वयं के नाम पर किया। ये थे - मढ़वा राजगढ़ के समीप बीरसागर, गढ़कुढ़ार में सिंह सागर तथा दिनांरा में देवसागर।[१२] जबकि चौथे जलाशय का नाम उन्होंने समुद्रसागर रखा। संभवतः इस जलाशय की विशलता को देखते हुए ही इसका नाम समुद्रसागर रखा जाना उचित समझा गया होगा। सनुद्रसागर का निर्माण बीरसिंहजूदेव ने बड़ी कल्पनाशीलता के साथ कराया था। यह स्थान ओरछा से टेहरी (टीकमगढ़) के मध्य स्थित था तथा इसके दोनों ओर ऊँची पहाड़ियाँ बड़ा मनोरम दृश्य प्रस्तुत करती थीं। साथ ही पहाड़ियों के होने से तालाब को प्राकृतिक रूप से गहराई भी मिल रही थी। समुद्रसागर पर एक बाँध भी बनाया गया है, जिससे इसकी जल संग्रहण क्षमता बढ़ी है।

जलाशय निर्माण योजना एवं तकनीक

जलाशय निर्माण तकनीक पर रचित ग्रंथ विश्व बल्लभ के उल्लास २ के जलाशय निरूपण में किये गये उल्लेख के अनुसार आकार भेद के आधार पर १००० दण्ड (१८२८.८ मीटर) लम्बा तालाब श्रेष्ठ, ६१४.४ मीटर लम्बां तालाब मध्यम तथा ४७५.२ मीटर लम्बा तालाब कनिष्ठ श्रेणी का होता है। इसी ग्रंथ के अनुसार जल की उपस्थिति के प्रमाण के बिना भी सरोवर बनाये जा सकते है। इस ग्रंथ के उल्लास-१ में वर्णन है कि दो पहाड़ियों के बीच या पहाड़ी की घाटी को बाँधकर कम व्यय में तालाब का निर्माण किया जाये। जहाँ आस-पास अधिक जमीन हो तो उस्की जलभराव क्षमता बढ़ सकती है। ऐसे सरोवर अच्छे माने जाते है।[१३]

समुद्रसागर बुंदेला शासकों की जलाशय निर्माण तकनीक का श्रेष्ठ उदाहरण है। राजा बीरसिंहजूदेव बुँदेला ने इस जलाशय का निर्माण दो पहाड़ियों के मध्य करवाया था। समुद्रसागर जलाशय के निर्माण की योजना के अंतर्गत् स्थल के चयन के लिये जहाँ बुँदेला राज्य की राजधानी ओरछा से टेहरी (वर्तमान टीकमगढ़) मुख्य मार्ग से लगभग ८ किमी. दूर एक सुरक्षित स्थान का चयन किया गया, वहीं दो पहाड़ियों के बीच के स्थान का चयन भी तकनीकी दृष्टि से उचित था, क्योंकि इससे इस जलाशय को प्राकृतिक रूप से गहराई मिली है। इस जलाशय के लिये जल के स्रोत की उपलब्धता का भी जलाशय निर्माण योजना में अवश्य विचार किया गया होगा। इस महत्वपूर्ण समस्या का समाधान इस क्षेत्र में ही उपलबध था। जलाशय में जत के स्रोत के लिये स्थानीय नदी बरगी नदी का सहारा लिया गया था ताकि जलाशय में नदी के माध्यम से वर्षाकाल में जल की आपूर्ति हो सके।[१४] कारी टोरन से निकली यह बरगी नदी दिगौड़ा, बिजरावन, नादिया, बिगा, कुर्राई से होते हुए नदनवारा पहुँचती है तथा

समुद्रसागर में मिलती है। यहाँ इस जलाशय के निर्माण के लिये अन्य जल-स्रोतों की भी कमी नहीं थी। बम्हौरी नाला, छिपरी नाला, बिसल्ली पट्ठा नाला, बिरौरा-खरारा नाला, ज्यौरा-मनिया-सकेरा का हगा नाला, बँधा-बिंदारी का हाइया नाला तथा रामनगर का ऐंचा नाला आदि ऐसे छोटे-बड़े नाले थे जो इस जलाशय में अपना जल छोड़ते थें।[१५] इन जल-स्रोतों के माध्यम से ही समुद्रसागर में विपुल जलराशि का संग्रहण किया जाना संभव हो पाता है।

समुद्रसागर तालाब का फैलाव लगभग १८ किमी. क्षेत्र में है तथा इसकी गहराई अधिकतम लगभग १०० फीट है। इस जलाशय के चारों ओर बसे हुए गाँवों में रमपुरा, गरार खिरक, ज्यौरा, रानीगंज, लाखरौन, प्रतापपुरा, पठार, बम्हौरी, राजनगर, बिंदारी, बँधा तथा रतनगाँव आदि प्रमुख है।[१७] इस जलाशय पर एक विस्तृत बाँध का निर्माण किया गया था, जो गणेश बाँध के नाम से जाना जाता है। इस बाँध पर भगवान गणेश के मंदिर की स्थापना के कारण इसका नाम गणेश बाँध रखा गया। इस बाँध की लम्बाई ५६० फीट अर्थात् ५ चैन ६० कड़ी है।[१८] जबकि इसकी चौड़ाई ६ फीट है। इस बाँध की ऊँचाई तल से लगभग ६० फीट हैं, जबकि पानी के ऊपरी तल से ऊँचाई ३० फीट है। बाँध से नीचे तक जल में उतरने के लिये बाँध के आंतरिक पार्श्व में शंक्वाकार दोहरी सीढ़ियाँ बनी हैं, जिनकी चौंडाई लगभग ५ फीट हैं। १५ फीट तक नीचे सीढ़ियों पर उतरने के बाद पुनः ४-५ फीट का आधार बनाया गया है और वहीं से नीचे तल तक जाने के लिये सोपान बने है। बाँध को बड़े-बड़े पत्थरों, लोहा, चूने, मिट्टी आदि से बाँधा गया है। बाँध को बनाने में विशेष कलाकारी का उपयोग नहीं किया गया है, किंतु उसे मजबूती प्रदान करने के दृष्टिकोण से जलाशय निर्माण एवं बाँध निर्माण तकनीक का प्रयोग अवश्य किया गया है। यही कारण है कि लगभग ४०० वर्षों के बीत जाने के बाद भी यह जलाशय एवं बाँध अपनी सुरक्षित स्थिति में है। गणेश बाँध इस जलाशय का मुख्य प्रवेश स्थल है, जबकि नदनवारा से लगभग २ किमी. दूरी पर स्थित गोरीखेरा गाँव से भी इस जलाशय में प्रवेश किया जा सकता हैं। गोरीखेरा गाँव की ओर भी जलाशय को बाँधने के लिये एक छोटी दीवार बनाई गई थी। हालाँकि वर्षा ऋतु के दौरान यह दीवार डूब क्षेत्र में आ जाती है।[१९]

समुद्रसागर जलाशय के जल को आस-पास के गाँवों में पहुँचाने तथा उसका अधिक-से-अधिक उपयोग करने के उद्देश्य से स्वतंत्रता प्राप्ति के पश्चात् तत्कालीन प्रदेश सरकारों ने इस जलाशय से तीन नहरों का निर्माण किया। प्रथम पंचवर्षीय योजना के अंतर्गत् इस परियोजना के लिये ११.०६ लाख रूपये की व्यवस्था की गई थी। यह परियोजना इस पंचवर्षीय योजना में पूर्ण नहीं हो सकी थी, अतः द्वितीय पंचवर्षीय

योजना में पुनः इस मद मे राशि मुहैया कराकर इस परियोजना को पूर्ण किया गयां।[२०] इसमें से एक नहर एल.वी.सी. लगभग ६ किमी. है, जो बम्हैरीखेरा, खाकरौन, नदनवारा गॉव के क्षेत्रों को सिंचाई की सुविधा उपलब्ध कराती है। इसी प्रकार द्वितीय नहर आर.वी.सी. १८ किमी. लंबी है, नदनवारा से चलकर पंचमखेरा ममौरा, रौतेरा, जेरोन, बुर्दरा, पाराखेरा, बाराबुजुर्ग, खदरी, ककावनी, मजल, लुहरगुँवा सहित लगभग १८ गॉवों की भूमि को सिचित करती है। इन नहरों के अतिरिक्त एक अन्य तीसरी नहर गोराखेरा से केसरगंज गॉव को जोड़ती है और इसकी लंबाई लगभग ३ किमी. है।[२१] जलाशय से निकली ये नहरें अपनी प्रारंभिक अवस्था में पक्की बनी हुई है, आगे चलकर ये कच्ची है। इनकी चौंडाई तल पर लगभग ४–५ फीट तथा ऊपर लगभग १० फीट है। इसीप्रकार इनकी गहराई लगभग ७–८ फीट है।

सामाजिक–आर्थिक महत्व

समुद्रसागर स्थित गणेश बॉध पर मकर संक्रांति पर प्रत्येक १४ जनवरी को विशाल मेले का आयोजन होता है, जिसमें हजारों लोग शामिल होते हैं।[२२] यहॉ पर विभिन्न अवसरों पर आसपास के निवासी अपनी सामाजिक परंपरा एवं रीति–रिवाजों की पूर्ति के लिये उपस्थिति दर्ज कराते है। मोर छठ के दिन यहॉं नव ब्याहता वर–वधू के परिवार वाले उनके मोरों का विसर्जन करने आते है। समुद्रसागर नदनवारा में प्रत्येक बुधवार को साप्ताहिक बाजार (हाट) का आयोजन होता है, जिसमें आस–पास के कई गॉववासी एकत्र होते है।[२३]

इस विशाल जलाशय में कई जल जन्तु पाये जाते हैं, इनमें कई प्रकार की मछलियॉं हैं। बाम, कतला, रोहू, पड़ोन, कटर, सोंरा, खड्डिया, महासीर, सूजा, पापता, बोखरू, चपटरा, गोरिया आदि मछलियॉं बड़े पैमाने पर यहॉं उत्पादित की जाती हैं। यहॉं कछुआ, पातर तथा परिनया सॉप भी बहुतायत में पाये जाते है।[२४]

इस जलाशय के आस–पास एक विशाल घना जंगल भी है, जो समुद्रसागर में सिल्ट को एकत्रित होने से रोकने में सहायक सिद्ध होता है। इस जंगल में बरगद, महुआ, आम, कवा, यूकेलिप्टस, सागौन, करधई, सलाई, खैर, तेंदू, नीम, पीपल आदि वृक्ष बहुतायत में पाये जाते हैं।[२५] इस जंगल की उपस्थिति से यहॉं का मौसम भी बड़ा खुशगवार रहता है। समुद्रसागर के निर्माण के फलस्वरूप इस क्षेत्र में जलाशय के आस–पास की जलोढ़ मिट्टी में चीमरी, तरबूज, ककड़ी, खीरा, टमाटर, भिंडी, बैंगन आदि फल–सब्जियों का उत्पादन बड़े पैमाने पर होता है।[२६]

समस्यायें

समुद्रसागर का वर्तमान स्वरूप बहुत अच्छा नहीं कहा जा सकता है। गणेश बॉध की स्थिति जर्जर होती जा रही है। उसके किनारे ढह चुके है। नियमित रूप से रखरखाव न हो पाने के कारण बॉध के ऊपर गढ़ढे हो गये है, जिनमे से होकर पानी बॉध में बैठ रहा है। इस जलाशय में आसपास से बहकर आने वाले नालों के साथ मिट्टी भी एकत्रित हो रही है, जो इसकी गहराई को प्रभावित कर रही है। इस मिट्टी अर्थात् गाद को निकालने के लिये प्रशासन द्वारा कोई उपाय नही किये गये है। जलसंसाधन विभाग जिला टीकमगढ़ द्वारा इस जलाशय की सुरक्षा एवं रखरखाव के लिये दो चौकीदारों की नियुक्ति की गई है, जो अपनी-अपनी पारी में कार्य करते हैं। ये चौकीदार ही इस जलाशय, बॉध एवं मंदिर की सुरक्षा का कार्य करते है। दस वर्ष पूर्व गणेश मंदिर से हुई मूर्तियों की चोरी की घटना से यह अनुमान लगाया जा सकता है कि यह महत्वपूर्ण क्षेत्र कितना सुरक्षित है। इस जलाशय को तकनीकी रूप से सुरक्षित करने के लिय विभाग द्वारा अपने अभियंताओं को दायित्व सौंपे गये है, किंतु उनके द्वारा नियमित रूप से जलाशय का सर्वेक्षण किया जाता होगा अथवा इसके विकास के लिये कोई नई योजना तैयार की गई होगी, इसमें संदेह है। जलाशय से निकाली गई नहरों की दीवारों में भी जगह-जगह गढ़ढे हो रहे है तथा उनमें मिट्टी जमा हो रही हे। नदनवारा गॉव के आस-पास स्थित पायरोफिलाईट, डायोस्फर खनिज की खदानों में निरंतर अवैध उत्खनन हो रहा है, जिससे इस क्षेत्र में असामाजिक तत्वों की उपस्थिति रहती है। इसीप्रकार यहॉ स्थित जंगल से वृक्षों की अवैध कटाई हो रही है, जिससे जलाशय में कटान की समस्या पैदा हो सकती है।

निष्कर्ष एवं सुझाव

समुद्रसागर को देखकर कोई भी इसे प्रथम दृष्टया एक झील के रूप में निरूपित करेगा। निःसंदेह इसकी विशालता अकल्पनीय हैं। बुँदेला शासक बीरसिंहजूदेव ने अपनी कल्पनाशीलता एवं दूरदर्शिता का उपयोग करते हुये इस जलाशय का निर्माण कराकर दूर-दूर तक गॉवों में सिंचाई की व्यवस्था उपलब्ध कराई थी। जलाशय का निर्माण तत्कालीन प्रचलित निर्माण तकनीकी के आधार पर कराया गया, हालॉकि इसकी निर्माण पद्धति का उल्लेख किसी तत्कालीन स्रोत में प्राप्त नहीं होता है, इसलिये जलाशय का भौतिक रूप से निरीक्षण के उपरांत ही इस संबंध में तथ्य प्रस्तुत किये गये है। समुद्रसागर के अस्तित्व को बचाने के लिये प्रशासन को गंभीरता के साथ उसके संरक्षण में रूचि प्रदर्शित करनी होगी। इस हेतु अत्यंन्त आवश्यक है कि इस जलाशय के बॉध का अविलंब जीर्णोद्धार किया जाये।, जलाशय के अंदर एकत्र हो रही गाद अर्थात्

सिल्ट को निकालकर आसपास के गॉवों में कृषियोग्य भूमि पर डाला जाये ताकि इस भूमि की उर्वरता बढ़ सके। इसीप्रकार इस जलाशय में मछली पालन के व्यवसाय को उन्नत करने का प्रयास किया जा सकता है। समुद्रसागर की विशालता एवं इस क्षेत्र की विशेषताओं को देखकर विचार किया जा सकता है कि इस जलाशय को केंद्र बनाते हुये इस क्षेत्र का विकास रोमॉचक पर्यटन, पारिस्थतिकी पर्यटन एवं ग्रामीण पर्यटन के रूप में किया जा सकता है। इसके लिये मध्य'-प्रदेश पर्यटन विकास निगम, तथा जिला प्रशासन संयुक्त रूप से योजना का निर्माण कर सकते है। ऐसा करने से समुद्रसागर नामक इस विशाल जलाशय को सदियों तक अक्षुण्ण रखा जा सकता है।

संदर्भ एवं टिप्पणी

१. हड़प्पा सभ्यता के अंतर्गत् मोहनजोदड़ो में एक विशाल स्नानागार की प्राप्ति हुई थी, जो उस काल में विभिन्न उद्देश्यों से सामाजिक एवं सार्वजनिक कार्यों में उपयोग में आता था।

२. श्रीवास्तव, बी.के., सुदर्शन झील : प्राचीन भारत में जल प्रबंधन का एक सशक्त उदाहरण, संधान-७, संपादक-सुरेश मिश्र, प्रोसीडिंग्स, ११वीं संगोष्ठी, २००८, डा. भगवानदास गुप्त स्मृति शोध संस्थान, झॉसी, पृ. ४३

३. टीकमगढ़ जिला गजेटियर, १९९५, पृष्ठ ५

४. वही।

५. त्रिपाठी, के.पी., बुँदेलखंड का बृहद इतिहास, टीकमगढ़, पृष्ठ ४४;

गौर, ठा. लक्ष्मणसिंह, ओरछा का इतिहास, ओरछा, पृष्ठ ८६

६. टीकमगढ़ जिला गजेटियर, १९९५, पृष्ठ ४

७. वही, पृष्ठ ३५२

८. वही, पृष्ठ १४४

९. वही, पृष्ठ ४

१०. ईस्टर्न स्टेट गजेटियर (बुँदेलखंड), १९९५, भोपाल, पृष्ठ ३

११. टीकमगढ़ जिला गजेटियर, १९९५, पृष्ठ ५४

१२. त्रिपाठी, के.पी., बुँदेलखंड का बृहद इतिहास, टीकमगढ़, पृष्ठ ४४

१३. राणावत, डा. ईश्वरसिंह, मध्यकालीन जलाशय निर्माण तकनीकी, संधान-७, संपादक-सुरेश मिश्र, प्रोसीडिंग्स, ११वीं संगोष्ठी, २००८, डा. भगवानदास गुप्त स्मृति शोध संस्थान, झाँसी, पृ. १, २, ३

१४. टीकमगढ़ जिला गजेटियर, १९९५, पृष्ठ ४

१५. जल संसाधन विभाग जिला टीकमगढ़ द्वारा समुद्रसागर जलाशय की सुरक्षा हेतु नियुक्त गार्ड श्री आशाराम यादव द्वारा दी गई जानकारी के आधार पर।

१६. वही।,

१७. वही।,

१८. वही।,

१९. गोराखेरा गाँव के स्थानीय निवासियों द्वारा दी गई जानकारी के अनुसार।,

२०.टीकमगढ़ जिला गजेटियर, १९९५, पृष्ठ ११२

२१. वही; शोधार्थी द्वारा स्वयं किया गया सर्वेक्षण।,

२२.टीकमगढ़ जिला गजेटियर, १९९५, पृष्ठ ३५२

२३. वही।,

२४.ईस्टर्न स्टेट गजेटियर (बुंदेलखंड), १९९५, भोपाल, पृष्ठ ३ मत्स्य विभाग, जिला टीकमगढ़ के अधिकारियों से प्राप्त सूचना के आधार पर।

२५.वही, पृष्ठ ४;

२६.स्थानीय निवासियों द्वारा दी गई जानकारी के अनुसार। चीमरी शब्द स्थानीय भाषा मे खरबूजे अथवा खरबूजे जैसे फल के लिये प्रयुक्त किया जाता है।

महाराणा राजसिंह द्वारा १७वीं शताब्दी में निर्मित राजसमुद्र झील एवं उसमें प्रयुक्त तकनीकी

डॉ. ईश्वरसिंह राणावत

यह झील उदयपुर से ६६ किमी[१] उत्तर तथा उत्तर-पश्चिम में और कांकरोली के उत्तर में २५०४' उत्तरी अक्षांश तथा ७३०५३' पूर्वी देशान्तर पर स्थित है। यह ४.८ किमी लम्बी तथा २.४ किमी चौड़ी है और ४९९.२ वर्ग किमी भूमि का जल इसमें आता है। यह बांध दक्षिण-पश्चिम में निर्मित है[२] तथा इसका क्षेत्रफल ७.७६ किमी है।

सर्वप्रथम गोमती नदी पर महाराणा उदयसिंह ने सेतु बांधने का प्रयास किया था।[३] प्रताप को संघर्ष से समय नहीं मिला था। अतः उसके समय तो संभवतः इसके लिए प्रयास नहीं किये गये हों परन्तु १६१५ ई. की मेवाड़-मुगल सन्धि से शान्ति हो जाने से महाराणा अमरसिंह ने इस ओर अपना ध्यान आकृष्ट कर विशाल बांध बनाने की योजना बनायी, परन्तु नदी के तेज प्रवाह के कारण वह स्थायी नहीं रहा।[३]

संवत १६९८ (१६४१ ई.) में राजसिंह ने अपने कुंवरपदे के समय विवाह के लिए जैसलमेर जाते समय वहां तालाब बनवाने का विचार किया।[४] उसकी योजनानुसार तालाब बनाने पर १६ गांवों की सीमा इसमें आती थी।[६] अपने राज्यकाल में सं. १७१८ मार्गशीर्ष (नवम्बर, १६६१ ई) को रूपनारायण के दर्शन को जाते समय पुनः उस स्थान को देखा और वहां तालाब बनाने का निश्चय किया।[७]

राजसमुद्र बनाने से सम्बन्धित जनश्रुतियां

१. राजसिंह ने एक पुरोहित, एक राणी, एक कुंवर और चारण को मार डाला था। अतः ब्राह्मणों की सम्मति से इन नृशंस हत्याओं के प्रायश्चित स्वरूप राणा ने इस तालाब को बनाने का निर्णय लिया था।[८]

२. विवाह के लिए जैसलमेर जाते समय गोमती नदी के वेग के कारण राजसिंह को तीन दिन वहां रुक जाना पड़ा। इसलिए इसे बनाने का निर्णय लिया।[९]

३. सं. १७१७ (१६६१ ई.) में भंयकर दुर्भिक्ष से पीड़ित हुई प्रजा के असीम कष्ट को ध्यान में रखकर राजसिंह ने इस झील का निर्माण करवाया था।[१०]

उपरोक्त तथ्यों का विश्लेषण करने पर तीसरा बिन्दु ही सही है, क्योंकि गोमती नदी से भी अधिक अनेक भयावह नदियां मेवाड़ में हैं। हत्या की घटनाएं भी बांध निर्माण के बाद की होना प्रमाणित हो चुकी हैं।[११] राजसमुद्र का निर्माण राजपूताना में प्रथम अकाल-राहत कार्य था।[१२] इसके निर्माण के समय वस्त्र, काष्ठ एवं पाषाण के मण्डप एवं कोष्ठ बनाये गये थे।[१३] यह विविध कार्य दुर्भिक्ष में महाराणा द्वारा बहुसंख्यक जनता को रोजगार उपलब्ध करवाने की मंशा को दर्शाते हैं।

महाराणा ने रणछोड़दास से सरोवर बांधने हेतु सलाह ली। पुरोहित ने तीन शर्तें रखी।[१४] १. कार्य के प्रति पूर्ण श्रद्धा हो २. प्रचुर मात्रा में धन व्यय किया जाये ३. दिल्लीपति से विरोध न हो। महाराणा ने शर्तें मन्जूर की।

मुहूर्त : गोमती नदी पर जलाशय बनाने का माघ कृष्णा ७, बुधवार, संवत १७१८ (१ जनवरी, १६६२ ई.) को मुहूर्त कर नींव की खुदाई प्रारम्भ की।[१५] कार्य की विशालता को देखते हुए तालाब के कार्य हेतु विभिन्न समितियों का गठन कर योग्य व्यक्तियों की नियुक्तियां की गयी। नियुक्त अधिकारियों को जलाशय के नाप एवं जांच पड़ताल के लिए भेजा गया।[१६] स्वयं राजसिंह ने गोगूदा में रहते हुए कार्य को देखा।[१७]

मजदूरों ने नाना प्रकार के औजारों से खुदाई प्रारम्भ की। करोड़ों मनुष्य पृथ्वी खोदने लगे। मिट्टी के बने ढ़ेरों से पृथ्वी पर बड़े-बड़े पर्वत बन गये।[१८] पचास हजार बैलगाड़ियां, एक लाख भैंसे, एक लाख खच्चर और दो लाख बेलदार पत्थर, चूना, मिट्टी ढोने के लिए लगाये गये और कमठाणों पर कार्य करने के लिए चार लाख मजदूर लगाये गये।[१९]

उपरोक्त वर्णन को अतिशयोक्तिपूर्ण मानते हुए मुहूर्त जो तीन वर्ष पश्चात् १७ अप्रेल, १६६५ ई. को किया गया था। उस वक्त ६०,००० कारीगर, मजदूरों को रोजगार मिलना बताया गया है।[२०]

कार्य की विशालता विवरण से हमें प्राप्त होती है यद्यपि यह अतिशयोक्तिपूर्ण लगता है, परन्तु विभिन्न स्रोतों, सर्वे[२१] एवं अन्य तालाबों[२२] की लागत को ध्यान रखते हुए तथ्यों का विश्लेषण करने पर हम पाते हैं कि ३ वर्ष पूर्व जब मुहूर्त हुआ। उस समय नींव खोदने में अधिक मजदूरों की जरूरत होती है। अतः उस समय काम करने वालों की संख्या ६०,००० से अधिक ही रही होगी। राजप्रशस्ति तथा राजविलास में किया गया वर्णन निश्चित ही अतिशयोक्तिपूर्ण है।

नींव से जल निकासी : नींव में पानी आ जाने पर चक्रवाले रहटों से बैल जोतकर, एक के ऊपर एक करके अनेक प्रकार के रहट लगाकर जल निकाला गया। तत्कालीन भारत में जल निकालने[२३] के सभी उपायों से जल निकाला गय। गुणवान सूत्रधारों तथा जानकार लोगों द्वारा जल निकालने के तरीकों को भी अपनाया गया।[२४]

वैशाख शुक्ला १३, सोमवार संवत १७२१ (चैत्रादि सं. १७२२) १७ अप्रेत, १६६५ ई. को नींव भरने का मुहूर्त किया।[२५] चेजागर पत्थर और चूना मिश्रित सामग्री से दीवार बनाने लगे, सहस्रों पुरुष शिलाएं उठाने के कार्य में लगे,[२६] बड़े-बड़े हाथी चूना लाये।[२७] कई श्रमिक खानों से पत्थर निकालने, उन्हें चौकोर और सुघड़ बनाने तथा गाड़ियों में पत्थर भरने के कार्य में जुटे हुए थे।[२८] महासेतु का पहले 'शरीबंध[२९] तथा इसके पश्चात् सुदृढ सेंभरोबन्ध[३०] बांधा गया।[३१]

कांकरोली सेतु का निर्माण

संवत १७२६ वैशाख शुक्ला, त्रयोदशी (३ मई, १६६९ ई.) सोमवार को सेतु निर्माण का मुहूर्त हुआ तथा सेतु को चूने में भीगी हुई बड़ी-बड़ी शिलाओं से ऊपर तक भर दिया।[३२]

मुख्य सेतु : सं. १७२६ (१६६९ ई.) में तड़ाग में आषाढ़ से पूर्व ज्येष्ठ में वर्षा होने से नया जल आ गया।[३३] इसी वर्ष आठ वर्ष पांच माह और छह दिन में सूत्रधारों ने मुख्य सेतु की नींव को भरकर भित्ती (दीवार) के रूप में ऊपर उठाकर उसे सुदृढ़ बना दिया।[३४]

इस वर्ष आये नये जल को चतुष्की[३५] खोदने वाले मनुष्यों ने अनेक चतुष्कियां खोदकर बाहर निकाल दिया।[३६] तत्पश्चात् सेतु के मध्य भाग को चतुष्कियों से निकली मिट्टी के ढ़ेरों से भर दिया।[३७] मुख्य सेतु[३८] पर राजसिंह ने संगी-कार्य का मुहूर्त निकलवाया। यहां प्रयुक्त पत्थर बड़े-बड़े चिकने और सफेद रंग के थे, उनके जोड़ों में चूना भरकर उन्हें मजबूत बनाया जाने लगा। इस प्रकार सूत्रधारों के निरन्तर कार्य करते रहने पर संगी कार्य पूरा हो गया[३९] एवं राजसमुद्र पूर्ण हुआ।

राजसमुद्र के सम्पूर्ण सेतु की लम्बाई ३९०९.१० मीटर है। गजधरों ने इस सेतु की लम्बाई को गाला योग से आठ हजार गज (४८७६.८ मीटर) सिद्ध किया है। विश्वकर्मा ने बताया है कि तड़ागों की सर्वाधिक लम्बाई छह हजार गज (३६५७.६ मीटर) होनी चाहिए।[४०]

राजसमुद्र की ओटाएं - जल निकास मार्ग

बासोल गांव के पार्श्व में बने सेतु पर तीन ओटाएं (जल-निकास मार्ग) हैं। इनसे गांवों में पानी ले जाया जाता था।[४१]

ओटा नं.	लम्बाई (मीटर)	ऊंचाई (मीटर)	चौड़ाई (मीटर)
१.[४२] १५२.४	६.६६	०.६१४	
२.[४३] १५२.४	६.६६	१.५२४	
३.[४४] १८२.८८	६.०६६	१.२१६	

राजसमुद्र में जलमग्न गांव[४५] : सिवाली, भिगावदा, भाना, लुहान, वासोल और गुड़ली।

राजसमुद्र में निम्न गांवों की सीमाएं डूबी हैं[४६] : मोरचणा, पसूंद, खेड़ी, छापरखेड़ी, तासोल और मंडावर।

जल प्राप्ति के स्रोत[४७] : गोमती, ताल और केलवा नदी

रामसमुद्र में डूबे जलाशय[४८] : कांकरोली, लुहान और सिवाली के ३० जलाशय जिनमें निवान, वापी एवं कूप सम्मिलित हैं।

गोमती तथा ताल नदी में बाढ़ : १६७३ ई. में ताल नदी में अचानक आयी बाढ़ से नदी के किनारे के मकान जलमग्न हो गये। गोमती में अचानक आये पानी से रात में नवीन तड़ाग आठ हाथ (४.८७ मीटर) भर गया।[४६]

नौकारोहण : २७ जुलाई, १६७४ ई. को सरोवर में लाहौर और सूरत से आये सूत्रधारों ने बड़ी-बड़ी नौकाऐं तैराईं।[५०]

प्रतिष्ठा : माघशुक्ला १५ सं.१७३२ (चैत्रादि सं. १७३३) २० जनवरी, गुरुवार, १६७६ ई.[५१] को राजसमुद्र की प्रतिष्ठा की गयी।[५२] मुख्य शिल्पी को २५,०००/- रुपये दिये गये।[५३] राजसिंह ने जलाशय का जन्म नाम "राजसागर" और द्वितीय नाम राजसमुद्र रखा।[५४]

रामसमुद्र निर्माण एवं उत्सव आदि पर व्यय

माघ कृष्णा सप्तमी, बुधवार, संवत १७१८, (१६६१ ई. से संवत १७३५ (१६७८ ई.) तक इस झील के निर्माण तथा उत्सव आदि पर व्यय[५५]

प्रथम पक्ष में हुआ व्यय :

रामसिंह के द्वारा[५६]	:	२७,३६,४६७.५० रु.
महाराणा के काका के निरीक्षण में[५७]	:	५,०४,८८०.२५ रु.
मोहनसिंह सिसोदिया की देखरेख में[५८]	:	२,१२,५३८.२५ रु.
सांवलदास पंचोली के हस्ते[५६]	:	४,७८,१०७.०० रु.
चतुष्कियों से निकली हुई मिट्टी की मजदूरी लेखे[६०]	:	३२,६०१.२५ रु.
प्रतिष्ठा में हुए रुपयों का योग[६१]	:	७,००,००१.०० रु.
प्रथम पक्ष में हुए रुपयों का योग[६२]	:	४६,६४,६२५.२५ रु.

ऊपर वर्णित राशि का फिर से ब्यौरा

राजसमुद्र के निर्माण कार्य निमित्त वेतन खर्च[६३]	:	३२,०२,८८०.२५ रु.
राजसमुद्र के काम पर उपस्थित रहने वाले ठाकुरों के खिराज के[६४]	:	७,६१,७७४.०० रु.

		३९,६४,६२५.२५ रु.
प्रतिष्ठा पर व्यय	:	७,००,००१.०० रु.
कुल योग	:	४६,६४,६२५.२५ रु.
दूसरे पक्ष में हुआ व्यय[६५]	:	१,०५,०७,६०८.०० रु.

यदि **प्रथम पक्ष में राजसमुद्र** का निर्माण कार्य एवं दूसरे पक्ष को कुल व्यय माना जाये तो :-

कुल व्यय	:	१,०५,०७,६०८.०० रु.
झील पर व्यय	:	४६,६४,६२५.२५ रु.
दान, इनाम आदि पर खर्च	:	५८,४२,९८२.७५ रु.

यदि **प्रथम तथा द्वितीय पक्ष का खर्च** भिन्न-भिन्न माना जाये तो :

राजसमुद्र के निर्माण पर व्यय	:	४६,६४,६२५.२५ रु.
दान, इनाम आदि पर व्यय	:	१,०५,०७,६०८.०० रु.
कुल व्यय[६६]	:	**१,५१,७२,२३३.२५ रु.**

उपरोक्त व्यय के अतिक्ति क्षत्रियादि, जागीरदारों द्वारा चौकड़ी कार्य में लगा व्यय, तड़ाग में ब्राह्मण, क्षत्रिय एवं अन्य लोगों द्वारा खर्च किया गया धन राजसिंह द्वारा प्रदत्त गौ, पृथ्वी, स्वर्ण, रजत, अन्न-वस्त्र, अश्व और गज आदि के दानों पर हुआ व्यय भी प्रभूत था। जिसकी गणना करना दुष्कर कार्य था।[६७] राजसमुद्र निर्माण कार्य के वर्षवार (१६६१ ई. से १६७७) तक के व्यय का ब्यौरा एक अन्य समकालीन रचना में दिया गया है। इस अनाम रचना में निर्माण कार्य पर कुल व्यय ४४,२५,८३८ रु. बताये गये हैं। जो राजप्रशस्ति में दिये गये व्यय से २,३८,७८७ रु. २५ पैसे कम थे।[६८]

यह बांध राजनगर की खान के संगमरमर पत्थर का बना हुआ है। राजसमुद्र[६९] की पाल, उसके घाटों, घाटों की सीढ़ियों और सीढ़ियों के बीच में बने परिधों तथा घाटों के आजू-बाजू बने परिधों के ताकयुक्त मिट्टों का बनाया जाना निर्माण प्रक्रिया की दृष्टि से भी अनोखा है। इस पाल के घाट की सीढ़ियों को भारतीय स्थापत्य की संज्ञा में "कुण्ड" कहा जाता है, नौ-नौ की संख्या समूह में है। ऊपर से नीचे तीन-तीन समूहों को मिलाकर इस पाल के कुण्ड भाग बने हैं। इस प्रकार इस पाल के कुण्ड भाग में ऊपर के परिध के पश्चात् पूर्व से पश्चिम की तरफ क्षैतिज स्थिति में बनी नौ सीढ़ियां, फिर परिधि फिर इसी प्रकार बनी नौ सीढ़ियां फिर परिध और फिर इसी रीति से बनी नौ सीढ़ियां विद्यमान हैं।[७०]

इस प्रकार पूर्व-पश्चिम दिशा में घाटों पर सत्ताईस-सत्ताईस सीढ़ियां बनी हैं। इसके पश्चात् कुण्ड की सीढ़ियों का क्रम बदल गया है। इन सत्ताईस सीढ़ियों के पश्चात् पूर्व से पश्चिम दिशा की तरफ बढ़ने वाली सीढ़ियों के स्थान पर मकान की दीवार में बनाये जाने वाले जीने (सीढ़ी) की तेरह छोटी सीढ़ियां बनी हैं, जिनकी दिशा उत्तर-दक्षिण में है। उन पर होकर तालाब के जल तक जाने के लिए पूर्व अथवा पश्चिम की ओर मुंह करके उतरा जाता है। ऐसी बनी सीढियों की संख्या भी नौ-नौ ही हैं।[७१]

जलाशय निर्माण में मुख्य शिल्पियों में प्रथम गजधर-प्रारूप ढांचा बनाने वाले तथा द्वितीय सूत्रधार अर्थात प्रबन्ध करने वाले होते थे।[७२] निर्माण पूर्व अधिकारियों को जलाशय के स्थल का चुनाव नाप एवं जाँच पड़ताल हेतु भेजा जाता था। महाराणा स्वयं भी कई बार जलाशय निर्माण के समय उपस्थित रहते थे।[७३] मालवा आदि से अच्छे कारीगर, मजदूर बुलाये जाते थे। पत्थर, लोहा आदि बांध निर्माण से संबन्धित सामग्री को उपयुक्त स्थानों से मंगवाया जाता था।[७४]

मेवाड़ में भूमिगत जल का सही आंकलन करने में सिद्धहस्त व्यक्तियों द्वारा बताये गये स्थान पर कुएं, बावड़ियां आदि खोदे जाते थे। नदियों एवं सरोवरों के रिसाव क्षेत्र में इनका निर्माण अधिक किया जाता था, क्योंकि वहां जल की उपलब्धता निश्चित होती थी।[७५]

मध्यकाल में जलाशय निर्माण में चूने का प्रयोग किया जाता था। अतः सीमेन्ट एवं चूने की तुलना की गई है।[७६]

क्र.सं.	चूना	सीमेन्ट
१. **तराई**	जल से तराई की आवश्यकता कम रहती है। २-१२ दिन तक जमने की अवस्था में इसमें दरारे नहीं पड़ती है।	इसको लगाने के १२-२४ घंटे के पश्चात् ४-७ दिन तक तराई की आवश्यकता होती है। इसके अभाव में चिनाइ में दरारे पड़ जाती है।
२. **सिकुड़ना**	जल के साथ मिलने पर चूना फैलता है। सख्त होने की प्रक्रिया २ से १० दिन तक चलती है। चलती है।	जल के साथ मिलते ही कठोर होकर सिकुड़ता है। यह अवस्था २-३ वर्ष तक
३. **अवधि**	इसकी अवधि ४०० से १००० वर्ष वर्ष मानी जाती है।	इसकी अवधि ४० से १०० आंकी जाती है।
४. **रिसाव**	चूने के कार्य[७७] में रिसाव की गुंजाईश कम रहती है।	सीमेन्ट में रिसाव की सभांवना अधिक रहती है।
५. **रसायन प्रतिक्रिया**	चूने में केमिकल रिक्शन कम होने से उसकी अवधि अधिक है।	सीमेन्ट बनाने में प्रयुक्त रसायन इसकी अवधि कन कर देते हैं।

बांधों के निर्माण में निम्नलिखित बातों का ध्यान रखना चाहिए[७८]-

१. जलपूरित जलाशय में शिल्ट की मात्रा आवश्यकता से अधिक नहीं होनी चाहिए। कोई भी जलाशय अत्यधिक सिल्ट आने के कारण असफल हो सकता है। मेवाड़ में निर्मित जलाशयों में शिल्ट की मात्रा आलोच्यकाल में वनों की अधिकत के कारण कम रही थी। इसके साथ ही नदियों का घुमाव इस मात्रा को सीमित रखने में सहायक रहा था।

२. जल-निकास की व्यवस्था : राजसमुद्र[७९] में तीन जल-निकास मार्ग रखे गये थे।

द्रवगति विज्ञान एवं गणित के आधार पर बांध की स्थिरता हेतु आधारभूत आवश्यकताएं[८०]-

१. बांध जिस नींव पर बना है, वह ठोस पत्थरों पर होनी चाहिए।

२. बांध का वजन एवं बांध पर जल के दबाव के परिणामी बल मिलने के स्थान की बांध से दूरी, बांध की चौड़ाई की दो तिहाई से कम होनी चाहिए।

राजसमुद्र झील की तकनीकी-

१. **कठोर चट्टानों पर नींव का निर्माण** : राजसमुद्र में जल के विभिन्न तरीके अपनाकर कठोर चट्टानों के आने तक नींव को खोदी गयी थी।[८१] मुख्य बांध के अतिरिक्त पीछे की तरफ एक दीवार[८२] बनाकर बीच वाले हिस्से में मिट्टी, पत्थर इत्यादि भरवा दिए जाते थे। इसमें वृक्ष, बाग आदि लगा दिये जाते थे। पेड़-पौधे तथा यह क्षेत्र बांध की सुदृढ़ता में सहायक थे।

२. राजसमुद्र के मुख्य बांध की चौड़ाई ३३.४४ मीटर है। बांध के वजन तथा जल के दबाव का परिणामी बल मिलने के स्थान की बांध से दूरी ११.१७ मीटर है। यदि यह २२.२८ मीटर से कम होती, फिर भी बांध की सुदृढ़ता निश्चित थी, परन्तु यह ११.१७ मीटर ही आता है। अतः यह बांध पूर्णतः सुरक्षित है।[८३]

संदर्भ

१. सेन्सस-उदयपुर; पृ. २-३

२. मेवाड़ रेजीडेन्सी; पृ.६

३. राजप्रशस्ति; सर्ग २; श्लोक २१

४. राजविलास; विलास ८, पद्य ११०

५. राजप्रशस्ति; सर्ग ६; श्लोक ३-५

६. उपरोक्त; सर्ग ६; श्लोक ५-६; इसमें धोयन्दा, सनवाड़, सिवाली, भिगावदा, मोरचणा, पसूंद, खेड़ी, छापरखेड़ी, तासोल, मंडावर, भांण, लुहाणा, बांसोल, गुढली, कांकरोली एवं मढ़ा नामक गांव शामिल थे। (राजप्रशस्ति; सर्ग ६, श्लोक ६-७)

७. राजप्रशस्ति; सर्ग ६; श्लोक ६-१०

८. वीर विनोद; भाग २, पृ. ४४५-४६

९. ओझा; उ.रा. का इतिहास; भाग २, पृ. ५७०

१०. राजविलास; विलास ८, पद्य ११३-३९; जेम्स टॉडकृत; राजस्थान का इतिहास पृ. २३३; वीर विनोद में वर्णन है कि दुर्भिक्ष के बाद चार-पांच वर्ष तक वर्षा की कमी रही थी। (वीर विनोद; भाग २, पृ. ४४६)

११. डॉ. बी.एम. जावलिया; राजसमुद्र झील का निर्माण व्यय (मज्झमिका, १९७९-८०, पृ.१५-१६)

१२. जेम्स टॉडकृत; राजस्थान का इतिहास; पृ. २३३; वीर विनोद; भाग २, पृ. ४४६; मेवाड़ रेजीडेन्सी; पृ. ६

१३. राजप्रशस्ति; सर्ग १२; श्लोक १६-१९

१४. राजप्रशस्ति; सर्ग ९; श्लोक १०-११

१५. उपरोक्त; सर्ग ९; श्लोक १४

१६. राजप्रशस्ति; सर्ग ९, श्लोक १९, २१ तथा शिला २५ के अन्त में मेवाड़ी में दी गयी अतिरिक्त जानकारी; पृ. २६४

१७. उपरोक्त; सर्ग १, श्लोक १०

१८. उपरोक्त; सर्ग ९, श्लोक १७-१९

१९. राजविलास; विलास ८, पद्य १४१-४२

२०. आर.वी. सोमानी; हिस्ट्री ऑफ मेवाड़; पृ. २९५

२१. स्वयं द्वारा राजसमुद्र बांध की सर्वे

२२. जयसमुद्र निर्माण में १८ लाख रुपये लगे। (जयसमुद्र प्रशस्ति; सर्ग १८, ह.ग्र.); उदयसागर निर्माण में १,७४,७८१ रु. उद्यापन सहित कुल ३,११,०९७/- रु. व्यय हुए। (चित्तौड़-उदयपुर पाटनामा; भाग ३, पत्र संख्या २२३ अ)

२३. चरस (चड़स), उलीचना, ढो, ढोकली, सूपड़ा आदि जल निकासी के तत्कलीन तरीके थे, जो ग्रामीण इलाकों में आज भी प्रचलित हैं।

२४. राजप्रशस्ति; सर्ग ९, श्लोक २४-२९

२५. राजप्रशस्ति; सर्ग ९; श्लोक ३४-३७, इंडियन एफेमरिज; भाग ६, पृ. १३२

२६. राजविलास; विलास ८; पद्य १४४

२७. राजप्रशस्ति; सर्ग ६; श्लोक ३६

२८. राजविलास; विलास ८; पद्य १४५

२६. शरीबंध - कच्चा बांध

३०. सेंभरोबन्ध - पक्का बांध

३१. राजप्रशस्ति; सर्ग ६; श्लोक ४५

३२. इंडियन एफेमरिज; भाग ६, पृ. १४०; राजप्रशस्ति; सर्ग २; श्लोक १०-११

३३. राजप्रशस्ति; सर्ग १०; श्लोक १२

३४. राजप्रशस्ति; सर्ग १०; श्लोक १३-१४

३५. चतुष्की - चौकड़ी

३६. राजप्रशस्ति; सर्ग १०, श्लोक १६

३७. उपरोक्त; सर्ग १०, श्लोक १८-१६

३८. मुख्य सेतु - नौ चौकी बांध

३६. राजप्रशस्ति; सर्ग १०, श्लोक ३८-३६

४०. उपरोक्त; सर्ग १२, श्लोक ११-१३; इस झील के नौ चौकी बांध तथा द्वारकाधीश मन्दिर के बीच एक साथ कई चड़स चलने के चिन्ह आज भी देखे जा सकते हैं।

४१. राजप्रशस्ति; सर्ग १२, श्लोक ४ तथा भूमिका, पृ. ६६

४२. राजप्रशस्ति; सर्ग १२, श्लोक १

४३. उपरोक्त; सर्ग १२, श्लोक २

४४. उपरोक्त; सर्ग १२, श्लोक ३

४५. उपरोक्त; सर्ग १२, श्लोक ७

४६. उपरोक्त; सर्ग १२, श्लोक ८

४७. राजप्रशस्ति; सर्ग १२, श्लोक ६

४८. उपरोक्त; सर्ग १२, श्लोक १०

४६.उपरोक्त; सर्ग १२, श्लोक २५-२७

५०.राजप्रशस्ति; सर्ग १२, श्लोक ३६-३७

५१.इंडियन एफेमरिज; भाग ६, पृ. १५४

५२.राजप्रशस्ति; सर्ग १८, श्लोक ४०

५३.उपरोक्त; सर्ग २०, श्लोक ३०; उद्धृत; ओझा; उ.रा. का इतिहास, भाग २, पृ. ५७३; मुख्य शिल्पी को २५०००/- रुपये दिये जाने का वर्णन सत्य नहीं है।

५४.उपरोक्त; सर्ग १५, श्लोक २६-३०

५५.राजप्रशस्ति; सर्ग २१, श्लोक १

५६.उपरोक्त; सर्ग २१, श्लोक ३-४

५७.उपरोक्त; सर्ग २१, श्लोक ५

५८.उपरोक्त; सर्ग २१, श्लोक ६-७

५९.उपरोक्त; सर्ग २१, श्लोक ७-८

६०.उपरोक्त; सर्ग २१, श्लोक ६-१०

६१.उपरोक्त; सर्ग २१, श्लोक ११

६२.उपरोक्त; सर्ग २१, श्लोक २

६३.उपरोक्त; सर्ग २१, श्लोक १२-१३

६४.उपरोक्त; सर्ग २१, श्लोक १४-१५

६५.राजप्रशस्ति; सर्ग २१, श्लोक २२

६६.राजप्रशस्ति के सम्पादक मोतीलाल मेनारिया ने रुपये १,५१,७२,२३३.२५ के व्यय को प्रमाणिक माना है। (राजप्रशस्ति; भूमिका, पृ. ३५)

६७.राजप्रशस्ति; सर्ग २१, श्लोक १८-२१ तथा २३; प्रशस्तिकार रणछोड़ भट्ट ने साफ लिखा है कि इस ब्राह्मण को उक्त आंकड़ों के अतिरिक्त इसमें क्षत्रियों, ब्राह्मणों के लगे हजारों, लाखों और करोड़ों की अनेक संख्याएं ज्ञात हुई हैं। मैनें यहां केवल उक्त लोगों द्वारा लगे धन की संख्या बतायी है। (राजप्रशस्ति;सर्ग २१, श्लोक २३)

६८.यह रचना प्राच्य विद्या प्रतिष्ठान, उदयपुर में ग्रंथाक २६७ पर उपलब्ध है; डॉ. बी.एम. जावलिया; राजसमुद्र झील निर्माण व्यय से सम्बन्धित एक संस्कृत काव्य (मज्झमिका; १६७६-८०, पृ. १८-२२)

६६.महाराणा फतहसिंह ने १,८१,४३३.७५ रु. व्यय कर राजसमुद्र पाल की मरम्मत तथा नहर निर्माण कार्य करवाया। (महाराणा फतहसिंहकालीन हकीकत बहिड़ा; भाग २, पृ. २७३; फाईल सं. २५०; रा.रा. अभिलेखागार, उदयपुर); यह झील कई वर्षों से पूरी नहीं भरी है। १८८४-८६ में नहरें बनाकर इस झील से लगभग २०० एकड़ भूमि की सिंचाई होती है। ८०,००० की आबादी वाले नगर के लिए प्रतिदिन ५० लाख लीटर जल, जलदाय विभाग द्वारा वितरित किया जा रहा है। जे.के.टायर इन्डस्ट्रीज का जल आपूर्ति स्रोत भी यही है। (मेवाड़ रेजीडेन्सी; पृ.६ : रमेश आचार्य; क्या कभी भरेगा राजसमन्द; राज. पत्रिका; २४ अगस्त, १६६६, पृ. १०)

७०.डॉ. राजशेखर व्यास; मेवाड़ की कला और स्थापत्य; पृ. २२६

७१.वही, पृ. २२६

७२.श्रीराम शर्मा; महाराणा राजसिंह एण्ड हिज टाईम्स; पृ. ४६

७३.राजप्रशस्ति; सर्ग १, श्लोक १०; सर्ग ६, श्लोक ६ व १६-२१; जयसमुद्र प्रशस्ति; सर्ग १२

७४.वीर विनोद; भाग २, पृ. ६६७

७५.आवरगढ, उदयपुर, गोगून्दा, चावण्ड आदि का स्वयं द्वारा सर्वे।

७६.अनुपम मिश्र; राजस्थान की रजत बूंदे, पृ. १०४

७७.चूने में संयोजी गुण नहीं होता, लेकिन जब उसे पीसकर काम में लिया जाता है, तो यह कई ऐसे यौगिक बनाता है। जो बहुत संयोजी है, अर्थात मजबूत बन जाता है। (गुरचरनसिंह; भवन-निर्माण तकनीकी; पृ. ३६४) **गरट - एक गोल बड़ा पत्थर बैलों की सहायता से चूने को पीसने के लिए काम में लिया जाता था, जो गरट कहलाता था।**

७८.डॉ. विद्यासागर दुबे और डॉ. प्रभाशंकर मिश्र; भू-विज्ञान एक परिचय; पृ. ५१५

७६.राजप्रशस्ति; सर्ग १२, श्लोक ४

८०. एस.रामामरुथम; स्ट्रेन्थ ऑफ मेटेरियल्स; पृ. ३३७-३८, सुशील कुमार; बिल्डिंग कन्सट्रक्शन; पृ. ८, १०१; वी.एन.एस. मूर्ति; सोइल मेकेनिक्स एण्ड फाउण्डेशन इंजीनियरिंग; पृ. ५८८;राजीव शर्मा; राजसमुद्र बांध : १७ वीं शताब्दी की अभियांत्रिकी की उपलब्धि (प्रोसिडिंग्स ऑफ इंडियन हिस्ट्री कांग्रेस; पृ. २२१-२३, १९९२-९३)

८१. राजप्रशस्ति; सर्ग ६, श्लोक २४-२६

८२. राजप्रशस्ति ; सर्ग ११; श्लोक ११-१२ व ३२-३३; ओझा; उदयपुर राज्य का इतिहास; भाग १; पृ. ५; मेवाड़ रेजीडेन्स; पृ. ६

८३. एम.रामामरुथम; स्ट्रेन्थ ऑफ मेटेरियल्स; पृ. ३३५-४१; सुशील कुमार; बिल्डिंग कन्सट्रक्शन; पृ. ८, १०१; वी.एन.एस. मूर्ति; सोईल मेकनिक्स एण्ड फाउण्डेश्न इंजीनियरिंग; पृ. ५८८

सल्तनत कालीन जल प्रबन्धन (दिल्ली के सुल्तानों के विशेष सन्दर्भ में)

डॉ. अशोक कुमार सिंह एवं अविनाश कुमार दुबे

मनुष्य ने सर्वप्रथम जल संचय के लिये कूप व जलाशय का निर्माण किया। कालान्तर में जल के प्राकृतिक स्रोतों नदियों प्रपातों एवं झीलों से नहरें निकाली जाने लगी। दिल्ली के सुल्तानों ने भी इस दिशा में सराहनीय प्रयास किये हैं।[१]

कुँआ- सल्तनत काल में भी पीने के जल के लिये कुँआ ही सर्वोन्तम साधन थ। लगभग प्रत्येक नगर एवं गाँव में कुँआ था। शिहाबुद्दीन अल उमरी के अनुसार प्रायः सात हाथ नीचे पानी मिल जाता था।[२] बाबर भी समर्थन करते हुये लिखता है कि "हिन्दुस्तान में पुरवे, गाँव तथा नगर क्षण भर में बस भी जाते हैं और उसी प्रकार नष्ट भी हो जाते हैं। यदि उन्हें किसी स्थान को आबाद करना होता है तो उन्हे न नहर खोदने की आवश्यकता पड़ती है और न बन्द बनवाने की, कारण कि यहाँ वर्षा के सहारे पर ही कृषि होती है और जनसंख्या की तो कोई सीमा ही नहीं। लोग एकत्र हो ही जाते हैं। कुँआ अथवा तालाब खोद लेते हैं।"[३]

मुहम्मद तुगलक ने अपने शासनकाल में दुर्भिक्ष के समय कुँए खुदवाने का आदेश दिया था।[४] सल्तनत कालीन ऐतिहासिक ग्रन्थों के अतिरिक्त तत्कालीन अभिलेखों में कुँआ निर्माण कराये जाने,[५] उन्हें साफ करने[६] एवं उनके मरम्मत किये जाने[७] आदि का प्रचुर उल्लेख मिलता है। उत्तर प्रदेश में अपनी यात्रा के दौरान इब्नेबत्तूता ने एक कच्चे कूप का उल्लेख किया है[८] जिससे अनुमान लगाया जा सकता है कि प्रायः कुँआ खोदने के उपरान्त उनमें पकी हुई ईटें थी या पत्थर लगाये जाते थे[९] किन्तु कुछ कुँओं को कच्चा ही छोड़ दिया जाता था। कुँओं से पानी खींचने के लिए रस्सी का प्रयोग किया जाता था। इब्नेबत्तूता ने एक स्थान पर मूँज से बनी रस्सी का उल्लेख किया है।[१०] इस रस्सी के सहारे लोग लोटा, बाल्टी या घड़े को बाँध देते थे और कुँए में जल भरने के उपरान्त उसे ऊपर खींच कर उसका उपयोग करते थे।[११]

पानी खींचने के लिये अनेक कुँओं पर लकड़ी के सहारे चर्खियाँ लगी होती थीं जिनकी सहायता से पानी निकालना सरल हो जाता था। शिहाबुद्दीन अल उमरी ने चर्खियाँ लगे कुँओं का उल्लेख किया है।[१२] कुँओं का निर्माण जल के स्वयं उपयोग करने तथा सार्वजनिक उपयोग के लिए किया जाता था किन्तु **फुतूहाते फीरोजशाही** के एक सन्दर्भ के अनुसार विपरीत मौसम में लोग कुँआ खोदकर जल को बेंचते भी थे।[१३]

आगरा, चन्दवार, बयाना आदि क्षेत्रों की यात्रा के समय बाबर ने चरस पद्धति का उल्लेख किया है। कुँए के दोनों किनारे पर दो शाखाओं वाली लकड़ी की सहायता से चर्खी लगायी जाती थी। इसकी सहायता से चमड़े के बड़े थैले को रस्सी के माध्यम से कुँए में ड़ाला जाता था और पानी भर जाने पर बैलों के द्वारा खींचा जाता था। तत्पश्चात् इस जल को खेतों तक पहुँचाने की व्यवस्था की जाती थी।[१४]

लाहौर, दीपालपुर, सरहिन्द आदि इलाकों में रहट से भी पानी खींचा जाता था। दो रस्सियों के बीच-बीच में लकड़ी बाँधकर घड़े लगाये जाते थे और उन्हें कुँए पर लगी चर्खी पर रख दिया जाता था। इस चर्खी के एक दूसरी धुरी से एक अन्य चर्खी लगी होती होती थी जिन्हें दाँतेदार चर्खी के माध्यम से घुमाया जाता था। घुमाने का कार्य बैल करते थे। इस प्रकार कुँए का जल एक चौड़े पात्र में गिरता था जिन्हें नालियों के माध्यम से खेतों तक पहुँचाया जाता था।[१५] आधुनिक काल में इसके लिए लोहे के चैन एवं डब्बों का प्रयोग किया जाता है। इसका पहला उल्लेख परोक्ष रूप से इब्नेबत्तूता ने तत्पश्चात् बाबर ने इसका विस्तृत वर्णन किया है।[१६] इरफान हबीब ने भी अपनी पूर्व मान्यता में संशोधन करते हुए कहा है कि भारत में रहट के प्रवेश का समय तुर्कों के विजय काल और उसके तुरन्त बाद की तेरहवीं और चौदहवीं शताब्दियों में ही निर्धारित करना काफी उचित होगा।[१७] इक्तिदार हुसैन सिद्दीकी के अनुसार बाबर द्वारा वर्णित स्थानों के अतिरिक्त उत्तर भारत के अनेक स्थानों पर भी रहट के संदर्भ प्राप्त होते हैं।[१८]

इब्नेबत्तूता ने कोल (आधुनिक अलीगढ़) के आस-पास एक विशेष कुँए का उल्लेख करते हुए कहा है कि भारतवर्ष में बाईं भी होती है जिसका अर्थ चौड़ा कूप होता है। यह पत्थर की बनी होती हैं और उसमें जल की सतह तक उतरने के लिए सीढ़िया बनी होती हैं। कुछ बाईं (बाउली अथवा बाड़ी) में पत्थर के गुम्मद, मेहराब और बैठने के भी स्थान बने होते हैं। उसका कहना है कि मुहम्मद तुगलक के शासन काल में मलिक तथा अमीर लोग जल के अभाव वाले मार्गों में ऐसी बावड़ी बनवाने में अपना परम सौभाग्य मानते थे। इब्नेबत्तूता ने आगे अनेक स्थानों पर ऐसे चौड़े

कूपों का उल्लेख किया है।[१९] मालाबार की यात्रा के समय इब्नेबत्तूता ने जुरफत्तन में एक विशाल बाईं का उल्लेख किया है।[२०] शिहाबुद्दीन अल उमरी ने ऐसी ही बाबड़ी का वर्णन किया है। **बाबरनामा** में भी बाबड़ी का उल्लेख मिलता है। इक्तिदार हुसैन सिद्दीकी का विचार है कि सल्तनत काल में ऐसे चौड़े कूपों के अनेक उल्लेख दिल्ली साम्राज्य एवं क्षेत्रिय राज्यों में भी मिलते हैं।[२२] ऐसे चौड़े कूपों की विशेषता यह होती है कि बिना किसी साधन के व्यक्ति या जानवर सीढ़ियों से उतर कर जलस्तर तक पहुँचे सकते थे और अपनी आवश्यकता की पूर्ति कर सकते थे। आज भी उत्तरी भारत में अनेक स्थानों पर ऐसे कूप दृष्टिगोचर होते हैं।

भारत में गाँव व नगर के अतिरिक्त दुर्गों में भी जल संचय के लिए कुँओं का निर्माण किया जाता था। इब्नेबत्तूता ने पहाड़ी पर स्थित ग्वालियर दुर्ग का वर्णन करते हुए लिखा है कि उसकी परिधि के भीतर २० कुँए थे।[२३] उत्तर प्रदेश के मिर्जापुर जिले में स्थित चुनार के सुप्रसिद्ध दुर्ग में भी एक कुँआ है। मान्यता के अनुसार दुर्ग से स्पर्श करती हुए गंगा नदी से इस कुँए में पानी पहुँचता है।

जलाशय/सरोवर (हौज़)– भारत में प्राचीनकाल से ही जलाशय निर्माण का इतिहास रहा है। तुर्क लोगों ने जब उत्तरी भारत पर विजय प्राप्ति की तो उन्होंने अपने लोगों के लिए कुछ एक नगरों का पुनर्निमाण कराया। साथ ही अनेक नये नगर भी बसाये। दिल्ली में तथाकथित राय पिथौरा के किले के पास आरम्भिक भवन व दुर्ग बनाये गये। आगे दिल्ली नगर का उत्तर एवं उत्तर-पूर्व में विकास होता रहा। एच०सी० वर्मा ने दिल्ली का उत्तर एवं उत्तर-पूर्व में विकास के कारण को यमुना नदी के जल की उपलब्धता से जोड़ा है, क्योंकि नवनिर्मित नगरों की उत्तरोत्तर वृद्धि होती जनसंख्या के लिए विस्तृत पैमाने पर जल की आवश्यकता थी।[२४]

दिल्ली के सुल्तानों में शम्सुद्दीन इल्तुतमिश पहला शासक है जिसने राजधानी दिल्ली में महरौली के पश्चिम में एक विशाल जलाशय का निर्माण कराया। इसका प्रथम उल्लेख अमीर खुसरो के ग्रन्थ **केरानुस्सादैन** में मिलता है। अमीर खुसरो लिखता है कि सुल्तान ने दो पहाड़ियों के मध्य एक पत्थर का हौज बनवाया था जहाँ से शहर वालों को पीने के लिए अच्छा जल उपलब्ध होता था। इसका जल इतना स्वच्छ था कि बालू के कण भी गिने जा सकते थे। लेखक के अनुसार पथरीली भूमि के कारण हौज का जल भूमि के भीतर प्रवृष्ट नहीं हो सकता था। यमुना नदी से हौज तक बहुत सी नहरें निकाली गई थी। हौज के बीच एक चबूतरा बना हुआ था जिस पर एक भवन भी निर्मित था। उसके चारों ओर लोग मनोविनोद के लिए शिविर लगाया करते थे।[२५] इस हौज को हौज़ेशम्सी, हौजे सुल्तान या हौजे सुल्तानी के नाम से जाना जाता था।[२६]

अलाउद्दीन खल्जी के शासन काल में इस हौज की सतह टूट जाने से यह पूर्णतया सूख गया। सुल्तान ने सर्वप्रथम इसे साफ कराने का निर्देश दिया। किन्तु इससे कोई लाभ नहीं हुआ। फलस्वरूप दिल्ली निवासियों को जल संकट से जुझना पड़ा। सुल्तान ने तालाब के जिर्णोद्धार के लिए दूसरा उपाय सोचा। उसके आदेशानुसार हौज के चबूतरे के चारों ओर दो-दो, तीन-तीन सौते खोदे गये। फलस्वरूप थोड़े ही दिनों में पानी चबूतरे तक पहुँच गया।[२७]

इब्नेबत्तूता के अनुसार यह हौज दो मील लम्बा तथा एक मील चौड़ा था। उसके पश्चिम में ईदगाह के समान पत्थर के घाट बने हुए थे। हौज़ में जब जल अधिक हो जाता था तो लोग नौका में बैठकर ही चबूतरे तक जा सकते थे। वह यह भी कहता है कि जब हौज़ के किनारे सूख जाते थे तो लोग उनमें गन्ना, ककड़ी, तरबूज, खरबूज आदि बो देते थे।[२८] फीरोजशाह के शासनकाल में हौजेशम्सी में आने वाले जल को कुछ लोगों ने बाँध दिया। फलस्वरूप पुनः जल का संकट उत्पन्न हो गया। सुल्तान ने दुष्टों को कठोर दण्ड देकर हौज में आने वाले जलधारा को खुलवा दिया।[२९] प्रतीत होता है कि बाबर के काल तक यह जलाशय उत्तम दशा में स्थित रहा।[२९]

हौज़े शम्सी के सूखने एवं सीरी नगर के निर्माण के कारण अलाउद्दीन खल्जी को एक अतिरिक्त जलाशय की आवश्यकता पड़ी। फलस्वरूप दिल्ली से ६ मील दक्षिण एवं कुतुबमीनार से २ मील उत्तर- पश्चिम में दिल्ली-गुड़गाँव मार्ग के दाईं ओर उसने एक विशाल जलाशय का निर्माण कराया।[३१] जिसे हौज़े खास या हौजे अलाई कहा जाता है।[३२] इब्नेबत्तूता के अनुसार देहली और दारूलखिलाफा के मध्य में हौजे खास है जो हौज़े शम्सी से भी बड़ा है। इसके किनारे पर लगभग ४० गुम्बद हैं। इसके चारों ओर गायक रहते हैं। इसी कारण यह स्थान संगीत नगर कहलाता है।[३३] फीरोज तुगलक के शासनकाल में इसी हौज के किनारे मदरसा-ए-फीरोजशाही की स्थापना की गई थी।[३४] इस विशाल एवं आवासीय मदरसा की स्थापना के पीछे हौज अलाई में पानी की प्रचुरता मुख्य कारक रहा होगा। यद्यपि फीरोज तुगलक के शासनकाल में यह हौज़ मिट्टी से भर गया था और सूख गया था। सुल्तान ने इस हौज़ को पुनः खुदवाया। फलस्वरूप यह हौज़ में वर्षपर्यन्त जल भरा रहने लगा।[३५] दिसम्बर १३९८ में तैमूर जब दिल्ली पहुँचा तो उसने हौजे खास को देखा। उसके अनुसार यह जलाशय वर्षपर्यन्त जल से भरा रहता है। दिल्ली के समस्त निवासी इसी से जल प्राप्त करते हैं।[३६] बाबर ने भी अपनी आत्मकथा में हौज़े खास का उल्लेख किया है।[३७]

गयासुद्दीन ने दिल्ली में जब तुगलकाबाद का निर्माण कराया तो वहाँ के निवासियों के लिए जल उपलब्ध कराने हेतु उसने एक हौज बनाने का आदेश दिया।[३८] मुहम्मद

तुगलक ने नवनिर्मित आदिलाबाद (दिल्ली) एवं दौलताबाद (देवगिरि) के नागरिकों के लिये नये जलाशयों का निर्माण कराया।[३९] फीरोज तुगलक ने भी हिसार फीरोजा नगर एवं दिल्ली में फीरोजाबाद नगर बसाये जाने के उपरान्त वहाँ के निवासियों के लिये जलाशयों (हौज़) का निर्माण कराया।[४०]

सल्तनतकाल में गुलाम शासकों के समय दिल्ली में हौज़े रानी[४१] खलजी काल में हौज़े बहत,[४२] मुहम्मद तुगलक के समय देवगिरि में हौज़े सुल्तान,[४३] फीरोज तुगलक के समय दिल्ली में हौज़े तुगलकशाह, हौज़े कुतलुग खाँ, हौज़े शाहजादा मुबारक खाँ,[४४] सैयद काल में हौज़े रानी[४५] जैसे विशाल जलाशयों का उल्लेख मिलता है किन्तु इनके सम्बन्ध में विस्तृत वर्णन प्राप्त नहीं होता है। समकालीन ऐतिहासिक ग्रन्थों के अतिरिक्त तत्कालीन यात्रा-वृतान्तों में अनेक जलाशयों का उल्लेख प्राप्त होता है[४६]। इसके अतिरिक्त समकालीन अभिलेखों में भी जलाशयों के निर्माण का विवरण मिलता है[४७]। सल्तनत काल में दुर्गों के भीतर भी जल की उत्तम व्यवस्था हेतु जलाशय बनाये जाते थे। इब्नेबत्तूता ने जहाँ ग्वालियर दुर्ग में जलाशय का उल्लेख किया है वहीं बाबर ने चन्देरी दुर्ग का वर्णन करते हुए लिखा है कि उसके भीतर एक चट्टान काटकर हौज़ बनाया गया है।[४९]

इब्नेबत्तूता ने दिल्ली निवासी शेख शहाबुद्दीन का उल्लेख करते हुए लिखा है कि उसके घर में स्नानागार था। शिहाबुद्दीन अल उमरी ने दिल्ली नगर में अगणित स्नानागार का उल्लेख किया है। इसी प्रकार देवगिरि शहर के प्रत्येक बस्ती में प्रत्येक श्रेणी के लोगों की आवश्यकतानुसार स्नानागार होने का उल्लेख किया है। नगरवासी समीपस्थ कुँओं अथवा जलाशयों से जल भरकर ले जाते थे।[५१] बरनी के ग्रन्थ **तारीखे फीरोजशाही** में हौज़े सुल्तानी के प्रसंग में भिश्तियों एवं जल भरने वाली दासियों का उल्लेख आता है।[५२] इससे स्पष्ट है कि नगर के सम्भ्रान्त परिवारों में जलाशयों से जल भरकर ले जाने का कार्य भिश्ती लोग या दासियाँ करती थी। स्नानागारों में और घरों में जल एकत्र करने के लिये धातु या मिट्टी के बड़े-बड़े पात्र रहे होंगे। इब्नेबत्तूता ने एक स्थान पर लिखा है कि दौलताबाद शहर गंगा नदी से ४० दिन की दूरी पर स्थित होने पर भी सुल्तान के निवास के समय उसके प्रयोग के लिये गंगा जल पहुँचाया जाता था।[५३] निश्चित तौर पर जल सुरक्षित रखने के लिये बड़े-बड़े पात्र रहे होंगे। उच्च्व वर्ग के लोगों के घरों पर 'आबदार'[५४] नामक सेवक लोगों तक जल उपलब्ध कराता था।

बाँध व नहर :- जल प्रबन्धन के दृष्टिकोण से बाँध व नहरों का निर्माण इस काल की महत्वपूर्ण विशेषता थी। सर्वप्रथम इल्तुतमिश द्वारा दिल्ली में निर्मित हौजे शम्सी

में यमुना नदी से नहर के माध्यम से जल लाने की व्यवस्था का विवरण प्राप्त होता है।[५५] खलजी काल में मुल्तान के मुक्ता पद पर रहते हुए गाजी मलिक ने उस प्रदेश में रावी नदी से झेलम नदी तक नहर का निर्माण करवाया।[५६] जियाउद्दीन बरनी ने गयासुद्दीन तुगलक की प्रशंसा करते हुए लिखा है कि उसके पास बड़ी-बड़ी नहरें खुदवाने, कृषि को सर्वसाधारण के लिये सुगम बनाने, अकृषि कर भूमि को उर्वरा बनाने के अतिरिक्त कोई कार्य नहीं था। आगे वह कहता है कि यदि उसकी अकाल मृत्यु न होती तो वह गंगा तथा यमुना के समान न जाने कितनी लम्बी नहरें खुदवा देता।[५७] ऐनुलमुल्क अब्दुल्ला ऐने माहरू के पत्र संग्रह **इन्शाये माहरू** में नासिरवाह, कुतुबुवाह आदि नामक नहरों की खुदाई एवं मरम्मत किये जाने का प्रसंग मिलता है।[५८] इब्नेबत्तूता ने दिल्ली निवासी शेख शहाबुद्दीन के विषय में लिखता है कि उसने अपने खेतों के लिये यमुना से जल लाने का प्रबन्ध किया था।[५९]

फीरोज तुगलक का शासनकाल बाँधों एवं नहरों के लिये विख्यात है। शम्स सिराज अफीफ के अनुसार उसने बन्द (बाँध) फतह खाँ, बन्द मालजा, बन्द महिपालपुर, बन्द शकूरखाँ, बन्द सालौरा, बन्द सहपना, बन्द वजीराबाद आदि बाँधों का निर्माण कराया। यद्यपि इसके सम्बन्ध में विस्तृत विवरण नहीं प्राप्त होते हैं।[६०]

बरनी ने लिखा है कि फीरोज के काल में गंगा तथा यमुना नदी के समान लम्बी-लम्बी नहरें ५० से ६० कोस से खोदी गई जो उन क्षेत्रों से गुजरती थी जहाँ तालाब तथा कुँए न थे।[६१] किन्तु लेखक ने नहरों का स्पष्ट वर्णन नहीं किया है। अफीफ ने दो नहरों का उल्लेख किया है जो सुल्तान ने नवनिर्मित हिसार फीरोजा नगर तक जल पहुँचाने के लिये निर्मित कराया। इनमें से प्रथम रजीवाह यमुना से एवं द्वितीय उलुगखानी सतलज नदी से निकालकर करनाल होते हुए लगभग ८० कोस दूर स्थित हिसार फीरोजा तक पहुँचायी गई।[६२] आर०सी० जौहरी **सीरत-ए-फीरोजशाही** एवं **तारीखे मुबारकशाही** के अध्ययन करने के उपरान्त इस निष्कर्ष पर पहुँचते हैं कि सुल्तान ने कुल पाँच नहरों का निर्माण कराया था। (१) १३५५ ई० में सतलज से झज्झर (रोहतक जिले में स्थित) तक ४८ कोस तक (२) १३५६ ई० में यमुना से मंडाती और सिरमूर पहाड़ी से नहर निकाल कर अन्य नहरों का पानी गिराकर हाँसी से होते हुए अरासीन तक जहाँ हिसार फीरोजा नगर बसाया गया था। (३) घग्घर से सरसुती दुर्ग होते हुए हरनी खेड़ा तक (४) यमुना से बुधी (बुधनी) के निकट से फीरोजाबाद तक (५) कठिन परिश्रम कर सरस्वती एवं सलीमा को नहरों से मिलाया।[६३] इक्तिदार हुसैन सिद्दीकी ने बरनी एवं **सीरत-ए-फीरोजशाही** के अध्ययन के उपरान्त यह निष्कर्ष निकाला है कि गंगा नदी से भी नहर-ए-गंगा निकाली गई

थी।[६४] सुल्तान ने वृहद भू-भाग पर पानी की व्यवस्था करने के उपरान्त उलेमा लोगों के अभिमत से जलकर (हक्-ए-शर्ब) दस प्रतिशत लगाया।[६५] इस प्रकार सुल्तान के प्रयासों के परिणामस्वरूप हजारों एकड़ भूमि में खेती व सिंचाई होने लगी जिससे अनाज और फलों के उत्पादन में वृद्धि हुई। साथ ही पानी के लिये निरन्तर भटकने वाले खानाबदोश जीवनयापन करने वाले लोगों ने नहरों के किनारे स्थायी निवास बना लिये।[६६] उन्नीसवीं शताब्दी में अंग्रेज अभियन्ताओं ने फीरोज के द्वारा खुदवाये गये कुछ नहरों की खोज कर उन्हें पुनर्जीवित किया।[६७]

इस प्रकार स्पष्ट है कि दिल्ली के सुल्तानों ने नवनिर्मित नगरों की उत्तरोत्तर वृद्धि होती जनसंख्या, सामान्य प्रजा एवं कृषकों की जल की समस्या के निदान हेतु कुँए, जलाशयों एवं नहरों का वृहद स्तर पर निर्माण कराया। उनके उचित जल प्रबन्धन से ही लोगों को पीने की पानी की समस्या से छुटकारा मिला वहीं सिंचाई से वंचित भूमि तक जल की व्यवस्था हो जाने से अन्न एवं फलों के उत्पादन में वृद्धि हुई। इस काल की विशेषता यह थी कि जहाँ सिंचाई के साधनों में नवीनतम तकनीक का प्रयोग हुआ, वहीं वृहद स्तर पर नहरों के निर्माण से एक बड़ी जनसंख्या को पानी सर्वसुलभ हो गया।

संदर्भ सूची

१. इक्तिदार हुसैन सिद्दीकी ने भारतीय इतिहास काँग्रेस के कुरूक्षेत्र अधिवेशन (१९८१) में 'वाटरवर्क्स एण्ड इरीगेशन्स सिस्टम इन इण्डिया ड्यूरिंग प्री-मुगल टाइम्स' शीर्षक से महत्वपूर्ण शोध पत्र पढ़ा था। संयोगवश वह प्रकाशित नहीं हो सका। यही शोध पत्र **इस्लामिक कल्चर,** भाग ६८, १९८४ में प्रकाशित हुआ है।

२. शिहाबुद्दीन अल उमरी, **मसालिकुल अबसार फी ममालिकुल अमसार,** अंग्रेजी अनुवाद, इक्तिदार हुसैन सिद्दीकी व काजी मुहम्मद अहमद (अलीगढ़, १९७१), पृ० ३६

३. बाबर, ***बाबरनामा,*** हिन्दी अनु०, सैयिद अतहर अब्बास रिजवी, **मुगलकालीन भारत-बाबर** (अलीगढ़, १९६०), पृ० १७१-१७२

४. जियाउद्दीन बरनी, **तारीखे फीरोजशाही** (कलकत्ता, १८६०-६२), पृ० ४८३; मेंहदी हुसेन (सं) **द रेहला आफ इब्नेबत्तूता** (बड़ौदा, १९६३), पृ० ८८

५. **एपिग्राफिया इण्डो-मुस्लिमका**, १९१५-१६, पृ० १७-१८; १९०९-१०, पृ० २८; १९३१-३२, पृ० १८; १९२३-२४, पृ० २४; १९१९-२०, पृ० ६

६. **एपिग्राफिया इण्डो-मुस्लिमका**, १९३७-३८, पृ० ६

७. **एपिग्राफिया इण्डो-मुस्लिमका,** १९१५-१६, पृ० १७८

८. **द रेहला ऑफ इब्नेबत्तूता**, पृ० १५६

९. **एपिग्राफिया इण्डो-मुस्लिमका**, १९३७-३८, पृ० ६

१०. **द रेहला ऑफ इब्नेबत्तूता** पृ० १५६

११. वही, पृ० १५६-१५७

१२. **मसालिकुल अबसार** (सिद्दीकी), पृ० ३६

१३. फीरोजशाह तुगलक, **फुतूहाते फीरोजशाही** (अलीगढ़, १९५४), पृ० १२-१३

१४. **बाबरनामा** (रिजवी), पृ० १७१

१५. वही, पृ० १७१-१७२, २१२-२१३

१६. **द रेहला ऑफ इब्नेबत्तूता**, पृ० १७२; **बाबरनामा** (रिजवी), पृ० १७०-१७१

१७. इरफान हबीब, 'प्रौद्योगिकी परिवर्तन एवं समाज,' **मध्यकालीन भारत**, अंक १, पृ० ३१; द्रष्टव्य, **इस्लामिक कल्चर**, भाग ६८, १९८४, पृ० ८-११

१८. **इस्लामिक कल्चर**, भाग ६८, पृ० १०

१९. **द रेहला ऑफ इब्नेबत्तूता**, पृ० १५५

२०. वही, पृ० १८७

२१. **मसालिकुल अबसार** (सिद्दीकी), पृ० ६२-६३; **बाबरनामा** (रिजवी), पृ० २१२-२१३

२२. **इस्लामिक कल्चर**, भाग ६८, १९८४, पृ० ११-१२

२३. **द रेहला ऑफ इब्नेबत्तूता**, पृ ४५

२४. एच०सी० वर्मा, **डायन्मिक्स ऑफ अरबन लाइफ इन प्री-मुगल इण्डिया** (नई दिल्ली, १९८६), पृ० १८५-१८६

२५. अमीर खुसरो, **केरानुस्सादैन** (अलीगढ़, १९१८), पृ० ३२-३३ मिनहाज ने इस हौज का उल्लेख मात्र किया है, मिनहाज-उस-सिराज, **तबकाते नासिरी** (कलकत्ता, १८७३-८१) , पृ० १९५

२६. एसामी, **फुतूहुस्सलातीन**, अं० अनु० मेहदी हुसैन, भाग २(एशिया पब्लि०, १९७६) पृ० २२७; जियाउद्दीन बरनी, **तारीखे फीरोजशाही**, (कलकत्ता, १८६०-६२), पृ० ५६; अमीर खुसरो, **खजाइनुल फुतूह**, अं०अनु०, मुहम्मद हबीब, **क्लेक्टेड वर्क्स ऑफ प्रोफेसर मुहम्मद हबीब**, (सं०) के०ए० निजामी, भाग २ (पिपुल्स पब्लि०, १९८१), पृ० १६१

२७. **खजाइनुल फुतूह** (हबीब), पृ० १६२

२८. **द रेहला ऑफ इब्नेबत्तूता**, पृ० २८

२९. **फुतूहाते फीरोजशाही**, पृ० १२; **सीरत-ए-फीरोजशाही** (खुदाबक्श पाण्डुलिपि सं० ५४७), फोलियो ७७

३०. **बाबरनामा** (रिजवी), पृ० १५६

३१. वही, टि० ५

३२. **द रेहला ऑफ इब्नेबत्तूता**, पृ० २८; **तारीखे फीरोजशाही** (बरनी), ४९७

३३. **द रेहला ऑफ इब्नेबत्तूता** पृ० २८

३४. **दीवाने मुतहर कड़ा**, सैयिद अतहर अब्बास रिजवी, **तुगलुक कालीन भारत**, भाग २, (अलीगढ़, १९५७), पृ० ४०६

३५. **फुतूहाते फीरोजशाही**, पृ० १२-१३

३६. शरफुद्दीन अली यजदी, **जफरनामा**, भाग २ (कलकत्ता, १८८५-८८) पृ० १०९; तैमूर, **मुलफुजात-ए-तीमूरी**, इलियट व डाउसन, **भारत का इतिहास**, भाग ३ (आगरा, १९८४), पृ० ३१५; तैमूर ने भ्रमवश फीरोज तुगलक को हौज़े खास का निर्माता कहा है।

३७. **बाबरनामा** (रिजवी), १५६

३८. एसामी, **फुतूहुस्सलातीन**, भाग-एक पृ० ६२२

३९. **इस्लामिक कल्चर**, भाग ६८, १९८४, पृ० ४

४०. यहिया, **तारीखे मुबारकशाही**, अं०अनु०, के०के० बसु (बड़ौदा, १९३२), पृ० १३०-१३१

४१. **तबकाते नासिरी**, पृ ३१६

४२. अमीर खुसरो, **तुगलकनामा**, सैयिद अतहर अब्बास रिजवी, **तुगलुककालीन भारत**, भाग १ (अलीगढ़, १९५५), पृ० १८८

४३. अमीर खुर्द, **सियरूल औलिया**, सैयिद अतहर अब्बास रिजवी, **खलजी कालीन भारत**, भाग १ (अलीगढ़, १९५५), पृ० १४९

४४. **सीरत-ए फीरोजशाही**, उद्धृत, **इस्लामिक कल्चर**, भाग ६८, १९८४, पृ० ५, १७ व टि० २७

४५. **तारीखे मुबारकशाही** (बसु), पृ० २४७

४६. **द रेहला ऑफ इब्नेबत्तूता**, पृ० १५६; **जफरनामा**, भाग २, पृ० ६७, ७७; **मसालिकुल अबसार** (सिद्दीकी), पृ० ३६

४७. **एपिग्राफिया इण्डो-मुस्लिमका**, १९२३-२४, पृ० १६, २०; १९३३-३४, पृ०३

४८. **द रेहला ऑफ इब्नेबत्तूता**, पृ० ४५

४६. **बाबरनामा** (रिजवी), पृ० २६८

५०. **द रेहला ऑफ इब्नेबत्तूता**, पृ० ८७

५१. **मसालिकुल अबसार** (सिद्दीकी), पृ० ३२, ३६

५२. **तारीखे फीरोजशाही** (बरनी), ५६

५३. **द रेहला ऑफ इब्नेबत्तूता**, पृ० ४

५४. **दीवाने मुतहर कड़ा, तुगलुककालीन भारत**, भाग २, पृ० ४०७

५५. **केरानुस्सादैन**, पृ० ३२

५६. **तुगलकनामा, खलजी कालीन भारत**, पृ० १८७

५७. **तारीखे फीरोजशाही** (बरनी), पृ० ४४२

५८. ऐनुलमुल्क अब्दुल्लाह ऐने माहरू, **इन्शाये माहरू** (अलीगढ़, तिथिरहित), पत्र सं० ११४

५६. **द रेहला ऑफ इब्नेबत्तूता**, पृ० ८७

६०. शम्स सिराज अफीफ, **तारीखे फीरोजशाही** (कलकत्ता, १८६०), पृ० ३३०

६१. **तारीखे फीरोजशाही** (बरनी), पृ० ५६७

६२. **तारीखे फीरोजशाही** (अफीफ), पृ० १२७

६३. **तारीखे मुबारकशाही** अं०अनु०, पृ० १३०-१३१; आर०सी० जौहरी, **फीरोज तुगलक**, (आगरा, १६६८) , पृ० १०५; सलीमा का आधुनिक नाम खानपुर का नाला है।

६४. **इस्लामिक कल्चर**, भाग ६८, १६८४, पृ० १३-१४

६५. **तारीखे फीरोजशाही** (अफीफ), पृ० १२६-१३०

६६. **तारीखे फीरोजशाही** (बरनी), पृ० ५६७-५७०

६७. आर०सी० जौहरी, पूर्व उद्धृत, पृ० १०५-१०६

गोंपाचल गढ़ का शिवमंदिर और अस्सी खम्बा बावड़ी

डॉ. मीना श्रीवास्तव

११०० से १८०० ई० के मध्य ग्वालियर में कच्छपघात, प्रतिहार, गुलम वंश, खिल्जी वंश, तुगलक वंश, तोमर वंश, मुगल वंश, सूरी एवं सिंधिया वंश का आधिपत्य रहा था। मध्यकालीन ग्वालियर गढ़ में इन शासकों ने साहित्य, संगीत और स्थापत्य कला की त्रिवेणी प्रवाहित की साथ ही साथ जल प्रबन्धन के क्षेत्र में भी अद्वितीय वैज्ञानिक और व्यवहारिक विधि अपनाई। इसके प्रत्यक्ष प्रमाण सूरजकुण्ड, गंगोलाताल, जौहरताल, एक खम्बा बावड़ी, गोल बावड़ी, एक पत्थर बावड़ी, अस्सी खम्बा बावड़ी, अनार बावड़ी, मानसरोवर, रानीताल, चेदीताल, कटोराताल, नूरसागर, शरद बावड़ी, मोतीझील[१] आदि जल स्त्रोत थे। इनमें से कुछ आज भी हैं यद्यपि इनका जल वर्तमान स्थिति में काई लग जाने एवं दूषित होने के कारण पीने के लिये उपयोग में नहीं आता है परन्तु ये तत्कालीन स्थिति में उत्तम जल-व्यवस्था को दर्शित करते हैं। अनेक कुंओं का निर्माण भी इस काल में हुआ। १३४२ ई० में इब्नवतूता ग्वालियर आया उसने लिखा है कि - कालियूर (ग्वालियर) का किला एक ऊंची पहाड़ी पर स्थित है। इसके अन्दर पानी के हौज हैं। किले की दीवार से मिले हुए लगभग २० कुंए हैं।[२] डूंगरसिंह द्वारा निर्मित किये गये एक कुंए का पानी मीठा एवं हाजमी था जो उरवाई गेट के पास स्थित है। इस कुंए का पानी औषधि के रूप में प्रयुक्त होता था और बिना राजाज्ञा के उसका उपयोग नहीं किया जा सकता था और निश्चित मात्रा में ही प्राप्त हो पाता था। बाबर ने बाबरनामा में उल्लेख किया है कि उरवा के भीतर दो अन्य झीलें हैं।[३]

उपर्युक्त जलस्त्रोतों में गोपाचल गढ़ में स्थापित अस्सी खम्बा बावड़ी भी अपने-आप में महत्वपूर्ण स्थान रखती है। इस बावड़ी एवं यहां पर स्थापित शिवमंदिर पर पहुंचने के लिये पूर्व दिशा का रास्ता जो पुराने शहर ग्वालियर में स्थित है उपयुक्त प्रतीत होता है। हथियापोर द्वार से प्रवेश करने पर बेजोड़ शिल्पकला को प्रदर्शित करता हुआ मानमंदिर स्थापित है। जिसके पास ही दुर्ग की पश्चिम दीवार से लगी हुई अस्सी खम्बा बावड़ी निर्मित है। इस बावड़ी के निर्माणकर्ता का यहां पर कोई भी अभिलेख प्राप्त

नहीं होता है परन्तु जनश्रुति यह है कि ' राजा मानसिंह के समय यह शिव मंदिर था वे प्रातःकाल भगवान शिव की आराधना के लिये आया करते थे।''[४] इसी शिव मंदिर से लगी हुई एक वृत्ताकार बावड़ी निर्मित है। जो गोलाई में लगभग ६० फुट होगी और इसकी गहराई ८० और १०० फुट के लगभग विदित होती है। इस बावड़ी में मुख्य रूप से ३ स्तर हैं। बावड़ी में अंदर जाने के लिएं ६-६ कुल १८ सीढ़ियां हैं। नीचे पानी तक पहुंचने के लिए इतनी ही सीढ़ियां और हैं। प्रथम तल में पहुंचने पर यहां ३२ खम्बों से घिरा हुआ दालान एवं छज्जा मिलता है। ये खम्बे लगभग २२ फुट लम्बे हैं। मध्य भाग में दो दरवाजे हैं इनमें से और नीचे तृतीय तल और पानी तक पहुंचने के लिए सीढ़ियां हैं। तृतीय तल में दो द्वार हैं। इन द्वारों तक बावड़ी में आज भी लबालब पानी भरा है। यह उल्लेख प्राप्त होता है कि - मान मंदिर के लिये इस बावड़ी से जल आपूर्ति होती थी।''[५] इन सभी द्वारों की ऊंचाई लगभग २० फुट और चौड़ाई ६ फुट है। ८० फुट की गहराई के बाद पानी भरा है। कमल की पंखुड़ियों की आकृति से आवृत्त गोल खम्बों के ऊपरी भाग में शिल्पांकन दृष्टव्य है। बावड़ी शिलाखण्डों से बनाई गई है। बावड़ी के तीन ओर लगभग ८ फुट ऊंची दीवार बनी है।

उपर्युक्त संपूर्ण विवरण से स्पष्ट होता है कि गोपाचल गढ़ पर स्थापित शिवलिंग जो अस्सी खम्बा मंदिर में स्थापित था वह किले की पश्चिम दिशा में सिंधिया काल में कोटेश्वर महादेव के नाम से स्थापित हुआ और यहां पर जीवाजीराव सिंधिया ने पुत्र रत्न प्राप्ति की मनोकामना पूर्ण होने पर मंदिर को भव्य रूप प्रदान किया । साथ ही यह भी सत्य है कि गोपाचल गढ़ की अस्सी खम्बा बावड़ी शिवमंदिर था । इसके अवशेष आज भी मंदिर के मध्य में स्पष्ट दिखलाई देते हैं । कुछ विद्वानों ने इस बावड़ी एवं मंदिर के संबंध में अपने शोध परक मत प्रस्तुत किये हैं वे इस प्रकार से हैं :-

आर्थर ह्यूज जो राजस्थान कॉलेज जयपुर में प्राचार्य थे उन्होंने अपनी पुस्तक ग्वालियर में इस भवन को ''चित्रशाला'' बतलाया है।[६] लाल बहादुर सिंह के अनुसार ''अस्सी खम्बा बावड़ी के पास उत्तरी भाग में बावड़ी से जुड़ा हुआ स्तम्भों पर आधारित एक विशाल भवन हैं जो आजकल रहीमदाद का मदरसा नाम से प्रसिद्ध है। २४ सितम्बर १५२८ ई० [७] को बाबर ने प्रस्थान किया और २७ सितम्बर १५२८ को मानसिंह और विक्रमादित्य तोमर के भवनों का निरीक्षण किया। उसने ८० खम्बा बावड़ी के संबंध में बाबरनामा में लिखा है कि- ' इन भवनों की सैर के उपरान्त हम लोग रहीमदाद द्वारा तैयार कराए गए मदरसे में पहुंचे। उसे उसने एक बड़े ''हौज''

के किनारे बनवाया था।" हरिहर निवास द्विवेदी के अनुसार- " मानमंदिर के सामने बायीं ओर कोई बहुत बड़ा मंदिर था। बाबर के गोपाचल गढ़ के सूबेदार रहीमदाद खां ने उसका अग्रभाग तुड़वा कर वहां मेहरावदार द्वार बनवा दिया और उसका नाम 'रहीमदाद का मदरसा' रख दिया। यहां कुरआन शरीफ पढ़ाया जाने लगा। यह मंदिर संभवतः डूंगरेन्द्रसिंह के समय बना था। बाबर ने जिस हौज का वर्णन किया है वह हौज नहीं बावड़ी है। पूरा निर्माण भी रहीमदाद ने नहीं कराया था। पुराने मंदिर के सामने उसने दरवाजा मात्र बनाया था।[८]

उपर्युक्त संपूर्ण विवरण एवं प्राप्त उल्लेखों तथा अस्सी खम्बा मंदिर एवं बावड़ी से प्राप्त प्रमाणों से हम इस निष्कर्ष पर पहुंचते हैं कि यह अस्सी खम्बा बावड़ी शिवमंदिर था। जिसका निर्माण तोमर शासक द्वारा किया गया था। बाबर के समय में इस मंदिर में कुछ हेर-फेर किये गये और औरंगजेब की धार्मिक असहिष्णुता की नीति के परिणामस्वरूप यह शिवलिंग गोपाचल गढ़ से नीचे फेंक दिया गया जो सिंधिया काल से 'कोटेश्वर महादेव' के भव्य मंदिर में स्थापित हो गया। वर्तमान में यहां अनेक श्रद्धालु आते हैं और प्रतिदिन पूजा-अर्चना होती है।

संदर्भ

१. सिंह, लाल बहादुर- ग्वालियर मार्ग निर्देशिका, पृ.क्रं. २१ एवं जैसल महेश्वरी हरिवल्लभ- ग्वालियर इतिहास संस्कृति एवं पर्यटन, पृ.क्रं. २१, २२, २८, ३१ व ३५

२. द्विवेदी, हरिहर निवास- ग्वालियर के तोमर, पृ.क्रं. १५

३. रिजवी, सैयद अतहर अब्बास- मुगलकालीन भारत बाबर (जहीरूद्दीन मुहम्मद बाबर पादशाह- बाबरनामा) पृ.क्रं. २७७

४. श्रीवास्तव, प्रदीप के.- ग्वालियर दुर्ग का इतिहास, पृ.क्रं. ६६

५. श्रीवास्तव, प्रदीप के.- ग्वालियर दुर्ग का इतिहास, पृ.क्रं. ६८

६. श्रीवास्तव, प्रदीप के.- ग्वालियर दुर्ग का इतिहास, पृ.क्रं. ६८

७. सिंह, लाल बहादुर- ग्वालियर, पृ.क्रं. २०

८. द्विवेदी, हरिहर निवास- ग्वालियर के तोमर, पृ.क्रं. ३४४ व ३५७ एवं गौरी, गुलाब खां- ग्वालियर का राजनैतिक एवं सांस्कृतिक इतिहास, पृ.क्रं. १४७

१७-१८वीं सदी की जलाश्य अभियांत्रिकी : अलवर रियासत के सिलीसेढ़, जयसमन्द और देवती बांध के सदंर्भ में

डॉ. अनुराधा माथुर

अलवर राज्य अरावली पर्वत श्रृंखला के उत्तर पश्चिम विस्तार क्षेत्र में स्थित है जो कि दिल्ली से गुजरात तक निरंतर एवं बाधा रहित फैली हुयी है।

अलवर की प्राकृतिक भौगोलिक स्थलाकृति ने यहां के शासकों को कई छोटे बड़े भूतल जल माध्यमों के निर्माण को प्रभावित किया। घाटी में स्थित होने के कारण अलवर मे जल स्त्रोत काफी संख्या में विद्यमान थे। सतत प्रवाही बड़ी नदी के अभाव ने भी शासकों को भूतलीय जल और मानव निर्मित जलाश्यों, बावडियों, कुण्डों और कुओं पर निर्भर करा। जल प्राप्ति का मुख्य स्त्रोत वर्षा जल था। १६ व १७वीं सदी में अच्छी वर्षा स्तर ने मानव निर्मित झील और जलाश्यों के निर्माण कार्य को प्रगति दी। अलवर के भौगोलिक अध्ययन से पता चलता है कि इस क्षेत्र में मुख्य रूप से दो समानांतर पश्चिममुखी और पूर्वमुखी ढाल हैं जो कि एक दूसरे के विपरीत परन्तु दोनों के मध्य एक संकरी घाटी का निर्माण करते हैं।[१] इस वजह से अरावली पर्वत श्रृंखला का जल दोनों तरफ बहता या फैलता है तथा अन्य भागों की जल आपूर्ति करता है। पहाडियों का ढलान होने के कारण ही यहां पर बारहमासी नदी एक भी नहीं है। इस तथ्य को ध्यान में रखते हुए यहां कई जल स्त्रोतों को विकसित, जल संग्रहण के लिये जलाश्यों का निर्माण, संग्रहण की नयी तकनीक तथा प्रबंधन की भी व्यवस्था की जिसकी पुष्टि इस क्षेत्र में विद्यमान जल संसाधनों से होती है - जैसे जलाश्य, सागर, झीले, कुंड कुएं, बावडी एवं बांध।

जलाश्यों के माध्यम से ही भूमिगत जल का स्तर ऊंचा उठाने का कार्य संभव था क्योंकि जलाश्यों में निरन्तर जल भूमि की दरारों के माध्यम से भूजल स्तर को बढ़ाता है तथा वर्षा जल को संग्रहित रखने का भी यही एक उपाय था।[२]

जल स्त्रोतों के महत्व और वर्षा जल की उपयोगिता को दृष्टि में रखते हुए जल संचयन की नई परम्परा जलाश्यों पर बांध निर्माण को विकसित किया ताकि वर्षा ऋतु पश्चात रबी की फसल की बुवाई में इन बांधों से सिंचाई की जा सके तथा प्रजा की जल आपूर्ति संभव हो। इस तकनीक के अन्तर्गत राज्य में ३ तरह के बांध बनाये गये। **(a)** डूब में आने वाले बांध **(b)** संचित बांध **(c) Diversion** बांध। अलवर राज्य में सबसे प्राचीन बांध राजगढ़ तहसील में बांध भगोला है जिसका निर्माण १४५ ई. में गुर्जर मुखिया द्वारा कराया गया था। बांध तालाव भी इसी का समकालीन है जो कि राजगढ तहसील में ग्राम टहला के समीप है। इस प्रकार अलवर में १३ और रियासत के अन्य भागों को मिलाकर कुल १३६ बांध थे।

सिलीसेढ़

अलवर शहर से १३ किमी की दूरी पर तीन ओर पहाड़ियों से घिरा सिलीसेढ़ जलाश्य है। प्राचीन ग्रन्थों अनुसार दो पहाड़ों के बीच या पहाड़ी की घाटी को बांधकर कम व्यय में तालाब बनाये जायें तथा जहां आसपास अधिक जमीन हो तो उसकी जलभराव क्षमता बढ सकती है। ऐसे जलाश्य ही अच्छे माने जाते थे।[३] सिलीसेढ़ इसका अच्छा उदाहरण है। ग्रन्थों में ही निर्देश है कि पाल पर राज प्रसाद बनाये जाने चाहिये। जलाश्यों पर भवन बनाकर उनमें जाने का रास्ता भी बनाना चाहिये तथा खोदते समय कच्चे व पक्के पत्थर का ध्यान रखना चाहिये।[४] इसी वास्तु नियम को ध्यान में रखकर इस जलाश्य पर महल का निर्माण महाराजा विनय सिंह के द्वारा १८४४ में किया गया था। इस भवन की चार मंजिले है। जिसमें से एक जलाश्य के पानी की सतह के समकक्ष है तथा ३ मंजिले सतह के ऊपर भूमि पर बनी है।

यह तालाब बहुत बड़ा है तथा इसका जल ग्रहण क्षेत्र ५२.८० वर्गमील है। यहां पर औसत वर्षा २५° है। इसमें पानी पैतपुरा, ठेलाबास, पैतपुर छोटा, रिगसपुरी, किशनपुर जागीर इत्यादि के पहाड़ों से आता है। जलाश्य के तीनों ओर पहाड़ो ने इसे नैसर्गिक रूप से बांध दिया और जल के महत्व को समझते हुए महाराज विनयसिंहजी ने इस पर बांध का निर्माण करवाया तथा शहर की आपूर्ति के लिये इसमें से नहरें निकलवायीं।[५] मुख्य नहर की लंबाई २६.५० किमी थी जिसको ऊपरी और निचली नहरों में बांटा गया। बांयी ऊपरी नहर १४ किमी लंबी थी जो अलवर नगर में लाल डिग्गी में जुबली टैंक तक पहुंचती थी तथा दांयी निचली नहर वर्तमान सरस डेयरी से होकर मंगल विहार तक १२.४८ किमी थी। इसी दायीं नहर से एक सहायक नहर ३.५२ किमी की विनय विलास महल तक आगे ले जायी गयी जो महल और उसके आसपास के क्षेत्र की आपूर्ति का एक महत्वपूर्ण साधन बनी रही। बायीं ऊपरी नहर

की जल क्षमता ४०,२०० मिलीयन घनफीट और दायीं निचली नहर की ४५,००० मिलीयन घनफीट जल क्षमता थी और निकासी क्षमता १० क्यूसेक्स थी।

इस बांध की लम्बाई ३१२.४२ मीटर है। यह ११.२२ मीटर ऊंचा और चौड़ा है इसकी अधिकतम निकासी क्षमता २६०० क्यूसेक है तथा बाई वाश या निकासी (मार्ग) की लम्बाई १९८.१२ मीटर है। इस बांध की भराव क्षमता ४२८.७० मिलीयन घनफीट और जल निकासी के पश्चात ६३.३० मिलीयन घनफीट बना रहता है। बांध का ऊपरी बैंक स्तर ३२.९ मीटर अधिकतम जल स्तर ३१.२४ मीटर और पूर्ण भराव स्तर ३०.४८ मीटर है जिसकी जल क्षमता ४६२.० मिलीयन घनफीट है। इसका नहर निकासी स्तर २१.७१ मीटर है। इस जलाश्य के द्वारा ३०३२ एकड भूमि सिंचाई के लिए निश्चित की गयी है जिसमें से २७७७ एकड भूमि क्षेत्र कृषि योग्य है। वास्तव में १७८४ एकड भूमि ही सिंचित होती है। इसमें से ७६ एकड़ भूनि पेटाकाश्त यानि डूब में आई भूमि है।[६]

जयसमंद

अलवर से ६ किमी दक्षिण दिशा में ग्राम बल्लान और लिवारी की पहाडियों की तलहटी में महाराजा जयसिंह जी के द्वारा १९१० ई. में रूपारल नदी के बेसिन पर जयसमन्द निर्मित कराया गया। इस जलाश्य में पानी की आवक उपरोक्त पहाड़ियों तथा सिलीसेढ़ के अतिरिक्त पानी से होती है। यह एक प्रकार क श्रृंखलाबद्ध बांधो की श्रेणी के अन्तर्गत आता है जिसमें सिलीसेढ़ के पूर्ण भराव उपरांत ऊपरा (चादर) चलने पर नीचे स्थित जयसंमद में पानी चला जाता है। यह श्रृंखला निरंतर चलती रहती है।[७]

जयसमन्द बांध पर कतारबद्ध लाल पत्थर की १५ कलात्मक छतरियां है जो कि इण्डो सारसैनिक शैली से निर्मित है। छतरियां एक बंद और एक खुली बनायी गयी हैं। सम्भवतः बंद छतरियां अधिकारीगणों के लिए और खुली छतरियां सेवाकारों के लिये बनी थी। नवे क्रमांक की छतरी बहुत ही कलात्मक पच्चीकारी और कटाई तथा बेलबूंटों से सज्जित है जो महाराजगण के लिये निर्मित की गयी थी।

जयसंमद का जल ग्रहण क्षेत्र ६९.४१० वर्गमील है। इस क्षेत्र में औसत वर्षा २५ इंच है जिससे ११६७.० मिलीयन घनफीट पानी की आवक है। औसत वर्षा का मानक स्तर अधिक होने से तथा पानी की अच्छी आवक ने इस स्थल को बांध बनाने के लिए उपयुक्त बनाया। इस बांध की लम्बाई १४ किमी, चौडाई १०.२० मीटर ऊंचाई १०.०६ मीटर है। बांध का ऊपरी बैंक स्तर ६४.६३ मीटर है तथा अधिकतम जल

स्तर ६३.११ मीटर है। इसका पूर्ण भराव स्तर ६१.५८ मीटर है जिसकी क्षमता ६५२ मिलियन घनफीट पानी की थी जो अब ८२० मिलियन घनफीट भराव क्षमता रह गयी है। निकासी मार्ग की लम्बाई २७४.३६ मीटर तथा अधिकतम निकासी क्षमता १४५०० क्यूसेक्स है। अधिक वर्षा या बाढ़ के हालात में ८५५ क्यूसेक्स जल निकासी की क्षमता रखता है। प्रारंभ में इस बांध की भराव क्षमता ८७६.५० मिलियन घनफीट थी जो अब ७७७.०० मिलियन घनफीट हो गयी है।[८]

सिंचाई के महत्व को देखते हुए इस जलाश्य से भी नहरें निकाली गयी है। मुख्य नहर नं० एक ४.६५ किमी और मुख्य नहर नं० दो १.७७ किमी लम्बी है। दांयी नहर से सहायक नहरें देसूला, भजीट, खानपुर और ईटाराणा निकाली गयी। बांयी नहर की दादर और महुआ सहायक नहरे है। ये कुल १६.५० किमी लम्बी है। मुख्य नहर निकासी स्तर ५४.५७ मीटर है। इन सहायक नहरों से ३१७१.६ हैक्टेयर भूमि पर काश्त की जाती है।[९]

जयसमंद से ५५६०.४० हैक्टेयर भूमि में कृषि की जा सकती है पर वास्तव में ४७६०.२८ हैक्टयर पर कृषि हो रही है। सिंचित क्षेत्र ३६६३.६ हैक्टेयर क्षेत्र है इस प्रकार ७६ प्रतिशत सिंचित क्षेत्र है। जिससे गेहूं (२६६० हैक्टेयर), चना १०२२ हैक्टेयर, सरसों २५२२ हैक्टेयर, जौं १६७ हैक्टेयर अन्य ६८७ हैक्टेयर भूमि पर फसल पैदा हो रही है। जयसमन्द के पानी से २८ गांव लाभान्वित हो रहे है।[१०]

देवती बांध

१६वीं सदी का बड़ गुर्जरों द्वारा निर्मित देवती बांध प्राचीन बांधो में से एक है। दो पहाड़ियों के बीच के स्थान पर पानी की रोक कर बांध का निर्माण किया गया। नरूका शासकों के प्रारंभिक राजगढ, माचेडी और राजपुर के आधे गांव की जल आपूर्ति का यह एक महत्वपूर्ण साधन था। अलवर के दक्षिण में वर्तमान राजगढ़ तहसील के अन्तर्गत देवती गांव में बाणगंगा बेसिन पर यह जलाश्य और बांध स्थित है।

इसका जलग्रहण क्षेत्र १५.२० वर्गमील है। औसत वर्षा स्तर चूंकि अधिक (२८ इंच) है अतएव पानी की आवक यहां २३७ मिलियन घनफीट है। इस बांध की लम्बाई १८६.०२ मीटर है। बांध का ऊपरी बैंक स्तर ३२.७७ मीटर है। बांध का अधिकतम जलस्तर ३१.८२ मीटर है और पूर्ण टैंक स्तर ३०.४८ मीटर है। अधिकतम जलस्तर के ऊपर ६५ सेमी फ्री बोर्ड दिया गया है। पूर्ण टैंक स्तर पर इसमें २१४.० मिलियन घनफीट पानी की भराव क्षमता है। जलाश्य से बाईपास या निकासी मार्ग की लम्बाई ५.४६ मीटर है जिसकी निकासी क्षमता ४७५.० क्यूसेक्स है। इसकी जल भराव क्षमता

२०७.७० मिलियन घनफीट है जो कि निकासी के पश्चात ६.३ मिलियन घनफीट रह जाता है। अधिक भराव या बाढ़ की स्थिति में ६१४४ क्यूसेक्स जल निकासी की क्षमता यह बांध रखता है। इस बांध से भी नहरें निकाली गयी है। बांध का नहर निकासी स्तर २६.५२ मीटर है।[11]

इस प्रकार इस बांध के द्वारा १२१३ एकड़ भूमि क्षेत्र लाभान्वित होता है। कुल सिंचित क्षेत्र १००६६ एकड़ है परन्तु काश्त योग्य मात्र ४०६० एकड और सिंचित क्षेत्र २००० एकड़ भूमि है जो नहरों द्वारा लाभ प्राप्त कर रही है।[12]

जलाश्य अभियांत्रिकी

अलवर के जलाश्य निर्माण में प्राचीन जलाश्य निरूपण तकनीकी का पूर्ण प्रयोग किया गया है। प्राचीनकाल में हमें ६ प्रकार के जलाश्यों - चौकोर, त्रिकोण, लम्बे, अर्ध चन्द्राकार, चन्द्राकार और बहुकोणीय वर्णित मिलते है जिनमें से गोल, त्रिकोण और चौकोर को उत्तम माना गया है।

१. जलाश्य निर्माण के लिये स्थान विशेष की भौगोलिक स्थलाकृति सबसे महत्वपूर्ण और प्राथमिक तत्व है। पहाड़ियों के बीच घाटी को बांधकर जलाश्य निर्माण के प्रयोजन को उत्तम माना गया है ताकि कम व्यय में बड़े जलाश्य बनाये जा सके और अगर आस-पास भूमि भी रिक्त हो तो उसकी जलभराव क्षमता में वृद्धि हो सकती है जो कि अतंतः राज्य के हित में ही होगा। जल ग्रहण क्षेत्र चाहे छोटा हो मगर भराव क्षमता अधिक हो ऐसे जलाश्य उत्तम माने गये।[13] **अलवर में ऐसे ही स्थल का चुनाव कर बांधो का निर्माण करवाया गया। देवती बांध इसका एक उत्तम उदाहरण है।**

२. तीनों ही जलाश्यों से जल निकासी मार्ग रखा गया है। सिलीसेढ़ का जल निकासी मार्ग १९८.१७ मीटर है जिसकी जल निकासी क्षमता २६०० क्यूसेक्स है, जयसमन्द का निकासी मार्ग २७४.३६ मीटर लम्बा है जिससे १४५०० क्यूसेक्स जल निकाला जा सकता है। देवती का निकासी मार्ग ५.४६ मीटर और ४७५.० क्यूसेक्स जल निकासी क्षमता है।

३. जयसंमद, सिलीसेढ़ और देवती तीनों ही जलाश्यों की अत्यंत गहरी नींव यानि अंदर चटटानों के आने तक खोदी गयी थी तथा उसमें सीसा डालकर उसे भरा गया। जहां चटटान और पत्थर अधिक हो वहां **Fault Line** हमेशा जल के बहाव की सीधी दिशा में होनी चाहिए ताकि रिसाव नही हो। कोई भी बांध की सफलता सिल्ट की अधिक मात्रा इकटठा न होने पर निर्भर करती

है। अलवर के तीनों की बांधो में ऐसी सावधानी प्रारम्भ से ही बरती गयी है। जलाश्यों के जीरो स्तर से निचले स्तर तक सिल्ट के लिये स्थान रखा गया तथा निचले स्तर से निश्चित पैमाने तक तीनों ही जलाश्यों में **dead storage** स्तर निश्चित है जो हर स्थिति बना रहता है। **Live storage** स्तर से नहरें सिंचाई प्रावधान हेतु बनाई गई है।[१४]

४. जलाश्यों पर बांध की लम्बाई न्यूनतम अच्छी मानी गयी ताकि कम व्यय पर पानी के दबाव को बांधा जा सके तथा बांध के अंदर और बाहर की तरफ चूने का अच्छा लेप करना चाहिए। जल के साथ मिलने पर चूना फैलता है। १०-१२ दिन की जमने की अवधि मे इसमें दरारे भी नहीं पड़ती तथा रिसाव की गुंजाईश भी नहीं रहती।[१५] यह लेप लम्बी अवधि तक कायम रहता है। अलवर का सिलीसेढ और देवती बांध ऐसी अभियांत्रिकी का ज्वलंत उदाहरण है। यही कारण है कि ये बांध इतने वर्षों के बावजूद भी न तो टूटे और न ही रिसाव हुआ है।

५. सिलीसेढ़ और देवती बांध की नींव ठोस पत्थरों और चूनें से मिश्रित कर के बनी है जिससे बांध का वजन बढ़ा। बांध की मुख्य दीवार पत्थर की और पीछे की दीवार मिटटी की है। यह एक मिश्रित बांध है। पीछे की तथा मध्य के रास्ते में वृक्ष और पौधे लगाये गये है। इन वृक्षों की जड़े नीचे गहरी जाकर मिटटी और पत्थरों को रोके रखती है जिसने बांध को दृढता प्रदान की और आज भी बिना कटाव के कायम है। जबकि जयसमंद मिटटी का बांध है जिसके दोंनो किनारों को छोटे गोल पत्थरों से और मध्य में **core wall** को पत्थर की चिनाई से मजबूती देकर बांध को टिकाया गया है आगे और पीछे की दीवार मिटटी की बनी थी जो बांध की सुदृढ़ता में सहायक है।

बांध पर निर्मित छतरियां भी जल के दबाव को कम करने में सहायक रही क्योंकि जल के दबाव का वितरण हो जाता है।[१६] **सिलीसेढ में मुख्य बांध की दीवार से पहले जलाश्य में उतरने के लिए बनायी गयी १.५ फीट की चौडी सीढियां और मोटी दीवार ने भी बांध पर जल के दबाव को कम करके स्थायित्व प्रदान किया।**

६. अलवर के इन तीनों ही जलाश्यों के निर्माण में अभियांत्रिकी का एक नियम, भराव क्षेत्र अधिक हो, ने भी बांधो को स्थायित्व दिया है। पानी का दबावा सीधा बांध पर न पड़कर आसपास की पहाड़ियों पर भी रहता है।

७. बांध की अभियांत्रिकी का आधारभूत सिद्धान्त है कि बांध पर जल के दबाव और गुरूत्वाकर्षण बल का परिणामी बल बांध की चौड़ाई के मध्य तिहाई से गुजरना

चाहिये। अगर यह बल मध्य तिहाई से न गुजर कर अगर किनारों से कहीं निकलता है तो जलाश्य का सारा पानी धीरे-धीरे बह जायेगा अर्थात नही टिकेगा। सिलीसेढ़ और देवती बांध इस सिद्धान्त पर खरे उतरते हैं।

८. जयसंमद (मिटटी के बांध) के स्थायित्व का अभियांत्रिकी कारण यह है कि जलाश्य की सिल्ट की ऊपरी सतह इतनी अर्न्तगृही **(Saturated top surface)** है कि **Pharatic line** जल के अंदर ही बनी रही, वह ऊपरी सतह पर न आ पायी। जिससे पानी का रिसाव नही हो सका अन्यथा अत्यधिक सिल्ट की स्थिति में **Piping** के माध्यम से उसे बाहर निकालना पड़ता है।

उपरोक्त वर्णन से यह प्रमाणित होता है कि उत्तर मध्य काल में अलवर में निर्मित जलाश्यों में वर्तमान अभियांत्रिकी का पूर्ण ध्यान रखा गया और स्थायित्व के उन सभी तरीकों को अपनाया गया जिसके आधार पर आज भी ये जलाश्व अलवर, देवती और आसपास के गांवो की सिंचाई सुविधाओं को पूर्ण करते है। मजबूत बनाने के लिए प्रयोग में लिये गये साधन महंगे जरूर पड़े होगें परन्तु आज भी वह उसी अवस्था में खडे हुए है।

संदर्भ सूची

१. मेजर पाऊलेट कृत अलवर का गजट, १८७८, अनु. अनिल जोशी, कुसुम प्रकाशन अलवर पृष्ठ २७-२८

२. अनिल जोशी, अलवर दर्शन, शोध ग्रंथमाला प्रकाशन अलवर २००४, पृष्ठ १२१

३. चक्रपाणि मिश्र, विश्ववल्लभ, उल्लास -१, १५७७ उदृत - ईश्वरसिंह रापावत, राजस्थान के जल संसाधन, चिराग प्रकाशन, उदयपुर, २००४, पृष्ठ २२७

४. वही, उल्लास - २, श्लोक ४-३०

५. बांधों का तकनीकी आंकड़े रजिस्टर, सिंचाई विभाग, अलवर, पृष्ठ ६०

६. टेक्नीकल एस्टीमेट रजिस्टर, सिलीसेढ़ बांध, सिंचाई विभाग, अलवर

७. अनिल जोशी, वही, पृष्ठ १२५

८. बांधों का तकनीकी आंकड़े रजिस्टर, सिंचाई विभाग, अलवर, पृष्ठ ४६

९. टेक्नीकल एस्टीमेट रजिस्टर, जयसमन्द, सिंचाई विभाग, अलवर।

१०. वही। बालाना, महुआ, दादर, भजीट, केसरपुर, बुर्जा, खानपुर, गंडपुर, सालपुर, मदनपुरी, रूपबास, देवखेडा, ईटाराणा, ऊमरैण, लिवारी, पालका, गुजुकी, नांगल चरन, सालपुरी, नांगल रातावत, महुआकला, सोनावा, अलवर शहर, सामोला, भूगोर, देसूला, बेलाका।

११. बांधों का तकनीकी आंकड़े रजिस्टर, सिंचाई विभाग, अलवर, पृष्ठ ७८

१२. टेक्नीकल एस्टीमेट रजिस्टर, देवती बांध, सिंचाई विभाग, अलवर।

१३. विश्ववल्लभ, उल्लास - १

१४. अभियांत्रिकी के इस पैमाने का स्वंय द्वारा निरक्षण कर तथ्यों पर सही पाया गया।

१५. अनुपम मिश्र, राजस्थान की रजत बूंदे, गांधी शांति प्रतिष्ठान, नई दिल्ली १९९५, पृष्ठ १०४

१६. पी.एन.एस. मूर्ति, सोइल मेकेनिक्स एण्ड फांउडेशन इंजिनियरिंग, धनपतराम एण्ड संस, जांलधर १९७४, पृष्ठ ५८७-८८

१८वीं शताब्दी के अप्रकाशित स्रोतों के आधार पर मेवाड़ राज्य में वर्षा-विषयक मान्यताएँ एवं लोक विश्वास

डॉ. जे.के. ओझा एवं डॉ प्रियदर्शी ओझा

'जल ही जीवन है', 'जल है तो कल है' की शाश्वतता से कौन परिचित नहीं है? मेवाड़-राज्य में २-३ वर्षो के अन्तराल में अकाल पड़ता रहा है। अतः अकाल-दुष्काल की चपेट से बचाने के लिए यहाँ के शासक, सामन्त एवं शासित वर्ग ने सदैव प्रयास किये थे। इन प्रचार में 'प्राच्य विद्या प्रतिष्ठान उदयपुर' शाखा में सुरक्षित एवं संरक्षित १८ शताब्दी के दो अप्रकाशित ग्रन्थ 'शकुन संवत्सर सार' व शकुन 'समुच्चय सार' बड़े महत्त्वपूर्ण है जिसमें वर्षा-विषयक शकुन, मान्यताएं एवं विश्वास को समझा जा सकता है। इसके आधार पर मेवाड़ के लोग वर्षा-जल के बारे में आशान्वित रहते थे। यही विश्वास धीरे-धीरे लोक मान्यताओं में बदलता गया और इनसे संबंधित कहावतें भी प्रचलित हो गई, जो वर्षा के पूर्वानुमान को समझने में बड़ी सहायक हुआ करती थी। तब आधुनिक तकनीकी से युक्त मौसम विभाग का तो निश्चित ही अभाव रहा होगा किंतु प्रकृति में आए परिवर्तन को समझकर अनुभवी लोगों ने वर्षा के आने अथवा न आने, काल-सुकाल आदि की घोषणा कर, तद्नुरूप आगे की योजना बनाते थे कि यदि वर्षा अच्छी होने के आसार हैं तो उसके अनुरूप औषि संबंधी सामग्रियों की तैयारी करना प्रारम्भ कर दें। जल को सुरक्षित रखने के लिए ताल-तलैया की साफ-सफाई आदि कराना, कुओं, बावड़ियों की गाद-मिट्टी निकलवाना अदि कार्यों में निमग्न हो जाते थे और यदि अकाल के आसार हैं तो उसका सामना करने के लिए क्या किया जाय, इस जुगती में लग जाते थे।

प्रायः देखा गया है कि आधुनिक मौसम विभाग द्वारा जारी की गई उद्घोषणा असफल हो जाती है किन्तु इन ग्रन्थों में बताये गये आसार के आधार पर वर्षा की अत्यधिकता, न्यूनता, कमी अथवा सूखा, अकाल, महाकाल आदि को भी देखने व समझने का अवसर भी आया है। 'शकुन संवत्सर सार' या 'शकुन समुच्चय सार'

प्राच्य विद्या प्रतिष्ठान उदयपुर शाखा के ग्रन्थ सं. १६१७ पर उपलब्ध है। इस ग्रन्थ की रचना ताराचंद सुत हृदयानंद जोशी (सिखवाल ब्राह्मण) ने महाराणा संग्राम सिंह द्वितीय के समय १७३३ ई. में की थी। इसमें कुल ५२४. १ = ५२५ दोहे हैं। उनमें शकुनावली दी गई जिसमें विविध जीव, जन्तुओं, जानवरों, वृक्षादि, प्रऔति के लक्षणों के आधार पर वर्षा-ज्ञान का बोध कराया गया है।[1] अतः वर्षा से संबंधित पूर्वानुमान के लिए यह एक मौलिक अप्रकाशित स्रोत है। इसी भाँति ग्रन्थ संख्या १६५६ पर संग्रहित 'सद्-विचार' ग्रन्थ की रचना महाराणा अरिसिंह के शासन काल में १७६६ ई. में हुई तथा इसकी पुष्पिका में ग्रन्थकार अथवा रचयिता का नाम नहीं दिया हुआ है। यह गद्य रूप में सकुन विचारों से युक्त ग्रन्थ है। जिसमें बादलों, हवा के रुख, दिशाओं में चमकने वाली बिजली आदि विविध रूपों से वर्षा ज्ञान का परिचय कराया गया है।[2] यों भी देखा जाय तो १७३२ ई. से १७३४ ई. व १७६६ ई. अकाल के वर्ष थे, अतएव इन ग्रन्थों की रचना एवं प्रणयन कराया गया हो तो कोई आश्चर्य नहीं। प्रस्तुत शोध-पत्र इन दोनों अप्रकाशित स्रोतों के आधार पर प्रस्तुत करने का प्रयास किया है।

वायु के पश्चात प्राणी के लिए जल सर्वाधिक महत्त्वपूर्ण है। 'जल बिन सब सून' कृषि-प्रधान इस राज्य में चाहे कृषक हो अथवा अन्य प्राणी सभी की निगाहें आकाश की ओर आये बादलों को निहारता है कि काले मेघा कब वर्षा कर जल प्लावित कर दे। इसके लिए प्राचीन काल से ही कई ऐसी मान्यताएँ बनन लगी जिससे वर्षा-विषयक संभावनाएँ की जाती थी और जब उस मान्यता के आधार पर वर्षा हो जाती तो मान्यता धीरे-धीरे विश्वास में बदल जाती थी।३

पर्यावरण और भौगोलिक प्रभाव को आधार बनाकर भावी समय की संभावना स्वीकार किये जाने की लोक मान्यता भी १८वीं शताब्दी के मेवाड़ी समाज में व्याप्त रही है जैसे-वृक्षादि पर अधिक फूल लगने पर अतिवृष्टि, कम फल लगने पर कम वर्षा, दूब आदि। रोहिणी नक्षत्रा और ज्येष्ठ महीने में यदि जोर से धूप न पड़े तो अकाल पड़ेगा। औत्तिका नक्षत्र में बिजली की एक चमक भी पहले के सब अपशकुनों को मिटा देती है। अक्षय तृतीया (आखा तीज) पर रोहिणी न हो, रक्षा बंधन पर श्रावण नक्षत्रा नहीं हो और पौष की पूर्णिमा पर मूल नक्षत्रा न हो तो संसार पर विपत्ति आवेगी। यदि आर्द्रा के आरंभ में बूंदें पड़ जाये तो १५ दिन में अच्छी वर्षा होगी। आर्द्रा में हवा चले तो अकाल पड़ेगा। पुनर्वसु में वर्षा हो तो तालाब भर जायेंगे व पुष्य नक्षत्रा में वर्षा न हो तो फिर वर्षा होना कठिन है। यदि शुक्रवार को बादल आवे और शनिवार तक रहें तो निश्चित रूप से वर्षा होगी।

माघ महिने में पाँच मंगलवार, ज्येष्ठ मास में पाँच रविवार और भादवा में पाँच शनिवार होंगे तो भयंकर बीमारी फैलने का अनुमान किया जाता था। इसी तरह यदि आषाढ़ के महिने में चन्द्रमा, सोमवार, गुरुवार, अथवा शुक्रवार को उदय होता है तो वर्षा अधिक मानी जाती है। आषाढ़ के महीने में पुनर्वसु नक्षत्र रविवार के दिन हो और मगसर मास में अच्छे हवा चले तो सातों प्रकार के दलहन अनाज होते हैं अर्थात अच्छी वर्षा का अनुमान किया जाता है। श्रावण महीने की पूर्णिमा यदि क्षय तिथि हो, पौष महीने में मूल नक्षत्र नहीं हो और आषाढ़ मास के रोहिणी नक्षत्र में वर्षा न हो तो प्रजा घूमती फिरती है अर्थात वर्षा नहीं होती है। इसी तरह यदि ज्येष्ठ मास की अमावस्या रविवार की हो तथा लग्न सारणी में रवि से आगे चन्द्रमा हो तो वर्षा में सुकाल होता हैं यदि कर्क संक्रांति और मकर संक्राति एक ही वार के दिन मिलती हो तो अकाल पड़ता है। यह मिलन अनिष्ट का सूचक माना गया है। श्रावण का चन्द्रमा यदि काले रंग से युक्त हो तो उस वर्ष में कहीं सुकाल एवं कहीं अकाल, या चन्द्रमा श्वेत वर्ण का हो तो पूर्ण सुकाल और यदि चन्द्रमा निर्मल हो तो अकाल होता है। आषाढ़ महीने की पूर्णिमा यदि मूल नक्षत्रा हो और संयोगवश उसी योग में शनिवार हो तो निश्चित रूप से प्रजा बाहर जाती है अर्थात अकाल की पूर्ण संभावना बढ़ जाती है। द्वितीया का चाँद जाड़े में सोया हुआ, वर्षा में बैठा हुआ और गर्मी में खड़ा हो तो अच्छा और यदि सूर्य के चारों ओर कुण्ड तथा चन्द्रमा के चारों ओर जलेरी हो तो बहुत ज्यादा वर्षा होगी। यदि चैत्रा में छोटी-छोटी बूंदें गिर जाती है तो श्रावण में वर्षा नहीं होने का अनुमान कर लेते हैं। चैत्रा के शुक्ल पक्ष में प्रथम से नवमी तक बिजली नहीं चमकनी चाहिए। यही शुभ लक्षण है। यदि चैत्रा मास में बिजली चमके तो बैसाख में ऐसी वर्षा होगी कि ढाक के फूल तक धूल में मिल जाएंगे। बैसाख की अमावस्या को रेवती नक्षत्रा हो तो सुकाल हो, आश्विनी हो तो मध्यम हो और भरणी हो तो अकाल पड़े। ज्येष्ठ मास उतरते ही मेंढ़क बोलने लगे तो पानी जल्दी बरसेगा। ज्येष्ठ में मृगशिरा नक्षत्रा के अंत के दस दिनों में वर्षा हो जाये तो वर्षा के सभी नक्षत्र कमजोर पड़े जायेंगे। श्रावण कृष्णा पंचमी के बादल गड़गड़ावे तो चार माह तक वर्षा होगी। श्रावण कृष्णा एकादशी को रोहिणी नक्षत्रा हो उस वर्ष किसी प्रकार का अभाव नहीं रहेगा। फसल अच्छी होगी। श्रावण कृष्णा चौथ को बादल बरसे तो उपज सवाई होगी। भाद्र पद की छट को बिजली नहीं चमकने पर अकाल के आसार नजर आते हैं।7

आषाढ़ मास में चींटिया अपने दर से बाहर कण लेकर आती है। वर्षा बहुत है और यदि अपने दर में कण ले जाती है तो अकाल की संभावना बढ़ जाती है। टिटोड़ी चार अण्डे देती हैं ये अण्डे यदि ऊँचाई पर दिये गये हैं तो शुभ और जमीन

पर नीचे दिये गये हैं तो अशुभ है। ऊँचाई पर दिय गये अण्डों में से जितने अण्डे सीधे होते हैं उतने महीने वर्षा होती है। साँप, गोयरे, डींडू (जल सर्प), कीड़ी, मकोड़े अपना बिल छोड़कर जमीन पर घूमें, चींटीं मुँह में अण्डे लेकर अपना घर छोड़कर भूमि पर घूमती हो (चलती हो) तो बरसात होती है। मक्खियाँ शरीर से चिपटे, मकड़ी शोर करे तो वर्षा का अधिक जोर रहता है। चिड़िया यदि धूल में नहावे (खेले) तो वर्षा का योग बनता है और यदि जल में नहावे तो वर्षा चली जाती है। मेंढ़क से मेंढ़क लड़ते हों अथवा बगुला पंख पसार के बैठे तो दो-तीन दिन में चारों ओर से घटा चढ़कर आती है। गोबर में कीड़े देखकर ग्वाले बरसात होगी के बारे में कह देते हैं। कांवलियों (चील) के दल मिलकर यदि जमीन पर आकर बैठ जाते हैं तो चौथे अथवा पाँचवे दिन खूब वर्षा होती है। संध्या के समय पूर्व दिशा की ओर यदि गीदड़ (सियार) शोर करते हैं और वर्षा ऋतु हो तो अनन्त वर्षा होती है। यदि पपीहा पिउं-पिउं करने लगे और मोर बार-बार बोलने लगे तथा पंखों के छत्रा बनावें तो वर्षा इतनी अधिक होगी कि नदियाँ बहने लगेंगी। तीतरी जोर-जोर से चिल्लावे, सारस पर्वतों के शिखर पर घूमने लगे, गिरगिट बार बार रंग बदले, तो जोर से वर्षा होगी। यदि मक्खी, मच्छर और डाँस अधिक उत्पन्न हो तो जमाना अच्छा होगा और यदि विषैले जन्तु अधिक पैदा हो तो अकाल पड़ेगा। जिस वर्ष काले रंग की मकड़ियाँ अधिक दिखाई पड़े उस वर्ष अच्छी वर्षा होगी। पीतल, कांसा व लोहे के जंग लग जाने पर, सर्पों के वृक्षें पर चढ़ जाने पर, घोर काले पत्ते निकलने पर वर्षा आने का शुभ संकेत माना गया है।

पश्चिम दिशा में यदि संध्या काल में गिरिनार के समान ऊँचे-ऊँचे शिखर वाले बहुत से मेघ दिखाई दे तो ३, ५ अथवा ७ रात्रि तक एक द्रोण पानी वर्ष माना गया है। इसी भाँति यदि पानी ठण्डा नहीं लगे, पीने पर स्वाद न लगे, गर्मी (उमस) से शरीर काफी व्याकुल हो तो वर्षा जोर से आयेगी। पित्त प्रकृति का व्यक्ति गहन नींद लेवे तो बादलों के जोर के कारण वर्षा होगी। वात प्रकृति का आदमी गर्मी की वजह से सिर दर्द बतावे तो वर्षा ज्यादा होगी। यदि मक्खन उष्मा के कारण बिलोवणे में ही विलीन हो गया हो और छाछ के ऊपर न आवे तो वर्षा अवश्य होगी। इसी भाँति सुतार अपनी साल, बसोला, बींधनी, कुल्हाड़ी से लकड़ी छीलने में दिक्कत महसूस करता है तो अच्छी वर्षा के आसार बनते हैं। कुम्भकार भी गीली मिट्टी के बर्तन चाक पर से न उतरते देखकर वर्षा के आने की संभावना प्रकट करते हैं। ढोल, नगाड़े आदि चमड़े के बाजे ढंग से न बजने पर डोम तीन दिनों में वर्षा आने की कह देता है। भेड़ के मुँह से झाग निकले और वह हवा के सामने दौड़ती है तो जोरदार वर्षा होगी। आम के पेड़ों की डालियों में जिस दिशा में फल-फल नहीं लगे उस दिशा में वर्षा नहीं होगी और जिस दिशा में फूल-फल लगे हों उस ओर अच्छी वर्षा के योग

बनते हैं, यह स्थानीय आम्र-वृक्षों के योग हैं। बतकों का चिल्लाना, हवा की तरफ पीठ करके बकरी का बैठना आदि आने वाली घनघोर वर्षा के निशानात है।। मटकों का पानी गरम हो जाये तो समझो बहुत अच्छी वर्षा होगी। रात्रि में कौओं का बोलना तथा दिन में सियार का बोलना अकाल का द्योतक है। 'तीतर पंखी बादल' आकाश में दिखाई दे तो वर्षा निश्चित होगी। आषाढ़ मास में जंगल की घनबेरी और खेजड़ियों के सभी पत्ते गिर जावे तो अच्छा वर्ष होगा और यदि आधे पत्ते ही झड़े तो मिला-जुला जमाना होगा। यदि इनके पत्ते खूब हरे-भरे हो जावें, फल-फूल लगे, वट-वृक्ष की जटाओं से जौ अंकुर नहीं निकले तो समझो कि वर्षा बिल्कुल नहीं होगी और जोरदार अकाल पड़ेगा।८

इस प्रकार इन ग्रन्थों में वर्षा, सुकाल, अकाल से संबंधित पर्याप्त शकुन देखे जा सकते हैं जिनके आधार पर वर्षा का पूर्वानुमान लगाकर आने वाले समय की स्थिति के बारे में विचार अथवा चिंतन किया जाता था।

सन्दर्भ सूची

१. डॉ. प्रियदर्शी ओझा, १७वीं-१८वीं शताब्दी में मेवाड़ में जल-प्रबन्धन एक अध्ययन (अप्रकाशित शोध-प्रबंध) पृ. १०.

२. वही, पृ. १०.

३. वही, पृ. ७६.

४. प्राच्य विद्या प्रतिष्ठान उदयपुर, शाकुन संवत्सर सार (शकुन विचार) (अप्रकाशित) द्रष्टव्य; विश्वम्भरा, बीकानेर, वर्ष ३० २-३, पृ. ८०-८.

५. प्रा. वि.प्र. उदयपुर, शकुन संवत्सर शकुन सार (आप्रकाशित)

६. नक्षत्रा ९ हैं भरणी २५ अप्रैल से लगता है, औतिका ९ मई से; रोहिणी २३ मई से; मगसर ६ जून से; आर्द्रा २० जून से, पुनर्वसु ५ जुलाई से, पुष्य १९ जुलाई से; अश्लेषा १ अगस्त से; मेघा १६ अगस्त से।

७. द्रष्टव्य शकुन विचार.

८. वही; डॉ. प्रियदर्शी ओझा, १७वीं-१८वीं शताब्दी में मेवाड़ में जल-प्रबंधन एक अध्ययन पृ. ७७-७९. परम्परा भाग १४१-१४२. पृ. १२२-२३.

मेहरानगढ़ दुर्ग में जल - प्रबन्ध तकनीक

डॉ. एस. पी. व्यास एवं डॉ. मनोरमा उपाध्याय

राजपूताना का क्षेत्र, विशेषतः पश्चिमी राजस्थान प्रकृति के अमृत अर्थात् जल की प्राप्ति में भाग्यशाली नहीं रहा है । किन्तु प्रकृति की कृपणता को मारवाड़ के शासकों की जल-प्रबन्धन नीति ने समाप्त कर दिया । तपते रेगिस्तानी इलाके में पानी की एक-एक बूंद का महत्व था तथा इसे घी से अधिक महत्व दिया गया । चिड़ियानाथ के श्राप से ग्रसित (जैसा कि कथानक प्रचलित है) जोधपुर सदैव जल की कमी से पीड़ित रहा है । किन्तु यहां की जनता, शासकों, रानियों आदि द्वारा समय-समय पर विभिन्न जल स्त्रोतों - तथा - तालाब, झीले बावड़ियां, कुएं, झालरे आदि का निर्माण कर इस समस्या का समाधान करने का प्रयास किया ।

जोधपुर की स्थापना १४५६ ईस्वी में राव जोधा द्वारा की गई । यह २६. १६ उत्तर अक्षांश तथा १३.८ पूर्वी देशान्तर पर स्थित है तथा यह समुद्री तरह से २४१ मीटर ऊँचा है । ऐसा प्रतीत होता है कि नगर बसाने हेतु इस स्थान चयन पानी की उपलब्धता को देखकर किया गया था । साथ ही सुरक्षा को दृष्टि कोण भी था । चोखा-दईजर की पहाड़ियां इस स्थान को एक महत्वपूर्ण अंग है । यह तीस किलोमीटर लम्बी, पांच किलोमीटर चौड़ी (यह सर्वाधिक चौड़ाई है) तथा ऊचांई १२०-१५० मीटर (जमीन तल से) है।[१] प्रारम्भ में जोधपुर मसूरिया नाम की पहाड़ी पर दुर्ग का निर्माण करना चाहते थे किन्तु जल का समुचित प्रबन्ध ना होने के कारण यह विचार त्याग दिया (जोधपुर की नींव दिराई, सहर व किलो बणाय व साया, तिण री ख्यात - (हस्तलिखित)प्रो. एम. आर. डी मेहता संग्रह से) मसूरिया पहाड़ी जोधपुर के पश्चिम की तरफ स्थित है जहां समुचित मात्रा में बरसात नहीं होगी थी।

चोखा दईजर का पूरा इलाका बहुत सारे जल स्त्रोतों का आगोर (वाटर कैचनेन्ट क्षेत्र) है । इन्टैक द्वारा करवाये गये सर्वे के अनुसार इसका आगोर जोधपुर में प्रत्यक्ष रूप से दिखने वाले ५६ सतही जल स्त्रोतों (यथा - नाड़ी, तालाब, टांके और झोलें) तथा १५४ भूमिगत जल स्त्रोतों - (यथा कुएं - बावड़ी और झालरो) का फीडर रहा है।[२] अरावली की पहाड़ियों का विस्तार चोखा - दईजर की पहाड़ियों के रूप में यह

श्रेष्ठ आगोर का कार्य करता है । पहाड़ी का पत्थर बलुआ (सैण्ड स्टोन) होने के कारण पानी रिस कर जमीन के भीतर पहुंचता है । तथा पानी की सीरें भूमिगत जलस्तर को ऊँचा बनाये रखती हैं । यहां यह बात ध्यान देने योग्य है कि दुर्ग के कैचमेन्ट क्षेत्रों में तो जल स्त्रोतों का निर्माण किया ही गया, दुर्ग से दूर के कैचमेन्ट क्षेत्रों के पानी को भी इन जल स्त्रोतो तक पहुंचाने के लिये नहरों तथा बांधों का निर्माण किया गया । भूमिगत जल - प्रवाह क्षेत्रों में बस्तियों का निर्माण किया गया तथा कुओं - बावड़ियों का निर्माण कर आवासीय बस्तियों की जल आवश्यकताओं की पूर्ति की गई । साथ ही इन जल स्त्रोतों के पानी को मेहरानगढ़ दुर्ग के भीतरी तथा ऊँचाई वाले क्षेत्रों में पहुंचाया गया । प्रस्तुत शोध पत्र में माइक्रो स्टडी के अन्तर्गत दो बिन्दुओं का केस स्टडी के रूप में अध्ययन किया गया है ।[३] -

१- मेहरानगढ़ दुर्ग के मुख्य जल स्त्रोत - रानीसर - पदमसर की जल प्रबन्ध तकनीक तथा इसका जल किस प्रकार से दुर्ग की भीतरी क्षेत्रों तक पहुंचाया जाता था ।

२- दुर्ग के भीतर के क्षेत्र फ़तेहपोल से लगाकर जालोरी गेट तक के बसावट वाले क्षेत्र में कैचमेन्ट क्षेत्र से भूमिगत जल धाराओं के रूप में प्राप्त होने वाले जल का उपयोग किस प्रकार से किया गया ।.

रानीसर - पदमसर - जल प्रबन्ध तकनीक -

(अ) जोधपुर दुर्ग के निर्माण के साथ ही जल व्यवस्था के प्रयत्न आरम्भ हो गये थे । रानीसर का निर्माण राव जोधा की रानी जस्मादेवी ने जोधपुर के किले के निर्माण के साथ ही करवाया था । किले की पश्चिमी ढलान तथा उत्तरी पहाड़ियों की ढालनों में पानी के बहाव तथा आगोर क्षेत्र में इसका निर्माण किया गया । उत्तर तथा पश्चिम की तरफ के मार्ग को खुला रखा गया तथा पूर्व तथा दक्षिण में रिटेन्शन वॉल (बांध) का निर्माण किया गया है । रानीसर दो भागों में विभक्त है - जूना रानीसर तथा नया रानीसर । जूना रानीसर की दक्षिण - पूर्वी रिटेन्शन वॉल में बारी बनाकर पानी के बहाव को नये रानीसर में डाला गया है ।

(ब) इस तालाब का आगोर उस वक्त जरूरत से ज्यादा था (आस-पास की समस्त पहाड़ियों का यह आगोर क्षेत्र हैं), इसलिये इसमें पानी बहुत ज्यादा आता था तथा तालाब शीघ्र ही भर जाता था । इसका कोई ओटा नहीं होने से पानी मुख्य घाट पट्ट के ऊपर से निकल कर इसकी पोल में से होता हुआ जगत सागर / मालासर में जाता था । बाद में बखतसागर बन जाने पर इसके ओटे (ओवरफ्लो) का पानी बखतसागर में जाता था । राव मालदेव के समय-जब दुर्ग के परकोटे का विस्तार

किया गया तब रानीसर के पश्चिम ही तरफ घाट काटकर उधर ही पश्चिम की पहाड़ी में इस पानी को पदमसर में डाला गया ।

यहां यह बात ध्यान देने योग्य है कि रानीसर तथा पदमसर का फीडर नाला एक ही है । पदमसर, रानीसर के बाये हाथ में पड़ने वाले पहाड़ियों का कैचमेन्ट क्षेत्र भी है । सन् १५५१-५२ में (मालदेव के समय ही) जब किले का विस्तार किया गया तो उस समय रानीसर को किले की परिधि में ले लिया गया । इसके इर्द-गिर्द एक परकोटा भी बनवाया गया । इसके पीछे सोच यह थी कि युद्ध के समय में इसके पानी का सदुपयोग किया जा सके ।

(स) रानीसर का आगोर क्षेत्र काफी विस्तृत था तथा पट्टे की ऊँचई अधिक न होने के कारण (वर्षा थोड़ी सी अधिक होने पर) पानी बहकर बाहरी क्षेत्रों में चला जाता था । अतः तखतसिंह जी के समय (कि पानी का सर्वाधिक उपयोग दुर्ग तथा परकोटे की बसावट के लिये हो सके), इसका पट्टा बढ़ाया गया था । पूर्व में इसका ओवरफ्लो (स्थानीय भाषा में ओटा अथवा बाला) इतना जबरदस्त होता था कि मार्ग अवरूद्ध हो जाते थे । अतः कहावत प्रचलित हुई -

रानीसर पदमसर हुयग्या ओटे

व्यापारी हुयग्या टोंटे।४

इसका घाट (जो वर्तमान में है) ८ से १० फुट का है तथा ऊँचाई लगभग २० फीट । साथ ही दाहिने हाथ की तरफ रिटेन्शन वॉल बना दी गई थी जिससे अधिकाधिक ओवरफ्लो पदमसर में पहुंच सके । घाट को मजबूती प्रदान करने के लिये चौड़ी दीवारों का निर्माण किया गया है ।

(द) रानीसर के पट्टे के विकास के साथ ही रावटी, कागा-कागड़ी, सूरसागर की दूरस्थ पहाड़ियों के कैचमेन्ट क्षेत्रों में जमा होने वाले पानी को रानीसर - पदमसर तक पहुंचाने का प्रबन्ध किया गया । चूंकि उस समय ये बसावट वाले क्षेत्र नहीं थे अतः इस जल का उपयोग भी परकोटे के भीतर किया जा सके इसलिये इन नहरों को निर्माण किया गया । यह नहर रावटी के पश्चिम में फतेश्वर महादेव के मन्दिर व टांके के पास से होती हुई रावटी कागा-कागड़ी एवं सूरसागर की पूर्व की पहाड़ियों का पानी लेते हुए बनाई गई । इन सभी पहाड़ियों की ढलान पश्चिम में होने के कारण नहर के पानी के घुमाव देने के लिये बड़ी मजबूत दो-तीन दीवारे भी बनाकर पानी को रोका गया तथा दक्षिण की तरफ बनी नहर में डाला गया । इसके बाद

सिंगोड़े की बारी के पास हाथी नहर बनाकर, शहर के परकोटे के नीचे उसके पानी को तालाब में डाला गया।५

(य) दुर्ग के भीतरों क्षेत्रों में जल वितरण की समुचित व्यवस्था थी । चौकेलाव महल के पिछवाड़े की ओर एक विशाल चौड़ा और वर्गाकार गहरा कुआं अपने आप मे अद्‌भुत है जिसका निर्माण सं° १७८६ में महाराजा अभयसिंह ने करवाया था । इस कुएं की शिराएं रानीसर से जुड़ी हुई थी जिसके कारण यहां हमेशा विशाल जल भण्डार उपलब्ध रहता था रियासत - काल में रानी सर की बुर्जे पर रहट लगाकर इस कुए का पानी हौज तक पहुंचाया जाता था । उस हौज पर अरहटो की नाली तथा तांबे की घड़लियों बंधी रहती थी । उनके द्वारा एक स्तर से दूसरे स्तर की दीवार पर बनी जल की नालियों के द्वारा पहुंचाया जाता था ।

चौकेलाव तालाब पर एक अरहट द्वारा पानी के चौकेलाव महल की ऊँचाई तक ले जाया जाता था, तो दूसरा अरहट चौकेलाव महल बेरे (कुएँ) का पानी डेढ़ कंगूरा पोल के पास बने हौज तक लाता था और तीसरे अरहट डेढ़ कंगूरा पोल से ऊपर होता था जो वर्तमान में '' पुस्तक प्रकाश के ऊपर की दीवार पर बनी पत्थर की नाली के द्वारा जय पोल स्थित हौज में पानी एकत्र करता था ।

उनके अंत में फनत महल में जहां लिफ्ट खुलती है, वहां लगा विशाल कार्य अरहट जयपोल से पानी ऊपर खींचता था । इस प्रकार पाताल के पानी को बिना किसी विद्युत के ही पारम्परिक व्यवस्था से महलों तक सुगमता से ले जाया जाता था । इस कुएं की सीढ़ियों को देखकर कहा जा सकता है कि पानी को सीधा निकाला जाता था अथवा बैलों के द्वारा चड़स व सूंडियों से पानी निकाला जाता था।[६] दुर्ग के भीतर जल आवश्यकता की पूर्ति हेतु अन्य स्त्रोत थे - इमरती बावड़ी, पुरानी बावड़ी, नौसखा कुआ, झरनेश्वर का कुड़ तथा टांका, पतालिया टांका, बाबा भात्माराम जी का टांका, फतह महल का टांका, जनानी ड्योढी का टांका, बाड़ी के महलों का टांका, चांमुड़ा माताजी मन्दिर का टांका ।

रानीसर पदमसर कैचमेन्ट क्षेत्र में आज रूकावट होने से कितनी भी बारिश हो, किन्तु बाला नहीं बहता । सारा पानी रिसकर भूमि में पहुंचता है, इसने भूमिगत जलस्तर को इतना बढ़ा दिया है कि आज यह शहर के भीतरी क्षेत्रों में समस्या बन गया है ।

चेरिया पहाड़ी का ढलान उत्तर पूर्व से दक्षिण पूर्व की ओर है । अतः कैचमेन्ट क्षेत्र का पानी जो रिसकर भूमि में पहुंचता है इसी ढलान की ओर बहता है । पहाड़ियों सेण्ड स्टोन से निर्मित है अतः यहां नीचे पानी की शिराओं का विपुल भण्डार

बहता है । फतेह पोल से सिंवाची गेट, जालोरी गेट तक पहुंचने वाली शिराओं के आस-पास ही अधिसंख्य बसावट है तथा सड़क के दोनों ओर विपुल मात्रा नें कुए तथा बावड़ियों हैं ।

ये कुएं तथा बावड़िया इस क्षेत्र की बसावट की जल की आवश्यकताओं की पूर्ति करते है। पदमसर से जालोरी गेट होकर जाते हुए सड़क के बांई और निम्नलिखित जल स्त्रोत हैं ।

१- **चांद बावड़ी** - राव जोधा की चांद कंवर नाम की सोनगरी (चौहान) रानी ने फतेहपोल के पास चांद बावड़ी का निर्माण कराया था । इसे चौहान बावड़ी भी कहते हैं ।[७] मारवाड़ का इतिहास[८] से ज्ञात होता है कि राव जोधा की जसमादे नामक हाड़ी रानी ने यहां एक कुआ बनवाया था। मुणोत नैणसी की मारवाड़ रा परगना री विगत से (पृ. सं. ५८३/३६) ज्ञात होता है कि राव जोधा के चौहान रानो ने कुएं को विकसित कर एक बावड़ी बनवाई थी, जो पहले "चौहान बावड़ी " कहो जाती थी । किन्तु बाद में उसे चांद बावड़ी कहा जाने लगा ।

२- **जोशियों का बेरा** - यह कुंआ जोशियों के मौहल्ले में दीवान आसकरण जोशी द्वारा बनवाया गया था । इस कुंए का पानी मीठा है जो पाताल फोड़ (अथाह) होने की वजह से मात्र १५ फुट पर ही निकल आता है । वर्तमान में भी यहां पानी निकालने हेतु पम्प की आवश्यकता नहीं है । यहां के निवासियों का कहना है कि रानीसर-पदमसर की सीरे चलने के कारण पानी ऊपर रहता है तथा मीटा है ।[९]

३- **शेषकरण का कुंआ** - यह कुंआ नवचौकिया में कोतवाली के सामने की सड़क की पूर्व दिशा में एक बड़ के पेड़ के नीचे आया हुआ है । इस कुंए का निर्माण महाराजा तखतसिंह के काल में शेषकरण कोतवाल ने करवाया था । इस कुंए का दासा बहुत ऊँचा है अतः लोग सीढ़ियों पर चढ़कर पानी खींचते है । इस कुंए का निर्माप सिर्फ पीने का पानी हेतु किया गया था । आज भी इस पर चरखियां लगी हुई है, इन चरखियों के ऊपर छत बनी हुई है । पानी अत्यधिक मीठा और स्वच्छ है ।

४- **नाथावतों की बारी का बेरा** - इस बेरे का निर्माण नथावत जाति के किसी व्यक्ति ने नथावतों के बास (बस्ती/मौहल्ला) में करवाया था । पानी अटूट एवं मीठा है जिसका उपयोग आज भी पीने के लिये किया जाता है ।[१०]

५- **नीमला / नीम्बला कुंआ** - इस कुंए का निर्माण राव जोधा के समय श्रीमाली नीम्बा ने करवाया था । आज तक इसको पीपली वाला कुंआ भी कहते हैं । पानी विपुल मात्रा में है तथा पीने के उपयोग में लिया जाता है ।

६- **नाजर जी की बावड़ी** - यह बावड़ी जालोरी गेट और बाईजी के तालाब के बीच जालोरी गेट से कबूतरों के चौक के रास्ते पर स्थित है । इस बावड़ी का निर्माण नाजर मोहम्मद इलमास ने संवत् १८५६ में करवाया था। कहते है इस नाजर ने तीन बावड़ियां बनवाई थी । दूसरी बावड़ी सरदारपुरा की ईदगाह के अन्दर है तथा तीसरी कबूतरों के चौक के पास जुलाहों की बावड़ी कहलाती है । पूर्व में इस पर अरहट लगा हुआ था ।

सड़क के दाई ओर निम्नलिखित जल स्त्रोत है -

१- **जेता कुंआ** - यह कुंआ फतेहपोल कोतवाली के बीच आया हुआ है । इसका निर्माण मूथा जेता ने राव जोधा के समय करवाया था । पूर्व में इस कुएं का पानी केवल राजधराने द्वारा उपयोग में लिया जाता था । अनुमान है कि महाराजा तखतसिंह के समय अकाल के बाद इस कुएं से ब्राह्मणों पानी भरने की स्वीकृति मिली । कुआं बहुत गहरा है तथा पानी मीठा है ।

२- **कोतवाली का कुआं** - इस कुएं का निर्माण पंवार शेषकरण ने इस समय करवाया था जब जीवनदास गहलोत महाराजा मानसिंह का कोतवाल था । यह कुआं कोतवाली मुख्य द्वार के पास दायी ओर ऊँचे चबूतरे पर बना हुआ है । पानी खींचने हेतु चरखियां लगी हुई है । पानी मीठा तथा सतह काफी ऊँची है ।११

३- **मूथों का कुआं** - इस कुंए का निर्माण वेलजी कोचर ने अपने घर के समाने करवाया था, जिसे बाद में ब्राह्मण मूथा को दे दिया गया । यह कुआं मूथों की गली में आया हुआ है । इस कुएं की गहराई करीब ५० फुट है ।

४- **बालकिशन लालजी के मन्दिर का कुआं** - यह कुआं बालकिशन जी के मन्दिर में महाराजा विजयसिंह के समय निर्मित हुआ था । यह करीब १२५-१५० फुट गहरा है तथा पानी काफी ऊपर है । कुएं पर आज भी चरखियां लगी हुई है ।

५- **कुम्हारियां कुआं** - इस कुएं का निर्माण राव जोधा के समय कुम्हार खीमा ने करवाया था । इसलिये इसे कुम्हारियां कुआं पुकारा जाता है। कुंए में पानी बहुत है ।

६- **लाडजी का बेरा** - यह कुआं खाण्डा फलसा में आया हुआ है । पानी बहुत मीठा तथा अट्टू है । यहां के निवासियों का कहना है कि भयंकर अकाल के समय भी इस कुएं का पानी कभी समाप्त नहीं हुआ ।[१२]

७- **बोड़ों का बेरा** - इस कुएं का निर्माण किन्ही शिवलाल जी बोड़ा ने करवाया था । जो खाण्डा फलसा के रास्ते में भोली बाई के मन्दिर के पास आया हुआ है । पानी बहुत तथा मीठा है ।

उपरोक्त अध्ययन से यह ज्ञात होता है कि मेहरानगढ़ दुर्ग में जल प्रबन्ध तकनीक अत्यन्त उत्तम कोटि थी । मुख्य वाटर कैचमेन्ट क्षेत्र में बनाये गये रानीसर तथा पदमसर न केवल महल की जलीय आवश्यकताओं को पूर्ति करते थे वरन् इसकी बढ़ती हुई सीरे किले के भीतर की जनता की बसावट को भी पर्याप्त मात्रा में जल उपलबध करवाती थी ।

सन्दर्भ -

१- इन्टैक की सर्वे रिपोर्ट ।

२- वहीं ।

३- इस शोध पत्र का अध्ययन मूलतः भौतिक सर्वे पर आधारित है ।

४- प्रो. जहूरखां मेहर एवं डॉ. महेन्द्रसिंह नागर :
जोधपुर का ऐतिहासिक मेहरानगढ़ दुर्ग, पृ. ८२ मेहरानगढ, म्यूजियम ट्रस्ट, जोधपुर २००७

५- इन्टैक की सर्वे रिपोर्ट ।

६- मेहर एवं नगर : वहीं पृ. ८४-८५

७- वाई. डी. सिंह : राजस्थान के कुएं एवं बावड़ियां पृ. ६० राजस्थानी ग्रन्थागार, जोधपुर २००२

८- पं. विश्वेश्वरनाथ रेऊ : मारवाड़ का इतिहास भाग १ पृ. ६३ : मानसिंह पुस्तक प्रकाश २००५

६- वाई. डी. सिंह : वहीं पृ. ६६

१०- वहीं पृ. ६७

११-वहीं पृ. ६५

१२- वहीं पृ. ७१

कुम्भलगढ़ दुर्ग में जलप्रबंधन

डॉ. दिग्विजय भटनागर

कुम्भलगढ़ दुर्ग मेवाड़ का सबसे बड़ा और सुदृढ़ दुर्ग है। यह उदयपुर जिले से ८४ किमी उत्तर में स्थित है। अरावली के पहाड़ियों के पश्चिमी शाखा के एक घेरे में सादड़ी गांव के पास मेवाड़ और मारवाड़ की सीमा पर अवस्थित है। इसके निकट पिण्ड़वाड़ा, भाटोही, भुणोद आदि गांव स्थित है जहाँ जूही नदी निकलती है।[1]

मेवाड़ की भौगोलिक स्थिति के अनुसार यहाँ का जल ढ़लान (पहाड़ी क्षेत्रों) के कारण शीघ्र बहकर अन्य भागों की जल-आपूर्ति करता है। अतः यहाँ जल संरक्षण और जल संग्रहण जलाशयों के निर्माण के द्वारा ही किया जा सकता था। साथ ही भूमिगत जल का स्तर ऊँचा उठाने का कार्य भी जलाशयों के द्वारा संभव है।

महाराणा कुम्भ ने सैनिक उपयोगिता और निवास की आवश्यकता की पूर्ति के लिए १४४३ ई में दुर्ग का पुनः निर्माण प्रारम्भ किया जो १४५८ ई. में पूर्ण हुआ। डॉ. गोपीनाथ शर्मा ने लिखा है, "राणा कुम्भा ने कुम्भलगढ़ के किले का पहाड़ी श्रृंखलाओं से घेरे हुए स्थान में सुरक्षित किया। किले के भीतर ऊंचे से ऊंचे भाग का प्रयोग राजप्रासाद के लिए, नीचे से नीचे भाग को जलाशयों के लिए और समतल भाग खेती के लिए रखा गया। बची हुई भमि का उपयोग मंदिर और मकानों के निर्माण में किया गया।[2] इस दृष्टि से मेवाड़ के महाराणाओं ने मानवीय आवश्यकताओं कों पूरा करने के लिए प्राकृतिक संसाधनों (जल, खनिज वन आदि) का श्रेष्ठता से प्रबंधन किया है। मानव की प्राथमिक आवश्यकता 'जल' के सदुपयोग के लिए तालाब, सरोवर, नाडे, कूप आदि बनवाने में बहुत धन व्यय किया है।

दुर्ग पर जाने के लिए केलवाड़ा गांव से (बाणमाता का प्रसिद्ध मंदिर है) पश्चिम की ओर पहाड़ी नाल से होकर १ मील तंग टेढे-मेढ़े रास्ते को पार करने पर ७०० फीट की ऊँचाई पर किले का प्रथम दरवाजा "आरेट पोल" है। इससें पूर्व पहाड़ी दर्रे पर बना लखोला तालाब है। पास ही आरेट नामक छोटी बस्ती के नाम से ही इस द्वार का नामकरण कर दिया। इसके बाद क्रमशः हल्ला पोल, हनुमान पोल, राम

पोल, विजय पोल नामक दरवाजा स्थित है। हल्ला पोल से कुछ दूर जाने पर एक बावड़ी स्थित है जिसे बादशाही बावड़ी कहते है। विजय पोल के बाद समतल भूमि है जहाँ स्थापत्य कला के सुन्दर मंदिर, प्रासाद आदि भवन बने है। चक्रपाणि मिश्र ने विश्ववल्लभ में भूमि जल स्त्रोतों का पता लगाने की विधियाँ बतायी है। मिट्टी, चट्टानों तथा वनस्पति का निरीक्षण कर भूमिगत जल का पता लगया जाता था। भूमिगत जल को कुंए, बावड़ी आदि खोदकर आवश्यकतानुसार पेयजल के रूप उपयोग लिया जा सकता है। यह राज्यों की सीमाओं से परे पेय और उपयोगी जल का विशाल भण्ड़ार भूमिगत जल है। मण्ड़न ने भी भूमि, घर, नगर और दुर्ग का निर्माण का शास्त्रोंक्त विधि से वर्णन करते हुए जल की महत्ता को स्पष्ट किया है। मण्ड़न ने दुर्ग के आंतरिक स्थान को उपयोगी बनाने के लिए वहाँ जलाशय बनाने के लिए कहा है। जलाशय ऐसे स्थान पर बनाये जाए जहाँ बरसात का पानी आसानी से जमीन पर बहकर उस स्थान पर एकत्रित हो जाये और उस जलाशय से आस-पास की भूमि में अन्न उत्पन्न हो सके जिसके कारण दुर्ग आत्म निर्भर हो जाए।[३] राजवल्लभ में वर्णित है कि छोटी-बड़ी झोपड़िया (घर) पहाड़ियों के नीचे अनियमितता के आधार पर बसते थे। इन घरों के समूह के बीच में खुली जगह देखी जाती थी। यह गाँव या घरों के समूह अपेक्षाकृत ऊँची जगह पर होते थे जिससे घर के जल से मक्का, चावल की अपेक्षाकृत नीचे वाली भूमि पर सिंचाई हो सके।[४] इस प्रकार की व्यवस्था कुम्भलगढ़ दुर्ग में भवनों के जल का उपयोग कृषि उत्पादन बढ़ानें में किया गया था जो जल के उचित प्रबंधन का उदाहरण है।

कुम्भलगढ़ दुर्ग में ५ बड़े एवं २ छोटे तालाब, १२ बावडियाँ है। हनुमान पोल के नाले के पूर्वी तथा उत्तर-पूर्वी दिशा में पहाड़ों के पूर्वी हिस्से में एक-दूसरे से १०० से २०० मीटर दूर तालाब बने हुए है। यहाँ चार तालाब श्रृंखलाबद्ध एक के बाद दूसरा जल भराव क्षमता में उत्तरोत्तर बड़ा बनाया गया है जो समय की मार के कारण ध्वस्त हो गये है। तालाबों के जल आवक क्षेत्रों में सीढ़ियों से युक्त बावडियाँ बनी हुई थी।[५]

इन जलाशयों को परस्पर नालियों के माध्यम से जोड़कर सुन्दर व्यवस्था की गई।[६] इन्ही तालाबों मे मध्य ''मामादेव कुण्ड़'' स्थित है[७] जो मामादेव मंदिर या कुम्भश्याम मंदिर के पास स्थित है। कुम्भलगढ़ प्रशस्ति में कुम्भा द्वारा एक जलाशय बनाने का उल्लेख है। मामादेव नामक कुण्ड़ पर ही उसके पुत्र उदा ने १४६८ ई. हत्या कर दी गई। यह कुण्ड़ कुछ वर्षों पहले ऊपर के तालाब की पाल काट देने से पानी के बहाव में बह गया जो इतिहास की दृष्टि से एक महत्वपूर्ण क्षति है।[८] दनी वाटा पोल

के पास बामनवा नामक सरोवर स्थित है। बामन तलाई और दूध तलाई नामक दो छोटे तालाब भी बने हुए है।[६] बडे-बडे पत्थरों तथा चूने के प्लास्टर से निर्मित यह बांध सीढ़ियों से युक्त है। प्रत्येक बांध की बांयी ओर जल निकास की व्यवस्था है। महाराणा रायमल के बहिन रमाबाई ने कुम्भलगढ़ में कुण्डेश्वर के मंदिर के दक्षिण की पहाड़ी के नीचे एक सरोवर तथा योगिनीपत्तम (जावर) में रामकुण्ड़ बनवाया।[१०]

कुम्भलगढ़ दुर्ग की अन्य विशेषता है आंतरिक दुर्ग के रूप में ''कटारगढ़'' का बना होना है।[११] यहाँ पर भी अन्न भण्ड़ार, शस्त्रागार, हस्तशाला, बड़ा सरोवर और बावडिया बनी हुई है। कुम्भा महल के निकट आयताकार ईंटों व चूने के प्लास्टर से युक्त टांका बना हुआ है जिसमें सभी महलो तथा आवासों की प्रत्येक जल की बूंद को एकत्र करने की व्यवस्था है। ऐसे स्थान भी है जिनसे आभास होता है कि बावडियों और सरोवर से रहट या चड़स से पानी को ऊपर स्थित आवसीय मकानों तथा महलों में पहुँचाया जाता था।[१२]

लखोला तालाब - इस मनमोहक सरोवर का निर्माण महाराणा लाखा (१३८२-१४२१) ने करवाया था। यह केलवाड़ा गांव के पश्चिम में कुम्भलगढ़ के मार्ग पर पहाड़ी दर्रे पर बना हुआ है। इसकी लम्बाई ५ किमी तथा चौडाई १०० मीटर से ३००० मीटर तक है। प्रारम्भ में इसकी ऊँचाई ४० फीट थी वर्तमान में इसकी ऊँचाई ६० फीट है।[१३]

आड़ावाला - दुर्ग के प्रथम द्वार आरेट पोल और दूसरे दरवाजे हल्लापोल के मध्य आड़ावाला ढ़लान की समाप्ति पर जल से परिपूर्ण बहता हुआ नाला ''आड़ावाला'' स्थित है जो पीने के काम आता है।

बादशाही बावड़ी -हल्लापोल से कुछ दूर जाने पर एक बावड़ी आती है जिसे 'बादशाही बावड़ी' कहा जाता है। कहा जाता है कि महाराणा प्रताप और अकबर के सेनापति शाहबाज खाँ ने मार्च १५७८ ई. पर कुम्भलगढ़ पर आक्रमण के समय अपनी सेना के पानी पीने के लिए इस बावड़ी का निर्माण करवाया था। यह बावड़ी मुख से संकरी और पीछे से काफी चौड़ी है तथा पत्थरो से निर्मित है और मध्यकालीन स्थापत्यकला का महत्त्वपूर्ण नमूना है। यह बावड़ी राहगीरो, सैनिकों आदि के पानी-पीने और सिचांई में काम आती रही है।[१४] मध्यकाल में पेयजल के लिए बावड़ी, कुँओं का निर्माण किया जाता था क्योंकि कुँओं (कूपो) और बावड़ियों का जल प्राकृतिक रूप से फिल्टर होकर आता था।

राणा बावड़ी - रामपोल से उत्तर में पहाड़ी ढ़ाल उतरने पर एक बावड़ी आती है जो राणा बावड़ी कहलाती है। यह बावड़ी काफी बड़ी और चौकारे है तथा पत्थरों से निर्मित है। दुर्ग में पानी ले जाने का यही एक सुदृढ़ मुख्य स्त्रोत है।

मामादेव कुण्ड़ -बावड़ी से थोड़ा आगे चलने पर एक नाले के किनारे मामादेव का मंदिर है जो विष्णु का समर्पित है। इस मंदिर के पास ही मामादेव या नामदेव नामक सुन्दरकुण्ड़ है जिसका निर्माण महारणा कुम्भा ने १४६० ई. (वि.स. १५१७ मार्गशीर्ष वदि ५ सोमवार) में कराया था।

कुम्भलगढ़[१५] जैसे विशाल दुर्ग का निर्माण, सिंचाई, सैनिकों और आम जनता की प्राथमिक और द्वितीयक आवश्यकता की पूर्ति जल की बहुल्यता या जल के उचित प्रबंधन से ही भी संभव थी। महाराणा कुम्भा द्वारा कुम्भलगढ़ में केवल एक जलाशय का निर्माण इतिहासकारों और पुराविद्रों को आश्चर्य में अवश्य डालता है लेकिन कुम्भलगढ़ को अपनी राजधानी बनाने के पीछे महाराणा कुंभा का निश्चित उद्देश्य था कि पहले के भांति (जैसा कि माण्ड़लगढ़ और चित्तौड़गढ़ के घेरो के दौरान जल अन्न की कमी हो गई थी) रसद की कमी न हो। इसका प्रत्यक्ष उदाहरण महारणा कुंभा के शासन काल में कुम्भलगढ़ दुर्ग पर जोरदार आक्रमण हुए लेकिन दुर्ग अजेय रहा।[१६] १५७८ ई. को महारणा प्रताप के काल में शाहबाज खाँ ने नाड़ोल और केलवाड़ा की तरफ नाकाबंदी कर किले में रसद को रोक दिया[१७] और पीने के पानी के एक मात्र नौगुण नामक कुएं के जल को जहरीला कर दिया गया जिसकी वजह से शाहबाज खाँ दुर्ग को जीतने में सफल रहा।[१८]

इस प्रकार महाराणा कुंभा ने अपनी जल संरक्षण की नीति के लिए ऐसे स्थान को चुना जो घने वनों से आच्छादित था। वर्तमान में अधिक से अधिक वृक्षारोपण के सिद्धांत पर आधारित है। सतही जल का अधिक से अधिक उपयोग करने के लिए वर्षा के जल को तालाब, कुण्ड़, छोटे-बड़े सरोबर (नाड़े), प्राकृतिक नहरों द्वारा एकत्र करने का सफल प्रयोग किया। वर्षा जल के संग्रहण के साथ भूमिगत जल को बढ़ाने के प्रयास किये गये क्योकि बनास का उद्गम स्थल कुम्भलगढ़ के पास ही था।

महाराणा कुंभा द्वारा दुर्ग में यज्ञवेदी का निर्माण शास्त्रोक्त विधि से किया गया। यह वेदी दो मंजिल भवन है जिसके गुम्बद के नीचे भाग में धुआं निकलने के लिए चारों भाग है। यज्ञवेदी रामपोल के दाहिनी तरफ स्थित है। दुर्ग में यज्ञवेदी चारों तरफ दीवारों से सुरक्षित है तथा यज्ञवेदी के चारों ओर पंडितों व दर्शकों के बैठने की पूर्ण व्यवस्था है। यह वेदी न केवल प्राचीन यज्ञ परम्परा को दर्शाती है बल्कि कृत्रिम वर्षा के प्रयोजन को भी सिद्ध करती होगी। युर्जुवेद में यज्ञ जल को शुद्ध करने वाला बताया

गया है और यज्ञ द्वारा कृत्रिम वर्षा करने का उल्लेख है।[१८] इतनी विशाल यज्ञवेदी के निर्माण के पीछे कुम्भा का क्या मंथन रहा होगा। संभवतः कुंभा ने वैज्ञानिक तकनीक का प्रयोग करते हुए यज्ञवेदी का उपयोग जल की शुद्धता और कृत्रिम वर्षा जैसे कार्य के लिए किया हो तो अतिश्योक्ति नही होगी। यज्ञ द्वारा वर्षा में घी का विशिष्ट महत्व है। मेरा मानना है कि कुम्भलगढ़ क्षेत्र मे घी. दूध, वनस्पति आदि किसी भी खाद्य सामग्री की कोई कमी नहीं थी और आवश्यकता पडने पर इस प्रकार कृत्रिम वर्षा का प्रयोग क़िया भी गया होगा। यहीं कारण है कि महाराणा कुंभा और मण्डन जैसे शिल्पी ने इस यज्ञवेदी का निर्माण प्रयोगशाला के रूप में किया हो। यह यज्ञवेदी जल की समस्या के निवारण का एक वैज्ञानिक आधार पर है। अन्यथा इतनी विशाल यज्ञवेदी का दुर्ग में निर्माण का औचित्य दुविधापूर्ण है।

इसके अलावा मेवाड़ के जमीन में मिट्टी की मटकियां निश्चित दूरी पर गाढ कर फसल की सिंचाई की जाती थी। इस प्रविधि में मटकियों में पानी भर दिया जाता था और ऊपर ढक्कन लगाया जाता था। मटकियों में से रिसरिस कर जल फसल तक पहुंचता था। मटकों के खाली होने पर उन्हें पुनः भर दिया जाता था। संभवतः जल प्रबंधन की दृष्टि से दुर्ग में भी कृषि की यह व्यवस्था अपनाई गई थी।

इस प्रकार कुम्भलगढ दुर्ग सुरक्षा, आत्मनिर्भरता और जल की उपलब्धता में सर्वोपरि है। इस दुर्ग में उपलब्ध जल का अपनी आवश्यकता के अनुरूप उपयोग करना प्रबंधन का श्रेष्ठ उदाहरण है। दुर्ग के जल प्रबंधन में महाराणा, उनके परिवार, जागीरदार एवं अधिकारी वर्ग के साथ जन सामान्य ने भी पूर्ण सहयोग दिया। कुंभलगढ मेवाड़-मारवाड़ सीमा पर स्थित होने के कारण दोनों प्रदेशों की जल संग्रहण प्रविधियों का उपयोग भी यहां किया गया।

संदर्भ

१. जैम्स टॉड, ट्रेवल्स इन वेस्टर्न इण्डिया, स. गोपाल नारायण बहुरा, पृ. २१; मनोहर सिंह राणावत (स.), मुणहौत नेणसी री ख्यात, भाग-१, पृ ४-५; कुंभलगढ़ प्रशस्ति, श्लोक १३०-१४३

२. जी.एन. शर्मा, राजस्थान का सांस्कृतिक इतिहास, पृ. १४४

३. एकलिंग प्रशस्ति, श्लोक ५०-५१; कुंभलगढ़ प्रशस्ति, पृ. १३०-१४३; जी. एन. शर्मा, सोशियल लाइफ ऑल मिडिवल इण्डिया, पृ. ७०

४. मण्डन, राजवल्लभ, सर्ग-४, श्लोक ४६

५. कुंभलगढ़ प्रशस्ति, श्लोक १३५; कुंभा स्मारिका, १९९८-९९, पृ. ९९

६. के.एस. गुप्ता, गोपाल व्यास; जे.के. ओझा, राजस्थान का इतिहास, पृ. ३१-३३

७. कुंभलगढ प्रशस्ति, सर्ग १३१; रणछोड़ दास भट्ट, (सम्पादन देव कोठारी) अमरकाव्यम्, सर्ग-१०, श्लोक ३८, पृ. १६६; गौरीशंकर हीराचंद ओझा, उदयपुर राज्य का इतिहास, भाग-१, पृ. ३११, ३२१-२२, ३३४; नैणसी की ख्यात, भाग-१, पृ. ३६

८. गौरी शंकर असावा, कुंभलगढ अजेय दुर्ग, पृ. १८

९. कुंभा स्मारिका, १९९७-९८, पृ. ५२

१०. जावर के रामस्वामी मंदिर को प्रशस्ति, श्लोक १-२

११. कटारगढ़- ऐसा दुर्ग जो सीधी ऊंचाई पर स्थित हो तथा मुख्य दुर्ग के अंदर ही छोटा दुर्ग के रूप में हो तथा जो प्राचीर, द्वार आदि से सुरक्षित हो।

१२. ईश्वर सिंह राणावत, राजस्थान के जल संसाधन, पृ. ७५

१३. गौरी शंकर असावा, कुंभलगढ़ अजेय दुर्ग, पृ. १३

१४. गौरी शंकर असावा, कुंभलगढ़ अजेय दुर्ग, पृ. १४

१५. दुर्ग के चारों तरफ सुदृढ दीवार बनी हुई है जो लगभग ३६ किमी भू भाग को सुरक्षित करती है। यह दीवार काफी ऊंची और इतनी चौड़ी है कि उस पर लगभग ८ घुड़सवार एक साथ दौड़ सकते है। इस परकोटे में लगभग ७०० बुर्ज बने है और चारों दिशाओं में ४ बड़े-बड़े द्वार है। (गौरी शंकर असावा, कुंभलगढ़ अजेय दुर्ग, पृ. १३) इस दुर्ग में लगभग ५०,००० व्यक्ति रह सकते थे इतने लोगों के लिए पानी की आवश्यकता को पूरा करने के लिए एक विशाल तालाब भी बनवाया गया। (कालूराम शर्मा, मध्यकालीन राजस्थान का इतिहास, पृ. १०४)

१६. श्यामलदास, वीर विनोद, भाग-१, पृ. ३२४, ३२६ (१४४२ ई. में मालवा के सूल्तान महमूद खिलजी का आक्रमण हुआ तथा १४५७ ई. में गुजरात के सुल्तान कुतुबुद्दीन द्वारा कुम्भलगढ़ दुर्ग को घेरा)

१७. श्यामलदास, वीर विनोद, भाग-२, पृ. १५६-१५७

१८. हूकुम सिंह भाटी (सं.), रावल राणाजी री बात, पृ. ६८; राजेन्द्र शंकर भट्ट, मेवाड़ के महाराणा और शहंशाह अकबर, पृ. २८४

१९. यजुर्वेद १६/३८, प. वीरसेन वेदश्रमी, वैदिक परंपरा, पृ. ४१०

अहमदाबाद का कांकरिया तालाब

डॉ. अन्नपूर्णा शाह

गुजरात के पास विशाल समुद्र तट, साबरमती, मही, नर्मदा, तापी जैसी बडी नदियां एवं कई छोटी छोटी नदियां है। गुजरात के कई भागों में बारीश भी कम होती हैं। गुजरात के भोगोलिक इतिहास को देखा जाए तो गुजरात में सुखा एवं अतिवृष्टि दोनो देखने को मिलते हैं। बारीश की अनियमितता, कई भागोमें नदियों का अभाव, गरम एवं सूखी आबोहवाकी वजह से पानी की सुविधा के लिये जलाशयों का निर्माण प्राचीनकाल से गुजरात में हुआ है। ऐसे जलाशयों में तालाब, कुए वावडी और कुंड उल्लेखनीय है।

गुजरात के जलाशय कलापूर्ण है। यहाँ सबसे ज्यादा जलाशय सोलंकीकाल (६ वीं से १४वी सदी) एवं सल्तनतकाल में (१४ वीं से १६ वी सदी) निर्माण हुए हैं। यहां के जलाशयों के निर्माण में हिंदू स्थापतियों का बड़ा योगदान है। जलाशयों के साथ धार्मिक, सामाजिक एवं सांस्कृतिक जीवन जुड़ा हुआ होता है।

गुजरात की स्वतंत्र सल्तनतकी स्थापना के थोडे साल बाद गुजरात की राजधानी अणहिलवाड पाटण के बदले अहमदाबाद कर दी गई। अहमदाबाद साबरम्ती नदी के किनारे सुल्तान अहमदशाह पहले ने अपने नाम से ई.सं. १४११ में बनाया था।[१] तारीखे अमदशाही में इस शहर को धरती के मुख का तील कहा है।[२] युरोपीय यात्री बारबेसा ने अहमदाबाद को समृध्ध नगर कहा है। जो वावडी, तालाब, बगीचों से भरा है।[३] तारीखे फरिश्ता में भी इस शहर को हिंदुस्तानका सबसे सुंदर शहर कहा है।[४]

मीराते सिकंदरी में भी इस शहर को सबसे सुंदर शहर कहा है।[५] ऐसे समृध्ध एवम् सुंदर शहर के बीच कांकरीया तालाब नगीने जैसा दिखता है। जहाँगीरने इस शहर की मुलाकात ली तब उसे कांकरीया तालाब बहुत अच्छा लगा था, यहाँ उसने रोशनी एवं आतिशबाजी भी देखी थी।[६] अहमदशाह के बड़े बेटे महमूदशाह, के बड़े बेटे कुतुबुद्दीन ने इ.स. १४५१ अपने नाम से "होजे - कुतुब" (कांकरिया तालाब) बंधवाया जो भारत के प्रसिद्ध तालाबों में से एक है।

तालाब अलग-अलग प्रकार के होते है। राजवल्लभने आकारकी दृष्टि से तालाब के कई प्रकार बतलाये है।[७] जैसे की, अर्धचन्द्राकार, चारों और से बन्धा हुआ महासर, वृत्ताकार, चतुष्कोण, भद्र, सुभद्र इत्यादि ऐसेही विस्तारकी दृष्टिसे भी तालाब के जयेष्ठ, मध्यम, कनिष्ठ प्रकार कहे है। जैसे कि १००० हाथ वाला जयेष्ठ, ५०० हाथ वाला मध्यम, २५० हाथ वाला तालाब कनिष्ठ कहा जाता है। तालाब के बांध की उंचाई के आधार पर भी जयेष्ठ मध्यम कनिष्ठ प्रकार होते है।[८] ५०० हाथ उंचा बांध जयेष्ठ, २५० हाथ उंचा मध्यम और १२५ हाथ उंचा कनिष्ठ। तालाब के पानी तक पहुंचने के लिए तालाब के चारों और सीढियों की रचना की जाती है। तालाब में बरसात के पानी का संग्रह होता है। बरसात का पानी सबसे पहले नाले द्वारा रूद्रकूपों मे से होकर तालाब में जाता है। रूद्रकूप के मुखपर छलनी जैसी जालियाँ लगी रहती है। जिसकी वजह से तालाब में कचरा नहीं जाता और तालाब का पानी गंदा नहीं होता। कचरे की वजह से तालाब का स्तर उंचा नहीं आता। बड़े तालाबों के बीच में एक टेकरी बनाई जाती है। जिसे स्थापत्य की परिभाषा में बकस्थल कहा जाता है। बकस्थल हेतूपूर्वक की गई रचना है। यदि पानी तालाब में प्रबल वेगसे प्रवेश करेगा या बहेगा तो तालाब के सामने की दिवार से जोरसे टकरायेगा और दिवार के कमजोर होकर टूटने का डर लगा रहेगा। बकस्थल का काम पानीके प्रबल वेग को कम करने का है। भारत के कई तालाबों में बकस्थल की जगह मंदीर, महल, बगीचे बनाये गये है। तालाब के बीचमें आये बकस्थल तक जाने के लिए कुछ तालाबो पर पुल की रचना की जाती है।

भारत में तालाब निर्माण की परंपरा बहुत प्राचीन है। जलाशयों का श्रेष्ठ स्थापत्य गुजरात में पाया गया है। गुजरात के सोलंकीकाल के तालाबो में पाटण का सहस्त्रलिंग तालाब, घोलकाका मलाव तालाब, वीरमगाम का मनसुर तालाब उल्लेखनीय है। मध्यकालीन गुजरातके तालाबो में अमदाबाद का कांकरीया तालाब प्रसिद्ध है। इसका ऐतिहासिक स्थापत्यकीय, भौगोलिक एवम् सांस्कृतिक महत्व है।

अहमदाबाद का हवामान सूखा एवं गरम है। इस शहर के आसपास का भाग टेकरियों वाला एवम् उंचाई वाला है इस वजह से यहाँ के नीचाई वाले भागों के बीच पानी भर जाता है। कांकरिया तालाब भी गोरधनवाडी टेकरा विस्तार में बना हुआ है। जहाँ आसानी से बारिश के पानी का संग्रह हो जाता हे। कहा जाता है कि सोलंकी राजवी कर्णदेव ने कर्णावती नगरी में 'करणसूर' तालाब बनावाया था। यहाँ बसे अहमदाबाद का कांकरिया तालाब शायद करणसूर तालाब पर बनाया गया होगा। चूंकी करणसूर के कोई अवशेष यहाँ नहीं पाये गये।[९]

होजे-कुतुब का नाम कांकरिया तालाब रखने के पीछे एक अनुश्रुति प्रचलित है कि, यहाँ के प्रसिद्ध संत शाहआलम साहबने कंकर डाल कर इस तालाब की जगह निश्चित की थी। इस लिये इस जगह को कांकरिया नाम दिया गया। दूसरी अनुश्रुति यह है कि यहाँ की मुलाकात लेते समय शाहआलम साहब के पाँव में कंकर लगा था। इस लिये इस तालाब का नाम कांकरिया रखा गया होगा।[१०] इस तालाब के आसपास मकान एवं बगीचे बनाये गये।[११] इस तालाब के आकर्षक अंग उसकी बांध, उसकी सीढियाँ, मंडप, प्लेटफोर्म, नगीनावाडी, रूद्रकूप इत्यादि है। इस तालाब के निर्माण के लिए घांगध्रा और उत्तर गुजरात की खानों से रेतीला पत्थर मंगवाया गया था। मुगल राजवीरों के शासन दौरान इसके बकस्थल पर नगीना वाडी में बगीचा बनवाया गया था। जहाँगीर के सूबे सूजात खान ने (ई.सं. १६६४ से १७०३) इस तालाब का पुनरोद्धार करवाया था।[१२]

मराठा शासन में इस तालाब पर कोई खास ध्यान नहीं दिया गया था। क्योंकी १८१७ में गायकवाड ने अहमदाबाद अंग्रेजो को दे दिया था।[१३]

ब्रिटिश शासको ने इस जगह के आसपास रास्ते बनवाये, नगीना वाडी तक जाने के लिए पुल का निर्माण किया। नगीनावाडी को ठीक करवाया।[१४] ई.सं. १८७६ में यहाँ के कलेक्टर ए.ए. बोराडियल ने इस तालाब का पुनरोद्धार करवाया।[१५] १९५० में यह स्थल नगर आयोजन के अंतर्गत आने से गुजरात स्टेट के आरक्योलोजी डिपार्टमेन्ट ने इसकी मरम्मत १९५२ में करवाई। आज इस स्थल का प्रवासन हेतु खूब विकास हुआ है।

यह तालाब प्रथम नजर में गोल दिखाई देता है, परंतु यह ३४ बाजुओं वाला बहुकोणीय स्थापत्य है। इसकी हर एक बाजू ६० से ६५ मीटर जितनी लंबी है। हरेक बाजू से पानी तक जाने की सीढियाँ है। जो पीले रेतीले पत्थर की बनी है। तालाब के पानी तक जाने के रास्ते में सीढी पर पगथार बनी है। जो १.२ मीटर की बनी है। इसकी सीढीयों को मजबूती देने के लिए ६.६ मीटर के अंतर पर जमीन नें गहराई तक जाते पत्थर के आधार रखे हुए है। जो सीढीयों की सुंदरता को भी बढाता है। इस तालाब का ढलाव दक्षिण उत्तर की तरफ है। तालाब २ किलोमीटर के धेरावे में आया हुआ है। इस व्यास ६४.५४ मीटर है।[१६] तालाब के पूर्व तरफ बडा रूद्रकूप है, जो रेतीले पत्थर का बना है। इसके मुख पर नाले है। इन के बीच ८ मीटर का अंतर है। इन को मजबूती देने के लिए नक्सी कामवाले आधार दिये गये है गोल नाले १.८ मीटर व्यास के बने है। इन नालो के मुख पर बारीक और सुंदर नक्काशी काम वाली जालियाँ लगाई गई है। नालो में २.५ मीटर के अंतर पर दीवार की मजबूती

के लिए अर्ध स्तंभो की रचना है। नालोकी जालियाँ छलनी का काम करती है। इनकी वजह से तालाब में कूड़ा-करकट नहीं जाता। रूद्रकूप को उपर से छत से ढांक दिया है, जिस पर ८ स्तम्भ रख कर मंडप बनाया गया है। इसके दोनों तरफ नीचे तक जाने की सीढीयाँ है।[१७]

तालाब के चारों ओर पानी तक जाने के लिए प्लेटफोर्म भी बनाये गये है। जहाँ रोड लेवल से जा सकते है। इस तालाबके पूर्व तरफ के प्लेटफोर्म पर बार स्तंभो की बनी वेदीका है। इसके पश्चिम के प्लेटफोर्म की रचना देख कर कह सकते है कि इसे बादमें बनाया गया होगा। दक्षिण पश्चिम के प्लेटफोर्म पर धुम्मट वाली छतरी है। धुम्मट के स्तंभों पर फूल-बैल की बारीक नक्कासी की गई है।[१८]

इस तालाब का बकस्थल १०० ग १०० मीटर की बनी नगीनावाडी है। जो दक्षिण छोड से एक पुल की बनी है। यह पानी के स्तर से ६ मीटर उंचाई पर बनी है। जिसकी चारों ओर बनी पक्की दिवाले इसको मजबूती देती है।

इस तालाब की भव्यता स्थापत्यका मूल्य आज भी है। मंडप और प्लेटफोर्म वाला यह तालाब अपनेआप में श्रेष्ठ है आजभी यह अपने आस-पास के वातावरण के तापमान कम करता है। पर्यटन और मनोरंजन का बडा स्थल है। इस तरह इसका ऐतिहासिक, स्थापकीय, भौगोलिक, सामाजिक एवम् प्रवासन स्थलके रूप में महत्व है।[१९]

संदर्भ सूची

१. डॉ. हरी प्रसाद शास्त्री-आशापल्ली-कर्णावती - अहमदाबाद, विद्यापीठ- वर्ष २ पृष्ठ २११ -के. का. शास्त्री - आशापल्ली-कर्णावती - गुजरात नो राजकीय सांस्कृतिक इतिहास-ग्रंथ पृष्ठ ७७ से ८०
- डॉ. हरी प्रसाद शास्त्री-अमदावादनी स्थापना नो समय- जैन विद्यालय संवर्ण जयंती अंक भाग १

२. रत्नमणीराव भीमराव जोट - गुजरात नु पाटनगर अमदावाद पृष्ठ ५७
-मीराते अहमदी भाग २ अमदावाद १६३४

३. रत्नमणीराव भीमराव जोट - गुजरात नु पाटनगर अमदावाद पृष्ठ ११३

४. वही पृष्ठ ११४-११५

५. रत्नमणीराव भीमराव जोट - गुजरात नु पाटनगर अमदावाद पृष्ठ ६५

६. डॉ. हरी प्रसाद शास्त्री, अमदावाद गुजरातनु मसहुर पाटनगर-गुजरात नो राजकीय सांस्औतिक इतिहास-ग्रंथ सल्तनत काल पृष्ठ ६४

७. महादेव आर.-राजवल्लभ-अमदाबाद .१६६५,अध्याय ४ पृष्ठ ३३-३६

गोसाई नारायण भारती यशवंत- राजवल्लभ अमदावाद -१६११

८. गोसाई नारायण भारती यशवंत- राजवल्लभ अमदावाद -१६११ पृष्ठ ७६

9. Trivedi, R. K. "Special report on Ahmedabad city census India 1961 part-VII B, Delhi, 1965.

१०. आर. टी. सावलिया - गुजरातना सरोवरो, तळाव अने कुन्डो, ग्रंथ निर्मण बोर्ड अमदावाद २००१

११. मीराते सिकंदरी, बडोदा - १६६१

१२. डॉ. हरी प्रसाद शास्त्री, अमदावाद गुजरातनु मसहुर पाटनगर-गुजरात नो राजकीय सांस्औतिक इतिहास-ग्रंथ सल्तनत काल पृष्ठ ६५

13. Commissariant M.S.- History of Gujarat, Vol-II Oriental Long Man, 1957, page no. 61

14. Burgess-jass, The Mahammdan Architecture of Ahmedabad Part-1, 1412 to 1520, Archaeological Survey of Western India - 1900

15. Trivedi R. K. – Special report on Ahmedabad city census India 1961 part-VII B, Delhi, 1965, page no. 53

१६. डॉ. थोमस परमार - भारतनु नागरक स्थापत्य गु. युनि. अहमदाबाद १६८४ पृष्ठ ८१-८२

१७. व्यक्तिगत सर्वेक्षण - कांकरीया तालाब अहमदाबाद

१८. व्यक्तिगत सर्वेक्षण - कांकरीया तालाब अहमदाबाद

भानपुरा क्षेत्र में मध्ययुगीन ऐतिहासिक तालाब वापिकाएँ और उनका तद्‌युगीन महत्व

डॉ. प्रद्युम्न कुमार भट्‌ट

भानपुरा का क्षेत्र परिचय एवं अवस्थिति

चम्बल के तटवर्ती पूर्वी भाग में विस्तृत भानपुरा अंचल का मध्ययुगीन इतिहास सुख,समृद्धि कला के विकास के साथ तालाबों, वापियो और पर्वत क्षेत्र से निःसृत सदा नीरा जल धाराओं के जल प्रबंधन के लिये चर्चित रहा है।

भानपुरा अंचल के उत्तर और उत्तर पूर्व में पसरी प्राकृतिक पर्वतमाला जो विन्ध्यान समूह की श्रेणियाँ है, इनमें बारह माह जल से सम्पन्न रहने वाले निर्झरों के जल को बंधान बनाकर, रोका जाकर राजस्व व वन्य भूमि की हरीतिमा बनाई रखी जाती थी। इन निर्झरों से निःसृत जल धाराओं को झर के नाम से जाना जाता है। अंचल की प्रमुख झरों में आम्बाझर, गोलम्बा झर, बॉदरा झर, देवझर, नरसिंहझर, आमझरी, पीरखोह, चिब्बड़ नाला की माता झर प्रसिद्ध है।

अंचल के प्रमुख तालाब

१. संधारा का रामसर तालाब

२. सांवत कोटड़ी का तालाब

३. गढ़ी का तालाब

४. धांगा बगचांच का फूटा तालाब

५. नीमथूर का तालाब

६. कॅवला का फूल ताल

७. पिपल्दा का तालाब

८. बिल्ली खोह तालाब भानपुरा

९. कैथूली का तालाब

१०. रातागुराड़िया का तालाब

११. रायपुरिया का तालाब

इन्ही के साथ साथ सुजानपुरा, बम्बोरी, मोड़ी कुणा, गंगपुरा, मलासरी की देवपुश्करणी, सरवन का तालबा, सेठा, बर्रामा और बढ़ोद के मध्ययुगीन तालाब प्रसिद्ध थे जो गांधीसागर जलाशय में जल मग्न हो चुके है।

संधारा का रामसर तालाब

तहसील मुख्यालय भानपुरा से १६ कि.मी. दूर रामगंजमण्डी मार्ग पर ऐतिहासिक ग्राम संधारा अवस्थित हैं। इस ग्राम के पश्चिम में १३ वीं सदी का बना रामसर तालाब हैं जो पश्चिम के पहाड़ पर बसे रामगढ़ के भील राजा "रामा" द्वारा बनाया गया था। ऐसा लोक विश्वास है। यह तालाब मुख्यतः पहाड़ से निकले नाले के पानी को रोककर बनाया गया था। तालाब की विस्तृत पाल पर हरदोलजी, पीर के थानक और पुराने सुफियों की मजारें बनी है। इमली, वट, पीपल, जामुन व आम के वृक्ष इसकी ऐतिहासिकता बयान कर रहे है। मध्यकाल में यह २.५ कि.मी. लम्बा व लगभग इतनी ही चौड़ाई में विस्तृत था। १२ माह जल से परिपूर्ण रहता था। इस तालाब से विस्तृत क्षेत्र में सिंचाई होती थी। यहां अनाज का बडी मात्रा में उत्पादन होता था। इसीलिए संधारा एक व्यापारिक नगर के रूप में अनाज की मण्डी होकर प्रसिद्ध था। फ्रांसीसी यात्री ट्रैवरनियर ने इसका उल्लेख किया है।

तालाब के किनारे नील के होदे बने थे । जिनसे नील निकाली जाती थी। ब्रिटिश काल में भी इस तालाब से सिंचाई की जाकर गन्ना, जूट, तम्बाकू, अनाज का उत्पादन किया जाता था। यह तालाब संधारा के आर्थिक विकास का आधार था।

सन् १६१७ ई.वीं. मे फरवरी माह में मुगल सम्राट जहांगीर ने अजमेर से मालवा अभियान के दौरान इस तालाब के किनारे शाही केम्प लगाया था। साथ में नूरजहां भी थी। उसने **तुजुक ए जहाँगीरी** में इसका उल्लेख किया है।

इस तालाब की देखरेख के लिये ग्राम प्रमुख चौधरी, भूमिहीन डाकोटिया, (नाथपंथी) परिवार व ग्राम बलाई तैनात थे। ये पानी के बंटवारे व सिंचाई से होने वाली उपज की जानकारी रखते थे। पानी का बंटवारा धौरों द्वारा दूर तक होता था। ये धौरे अब विलुप्त हो चुके तालाब भी अतिक्रमण की भेंट चढ़ चुका है।

ग्राम में तेली जाति के बोहरा व सूद पर रूपया देने वाले गिलोची परिवारों का पानी के बंटवारे में दखल था। पानी का ज्ञान रखने वाले गजधरों व सिलावटों का सम्मान होता था।

सावंत कोटड़ी का तालाब

भानपुरा से ३० कि.मी. दूर वनांचल में (नावली से आगे) ड़िंगलाजगढ़ के पास सांवतकोटड़ी नामक ग्राम है। यहां पास-पास दो मध्य युगीन तालाब है। जो श्रृंखला बनाते है। पहले बड़ा ताल भरता है फिर इनके शेष जल से अगला तालाब भरता है। १३ वी १४ वी सदी के बने ये तालाब सामरिक दृष्टि से महत्वपूर्ण रहे है

चन्द्रावतों व मराठों ने ब्रिटिश सेनाओं के लिए सेना के तोपखाने के ढोने, माल असबाब ले जाने वाले हजारों पशुओं के लिए वन में इन्ही दो तालाबों से जल पूर्ति की जाती थी। इनके किनारे रक्षक सैनिकों की तैनाती थी। जिनके लिए कक्ष बने थे जो अवशेष रूप में है।

इनमें कमल, सिंघाड़े खूब होते थे । तालाब की पाल पर बड़े विशाल वृक्ष इसकी ऐतिहासिकता व उपयोग की निरंतरता को प्रकट करते है। सुदृढ़ व विस्तार तथा सामरिक अभिरक्षा की दृष्टि से ये बेजोड़ रहे है। ब्रिटिश व होल्कर सेनाओं के पड़ाव इन्ही के किनारे होते थे। इन्हें कोई प्रदूषित नहीं कर सकता था। चूंकि २४ घंटे यहां पहरेदार नियुक्त थे।

गढ़ी का तालाब - चन्द्रावतों के समय (धावद में आगम्न) इसका जीर्णोद्धार कराया जाकर इसे पक्का व खूबसूरत बनाया गया। गहराई, लम्बाई व चौड़ाई में यह तालाब सांवत के तालाब से दुगना बड़ा है। गहराई १५ पुरूष है । किनारे पर वरूण की प्रतिमा घाट पर लगी है। वीरों के थनक व सती स्तंभ भी पाल पर लगें है । सैन्य दृष्टि से इसका जल सामरिक कार्यो, सैन्य व राजकीय परिवारों के लिए किया जाता था। राजकीय कैम्प के श्रेष्ठियों के लिए तालाब का जल उपयोग में लाया जाता था।

सिंचाई भी की जाती थी व वन्य जीवन भी प्र्याप्त उपलब्ध था। अतः मध्ययुगीन वीरों व सैनिकों को शिकार आदि यहां सहज उपलब्ध था।

धागा बगचांच का फूटा तालाव - सांवत के पास गढ़ी तलाब है वहां से उत्तर में दो कि.मी. दूर यह फूटा तालाब है। इसकी पाल फूट चुकी है। वैसे यह वन प्रांत का सबसे बड़ा तलाव था। जो आज सिमट चुका है। २ कि.मी. लम्बाई में फैला सघन वृक्षावलियों से घिरा, प्रवासी पक्षियों व वन्य जीवन से पूर्ण था। सेनाओं के लिए यह

रिजर्व स्त्रोत के रूप में प्रयुक्त होता था। हिंगलाजगढ़ के सैन्य प्रबन्ध व सेना के लिए यह उपयोग में आता था।

कॅवला का तालाव (फूलताल) - भानपुरा से १० कि.मी. पश्चिम में ऐतिहासिक वैभव से सम्पन्न कॅवला स्थित है। इसका प्राचीन नाम कमलापुर था। इसके आसपास तालाबों तलाइयों की श्रृंखला विद्यमान है। चन्द्रावतों के प्रभावकाल में यह समृद्ध था। महाराणा संग्रामसिंह के काल में कॅवला से नील कमल के बीज मेवाड़ महाराणा द्वारा मंगाये जाने का उल्लेख "**वीर विनोद**" में आता है । जिससे इसका कमलापुर नाम सार्थक सिद्ध होता है। यहां का फूलताल नीलकमल के लिए प्रसिद्ध था। कॅवला परगने में ८४ ग्राम जुड़े थे।

पिपल्दा का तालाव - भानपुरा से १४ कि.मी. दूर पश्चिम में चम्बल के किनारे पिपल्दा ग्राम है। यहां का मध्ययुगीन तालाव कमल, सिंघाड़े व नीलकमल के लिए प्रसिद्ध रहा है। पिपल्दा तालाव का निर्माण गुर्जरों व मीणों द्वारा कराया गया । भीलों व कहारों का इस पर लम्बे समय तक नियंत्रण रहा । इससे सिंचाई भी होती थी।

बिल्लीखोह तालाब (भानपुरा) - भानपुरा के ईशानकोण में पहाड़ की तलहटी में १५ वीं सदी का तालाब बना है । बेल वृक्षों की बहुतायत के कारण इसे बिल्ली खोह तालाब कहा जाता है। भीलों के प्रभाव काल में इसका निर्माण हुआ । आज भी भील बस्ती के अवशेष इसके आसपास बिखरे पड़े है। होल्कर शासकों के समय शिकार व पर्यटन तथा जल क्रीड़ा के लिए यह प्रसिद्ध था। इससे सिंचाई भी की जाती थी। पक्का नेस्टा बना है । जिससे झरना बनता है। वन्य जीवन व प्रवासी पक्षियों के लिए यह सुरक्षित स्थल माना जाता था। पर्वत की तलहटी में वर्शा में नयनाभिराम दृश्य बनता है।

कैथूली का तालाब - भानपुरा से २३ कि.मी. दूर उत्तर पूर्व में पर्वत के नीचे प्राचीन ग्राम कैथूली बसा है। पर्वत के झरनों से निकलता जल यहां के तालाब में एकत्र होता है। तालाब के किनारे (मध्ययुगीन चन्द्रावतों) स्मारक बने है।

रातागुराड़िया का तालब - इसका निर्माण १५ वीं सदी में सौधिंया राजपूतों व मीणाओं द्वारा कराया गया । इसकी गहराई १५ पुरूष तक है । प्रवासी पक्षियों व सिंचाई के लिए इसका महत्व है। यह भानपुरा से ४ कि.मी. दक्षिण में स्थित है।

रायपुरिया का तालाब - बाबुल्दा से २ कि.मी. पश्चिम में रायपुरिया का मध्ययुगीन तालाब है । गाम की आबादी के लिए दैनिक कार्यो व पशुओं के लिए पेयजल उपलब्ध कराता है।

अंचल की प्रमुख बावड़ियाँ

(१) महेश्वरी की बावड़ी संधारा, (२) जोगनियां की बावड़ी संधारा, (३) फूटी बावड़ी संधारा, (४) छत्री वाली बावड़ी संधारा, (५) लक्ष्मीनारायण बावड़ी, नोमथूर, (६) खोजी की बावड़ी, नीमथूर, (७) ठगों की बावड़ी भानपुरा, (८) उपाध्याय की बावड़ी भानपुरा, (६) जत्तीजी की बावड़ी भानपुरा, (१०) शिवजी की बावड़ी कैथूली (११) देराणी जेठाणी की बावड़ियां कैथूली, (१२) गणेश जी की बावड़ी भैसोदा, (१३) खातन की बावड़ी खजूरना

इनमें से महेश्वरी की बावड़ी संधारा, जोगन की बावड़ी संधारा, ठग की बावड़ी भानपुरा, अपनी प्राचीनता, उपयोग, व इतिहास की दृश्टि से महत्वपूर्ण है ।

माहेश्वरी की बावड़ी, संधारा

ग्राम संधारा में ग्राम के पशचिम में रामसर के नीचे बनी १८ वी सदी की कलात्मक बावड़ी शिल्प, सुदृढ़ता, अलकृत तिबारियों, स्तम्बों, नक्काशीदार मेहराबों और हिन्दू वास्तुकला के प्रतीको व अलंकरणों से सुसज्जित है। बावड़ी के पास शिवालय है। जिसमें गौरी व गणेश की प्रतिमाऐं थी। जो १६८७ में चोरी हो चुकी है। बावड़ी से बगीचे तक सिचांई होती थी। होज और पक्की नालियां बनी है व परिसर में महेश्वरी परिवार के बुजुर्गो की छत्रियां बनी है। चौकीदार का कक्ष व बाग लगा था। इस बावड़ी का विवाह विशाल कुए से कराया गया था। कुए के मालिक का नाम शाह भीमराज था। इसका उल्लेख वहां लगे शिलालेख से मिलता है।

जोगनिया बावड़ी - संधारा में माहेश्वरी बावड़ी के पास दक्षिण में मठ है जो गुसाई परिवार के पास है। यहां शिलालेख लगा है। इससे शाहजादे औरंगजेब द्वारा गुसाई परिवार को भूमिदान का उल्लेख है। बावड़ी सादी बड़े-बड़े पत्थरों से निर्मित है। इससे सिंचाई होती थी। कहते है संवत ५६ के आकाल में इसी बावड़ी से पानी पूरे गांव को मिलता था।

नीमथूर की बावड़ी - लक्ष्मीनारायण मंदिर के पास १५ वी सदी की बावड़ी है जो मंदिर के पूजा पाठ हेतु जल उपलब्ध कराती है। ग्रामवासी भी इसी से पेयजल प्राप्त करते है। बावड़ी कलात्मक है।

ठगों की बावड़ी भानपुरा - भानपुरा नगर से १ कि.मी. पूर्व में १६ वें सदी की निर्मित ठगों की बावड़ी है। इसमें लेख है। भाषा स्पष्ट है। लेकिन ब्रिटिश अधिकारियों द्वारा ठगों को दण्ड देने का उल्लेख है। ऐसा बावड़ी के वर्तमान मालिक बताते है।

जत्तीजी की बावड़ी, भानपुरा - भानपुरा अंचल की सर्वाधिक महत्वपूर्ण और कलात्मक बावड़ी है। इसका निर्माण पूर्व मध्यकाल में हुआ । इससे जुड़ा शिवालय है। जिसमें विलक्षण शिवलिंग है और नंदी की विशालता इसकी सुदृढ़ता को बयान करती है। बावड़ी से सिंचाई होती थी। इसका निर्माण चौकोर पत्थरों से हुआ है। इसमें नीचे उतरने और पानी लेकर उपर आते व्यक्ति आपस में एक दसरे के बिना टकराये उपर तक जल कलश को ला सकते है। एक समय में १० व्यक्ति अलग-अलग रास्तों से बावडी से जल प्राप्त करते है। इसकी ज्यायमितिय आकृति और समतलता मध्ययुगीन वास्तुकला की श्रेष्टता दर्शाती है । भानपुरा अंचल में यह विशालतम बावड़ी है। वर्तमान में यह जत्ती परिवार के संरक्षण में है।

शेष बावड़ियों का कला, स्थापत्य, शिल्प की दृश्टि से महत्व है। ये हमारी सांस्कृतिक धरोहरें है। जो उपेक्षा की शिकार बनी हुई है।

निष्कर्ष

भानपुरा क्षेत्र में झरों की उचित देखभाल नहीं होने से अतिक्रमण व उपेक्षा के चलते अपना वजूद खोती जा रही है। आज भी ये प्रासंगिक है।

संधारा का रामसर, नीमथूर का तालाब, बिल्ली खोह का तालाब का ऐतिहासिक महत्व है। इनकी पाल पर इनके इतिहास की अंकन किया जाना चाहिये जिससे वर्तमान पीढ़ी को इनके महत्व का ज्ञान हो सकें।

भानपुरा क्षेत्र में तालाबों का उपयोग तीन प्रमुख कार्यो के लिए होता रहा है-

१. सैन्य व सामरिक महत्व - गढ़ी, सांवतकोटड़ी व हिंगलाजगढ़ क्षेत्र के तालाब सदियों से सैन्य काफिले, सेना के पशुओ व वन्य जीवन के लिए बहुआयामी महत्व के रहे है। आज भी इनके उपयोग की निरंतरता इनके कालजयी महत्व को रेखांकित कर रही है।

२. पेयजल व ग्राम्यजीवन के जलस्त्रोत के रूप में कॅवला, रातागुराड़िया बिल्लीखोह, नीमथूर के तालाबों का उपयोग होता रहा । ये आज भी जीवंत है व प्रासंगिक बने है।

३. सिंचाई के लिए - संधारा, रातागुराड़िया, रायपुरिया, कॅवला, कैथूली नावली के तालाब किसानों के लिए किसी वरदान से कम नहीं है।

इनका नियमित गहरीकरण, रखरखाव आवश्यक है। स्थानीय एजेंसियों को प्रशासकीय स्तर पर प्रशिक्षण दिया जाकर इनके सार्थक सांस्कृतिक प्रगति के सोपान रचे जा सकते है।

ये तालाब भानपुरा अंचल की आज भी सांस्कृतिक, सामाजिक सद्भाव, मेलजोल, तीज त्यौहार, पर्व, मेले, उत्सवों के जीवन केन्द्र बने है। अनेक परम्पराओं का अटूट सिलसिला इनसे जुड़ा है। तालाब मानव जीवन के उत्सव है। सांस्कृतिक जीवन के प्राण आधार है। इनकी रक्षा व देखभाल वर्तमान समय की आवश्यकता है।

संदर्भ

१. मालवा में युगांतर - डा. रघुबीरसिंह, पृ. ३३६, ३४०-इन्दौर

२. 'मालवा, मराठा कालीन रियासते, सं. डॉ. शचीन्द्रप्रसाद, पृ.१६०, १७५

३. मन्दसौर डि. गजेटियर, पृ. ३, भोपाल

४. मंदसौर डि. गजेटियर पृ. १२, २४, २५, भोपाल

५. आज भी खरे है तालाब - अनुपम मिश्र, पृ. २६, भोपाल

६. तुजुक-ए-जहागीरी - अनु. मथूरालाल शर्मा, पृ.१७१, १७२, भोपाल

७. भानपुरा पर्यटन विवरणिका - प्रद्युम्न भट्ट, पृ. ३ से ८

८. भीमसागर का शिलालेख

६. भानपुरा पर्यटन विवरणिका - प्रद्युम्न भट्ट, पृ. ५ से ८, भानपुरा

१०. भानपुरा पर्यटन विवरणिका - प्रद्युम्न भट्ट, पृ. ५ से १०, भानपुरा

११. मन्दसौर - जलाभिषेक रिपोर्ट २००३, मंदसौर

१२. वीर वीनोद - भाग दो, खण्ड दो- कविराजाश्यामल दास पृ. ६६०-६६१, वाराणासी

१३. भानपुरा पर्यटन विवरणिका - प्रद्युम्न भट्ट, भानपुरा १६६२

१४. भानपुरा पर्यटन विवरणिका - प्रद्युम्न भट्ट, भानपुरा १६६२

१५. जोगनिया बावड़ी का शिलालेख

१६. भानपुरा की बावड़िया लेख

१७. आज भी खरे है तालाब - अनुपम मिश्र पृ. ५६

१८. आज भी खरे है तालाब - अनुपम मिश्र पृ. ५५ से ५७

रायसेन दुर्ग की मध्यकालीन जलसंग्रहण प्रणाली

डॉ. ममता चंसोरिया

रायसेन के किले की मस्जिद, जो बारादरी के पास स्थित है में हमें एक फारसी अभिलेख प्राप्त होता है जिसकी तिथि ८९० हिजरी है।[१] जो इस दुर्ग पर मुस्लिम अधिकार की पुष्टि करता है।[२] एक अन्य अभिलेख में स्थानीय सरदार सिलहदी को सलाहदादु नाम से अंकन मिलता है।[३] १५४२ में रायसेन क्षेत्र एवं किला सिलहदी के पुत्र पूरनमल के आधीन आ गए। बाद में शेरशाह ने उस पर अधिकार कर लिया। अकबर के काल में रायसेन को सरकार में शामिल कर ३१ महालों में उपविभाजित कर दिया गया।[४]

जलसंग्रहण हेतु रायसेन दुर्ग में अनेक ताल एवं कुएं तो है हीं साथ ही अत्यन्त अनूठी एवं वैज्ञानिक जलसंग्रहण की प्रणाली भी देखने को मिलती है। पूरे रायसेन जिले में जल की प्रचुरता का कारण यहाँ की पौराणिक बेत्रवती (बेतवा) नदी रायसेन से १४ कि. मी. दूर पश्चिम में भोपाल मार्ग एवं उत्तर में विदिशा मार्ग से प्रवाहित होती है। नर्मदा नदी जिले के दक्षिण - पूर्वी सीमा के साथ-साथ बहती है।[५] साथ ही रायसेन जिला दो बड़ी नदियों गंगा एवं नर्मदा की अप्रवाह् द्रोणियों में स्थित है।[६]

इस तरह रायसेन के दुर्ग की जो स्थिति हम देखते है उसमें जल का बाहुल्य दो कारणों से हम पाते हैं --

१. वर्षा काल में पहाड़ की भौगोलिक स्थिति के कारण ऊपर से बहकर आने वाला जल (Surface flow on hills)

२. भूमि के अंदर स्थित जलधारा (Underground Spring)

रायसेन दुर्ग के ताल

राजा रोहिणी महल अथवा रानी महलः-

१. इस महल के सामने एक विशाल ताल है जो रानी ताल कहलाता है। यह ताल बावड़ी की तरह निर्मित है। इसकी योजना वर्गाकार है। इस ताल में छतरियों का

निर्माण भी किया गया है। इस ताल में पत्थर सीढ़ियाँ भी बनी हुई है। इसका निर्माण तत्कालीन सामग्री एवं ईंट गारे के द्वारा किया गया था।

मंदागंज तालः-

शिव मंदिर के झरोखे से दिखाई देने वाला मंदागंज ताल।[७] जनश्रुति है कि इस ताल में पारसमणि है। यह ताल काफी विस्तृत एवं वृहद चौकोर आकार का है एक बार इसे ढूढ़ने हेतु हाथियों को चेन बांधकर इस ताल मे उतारा गया जिसमे उनकी चेन तो सोने की हो गई किंतु पारसमणि नही मिली। यह ताल तत्समय जल संग्रहण का प्रमुख स्त्रोत था।

जौहर कुंड तालः-

सलहदी की पत्नी जो कि राणा सांगा की पुत्री थी, दुर्गावती ने सात सौ स्त्रियों के साथ जौहर करने के पूर्व इस कुण्ड मे स्नान किया था।[८]

हम्मामः-

हम्माम के निर्माण की परंपरा भारत मे मुसलमानों के आगमन से प्रारंभ होती है। हम्माम बारादरी के पृष्ठ भाग में स्थित है। हम्माम में प्रवेशद्वार मेहराबदार है। कुछ सीढ़ियों के पश्चात एक छोटा सा कक्ष है जिसमें निकास नालियाँ बनी है। इस कक्ष में एक टैंक बना है, जो गरम पानी के लिए इस्तेमाल किया जाता रहा होगा। हम्माम मे टैंक के पास एक छोटी सी खिड़की बनी है तथा पृष्ठ भाग में भट्टी के अवशेष है। हम्माम मे पानी का स्त्रोत पृष्ठ भाग में स्थित धोबी ताल से है यह ताल वर्तमान में पानी से भरा रहता है।[९]

पीने के पानी की जलसंग्रहण प्रणालीः-

बारादरी भवन मे जसंग्रहण की अनूठी प्रणाली के साक्ष्य आज भी देखे जा सकते है। बारादरी भवन जो कि मस्जिद (पामिका) के पास है। यहीं पास में एक बाग भी है। मस्जिद के पास एक कब्र है। यहाँ एक फारसी अभिलेख अंकित है कि मस्जिद, बाग एवं कब्र का निर्माण मलिक रादी जो मालिक छज्जू का पुत्र ा, ने करवाया था। बारादरी भवन की छत को एक ओर ढलान देकर बनाया गया है। इस ढलुआ छत पर पानी एक मिट्टी के बाहर निकले पाइप (Outlet pipe) द्वारा एकत्रित होकर नीचे गिरता था।[१०]

छत से पानी गिरकर भूतल पर स्थित पुनः ढलुआ (Slop) आयताकार पक्के चबूतरेनुमा फर्श पर गिरता था।

एक बड़े से छिद्र से नाली द्वारा एक नीचे स्थित टैंक में इकट्ठा होता था।

इस टैंक की क्षमता (Capacity) काफी ज्यादा है। यही अन्दर स्थित टैंक का (Underground Tank) पानी नीचे-नीचे ही दूसरें टैंक में इकट्ठा हो जाता था।

भूमिगत पाइप लाइन एवं गुरुत्वाकर्षण शक्ति द्वारा एकत्रित जल का किले के रिहायशी स्थलों में पहुँचना संभव था। उपर्युक्त दोनों ही टैंक काफी गहरे है जिसमें वर्ष भर पीने के जल का एकत्रीकरण किया जा सकता है।

निष्कर्षतः- हमने रायसेन की भौगोलिक स्थिति मे देखा कि ऊपर की वर्षा के जल के संग्रहण की प्रणाली एवं ताल तथा कुओं के निर्माण द्वारा भी जलसंरक्षण का कार्य यहां किया गया। इन तालों की गहराई काफी अधिक है। साथ ही अंदर के पानी के रिसाव को भी इकट्ठा इन तालों में किया गया। क्योंकि यह क्षेत्र बेतवा के पास है जिसकी सहायक नदियाँ, कलियासोत, अजनाल, रिछन, डाबर हलाली आदि है। अतः अंदर से भी पानी का रिसाव इन तालों मे होता था। रायसेन दुर्ग मे संग्रहित जल के दो उपयोग हम देखते है।

१. स्नान एवं दैनिक उपयोग तथ धार्मिक उद्देश्य के लिए तालों के जल का उपयोग।

२. पीने के लिए वर्षा के जल के एकत्रीकरण की प्रणाली द्वारा संग्रहित जल का उपयोग होता था।

यदि हम रायसेन दुर्ग की जल संग्रहण की प्रणाली की मध्ययुग की अन्य जल संग्रहण की प्रणालियों से तुलना करें तो उसमे सर्वप्रथम बुरहानपुर की जलसंग्रहण प्रणाली सर्वथा अनूठी है।

अकबर ने जलसंग्रहण एवं उसके महलों में प्रयोग के नए तरीके को इजाद किया पार्शियन व्हील की पद्धति में उसने पानी के न केवल सिंचाई अपितु ऊपर चढ़ाने हेतु वर्तमान साइकिल जैसी ही चैन लगवाई थी।[11]

Zig-Zag नहरों का प्रयोग खेतों में किया जाता था ताकि यह पानी खेतों में पहुँच सके। पानी नीचे के स्थलों से एक निश्चित ऊँचाई पर ले जाया जाता था। (Carried To a Height)

अकबर के समय के जलसंग्रहण एवं उसके उपयोग की प्रणाली की प्रमुख विशेषताएं थी --

* पार्शियन व्हील

* गियरिंग व्यवस्था (Gearing System)
* डक्ट (Duct)
* Zig-Zag नहरों का प्रयोग
* गुरूत्वाकर्षण शक्ति (Gravitational Force) से पानी नीचे के क्षेत्रों (Low lying places) में पहुचाया जाता था।

संदर्भ

१. भोपाल स्टेट गजेटियर सी. ई. लुआर्ड, भाग ३ कलकत्ता १६०८ - एवं जिला गजेटियर रायसेन, पी. एन. श्रीवास्तव, संस्कृति विभाग म. प्र. भोपाल प्रथम संस्करण पृष्ठ ३३६ रायसेन भोपाल से ४५ कि. मी. की दूरी पर भोपाल सागर राष्ट्रीय राजमार्ग पर अवस्थित है। रायसेन का किला तीन ओर से प्राकृतिक स्थिति में सुरक्षित है किंतु सुरक्षा की दृष्टि से किले का पश्चिमी भाग जो रामछज्जा पहाड़ी, क्षेत्र से जुड़ा हुआथा उसे काटकर किले से पृथक किया गया एवं घाटी का रूप दिया गया।

   रायसेन राजवासिनी या राजप्रासाद का अपभ्रंश है। यहाँ गोंड शासक रायसिंह ने शासन किया था। उसी के नाम पर यह नगर रायसेन नाम से विख्यात हुआ।

२. भोपाल स्टेट गजेटियर पृ. २०६-२१०

३. एपीग्रा .इण्डिका १६३३ - ३४ पृ. २४-२६ अभिलेख संख्या २४६।

४. इलियट डाउसन हिस्ट्री ऑफ इण्डिया किताब महल इलाहाबाद १६७५ जिल्द ४ पृ. ४६- १५ फरवरी १५२६ का दुर्ग में एकअभिलेख है जिसमें सिलहदी को सलाहदादु अंकित हुआ मिलता है। ये तोमर राजपूत थे जो पुरवैय्या कहलाते थे। आज भी रायसेन नगर में पुरवैय्या मुहल्ला है। रायसेन के किले के सरदार सिलहदी ने ३०,००० घुड़सवारों के साथ राणा सांगा को खानवा के युद्ध में सहायता दी थी।

५. एन एटलस ऑफ द मुगल एम्पायर-इरफान हबीब देलही ऑक्सफोर्ड यूनिवर्सिटी प्रेस ऑक्सफोर्ड, न्यूयार्क १६८२, पृ ३४ एवं घ्गजेटियर ऑफ मध्यप्रदेश, सीहोर एण्ड भोपाल, पी. एन. श्रीवास्तव, एस. डी. गुरू १६८६ पृ. ४४-

   अकबर के काल में हिन्दुस्तान के सुदृढ़ बुर्जो मे इसकी गणना की जाती थी अकबर ने रायसेन के किले मे मरम्मत हुतु ख्वाजा बहाउद्दीन, मुहम्मद, हाजी

मुहम्मद, अनूप राय, मुहम्मद मंसूर, मुहम्मद अबिद खान ए - दुर्रानी, गंगाराम (मुख्य मिस्त्री) द्वारा करवाया था, जिसका उल्लेख दुर्ग के उत्तरी दरवाज़े पर अंकित अभिलेख से मिलता है।

६. जिला गजेटियर रायसेन पी. एन. श्रीवास्तव, संस्कृति विभग प्रथम संस्करण पृ. १

७. वही पृ. ८-६

८. सर्वेक्षण पर आधरित

६. सर्वेक्षण पर आधरित

१०. बी. एन. मिश्रा द हिल फोर्ट ऑफ रायसेन प्राच्य प्रतिभा भाग ६-१० पृ. ८६।

११. अकबर, इरफान हबीब ऑक्सफोर्ड यूनिवर्सिटी प्रेस दिल्ली १६६७ पृ. १३६

महाराणा राजसिंह कालीन जल प्रबन्धन

डॉ. उषा पुरोहित

महाराणा राजसिंह का औरंगजेब से युद्ध होने के पूर्व तक (ई. सन् १६६२ से १६७६ ई.) का काल मेवाड़ के इतिहास मे शांति व समृद्धि का काल रहा। इसी काल में महाराणा ने राजसमुद्र झील का निर्माण करवाया था। आज भी यह झील राजसिंह के स्वर्णमय युग की याद दिलाती है। इसके निमार्ण से सम्बन्धित अनेक रोचक व महत्वपूर्ण तथ्य इतिहास में वर्णित है उनका यहाँ उल्लेख करना उचित प्रतीत होता है।

राजनगर के निकट दो पहाड़ियों के मध्य गोमती नाम की एक नदी बहती थी इस नदी के पानी को रोक कर एक विशाल तालाब बनाने की योजना महाराणा अमरसिंह प्रथम ने बनाई थी और उसने बांध बनवाने का कार्य भी आरंम्भ कर दिया था, किन्तु नदी के तेज वेग के कारण यह बांध स्थायी नहीं रह सका था।[1]

राजसिंह अपने युवराज पद में जैसलमेर के रावल मनोहरदास की पुत्री कृष्णकुँवरी से विवाह करने जैसलमेर गया। विवाह कर वापिस लौटते समय उसने राजनगर पर पड़ाव किया था। वर्षाऋतु होने के कारण गोमती नदी में बहाव काफी तेज था। उस समय राजसिंह ने गोमती नदी के पानी को रोक कर एक विशाल तालाब बनाने के लिए सोचा था।[2]

इस तालाब की परिधि में सोलह गाँवों की सीमा आ जाती थी।[3]

१६६१ ई. नवम्बर में महाराणा राजसिंह ने राज्यासीन होने के बाद रूपनारायण की यात्रा की। रूपनारायण का मन्दिर उदयपुर से लगभग ५३ मील उतर दिशा मे स्थित है। इस यात्रा से लौटते समय राजसिंह पुनः राजनगर में ठहरा। वहाँ उसने पुनः गोमती नदी के वेग को देखा, जिससे उसकी पुरानी स्मृति जाग उठी। उसने अब इस नदी के पानी को रोकने हेतु बांध बनवाने का मन में निश्चय किया।[4]

राजसमुद्र झील के सम्बन्ध मे एक यह बात भी प्रचलित है कि राजसिंह ने एक पुरोहित, एक राणी, एक कुँवर और एक चारण को मार दिया था, अतः ब्राह्मणों की

सम्मति से इन नृशंस हत्याओं के प्रायश्चित के रूप में राणा ने इस विशाल तालाब को बनाने का निर्णय लिया था।[5]

ई. स. १६६१-६२ के वर्ष में उदयपुर राज्य में भंयकर अकाल पड़ा। मेवाड़ी जनता भूख के मारे पूर्णतया संतृस्त थी[6] महाराणा राजसिंह ने राजसमुद्र झील के निर्माण का संकल्प तो पहले से ही कर रखा था, अतः अब भंयकर दुर्भिक्ष से पीड़ित लोगों की सहायता करने हेतु उक्त संकल्प को उसने तुरन्त मूर्तरूप में परिणित कर दिया।

गोमती नदी के जल को एकत्रित करने हेतु अनेक स्थानों पर बांध बनवाना आवश्यक था। राजसमुद्र के बांध की नींव खुदाई का कार्य वि. सं. १७१८ माघ बदि ७ (ई. सं. १६६२ ता. १ जनवरी) को प्रारम्भ हुआ। यहाँ हजारों मजदूर काम करते थे। कार्य की विशालता को देखकर राणा ने इस कार्य की पूर्ति हेतु अनेक विभाग बनाये और प्रत्येक विभाग पर अनुभवी व विशाल पात्र सरदार को नियुक्त किया, जो कार्य को सूचारू रूप से पूर्ण करवा सके।[7]

गोमती नदी के किनारों पर स्थित दोनों पहाड़ो के मध्य बाँध बनाने का कार्य आरम्भ हुआ। परिणामस्वरूप लगभग तीन मील लम्बा एवं डेढ़ मील चौड़ा सागर बना।

धनुषाकृति में निर्मित इस बाँध में लगभग १६५ वर्ग मील भूमि का जल एकत्रित होता है।[8] इस विशद् बाँध की दृढ़ता के स्थायी रखने के उद्देश्य से पक्की नींव लगाई गई। लेकिन नींव लगाने के समय जलाधिक्य के कारण समस्या का सामना करना पड़ा। अतः अनेक अरहटों द्वारा जल निकालने का कार्य किया गया एवं शुष्क भूमि में दृढ नींव स्थापित की गई।[5] सौन्दर्य का भी ध्यान रखा गया। पूरे बाँध पर राजनगर की खानों में उपलब्ध संगमरमर के पत्थर का प्रयोग किया गया। नीवं की खुदाई व पाल पर मिट्टी डालने का कार्य पूर्ण हो जाने पर श्रावणदि वि. सं. १७२१ (चैत्रादि १७२२) वैशाख सुदि १३, ई. सन् १६६५ ता. १७ अप्रेल को पुरोहित गरीबदास के पुत्र रणछोड़राय के हाथ से पंचरत्न सहित नीवं का पत्थर डाला गया और शुभ मुहुर्त में चुनाई का कार्य आरम्भ हुआ। आषाढ़ सुदि ४ ई. सन् १६७१ ता. ३० जून को इस जलाशय में नाव का मुहूर्त किया गया।[9] बांध के बन जाने पर गोमती, ताल (ताली) और केलवा की नदियों का पानी इनमें एकत्रित होने लगा।[10]

ई. सन् १७७६ में राजसमुद्र झील का निर्माण कार्य पूर्ण हुआ और इसी वर्ष १४ जनवरी को इसकी प्रतिष्ठा का कार्य आरम्भ किया गया।[11]

महाराणा राजसिंह के द्वारा राजसमुद्र झील के निर्माण के अतिरिक्त मेवाड़ की जनता के लिए सिंचाई-व्यवस्था के लिए इस पहाड़ी नगर में अपने शासन काल में समय-समय पर जल प्रबन्धन हेतु कुएँ व बावड़ियों व तालाबों का भी निर्माण करवाया, उनका यहाँ उल्लेख किया जा रहा है :- महाराणा राजसिंह ने अपने कुँवरपदें में ही उदयपुर नगर के अग्निकोण में स्थित कर्ण बावड़ी के समीप सर्वऋतु-विलास नामक महल और बावड़ी युक्त बाग का निर्माण करवाया।[९२]

वि.सं. १७१६ (ई. सन् १६५६) में देबारी के घाटे का कोट और दरवाजा तैयार करवाया करवाया तथा पास में बावड़ी और छोटा तालाब बनवाया।[९३]

वि. सं. १७१७ (ई. सन् १६६०) में महाराणा राजसिंह के काल में खवासणा सुन्दर ने उदयपुर से २११ मील ईशान कोण में पारडा ग्राम के पास एक सुन्दर बावड़ी बनवाई। इसकी प्रतिमा पर महाराणा ने न्यास गोविन्दराम व व्यास बलभद्र के भवाण ग्राम में ७५ बीघा जमीन दी। इस भूमि पर गोविन्दराम की मात ने बावड़ी कराई तथा यात्रियों की सुविधा के लिए एक सराय बनवाई।[९४]

वि. सं. १७२१ मार्गशीर्ष कृष्ण १०,१६६६ ई. ता. १५ नवम्बर को महाराणा राजसिंह ने अपनी माता राठौड़ राजसिंह मेड़तिया की बेटी और महाराणा जगतसिंह की रानी जनादे बाईजी राज (राजमाता) के नाम से तालाब बनाने का मुहूर्त बड़ी नामक ग्राम में किया, और वि० सं० १७२५ माघ शुक्ल १०, ई. १६६९ त. ११ फरवरी को प्रतिष्ठा करके उसका नाम 'जना-सागर' रखा। यह तालाब उदयपुर से वायव्य (उत्तरी-पश्चिमी) कोण में छः मील के फासले पर स्थित है।[९५]

वि. सं. १७२५ (ई सन् १६६८) में महाराणा राजसिंह के पुत्र कुंवर जयसिंह ने पीछोला तालाब के उतर अम्बावगढ़ के नीचे उदयपुर के पास रंग-सागर नामक तालाब बनवाया और उसकी प्रतिष्ठा के समय भी बहुत सा दान पुण्य किया।[९६]

वि. सं. १७२५ वैशाख शुक्ल ६ (ई. सन् १६६९ ता० २६ अप्रेल) को महाराणा राजसिंह के मन्त्री फतहचन्द ने बेड़वास गाँव में एक बावड़ी क निर्माण करवाया। इस बावडी के सामने एक सराय व एक महल भी बनवाया। इस बावडी के संलग्न १३ बीघों में एक सुन्दर उद्यान की व्यवस्था की गई। बावडी का पानी मीठा व आरोग्यवर्द्धक था।[९७]

महाराणा राजसिंह की रानियों ने भी प्रजा हित के लिए जल प्रबन्धन में बावड़ियों का निर्माण करवा कर अपना योगदान दिया। इनमें प्रमुखतः किशनगढ के राजा रूपसिंह की बेटी चारूमती महारानी राठौड़ ने वि. सं. १७३२ माघ शुक्ल ७ (ई. सं. १६७६

ता. १२ जनवरी) को राजनगर ग्राम के पश्चिम दिशा में सफेद पत्थर की बावड़ी बनवायी।[१८] और वि० सं० १७३२ (ई० सं० १६७५) में महारानी पंवार रामरसदेबाई ने देबारी के भीतर झरना सराय के निकट 'त्रिमुखी बावड़ी' का निर्माण करवाया।[१९]

महाराणा राजसिंह के काल में ही एकलिंगजी के पास स्थित इन्द्रसर (सरोवर) का जीर्णोद्धार किया गया। पुराने बांध के स्थान पर नये बांध के बनवाने की व्यवस्था की गई।

महाराणा राजसिंह द्वारा जब राजसमुद्र झील का निर्माण कार्य प्रारम्भ किया गया तब पुरोहित गरीबदास ने महाराणा कि सलाह दी थी कि इस झील के निर्माण काल में मुगल बादशाह से किसी प्रकार युद्ध नहीं होना चाहिए। यदि मुगलों से युद्ध हो गया तो यह जनोपयोगी कार्य सम्पूर्ण नहीं हो सकेगा।[२०] महाराणा इन विचारों से पूर्णतया सम्बन्ध बनाये रखने के लिए सतत् प्रयत्न किया, जिसके परिणामस्वरूप उसके काल में शान्ति रही और अनेक जन-कल्याण के कार्य सम्पत किये जा सके। जलाशय, बावड़ी, बगीचे, सराय आदि केवल राज्य की ओर से ही नहीं निर्मित किये गये वरन् राणियो, सभासदो, अनुचरो व सम्पन्न व्यक्तियों ने भी इस लोक-कल्याण के कार्य में हाथ बंटाया।

नव - निर्मित जलाशयों, बावड़ियों आदि से कृषि हेतु सिंचाई के लिए पानी दिया जाने लगा, जिससे उपज में वृद्धि हुई। राज्य में सर्वत्र सुरक्षा व व्यापारियों को राजमार्गो पर ठहरने आदि की सुविधाओं के फलस्वरूप व्यापार में उन्नति होना स्वाभाविक ही था। मेवाड़ में यह स्थिति ई. सं. १६७८ (औरंगजेब के युद्ध से पूर्व तक तक बनी रहीं।)

सन्दर्भ

१. मान - राजविलास, विलास ८, पद्य ११०

२. (अ) वीर विनोद, भागः २, खण्ड - १, पृ. ४४४.

(ब) राजप्रशस्ति, सर्ग-६, श्लोक- ३ और ७

३. (अ) वहीं, पृ. ४४५

(ब) वही, सर्ग, ६, श्लोक - ५-६, सोलह गांवों के नाम इस प्रकार है :-

घोयन्दा, सनवाड़, सिवाली, भिगावदा, मोरचणा, पसूंद, खेड़ी, छापर, खेडी, तासोल, मंडावर, भांण, लुहाणा, बंसोल, गुढली, कांकरोली और मढा।

४. मान - राजविलास, विलास - ८, पद्य ४, १११, ११२

५. वीर विनोद, भाग २, खण्ड - १, पृ. ४४४ - ४५

६. मान राजविलास, विलास ८, में कविमान ने इस दुर्भिक्ष का बड़ा मार्मिक वर्णन किया है:-

"विकल भयै नर अन्न बिनु, भूखहिं अभख भखंत ।

कंत तज़त निज कामिनी , कामिनी तजत सुकंत" ।।५।।

"मात पिता हूँ निठुर मन, बेचत बालक बाल।

ररबरि रंक करंक परि, दिसि दिसि रौर दुकाल" ।।६।।

७. राजप्रशस्ति, सर्ग ६, श्लोक - २१ -

८. (अ) जी.एन. शर्मा', राजस्थान का इतिहास, पृ. ५६६

(ब) राजसमुद्र और राजस्थान की १७ वीं श. की संस्कृति और समाज, शोध पत्रिका, भाग - ६, अंक - ३, पृ. ५४

६. राजप्रशस्ति, सर्ग - १०, श्लोक - २२-३०, वीर विनोद, पृ. ४४८

१०.वहीं, सर्ग - १२, श्लोक - ६

११.वहीं, सर्ग - १४ श्लोक - १३, मान - राजविलास, विलास ८, द्य १५४-५५,

"सुप्रतिष्ठा कीन सत दह संवत बतीसै उतम बरसै १ -- ।। १५४।।

मासोतम माह रच्यौ सु महोत्सव पोवन आये देवपती ।।१५५।।"

१२.वीर विनोद, पृ. ४४३ और ४७६',

१३.वहीं, पृ. ४७६, राजप्रशस्ति, पर्ग - ८, श्लोक २६-२८,

१४.वीर विनोद, भाग - २, खण्ड-१, पृ. ५७८। इस बावड़ी पर उत्कीर्ण प्रशस्ति।

१५.वीर विनोद, पृ. ६३५ - ३६, बड़ी के तालाब की प्रशस्ति।

१६.(अ) राजप्रशस्ति, सर्ग - ८, श्लोक ५१-५२

(ब) वीर विनोद, पृ. ४४८

१७.वहीं, पृ. ३८१-८३, बेडवास की बावड़ी की प्रशस्ति। यह बावड़ी उदयपुर से देबारी की तरफ जाने वाले मार्ग पर बनी हुई है।

१८.(अ) वहीं, पृ. ४४६', (ब) राजप्रशस्ति, सर्ग - १४, श्लोक - ११-१२,

१६.वहीं, पृ. ५५४ और ६३८ - ६४०, त्रिमुखी बावडी की प्रशस्ति।

२०.वीर विनोद, भाग - २, खण्ड - १, पृ. ४४४.

सागर का ऐतिहासिक तालाब : मध्ययुगीन भारत में जल प्रबंधन का एक सशक्त उदाहरण

डॉ. बी.के. श्रीवास्तव

सागर के तालाब के आगे ऐतिहासिक इसलिये जोड़ा गया है कि यदि यह तालाब न निर्मित किया जाता तो आज सागर का अस्तित्व भी शायद ही होता। यदि मिस्त्र नील नदी का उपहार है तो सागर लाखा बन्जारा तालाब का उपहार है। इस तालाब को लाखा बन्जारा तालाब इसलिये कहा जाता है क्योंकि इस तालाब के निर्माण का श्रेय उसी को जाता है। लाखा बन्जारा, बन्जारों का मुखिया था। इसे लाखा बन्जारा इसलिये कहा जाता था क्योंकि उसके पास एक लाख के लगभग बैल थे।[१] ये बन्जारे १६०० ई. के लगभग सागर[२] क्षेत्र में नमक एवं गुड़ का व्यापार करने आया करते थे।[३] यह क्षेत्र उस समय पानी की कमी से जूझ रहा था।[३]

जिस स्थान पर वर्तमान तालाब बना हुआ है एवं नगर बसा हुआ है उसे तीन ओर से विन्ध्य पर्वत माला घेरे हुए है।[४] चूँकि इस क्षेत्र में पहाड़ियाँ, ककरीली, पथरीली, रांकड़ जमीन है, अतः वर्षा का पानी ठहरता नहीं है और शीघ्र बह जाता है। यहाँ की जमीन शीघ्रता से पानी भी नहीं सोखती। यहाँ औसत वर्षा ११०० से १२०० मि. मी. के मध्य होती है।[५] चूँकि विन्ध्य शैल चट्टानों में जल संचय क्षमता अत्यधिक कम होती है अतः गरमी के मौसम में यह क्षेत्र पानी की कमी से जूझता है।[६]

छोटी-छोटी पहाड़ियों से घिरे सागर क्षेत्र में लाखा बन्जारा अपना पड़ाव डालता था। गर्मी के मौसम में बन्जारों के बैल पानी की कमी के कारण व्याकुल रहते थे। येन-केन प्रकारेण बन्जारे अपने बैलों की प्यास कुओं से पानी खींच कर शांत करते थे।[७] कुँए इस क्षेत्र में जल आपूर्ति का प्रमुख साधन थे। इन कुओं की गहराई ८ से २० फुट तक रहती थी। कठोर शैल वाला क्षेत्र होने के कारण कभी-कभी ये कुँए भी गरमी के मौसम में सूख जाते हैं।[८]

ह्यूरोज ने लिखा था कि - '**सागर का जबलपुर से अधिक महत्व है**। सेन्ट्रल इंडिया की तो यह आयुध शाला ही है जहाँ शस्त्रादि बनाए जाते हैं..... यहीं नहीं

सागर की स्थिति ऐसी है कि वह मध्य में है तथा पश्चिम से उत्तर-पूर्व एवं दक्षिण भारत के लिये संचार साधनों का यह माध्यम है। मंदसौर, कोटा, कालपी, लखनऊ के विद्रोही झाँसी से रीवा तक फैले हैं। **सागर ही ऐसा मुकाम है जहाँ पर सेन्ट्रल इंडिया की रियासती फौजें तथा ब्रिटिश सेना एकत्रित होकर विद्रोहियों का विनाश कर सकती है।**'[९] सागर की महत्वपूर्ण भौगोलिक स्थिति को दर्शाने वाला यह पत्र ह्यूरोज ने २१ दिसम्बर १८५७ को ब्रिटिश सरकार को लिखा था।

सागर ही नहीं समूचा बुन्देलखण्ड पानी की कमी से जूझता रहा है। ऋतु विज्ञानियों ने इसे अनिश्चितकालीन वर्षा वाला क्षेत्र माना है। इस क्षेत्र में नदियाँ भी है। बुन्देलखण्ड में प्रवाहित होने वाली दस नदियों के कारण पूर्व काल में इस भू-भाग को दर्शाण भी कहा जाता था।[१०]

पानी की कमी से निजात पाने के लिये बुन्देलखण्ड के चन्देल शासकों ने जल प्रबंधन की दिशा में महत्वपूर्ण प्रयास किये।[११] चन्देल राजाओं ने दक्षिणी बुन्देलखण्ड में बेतवा से केन नदियों के मध्य शुष्क, लम्बे, अविकसित क्षेत्र की वर्षाती सतही जल संग्रहण योजना बनाई। वर्षा का बहता पानी रोकने के भरपूर प्रयास किये।[१२] चन्देल शासकों ने अनावृष्टि से उबरने के लिये अनेक तालाबों का निर्माण कराया। चूँकि बुन्देलखण्ड एक पहाड़ी प्रदेश है एवं यहाँ तालाब निर्माण के सभी साधन सुलभ है। प्रत्येक मंदिर के साथ एक तालाब का निर्माण एक नियम सा बन गया था।[१३] चन्देल राजाओं ने कई तालाबों का निर्माण कराया, कुछ तालाबों का नाम तो राजाओं के नाम पर ही रखा गया है। चन्देल नरेश राहिल्य वर्मन ने सर्वाधिक तालाबों का निर्माण कराया। बाँदा से २६ मील दूर पहाड़ी पर स्थित रसिन ग्राम में अनेक सरोवरों का निर्माण कराया गया। एक किवदन्ती के आधार पर यहाँ ८० तालाब थे। जनरल कनिंघम ने अपनी रिपोर्ट में १६ तालाबों की एक अपूर्ण सूची दी है।[१४]

चन्देलों के बाद इस क्षेत्र में बुन्देला शासकों का उद्भव हुआ। चन्देलों द्वारा प्रारंभ तालाब निर्माण की परम्परा बुन्देला नरेशों ने भी अनवरत जारी रखी। ओरछा नरेश वीर सिंह जू देव 'प्रथम' (१६०५-१६२७ ई.) ने तालाब निर्माण की परम्परा को आगे बढ़ाया। उन्होंने वीर सागर, सिंह सागर एवं देव सागर आदि का निर्माण कराया।[१५]

इस तरह पानी की कमी को दूर करने के लिये तालाब निर्माण की परम्परा समूचे बुन्देलखण्ड में चल रही थी। इस परम्परा को देखते हुए लोकगायकों ने भी तालाब पर लोकगीत लिखे। जैतपुर के पास चन्देल शासक वाला वर्मन द्वारा ६ मील के घेर वाला गहरा वेला ताल बनवाया गया।[१६] इस तालाब पर लोक गायकों ने यह लोकगीत गाकर जन साधारण में तालाब निर्माण की चेतना जागृत की।

अलगरजी भरे बेलाताल, गगर मोरी न डूबे राम।
सासो की डूबे ननद की डूबै मोरी रई उतराय।
अलगरजी भरे बेला ताल; गगर मोरी न डूबे राम।
मॉई के रोय से नदिया बहत है, बाबुल के रोय बेलाताल।
अलगरजी भरे बेलाताल, गगर मोरी न डूबे राम।

इस प्रकार हम देखते हैं १६०० ई. के लगभग बुन्देलखण्ड में जल प्रबंधन हेतु तालाब निर्माण की परम्परा से जन साधारण भी वाकिफ था।

बन्जारे तो यायाबर होते हैं, उन्होंने समूचे बुन्देलखण्ड में घूम-घूम कर तालाब निर्माण द्वारा जल प्रबंधन का महत्व भली भांति समझा होगा। उन्होंने तालाब निर्माण का तरीका भी बखूबी देखा होगा। यही कारण रहा होगा कि लाखा बन्जारे ने पानी की कमी से निजात पाने के लिये तालाब के निर्माण का विचार बनाया।

इसी प्रेरक शक्ति के बल पर बन्जारों ने अदम्य उत्साह क परिचय देते हुये १६०० ई. के लगभग सागर के इस तालाब की खुदाई की।[१७] सागर के इस तालाब का रकबा ३९५ एकड़ है।

ऐसा नहीं है कि बन्जारों द्वारा सागर में ही तालाब बनवाया गया, भारत के अन्य क्षेत्रों में भी बन्जारों द्वारा तालाब निर्माण संबंधी कुछ रोचक किंवदन्तियाँ भी मिलती हैं। राजस्थान का झीलों की नगरी कहा जाने वाला उदयपुर नगर पिछोला झील के किनारे स्थित है।[१८]

कहा जाता है कि उदयपुर के महाराजा लाखा के समय पिछोला झील का निर्माण (१३८२-१४२८) एक छीतर नामक बन्जारे द्वारा करवाया गया था।[१९] के तालाब का निर्माण कराया था।

किसी राजा अथवा अभिजात वर्ग द्वारा निर्मित न होकर आम बन्जारों द्वारा निर्मित होने के कारण सागर का यह तालाब उपाश्रयी इतिहास लेखन की एक महत्वपूर्ण विषय वस्तु भी है। १७वीं शदी के पूर्वार्द्ध में जब यह तालाब बन्जारों द्वारा बनाया गया उस समय इस तालाब के आस-पास की पहाड़ियों पर कोई भी बस्ती नहीं थी। यहाँ आकर बसने वाले लोग पहले सागर से १० कि.मी. उत्तर की ओर झांसी मार्ग पर गढ़पहरा में रहते थे। इस समय गढ़पहरा में डांगी राजपूत राजाओं का राज्य था। गढ़पहरा के लोग भी उस समय पानी की कमी से जूझ रहे थे।[२०] बन्जारों द्वारा निर्मित तालाब में लबालब पानी भरा देखकर डांगी नरेश ऊदनशाह ने १६६०

ई. में इस तालाब के उत्तर-पश्चिमी तट पर सागर के किले का निर्माण कराया।[२१] गढ़पहरा में एक तो पानी की कमी थी और दूसरे उत्तर की ओर धामोनी से यहाँ निरन्तर बुन्देला आक्रमण हो रहे थे अतः लोग गढ़पहरा से सागर की ओर पलायन कर गये।[२२] सागर किले के पास स्थित परकोटा में सागर की प्राचीनतम बस्ती आबाद हुई।[२३] परकोटा का अर्थ शहर-ए-पनाह होता है।

वस्तुतः बंजारों ने बहुत ही वैज्ञानिक दृष्टिकोण से तालाब के निर्माण हेतु इस स्थान का चयन किया। चूँकि यह तीन ओर से पहाड़ियों से घिरा हुआ था अतः बारिश का पानी बह कर इसे लबालब भर देता है। चौथी ओर दांगी राजपूत राजाओं ने किले का निर्माण करा कर पानी को इस ओर से रोक दिया। जो स्थान पानी की कमी से जूझ रहा था उस स्थान पर जल प्रबंधन का एक सशक्त उदाहरण बन्जारों ने इस तालाब के निर्माण द्वारा प्रस्तुत किया। सागर के किले के दक्षिण में तालाब किनारे सुन्दर घाटों का निर्माण किया गया। किले के पश्चिम में एक मंदिर एवं चकराघाट स्थित है। इन घाटों पर खड़े होकर देखने पर एक अत्यन्त मनोहारी प्राकृतिक दृश्य दिखाई देता है। विद्वानों का मानना है कि तालाब के आस-पास बसने के कारण ही इस स्थान का नाम सागर पड़ा। इस तारतम्य में डॉ. हरीसिंह गौर का यह कथन उल्लेखनीय है-

'सागर को सागर इसलिये कहा जाता है क्योंकि यह एक तालाब के चारों ओर बसा है जो इसके ३०० एकड़ क्षेत्र में फैला हुआ है। एक समय यह गोलाकार तालाब काफी गहरा था व पानी से लबालब भरा रहता था। जिसको घेरें हुए निचली पहाड़ियों (टोरियों) पर सागर शहर बसा हुआ था वहाँ से इसे (तालाब को) देखने पर एक सुन्दर नज़ारा दिखता था।'[२४]

संदर्भ

१. राय बहादुर हीरा लाल, सागर सरोज, सरस्वती विलास प्रेस, नरसिंहपुर, १६२२, पृ. ११५.

२. उस समय सागर नगर बसा नहीं था, और न ही यहाँ तालाब था।

३. लक्ष्मी प्रसाद मिश्र, बंजारे का त्याग, मध्यप्रदेश संदेश, वर्ष ८५, अंक ७, १० अप्रैल १६८६, पृ. ६३.

४. सागर नगर, वही, पृ. ४४.

५. सागर संभाग : एक नजर में, वही, पृ. ३.

६. व.सु. कृष्णन, सागर गजेटियर, भोपाल, १९७०, पृ. ६.

७. बंजारे का त्याग, पूर्वोक्त, पृ. ६३.

८. सागर गजेटियर, पूर्वोक्त, पृ. ६.

९. राष्ट्रीय अभिलेखागार, पालीटिकल प्रासीडिंग्स, ३०-१२-१८५९, पंचम भाग, अनुक्रमांक ३५९, सर ह्यूरोज की ओर से ब्रिटिश सरकार के नाम पत्र २१-१२-१८५७.

१०. सुरेश तिवारी, 'सागर संभाग ऐतिहासिक दृष्टि', मध्यप्रदेश संदेश, पूर्वोक्त, पृ. ५.

११. वही, पृ. ६.

१२. काशी प्रसाद त्रिपाठी, बुन्देलखण्ड का सामाजिक आर्थिक इतिहास, समय प्रकाशन, दिल्ली, २००६, पृ. ४३.

१३. अयोध्या प्रसाद पाण्डेय, चन्देलकालीन बुन्देलखण्ड का इतिहास, हिन्दी साहित्य सम्मेलन, प्रयाग, १९६८, पृ. २११.

१४. वही, पृ. २१३.

१५. Eastern States (Bundelkhand) Gazetteers, C Edward, M.P. Govt. Gazetteer Department, 1994, p. 73.

१६. बलवंत सिंह (सं.), हमीरपुर गजेटियर, लखनऊ, १९८८, पृ. २६८.

१७. बन्जारे का त्याग, पूर्वोक्त, पृ. ६३.

१८. वही, पृ. ६३.

१९. कवि श्यामलदास, वीर विनोद, भाग-१, मोतीलाल बनारसीदास, नई दिल्ली, १९८६, पृ. ३०८.

२०. चित्तौड़-उदयपुर पाटनामा, भाग-३, पत्र संख्या, २१६ ब, २१७ अ.

२१. सागर नगर, पूर्वोक्त, पृ. ४४.

२२. स्वप्ना गुरू, सागर संभाग के प्रसिद्ध ऐतिहासिक दुर्ग, मध्यप्रदेश संदेश, पूर्वोक्त, पृ. २१-२२.

२३. सागर सरोज, पूर्वोक्त, पृ. १९५.

२४. वही, पृ. ४६.

गंगोलाताल एक ऐतिहासिक अध्ययन तोमर राजा उद्धरणदेव के संदर्भ में

डॉ. मधुबाला कुलश्रेष्ठ

ग्वालियर किले पर स्थित ८ तालों का उल्लेख मिलता है आज भी वे सभी ताल पानी के स्रोत के अच्छे साधन हैं। तालों के निर्माण के संबंध में ऐतिहासिक साक्ष्यों से जो जानकारी मिलती है वह यह कि जब ग्वालियर किले पर मानव-बस्ती के प्रयास शुरू हुए और उन्हें यहाँ पर रहने के लिए किला, दुर्ग, महल बनाने की आवश्यकता महसूस हुई तब यहाँ की चट्टानयुक्त जमीन को खोदकर पत्थर निकाले गए और इस तरह एक ओर किले की रक्षा दीवार, महल, मंदिर और दुर्ग बनते चले गए वहीं दूसरी ओर तालों, बावड़ियों का निर्माण होता गया और उसमें असंख्य नैसर्गिक स्रोत फूट पड़े और वे ताल उनके जीवन के साधन बन गए। इन्हीं प्रक्रियाओं से बना गंगोलाताल उनमें से एक है। किला पर स्थित सभी अन्य तालों से यह ताल प्राचीन माना गया है इसकी पुष्टि इस ताल से प्राप्त मूर्तियों, सामग्रियों, शिलालेखों से होती है।[1] गंगोताल की ऐतिहासिकता इस बात से अधिक है कि इस ताल से प्राप्त जो भी शिलालेख मिले हैं उन शिलालेखों में तत्कालीन राजा का नाम वंशगत भावीराजा तथा राजकुमारों के नाम, राजनीतिक घटनाओं का उल्लेख, शासन-काल की तिथि का वर्णन है, जिनके अध्ययन एवं अवलोकन से तत्कालीन राज्यकाल की घटनाओं का प्रमाणिक अध्ययन किया जा सकता है और तिथिक्रम का निर्धारण भी।

प्रस्तुत शोध पत्रा तोमर राजा उद्धरणदेव को केन्द्रित करते हुए तैयार किया गया है जो कि गंगोताल से मिले शिलालेख पर आधारित है। इस शोध पत्र के माध्यम से ग्वालियर में स्वतंत्रा तोमर राज्य की स्थापना में वीरसिंहदेव के साथ उद्धरणदेव का योगदान तथा एक राजा के रूप में उसके कार्यकाल (१४००-१४०२ ई.) में घटित राजनैतिक घटनाक्रम एवं धार्मिक कार्यों का उल्लेख करना मेरा प्रमुख उद्देश्य है।

ग्वालियर किले पर स्थित दाताबंदी छोड़ गुरुद्वारा के पीछे वर्तमान में गंदे पानी युक्त एक ताल दिखाई देता है वही ऐतिहासिक एवं प्राचीन गंगोलाताल है। पहले कभी

इस ताल तक पहुँचने का सड़क से तथा गुरुद्वारा मार्ग से जाने का रास्ता था लेकिन गुरुद्वारा के नवीन निर्माण कार्य और अतिक्रमण के चलते न तो वहाँ तक जाना संभव है और न ही उसे पहचानना। इस ताल की उपयोगिता की बात करें तो इस ताल ने किले पर स्थित मानव बस्ती के अस्तित्व को बसाने और बचाने में हर पल सहयोग दिया था इसमें बरसात का पानी एवं अन्य नैसर्गिक स्रोत से यह जल से परिपूर्ण बना रहता था जिसकी उपयोगिता और महत्ता को समय-समय पर प्रतिहार, तोमर राजाओं ने भी समझा था तभी तो उनके द्वारा विशिष्ट अवसरों पर ताल की सफाई कराने तथा अपनी विशिष्ट उपलब्धियों-युद्ध में विजय प्राप्त करने पर अथवा विशिष्ट पूजा-श्राद्ध आदि के अवसरों पर शिलालेख खुदाए जाने का उल्लेख ऐतिहासिक साक्ष्यों में दर्ज है। इस समय गंगोलाताल को एक ओर से गुरुद्वारा ने तथा दूसरी ओर सड़क मार्ग (तेली मंदिर के सामने) को घेरते हुए एक नया स्नान कुण्ड बनाकर घेर दिया गया है।[२]

गंगोताल के ऐतिहासिक महत्त्व की बात करें तो इस ताल में अंकित कई शिलालेख प्राप्त हुए हैं परवर्ती प्रतिहास कालीन नरवर्मन, तोमर कालीन, वीरसिंहदेव तोमर, उद्धरणदेव, मानसिंह तोमन राजाओं के समय के शिलालेख[३] इत्यादि परन्तु इस शोधपत्र में मेरा उद्देश्य ग्वालियर किले पर स्वतंत्रा तोमर राज्य की स्थापना में उद्धरणदेव के योगदान को बताना तथ १४०० से १४०२ ई. तक के संक्षिप्त कार्यकाल में उसके राजनीतिक, सामाजिक, धार्मिक कृत्यों और कर्त्तव्यों को शिलालेख के माध्यम से प्रकट करना है।

गंगोलाताल में वीरसिंहदेव तोमर द्वारा एक राजकीय शिलालेख आषाढ़ शुक्ल ५ विक्रम संवत् १४३८ अर्थात् ४ जून १३६४ ई. को खुदवाया हुआ मिला है।

इस शिलालेख की शुरुआत शिव की वंदना के साथ हुई है। शिलालेख को अंकित करने की तिथि आषाढ़ शुक्ल तिथि पंचमी दिन गुरुवार था। तोमर कुल में उदित होने वाले कमल और सूर्य के समान वीरसिंहदेव राजा हुए। शिलालेख की पाँचवी और छठवीं पंक्ति अधूरी है वे दोनों पंक्ति भी वीरसिंहदेव तोमर की वीरता को समर्पित हैं। शिलालेख की सातवीं पंक्ति में उद्धरणदेव का उल्लेख है जिसमें कहा गया है कि उद्धरेण सहित : अनेक शकों का विनाश किया गया। अर्थात् वीरसिंह को ग्वालियर गढ़ को प्राप्त करने से पहले शकों का विनाश करना पड़ा और इस कार्य में उसके पुत्रा उद्धरणदेव ने नेतृत्व किया और पूरा-पूरा योग दिया। आठवीं पंक्ति पुनः भग्न स्थिति में हैं केवल उसमें गोपाचल पढ़ने योग्य है। जिसका तात्पर्य ग्वालियर गढ़ से है। नवीं पंक्ति पुनः भग्न अवस्था में है जिसमें पं. लक्ष्मीधरसु का नाम अंकित है

इसी लक्ष्मीधरसु का संबंध दसवीं पंक्ति से है अर्थात् वीरसिंहदेव के राज्य काल में पं. लक्ष्मीधर नाम कोई श्रेष्ठ पुरुष था जो राजकार्य में तथा षट्कर्म में कुशल था जिसका संबंध संभवतः रणथंभौर के महाराजा हमीरदेव के प्रधान सभासद रघवदेव के प्रपौत्रा लक्ष्मीधर से है। पं. लक्ष्मीधर के निर्देशन में तालाब को साफ कराया गया और यह लेख अंकित कराया। शिलालेख की बारहवीं पंक्ति में प्रशस्तिकार ने राजा एवं कुल के प्रति आशा और निष्ठा व्यक्त करते हुए लिखा है कि जब तक कच्छप धरा को धारण करते रहेंगे तब तक उनके कुल का प्रताप 'सूर्य' अस्त नहीं होगा[४]

शिलालेख में वर्णित सातवीं पंक्ति का सीधा संबंध शोध पत्र की विषयवस्तु उद्धरणदेव से है। उद्धरणदेव सहित वीरसिंहदेव को ग्वालियर-गढ़ पर अधिकार करने से पहले असंख्य शकों का विनाश करना पड़ा। यह संकेत, तुगलक वंश के तत्कालीन सुल्तान, नासिरुद्दीन महमूद शाह के आक्रमण की घटना की ओर है जो कि २३ मार्च १३९४ ई. से अक्टूबर १४१२ ई. तक दिल्ली का सुल्तान रहा।[५]

नासिरुद्दीन महमूदशाह के आक्रमण से पहले की परिस्थितियों पर विचार करते हैं तो ग्वालियर-गढ़ पर तोमर राजाओं के उदय की शुरुआत मुहम्मद-बिन-तुग़लक़ के शासन काल में कमलसिंह द्वारा हो गई थी। फिरोजशाह तुग़लक़ के शासन काल में देववर्मा (देवब्रम्ह) ने प्रयास किए और फिर इसी शासन काल के अंतिम वर्षों में (१३७५ ई.) में वीरसिंहदेव के प्रयास हुए। वीरसिंहदेव द्वारा किए गए प्रयास लम्बे समय तक (लगभग जून १३९४ ई.) चले इस अवधि में नासिरुद्दीन महमूदशाह के शासनकाल में ऐसाह की जागीर की पुष्टि कराना १३९१-९२ में राजपूतों का संगठन बनाना और १३९२-०३ ई. में पुनः दूसरा संगठन बनाकर दिल्ली सुल्तान को भयाक्रांत करना परिणामस्वरूप कन्नौज हत्याकाण्ड हुआ। अलाउद्दीन सिकन्दरशाह हुमायूँ के शासनकाल २२ जनवरी १३९४ से ७ मार्च, १३९४ ई. के बीच वीरसिंहदेव को ग्वालियर-गढ़ का वैधानिक अधिपति बनाए जाने का फ़रमान मिला जिसके परिपालन में रानीपुरा की घटना घटित हुई और ग्वालियर किले के तुर्क हाकिम सिकन्दर खाँ तथा अन्य सहयोगियों की छल-प्रपंच रचकर हत्या हुई और मार्च १३९४ ई. में वीरसिंहदेव ने गोपाचलगढ़ पर आधिपत्य स्थापित कर स्वतन्त्रा तोमर राजवंश की नींव डाली। ७ मार्च १३९४ ई. को अलाउद्दीन सिकन्दरशाह की मृत्यु के बाद उसका छोटा भाई नासिरुद्दीन महमूदशाह २३ मार्च १३९४ ई. को गद्दी पर बैठा और अक्टू. १४१२ ई. तक सुल्तान पद पर रहा। ग्वालियर के तोमर राजाओं की स्वतंत्रा सत्ता पर नियंत्राण स्थापित करने के लिए उसने अप्रैल-मई के बीच में ग्वालियर पर आक्रमण किया।[६] जिसका उल्लेख तारीख़े-मुबारक़शाही और तबकाते-अक़बरी में भी मिलता

है[७] लेकिन युद्ध के परिणाम के संबंध में दोनों लेखक मौन हैं। इस घटना का प्रमाणिक साक्ष्य गंगोलाताल का यह अभिलेख है। यह शिलालेख मुस्लिम इतिहासकारों का युद्ध के परिणाम पर साधी गई चुप्पी को तोड़ता है और सत्य घटना को प्रकट करता है। नासिरुद्दीन महमूदशाह, यह वही 'शक' है जिसका निपात उद्धरणदेव के साथ वीरसिंहदेव ने किया।[८] उपरोक्त सभी घटनाओं की पुष्टि परवर्ती अभिलेखों और साहित्यिक साक्ष्यों से भी होती है। विजय की घटना तोमर शासक वीरसिंहदेव के लिए बहुत बड़ी उपलब्धि थी कि पिता और पितामह द्वारा तुर्कों के अत्याचार से मुक्ति दिलाने हेतु किए गए प्रयास में सन् १३७५ ई. से लगातार सन्नद्ध रहते हुए वीरसिंहदेव को जून १३६४ ई. में पूर्ण सफलता मिली और इसी उपलक्ष्य में गंगोलाताल की प्रशस्ति अंकित कराई गई।

गंगोलाताल का एक अन्य शिलालेख जो कि उद्धरणदेव के द्वारा विक्रम संवत् १४५८ आषाढ़ शुक्ल पंचमी को अंकित कराया गया अर्थात् १४ जून १४०१ ई. का शिलालेख है।[९] यह उद्धरणदेव के शासनकाल को समर्पित है। शिलालेख का आरंभ श्रीगणेश को नमस्कार करने से हुआ है। शिलालेख की तीसरी और चौथी पंक्ति के अनुसार आषाढ़ शुक्ल पंचमी विक्रम संवत् १४५८ को उद्धरणदेव राज्य कर रहे थे। चौथी और पाँचवीं पंक्ति के अनुसार इस शिलालेख के अंकन से १ वर्ष पहले आषाढ़ शुक्ल पंचमी विक्रम संवत् १४५७ अर्थात् २७ जून १४०० ई. में वीरसिंहदेव की मृत्यु हुई थी। उनके वार्षिक श्राद्ध के समय पितृदैवव्रते गंगोलाताल के सफाई कराई गई और यह शिलालेख अंकित कराया गया। छठवीं पंक्ति में नगर में प्रवाहित होने वाली स्वर्णरेखा नदी का उल्लेख है।

शिलालेख की अंकित सातवीं पंक्ति में उद्धरणदेव के गोपगिरि पर राजा के रूप में विराजित होने तथा पृथ्वी का उद्धार करने का उल्लेख है। जहाँ स्वर्ण रेखा नदी प्रवाहित है। आठवीं पंक्ति में पुनः शक गणं हत्वा अर्थात् शकों का विनाश कर पृथ्वी का उद्धार करने वाला कहा गया है शिलालेख की ग्यारहवीं पंक्ति में प्रशस्तिकार का नाम गयाधर वेनसूरिणा उल्लिखित है जिसका अर्थ मंदिर के आचार्य से है जो कि एक सनाढ्य ब्राह्मण थे उनका संबंध केशवदास के पूर्वज-दिनकर के पुत्रा गयाधर से है। अर्थात् वीरसिंहदेव की मृत्यु के बाद उद्धरणदेव ने अपने पिता के पुरोहित दिनकरराव को गया भेजा जहाँ उनके द्वारा पिण्ड दान कराया गया और उनके वापिस लौटने पर ग्वालियर-गढ़ पर उनका श्राद्ध किया गया और उस उपलक्ष्य में गंगोलाताल का उक्त लेख अंकित किया गया जिसके रचनाकार गयाधर आचार्य थे।[१०] गयाधर-वेन-सूरिणा का संबंध डॉ. संतलाल कटारे ने जैन धर्म से जोड़ा है क्योंकि

अगली पंक्ति माथुरान्वय कायस्थ शाखा के काष्टसंघी भट्टारक रहे हैं। इसी शाखा में ग्वालियर में भट्टारक देवसेन, धरमसेन आदि हुए जो कि रइधु से पहले के थे। कविप्रिया में वर्णित केशवदास के वंश परिचय के अध्ययन से तथा कष्टसंघी भट्टारकों के नामों के अवलोकन में[११] मिलते-जुलते नाम होने की वज़ह से यह संभावना बनती है कि केशवदास के पूर्वजों ने जैन धर्म अपना लिया हो अथवा वे इससे प्रभावित हों। गुलाब खाँ गौरी ने भी इसी तरह का अभिमत दिया है।[१२]

उद्धरणदेव के शिलालेख से उसके कार्यकाल की तिथि तथा वीरसिंहदेव के बाद तोमर वंश का अगला उत्तराधिकारी उद्धरणदेव के होने की पुष्टि होती है जबकि याह्या सिहरिन्दी ने तारीखे मुबारकशाही में वीरम को अगला उत्तराधिकारी बताया है। इसी तरह उसने तोमर के आक्रमणों को मुग़लों का उत्पात बताया है।[१३] ये दोनों ही उल्लेख असत्य और भ्रामक हैं।

निष्कर्ष रूप में कहा जा सकता है कि गंगोलाताल के दोनों शिलालेख तोमरवंश के उदय, उत्थान और विकास में उद्धरणदेव के योगदान की स्पष्ट झलक दिखाने में सक्षम है। राजनीतिक घटना क्रम, तिथि-निर्धारण, हिंदुओं के सामाजिक-धार्मिक कृत्यों में राजा की भूमिका, राजा के प्रजा के प्रति कर्त्तव्य एवं दायित्वों के बोध एवं निर्वहन का पूरा-पूरा विवरण शिलालेखों में मिलता है। ये शिलालेख यह भी बताते हैं कि गंगोलाताल एक जीवनोपयोगी जलस्रोत है। प्रजाहित में उसकी साफ-सफाई करवाना राजा का कर्त्तव्य है अतः तोमर राजाओं ने समय-समय पर कोई विशिष्ट उपलब्धि हासिल करने पर जनहित में यह कार्य उन्होंने बार-बार किया। स्वयं उद्धरणदेव ने भी इस कर्तव्य का पालन किया।

शिलालेखों के अवलोकन से यह भी स्पष्ट होता है कि तोमर राजा हिंदू धर्म, संस्कृति के पालक एवं पोषक थे। शिव और गणेश की वंदना करना, एक पुत्र के रूप में उद्धरणदेव का अपने पिता के साथ युद्ध में हिस्सा लेना, पिण्ड दान करना, श्राद्ध कर्म करना, इस बात के स्पष्ट प्रमाण हैं।

गंगोलाताल जहाँ राजा का, प्रजा के प्रति कर्तव्य को दर्शाता है वहीं वह राजा के प्रति प्रजा की भावना तथा उनके मन में छिपी मंगल आशा को अभिव्यक्त करता है। 'उद्धरणों महीम्' शब्द में यही भाव छपे हैं। उद्धरणदेव के समय तक उत्तर भारत में लगभग २०० वर्ष तक तुर्क शासन कर चुके हैं। इस अवधि में उनके द्वारा जनता पर जिस तरह का अत्याचार पूर्ण व्यवहार किया जा रहा था उससे कोई भी सुखी नहीं था। इस अत्याचार पूर्ण शासन से मुक्ति दिलाने का प्रयास कमलसिंह के द्वारा हुआ। कमलसिंह के इसी बीड़े को उसके पौत्रा वीरसिंहदेव और प्रपौत्रा उद्धरणदेव ने उठाया

और पूरा किया। शकों का निपात करके वीरसिंहदेव और उद्धरणदेव ने ग्वालियर की जनता के लिए जो कार्य किया था वह वैसा ही था जैसा कि वराहवतार रूपी विष्णु ने राक्षसों का विनाश करके मही अर्थात् पृथ्वी का उद्धार किया इसलिए प्रशस्तिकार गयाधर ने अपने राजा को वराहवतार के रूप में देखा और उनके प्रति यह इच्छा व्यक्त की कि वे इसी तरह राजा के कर्त्तव्यों का पालन करते हुए राज्य के निवासियों की रक्षा, तुर्कों से करते रहें और उन्हें शांतिपूर्ण प्रशासन और भयमुक्त जीवन दें।

सन्दर्भ स्रोत

१. द्विवेदी, हरिहर निवास : ग्वालियर दर्शन, मनीषा १६८०, पृ. ३५३।

२. सर्वेक्षण के आधार पर १२ सितम्बर २०१० एवं पूर्व सर्वेक्षण २०००।

३. गंगोलाताल से प्राप्त शिलालेखों के आधार पर।

४. शिलालेख क्रमांक-१ के अनुसार, जर्नल ऑफ दि ओरिएण्टल इन्स्टीट्यूट बड़ौदा १६७४ : द गंगोलाताल इन्सक्रिप्शन।

५. शिलालेख क्रमांक-२ तुलनात्मक वंश-वृक्ष के अनुसार।

६. कुलश्रेष्ठ मधुबाला, 'ग्वालियर में स्वतंत्रा तोमर राजवंश के संस्थापक : वीरसिंहदेव, शोध पत्र (प्रका.) जर्नल ऑफ दि मध्यप्रदेश इतिहास परिषद, अंक-२२, २००८, पृ. ८८ एवं परवर्ती ऐतिहासिक साक्ष्य के आधार पर।

७. याह्या, तारीखे मुबारक़ शाही

निजामुद्दीन : तबकाते अक़बरी

रिजवी, अतहर अब्बास : तुग़लक कालीन भारत, भाग-२, पृ. २१६, ३५७।

८. गंगोलाताल शिलालेख क्रमांक-१ के अनुसार-वीरसिंहदेव का शिलालेख आषाढ़ शुक्ल-५, वि. संवत् १४३८ अर्थात् ४ जून १३६४ ई.।

६. परिशिष्ट क्रमांक-३, गंगोलाताल शिलालेख आषाढ़ शुक्ल पंचमी विक्रम संवत् १४५८, अर्थात् १४ जून १४०१, उद्धरणदेव का शिलालेख।

१०.द्विवेदी हरिहरनिवास : ग्वालियर के तोमर, पृ. ४०-४१ एवं केशवदास रचित कविप्रिया में वर्णित केशवदास के वंश परिचय के अनुसार।

११.अनेकांत, जून १६६६, ग्वालियर के काष्टसंघी भट्टारक : राजा राम जैन, पृ. ६०-६६।

१२. गौरी, गुलाब खाँ : ग्वालियर का राजनैतिक एवं सांस्कृतिक इतिहास, पृ. ५०-५१।

१३.डॉ. रिजवी, अतहर अब्बास : उत्तर तैमूर कालीन भारत, भाग-१, पृ. ६।

हरियाणा राज्य में मध्यकालीन जल प्रबन्धनः विशेषकर झज्जर ज़िले के संदर्भ में

डॉ. विशाल कुमार शर्मा

झज्जर, समुद्रतल से लगभग ७०० फुट ऊचाई पर हरियाणा राज्य मे स्थित है। इसके पूर्व में दिल्ली, दक्षिण में रेवाडी, पश्चिम में चरखी दादरी और उत्तर में रोहतक स्थित है। झज्जर का जल स्तर बहुत नीचे है तथा जो जल प्राप्त होता भी है, वह बहुत खारा है।[१] इस क्षेत्र की जलवायु उपोश्ण कटिबंधीय, अंशतः गर्मी से झुलसी हुई तथा मानसूनी है। अप्रैल माह से जून तक झज्जर का क्षेत्र अत्याधिक गर्म रहता है। पश्चिम की ओर से गर्म हवाऐं बहती हैं प्रायः रेतीली आंधी आती रहती है। जार्ज थॉमस नामक प्रसिद्ध भाासक का कथन था कि 'आम तौर पर इस क्षेत्र की गर्मी स्वाथ्यकारक है लेकिन धूल भरी आंधी जब चलती है तो यूरोपीयन लोगों के लिए यहां का मौसम प्रतिकूल हो जाता है'।[२]

यदि झज्जर क्षेत्र की जन संपदा की बात की जाये, तो जान पड़ता है कि यहां सिचांई के लिए अनेक प्रकार की युक्तियों का प्रचलन था। ढ़ेकली, चड़स, रहंट, नहरें, तालाब व कुओं द्वारा सिचांई की जाती थी और जल प्रबंधन किया जाता था। यहां की नहरों में मुख्य रूप से सतलुज साहिबी, इंइरी, कन्सूरी, बदरों, नज़फगढ़ झील आदि आती हैं।[३]

सुल्तान फीरोज़शाह तुगलक, जिसका योगदान इस क्षेत्र में जल प्रबंधन के लिए मध्यकाल में सर्वाधिक रहा, द्वारा पश्चिमी युमना नहर बनवाई, यद्यपि कालांतर में अग्रेंज शासकों द्वारा इसका मार्ग बदल दिया। यदि सिंचाई की विभिन्न युक्तियों का वर्णन किया जाये तो 'चड़स' अत्यंत महत्वपूर्ण युक्ति थी जिसमे पानी को कुएं से निकालने के लिए कुएं के किनारे पर मजबूत लकड़ी के दो 'डाटवें बनवाये जाते थे उसके ऊपर एक चाक या चकला लगवाया जाता था और एक मजबूत 'सण की ता' बनाई जाती थी, जिसे भैंस की खाल से बने चड़स से बांध दिया जाता था एक ऊपरी सतह यानि कुएं की मुंडेर पर डामचा और अंतिम छोर की निचाई की ओर एक गूग,

पानी की गहराई जितनी लम्बी बनाई जाती थी जिसमें मजदूर या बैल दोनों ही प्रयोग में लाए जाते थे।[४]

रहट द्वारा पानी निकालने के लिए लोहे के एक गोल आकार वाले चक्र के साथ बाल्टियां जोड़ी जाती थीं। कुएं से पानी भरकर, बाल्टियां ऊपर आ जाती थीं और उल्टी होकर पानी खाली करके पुनः घूमती हुई पानी भरती।[५]

इस क्षेत्र में नहरों में सबसे पहला नाम सतलुज का आता है। सुल्तान फिरोज तुगलक १३५५ ई० में यह नहर झज्जर तक लाया था और मुगल सम्राट शाहजहां ने सन् १६३५ में इसकी मरम्मत कराई थी, यद्यपि वर्तमान में यह पूरी तरह विलुप्त हो गई है।[६] इसके अतिरिक्त साहिबी नदी जयपुर के उत्तर से निकलती हुई कोट क्रासिम के पास आकर, रेवाड़ी में मिलती है और आगे झज्जर पहुँचती है फिर दिल्ली में यमुना से मिल जाती है।[७]

"अकबर बांधी का बंधू ना रेवाड़ी जाँऊ
कोट तले तै पिकलू साक्षी नाम कहाऊ"

इन प्रमुख नहरों के अतिरिक्त झज्जर के पूर्वी किनारे पर नजफगढ़ झील होती थी, जो साहिबी, इन्द्ररी और कसूटी नदियों से भर जाती थी।[८] सन् १७९५ ई. में जार्ज थॉमस लिखते है कि "बड़ा अफसोस है कि नहर ए. बहिश्त की कोई मरम्मत नहीं कराई गई। ये स्वर्ग की नहर सूखी पड़ी है और कई जगहों पर तो इसे खत्म ही कर दिया गया है।"[९] सन् १८३३-३४ और १८३७-३८ ई० के सूखे में इस क्षेत्र को लोगों को पानी के महत्व और इस झील के महत्व का ज्ञान हुआ।

सतुलज नहर को झज्जर तक १३५५ ई. में लाने का श्रेय सुल्तान फीरोजशाह तुगलक को था।[१०] फिरोज ने पांच नहरें बनवाने का आदेश पारित किया था, ये नहरे थी-[११]

१. सतलुज से झज्जर तक

२. सिमौर की पहड़ियों से हांसी, आरसन और हिसार-फिरोजा तक

३. धग्गर वाया सरसूती किला से हरनी खेड़ा तक

४. सरस्वती से सलीमा तक

सुल्तान फिरोज तुगलक ने सन् १३६० में फिरोज कैनाल बनवाई थी, जिसे पुरानी युमना कैनाल भी कहते थे।[१२] इसे सिचांई चैनलों के माध्यम से धग्गर और सतलुज से

जोड़ा गया। पश्चिमी यमुना कैनाल पर जार्ज थामस ने अपने लेख में इसका विस्तार पूर्वक वर्णन किया है। उन्होनें स्पश्ट किया है कि युमना-सतलुज-घग्गर संपर्क कैनाल सन् १३६० में बनकर पूरी तरह तैयार हो चुकी।

झज्जर क्षेत्र की प्रमुख सतलुज यमुना संपर्क नहर के अतिरिक्त, मध्यकालीन जल प्रबंधन के कुछ अन्य श्रेष्ठ उदाहरण भी प्राप्त होते हैं। इस दृष्टि से सबसे पहला नाम दिल्ली झज्जर राजमार्ग पर स्थित सात मकबरों के एक समूह, जिन्हें पुरातत्व विभाग के रिकार्ड में STR-१, ३, ४, ५, ८, १० व १३ पर दर्ज किया गया है व STR-१२, आता है। STR-१२ के अनुसार पानी के एक बहुत तालाब का संदर्भ दिया गया है जो ५०० x ३०० मी० में फैला दर्शाया गया है, बुआ कलाल तालाब[१४] के नाम से विख्यात है।

इसमें लखौरी ईटों का व लाल पत्थर का प्रयोग किया गया था।[१५]

तालाब की पीछे की दीवार पर एक मेहराब बनी है जिसे भीतर से फूल पत्तियों से सजाया गया है।

इस तालाब को हसन भाहिद और बुआ कलाल की याद में कलाल खान ने लगभग १६३०-१६३५ ई० के मध्य बनवाया था।[१६] मुगल कालीन जल प्रबंध का यह तालाब एक उत्तम उदाहरण है।

इसी तालाब के निकट एक बावड़ी है जहां निरंतर पानी का स्त्रोत बना रहता था।

इस प्रमुख तालाब के अतिरिक्त झज्जर में १७ घाटों का एक विशाल तालाब है जो दुर्गामल ने १६२६ ई० में बनवाया था। साथ ही छुछकवास के महल में बना ऐतिहासिक तालाब भी मण्ध्यकालीन जल प्रबंधन का उत्तम उदाहरण प्रस्तुत करता है।[१७]

इन सुन्दर उदाहरणों के अतिरिक्त झज्जर क्षेत्र में दिल्ली फाजिल्का राश्ट्रीय मार्ग पर स्थित राहठ गोत्र के जाटों का बसाया नगर शरफाबाद (१७५५ ई.) है। मुगल बादशाह आलमगीर-II ने २५ ग्रामों सहित यह जागीर, फरूखनगर के दो बलूच बहादुर खान और ताज मुहम्मद को दी थी। जिन्होनें यहां बहादुरगढ़ नामक किले में नीवं रखी। बहादुगढ़ के नवाब ने अपने घर में एक कंचन तालाब बनवाया यह कंचन तालाब एक नाचने वाली के नाम पर बनवाया गया था। इसकी सीढ़ियों शीशे से बनवाई गई थीं।[१८] बहादुरगढ़ का ही एक अन्य तालाब 'भगवान दास तालाब' भी मध्यकालीन जल प्रबंधन का एक बेहतर नमूना है।

यह तालाब वैज्ञानिक दृष्टि से एक अजूबा था। इस तालाब से वर्षा का अतिरिक्त जल एक कच्चे जोहड़ की ओर निकल जाता था और तालाब का स्तर ज्यों का ज्यों बना रहता था।[१९]

झज्जर क्षेत्र में मध्यकालीन जोहड़ो का भी पता चलता हैं जिसमें सबसे पहला जोहड़ झज्जर के नवाब फैज अली खां ने बनवाया था। यहां कि मिट्टी बहुत चिकनी है।[२०] झज्जर से लगभग १५ कि.मी. पश्चिम में जहाजगढ़ नामक पर एक चमत्कारी जोहड़ है, जिसमें ऐसां माना जाता है कि, यहां के महंत स्नान करते थे। जिससे यहां का जल अत्यंत पवित्र हो गया है।[२१] इसके अतिरिक्त झज्जर सांपला रोड़ पर स्थित छारा ग्राम में एक चमत्कारी जोहड़ है जिसकी मान्यता है कि इसमें नहाने से पीलिया का असाध्य रोग समाप्त हो जाता है।[२२]

इस प्रकार झज्जर क्षेत्र, मध्यकालीन जल प्रबंधन के अनेक विशिष्ट उदाहरण समेटे हुए है। यहां के जल प्रबंधन की सबसे बड़ी विशेषता यह है कि यहां कच्चा और पक्का दोनों ही प्रकार का जल प्रबंधन देखने को मिलता है। इस क्षेत्र के मध्यकालीन शासकों द्वारा जहां एक ओर उच्च स्तरीय जल प्रबंधन किया गया, वहीं यहां के स्थानीय ग्रामीणों ने अपने अनुसार जल प्रबंधन कर इस क्षेत्र की जल की कमी को दूर करने का और उपलब्ध जल संसाधनों का अधिकतम उपयोग व संरक्षण करने का प्रयास किया।

संदर्भ

१. रोहतक डिस्ट्रिक्ट गजेटियर, (१६१०) पृ० २४

२. मैमोरीज़ ऑफ जार्ज थामस- (जार्ज थामस) पृ० २१-२३

३. हरियाणा की सांस्कृतिक विरासत - (लीलीधर 'दुखी') पृ० २०-२४

४. विकास का रचा इतिहास - पृ० (पअ) पैरा ७-८

५. हरियाणा एक सांस्कृतिक अध्ययन - पृ० २-५

६. रोहतक डिस्ट्रिक्ट गजेटियर - १६१०

७. रोहतक डिस्ट्रिक्ट गजेटियर - १६१०

८. रोहतक डिस्ट्रिक्ट गजेटियर - १६१०

९. पूर्वोक्त - जार्ज थामस

१०. रोहतक डिस्ट्रिक्ट गजेटियर - १६१०, पृ० २४, संदर्भ -तारीख़-ए मुबारकशाही (रिजवी)

११. तारीख-ए-मुबारकशाही - पृ० १६६, २०१, २०२ उद्धृत हरियाणा अन्शियंट एंड मिडिवियल (एच.ए. फड़के) पृ०१२०

१२. इम्पीरियल गज़ेटियर ऑफ इण्डिया भाग-प्ट, पृ० ३३

१३. 'पठान किंग्ज़' (जार्ज थामस का लेख) पृ० १२१

१४. भारतीय पुरातत्व विभाग के श्री जोगेन्द्र सिंह के दि.११/६/१० को हुए साक्षात्कार पर आधारित।

१५. उपर्युक्त

१६. उपर्युक्त

१७. भारतीय पुरातत्व विभाग के श्री जगमाल के दिनांक १४-६-१० को हुए साक्षात्कार पर आधारित।

१८. बहादुरगढ़ निवासी श्री नरेश कुमार के दिनांक १६-६-१० को हुए साक्षात्कार पर आधारित।

१६. उपर्युक्त

२०. झज्जर नगर के श्री राम मेहर सिंह के दिनांक १६-६-२०१० को हुए साक्षात्कार पर आधारित।

२१. ग्राम जहाजगढ़ के श्री सुभाश चंद्र के दिनांक १६-६-१० को हुए साक्षात्कार पर आधारित।

२२. ग्राम छारा के श्री राजेश के दिनांक १६-६-२०१० को हुए साक्षात्कार पर आधारित।

धार का मध्यकालीन जल प्रबंधन

डॉ. रमेशचन्द्र यादव

तीर्थ या मंदिरों की स्थापनायें भी या तो नदियों, प्राकृतिक झरनों के किनारे की गयी थी या निर्मित मंदिरों के आगे सरोवर या जल कुण्ड निर्मित किये, किन्तु उद्देश्य वही था, जल प्रबंधन या जल की उपयोगिता। गुप्तकाल से पूर्व मध्यकाल तक बड़े पैमाने पर मंदिरों का निर्माण हुआ, तो सरोवर भी स्थापित किए गये। नगर नियोजन हुआ, तो नदियों के जल का उचित प्रबंधन भी किया गया। परमार शासन काल में कुछ ऐसे भी नगर थे, जहाँ नदियाँ नहीं थी, किन्तु जल प्रबंधन उच्च कोटि का था। उनके महत्वपूर्ण उदाहरण खण्डवा एवं धार नगर है। परमार काल में खण्डवा नगर समरांगण सूत्रधार के सिद्धान्तों के अनुरूप नगर कोट, नगर द्वार सहित बनाया गया, जिसके चारों दिशाओं के कोने पर बड़े-बड़े जलकुण्ड स्थापित हुए, जो आज रामेश्वर कुण्ड, सूरज कुण्ड, पद्म कुण्ड एवं भीम कुण्ड के नाम से जाने जाते हैं।

मालवा की परमार कलीन राजधानी धार का भी जल प्रबंधन कम महत्व का नहीं है। नगर का "धारा" नाम भी, किसी जलधारा का सूचक है। प्रतिहार काल में धारा पद्रक ग्राम था, जिसे परमार काल में राजधानी का गौरव प्राप्त हुआ। परमारों से संबंधित ऐतिहासिक संदर्भों में धार को उनकी कुल राजधानी लिखा गया है।[१] परमार राजा सीयक हर्ष राष्ट्रकूट नरेश कृष्ण अकाल वर्ष के अधीन सामन्त के रूप में गुजरात के खेटक मण्डल (जिला खेड़ा) का शासक था, उसने ई. सन् ९७२ में अकाल वर्ष के उत्तराधिकारी खोटिगा को पराजित कर स्वतंत्र सत्ता स्थापित की।[२] उसके पुत्र वाक्पतिराज मुंज के शासन काल में धारा पद्रक को धारा नगरी बनाया गया।[३] मुंज ने धारा नगरी में तालाबों का निर्माण करवाया एवं देवी कालिका का मंदिर बनवाया। मंदिर के उत्तरी ओर के तालाब को आज भी मुंज सरोवर नाम से संबोधित किया जाता है। वाक्पतिराज मुंज ही वह महान निर्माता थे, जिसने कई स्थानों पर तालाबों का निर्माण करवाया था। मुंज के उत्तराधिकारी सिन्धुराज ने धारा नगरी के शिव मंदिर में स्फटिक के धारेश्वर लिंग की स्थापना करवाकर नगर प्रवेश किया।[४] धारा नगरी में भव्य भवनों का निर्माण हुआ, किन्तु उसकी सुरक्षा व

जल प्रबंधन का कार्य भी किया था, राजा भोजदेव परमार ने। भोजदेव ने ई. सन् १०१० से १०५५ तक का शासन किया और धारा नगरी की सांस्कृतिक धारा को सर्वत्र प्रवाहित किया। राजा भोज के समय धारा नगरी को सुरक्षित व भव्य नगरी के रूप में परिवर्तित किया गया। मार्तण्ड प्रासाद, सरस्वती सदन, मणिमरकत मण्डप के अतिरिक्त भवनों, सस्थाओं और देवालयों का निर्माण हुआ।[५] अलबरूनी ने धारा नगरी का विशद् वर्णन किया है।[६] राजा भोजदेव ने धारागिरि लोलोदूयान में मणिमरकत मण्डप एवं एक विशाल बावड़ी का निर्माण करवाया। नालछा का नलतड़ाग भी राजा भोज के समय निर्मित हुआ।

राजा भोज के बाद धारा नगरी पर निरन्तर आक्रमण हुए, जिसके कारण राजा भोज का जल प्रबंधन भी विछिन्न हो गया। जल प्रबंधन के लिए सुदर्शन झील के बाद एक बड़ा ऐतिहासिक उदाहरण भोपाल का विशाल तालाब है। राजा भोज ने इस विशाल झील का निर्माण करवाया, इसमें कई स्थलों पर बांधों का भी निर्माण करवाया था। पूर्वी ओर एक तरफ इसी झील के किनारे भोजपुर का शिव मंदिर था। दूसरी ओर इसी झील के दक्षिणी कोने पर भीम बैठका की गुफायें थी। मण्डी द्वीप एक द्वीप मात्र था। १६ वीं शताब्दी में माण्डू सुल्तान होशंगशाह ने इस विशाल झील पर भोपाल में बांध बंधवाकर भोपाल तक सीमित कर दिया।[७] राजा भोज ने धारा नगरी में "वारि परिखा" का निर्माण किया था। नगर के चारों ओर चार तोरण द्वार एवं नगर प्राकार का निर्माण करवाया था। तोरण द्वार के दोनों ओर बड़े-बड़े सरोवर थे, इनकी जलधारा एक दूसरे तालाब से मिली हुई थी, जो वारि परिखा का काम कर रही थी। भौगोलिक परिस्थिति के अनुसार धारा नगरी के चारों ओर लघुकाय पहाड़ियाँ है, भूमि का सामान्य ढाल पश्चिम की ओर है। इन पहाड़ियों के मध्य के पठारी भाग पर धारा नगरी की अनुपम रचना की गयी। वर्षा ऋतु में जो जल बहकर आता था, उसके लिए चारों ओर बड़े तालाब बने हुए थे। इन तालाबों का जल बढ़ने पर देवी तालाब से पानी नाले की ओर जाता था, जो आज भी जाता है, यही नाला आगे जाकर मान नदी में मिलता है।

धारा नगरी में १३ तालाब बनायें गये, इनमें कुछ तालाब परमार कालीन है तथा कुछ माण्डू सुल्तानों के समय बनाये गये। नगर के भीतर पेयजल के लिये कुऐं एवं बावड़ी थी, इनमें दो बावड़ी अस्तित्व में है। परमार काल में धारा नगरी के प्राकार के बाहर जो तालाब बनाये गये थे, इनमें से कई स्थानों पर आज धारा नगरी की बस्तियाँ बसी हई है, किन्तु कुछ तालाब आज भी अस्तित्व में है। स्थानीय लोग धारा नगरी के १२) तालाब की गिनती करते है, जिसका तात्पर्य १२ बड़े तालाब एवं एक छोटा तालाब है। धारा नगरी के मध्यकालीन तालाब निम्नानुसार है-

१. मुंजदेव तालाब

यह तालाब नगर के उत्तर-पश्चिमी कोने पर निर्मित विशाल तालाब है, इसका पानी देवी सागर तालाब एवं पूर्व के कुंजदेव तालाब में मिलता था। इस तालाब का निर्माण परमार नरेश वाक्पतिराज मुंज द्वारा करवाया गया, जिसके कारण इसका नाम मुंजदेव तालाब पड़ा।

२. कुन्जदेव तालाब

यह तालाब मुन्ज तालाब के पूर्व की ओर था, जो धारा गिरि वर्तमान धार किले तक विस्तृत था। इसी तालाब की भूमि पर नौगांव बस्ती एवं स्टेडियम है। इस तालाब का निर्माण परमार नरेश भोज के समय हुआ, किन्तु कुन्जदेव नाम क्यों पड़ा, यह स्पष्ट नहीं हो सका। राजा भोज देव के समय धारा गिरि पर एक सुन्दर शाही प्रमाद वन (उद्यान) विकसित हुआ था, जिसके लिये पानी की व्यंवस्था इसी तालाब से होती थी। इस शाही प्रमद वन में भोज ने अपनी बैठक ''मणिमरकत मण्डप'' का निर्माण करवाया था। परवर्ती परमारों ने इसे दुर्ग का रूप प्रदान किया।

३. भोज देव तालाब

इस तालाब का निर्माण राजाभोज देव परमार द्वारा करवाया गया। इस कारण इसे भोज देव तालाब कहा जाता है। यह तालाब नगर के उत्तर में पुराने गणपति मंदिर के सामने स्थित है।

४. देवी सागर तालाब

यह तालाब धार नगर के पश्चिम में कालिका माता मंदिर के समीप स्थित हैं। इस कारण इस तालाब को देवी सागर तालाब कहा जाता है। इस तालाब तथा मंदिर का निर्माण वाकपतिराज मुंज द्वारा करवाया गया था। प्राचीन तालाब के बांध व घाटों की मरम्मत मराठा काल में स्थानीय पंवार शासकों द्वारा मंदिर के जीर्णोद्धार के समय करवायी गयी। इस तालाब में व्यवस्थित सीढ़ियां युक्त घाट है, दक्षिणी ओर बांध है, जिसके ऊपर से अहमदाबाद रोड़ गुजरती है। परमार काल में सभी तालाब आपस में जुड़े हुये थे, वर्षा ऋतु में जल स्तर बढ़ने पर अतिरिक्त पानी इसी बांध से नाले में छोड़ा जाता था, जो आगे जाकर मान नदी में मिलता था।

५. फूटी पाल का तालाब

यह तालाब धार नगर में दक्षिण-पूर्व में वर्तमान बस स्टेण्ड के पास था। इसकी पाल फूटने के बाद मध्य काल में ही इस क्षेत्र में बस्ती बस गयी थी। संपूर्ण तालाब में कई बस्तियाँ है।

६. धूप तालाब

यह तालाब धार नगर के दक्षिण-पश्चिमी कोने पर श्मशान घाट के पास स्थित है। इस तालाब का निर्माण भी मध्य काल में हुआ है, किन्तु निर्माता की जानकारी प्राप्त नहीं होती है।

७. पूणियां तालाब

यह तालाब नगर के पूर्व में स्थित था, किन्तु आज माण्डव रोड़ पर स्थित पाटीदार अस्पताल के पीछे की जोशी कालोनी एवं अन्य बस्तियाँ इसी तालाब में बसी हुई है। इस तालाब की पश्चिमी पाल पर हनुमान मंदिर एवं सिटी कोतवाली है, इसके आगे बस स्टेण्ड है। मूलतः यह तालाब परमार कालीन है, किन्तु १८ वीं शताब्दी के बाद यह तालाब जल संग्रहण क्षेत्र की कमी के कारण सूख गया। इस क्षेत्र में पंवार शासकों द्वारा बनाई गयी सड़कों के कारण जल संग्रहण क्षेत्र समाप्त हो गया।

८. मंसूरी तालाब

यह तालाब नगर के बाहर माण्डव रोड़ पर बांयी ओर स्थित है। इसका निर्माण मध्य काल में माण्डू सुल्तानों के समय हुआ था। यह तालाब अभी तक अस्तित्व में था, किन्तु धीरे-धीरे इसको समाप्त कर भूमि अन्य उपयोग में ली जा रही है।

९. हिम्मतगढ़ तालाब

धार नगर के दक्षिणी ओर हिम्मतगढ़ नामक ग्राम के पास यह तालाब स्थित है। यह तालाब भी मूलतः परमार कालीन है। जो वारि परिखा का अंग है।

१०. लेण्डिया तालाब

यह तालाब राजा भोज के राजमहल राजमार्तण्ड प्रासाद के पास स्थित है। इसी प्रासाद को आज लाट मस्जिद कहते है। यह तालाब भी मूलतः परमार कालीन है।

११. सिद्धनाथ तालाब

यह तालाब धार नगर के बाहर इंदौर रोड़ पर दायीं ओर स्थित है। वर्तमान में इस तालाब के उत्तर में कर्मचारी कालोनी एवं दक्षिण-पश्चिम में हाऊसिंग बोर्ड की कॉलोनी बनी हुई है। वर्तमान में यह तालाब भी लगभग समाप्ति की ओर है।

१२. नटनागरा तालाब

यह तालाब धार से दक्षिण-पूर्व में पुराने माण्डव रोड़ अर्थात सलकनपुर नालछा मार्ग पर स्थित है। नगर की दक्षिण पूर्व की पहाड़ी तलहटी में एक बांध को बनाकर तालाब को बनाया गया है। इसके किनारे स्थित है नटनागरा मठ, जहाँ आज भैरव बाबा का मंदिर है। मूलतः यह नाथपंथी योगियों का है, जो परमार काल में १३ वीं शताब्दी ईस्वी में निर्मित हुआ। माण्डु सुल्तानों के समय इस मठ में सूफी सन्तों की मजलिसें भी हुआ करती थी।

१३. राम तलाई

यह छोटा तालाब है जो एस. पी. के बंगले के पास स्थित है। इसे लोग आधा तालाब कहते है।

उक्त तालाबों के अतिरिक्त दो महत्वपूर्ण बावड़ी भी है, जो मध्य कालीन जल प्रबंधन की देन है। इनमें धार किले के आगे नौगांव के पास तीन मंजिला बावड़ी है, जिसमें अभी भी जल की उपलब्धि है। इसका निर्माण १५ वीं शताब्दी ईस्वी में हुआ था। दूसरी महत्वपूर्ण बावड़ी धार दुर्ग पर स्थित है, जो मध्यप्रदेश पुरातत्व विभाग द्वारा संरक्षित है। यह बावड़ी भी परमार राजा भोज देव के समय निर्मित हुयी, कालान्तर में भी इसमें निर्माण होते रहे।

आज का धार दुर्ग राजा भोजदेव परमार के समय धार गिरि लीलोद्यान के नाम से शाही प्रमद वन हुआ करता था। इस स्थल के नैसर्गिक सौन्दर्य को देखकर राजा भोज ने यहाँ एक महल बनाया, जिसका नाम मणिमरकत मण्डप रखा गया है। यह स्थल राजा भोज के पठन-पाठन व चिन्तन का केन्द्र था। पारिजात मंजरी नाटक में इस का विशद वर्णन है। धाराधीश अर्जुन वर्मन के राजगुरू मदन उपाध्याय ने इस ग्रंथ की रचना की है।[८] यही धारागिरी जो १३ वी शताब्दी में जयसिंह द्वितीय के समय दुर्ग के रूप में परिवर्तित हुयी। इसी के दक्षिणी ओर स्थित है। वहाँ विशाल बावड़ी, जिसका निर्माण परमार काल में चट्टान को काटकर अर्थात शैलोत्कीर्ण किया गया है। इसकी सीढ़ियाँ भी शैलोत्कीर्ण थी। मुस्लिम काल में किले द्वारों, बैरक, पैरापेट वॉल का निर्माण हुआ, इसी समय माण्डू सुल्तान महमूद शाह खिलजी प्रथम ने ई. सन् १४४७-४८ में बावड़ी की सीढ़िया निर्मित करायी। दिल्ली सल्तनत काल में ई. सन् १३०५ से १४०५ तक १०० वर्षो तक मालवा के सूबेदार का निवास धार दुर्ग में रहा। विशाल सेना एवं अश्व आदि के लिये पेयजल हेतु इस बावड़ी का ही उपयोग होता था। पंवार शासकों के काल में बावड़ी के चारों ओर बनी भित्ति एवं सीढ़ियों की

मरम्मत करवायी गयी। बावड़ी में घाट, मण्डप बनाये गये। कालान्तर में बावड़ी अपने मूलरूप में नहीं रह सकी।

धार नगर के सभी जल स्त्रोत तत्कालीन शासकों के जलप्रबंधन का ही परिणाम है, किन्तु पर्यावरण की दृष्टि से जल प्रबंधन के लिये कितने सजग थे, यह बिन्दु भी विचारणीय है। प्राचीन काल में नदियों के जल को शुद्ध रखने के लिये गंदे पानी का विसर्जन नदियों की ओर नहीं होता था। शौच के लिये नदी या तालाब के जल का उपयोग नहीं होता था। घरों के गंदे पानी के निकास के लिये वलयाकार कूप सेफ्टी टेंक बनाए जाते थे। धार के लोगों ने इन तालाबों के जल को शुद्धि के लिये क्या किया एवं जल का क्या उपयोग किया? सभी तालाबों की भौगोलिक स्थिति का अध्ययन किया जाय, तो यह ज्ञात होता है कि, भूमि के सामान्य ढाल के अनुसार तालाबों का जल संग्रहण क्षेत्र उत्तरी ओर अधिक था। पूर्व से उत्तर होकर पश्चिम तक के तालाब आपस में जलवृद्धि के समय मिल जाते थे, किन्तु पूर्व की ओर तथा पश्चिम की ओर के तालाबों का अतिरिक्त जल दक्षिणी ओर के नालों में चला जाता था। दक्षिणी ओर के तालाबों के बीच में दूरी अधिक थी, इसी भाग में नालियों के माध्यम से नगर का जल विसर्जन होता है। दक्षिणी भाग पठार का अन्तिम कोना है, यहीं से प्राकृतिक खाइयां प्रारम्भ हो जाती है। अतः दोनों से जलधारा प्रवाहित होती रहती थी। यहीं जल धारा वारि परिखा का भी काम करती थी। तालाबों के जल को प्रमुखतया दो उपयोग होते थे। प्रथम भूमि की सिंचाई के लिये, किन्तु इसके प्रत्यक्ष अवशेष प्रकाश में नहीं आये। द्वितीय नगर में जलापूर्ति के लिये। दुर्भाग्य से धार नगर में परमार काल के नियोजन के अवशेष विद्यमान नहीं है, किन्तु धार किले के हमाम, शीशमहल व खरबूजा महल में जलप्रदाय व्यवस्था, माण्डव के जहाज महल की सर्पिल नायिां एवं हमाम आदि से यह अनुमान लगाया जा सकता है कि इन तालाबों का पानी नगर में किस-किस उपयोग में लिये जाता रहा होगा।

तलाबों के पानी को नालियों के माध्यम नगर में ले जाते थे, उस समय पक्की मिट्टी के पाइप बनाये जाते थे, जिससे पानी स्नानागारों में एवं महलों में ले जाया जाता था। नगर की कोट के किनारे जल प्रदाय नालिया बनाई जाती थी, जिससे नगर में सदैव जलापूर्ति होती रहे।

धार नगर एक मैदानी नगर था, जहाँ अथाह जल था, जिसकी धारा कभी बन्द नहीं होती थी उसी प्रकार कला व संस्कृति का केन्द्र बनाया था, राजा भोज ने, जो न केवल वास्तु के शिल्पी थे, अपितु महान लेखक भी थे, किन्तु दुर्भाग्य कहे धारा नगर का, कि इसकी ख्याति से ही ग्रहण लग गया और चालुक्य नरेश सोमेश्वर के १०४७

ई. के आक्रमण एवं कलचुरि कर्ण व अहिलवाड़ के चालुक्य भीम की संयुक्त सेना ने धारा नगरी की धारा को बन्द कर किया, भीषण युद्ध में धार नगरी ध्वस्त हो गई, राजा भोज का निधन हो गया। जब यह समाचार कवि विल्हण को मिला, जो धार नगरी की ओर जा रहे थे, तो उनके मुख से निकला "अंशधारा निराधारा निरालम्बा सरस्वती पंडिता खण्डिता भोज राजा दिवंगता"।

परवर्ती परमारों के शासन काल में ही नगर के ध्वस्त होने पर दुर्ग का महत्व बढ़ गया और राजधानी माण्डव बनायी गई। इसी समय पूर्वी ओर तालाबों का जल संग्रहण कम हो गया। माण्डू सुल्तानों के समय धार सूफी सन्तों का केन्द्र था। धार व माण्डव में उनके कई हुजरे खानकाहे बनी, इनके पास तालाबों व बावड़ियों का भी निर्माण हुआ। माण्डव दुर्ग पर बने हुए स्मारक जो महल शब्द से सम्बोधित होते है, वे सभी सूफी सन्तों के हुजरे खानकाहे थी, जो बाद में मकबरे बन गये। प्रत्येक मकबरा या खानकाह के पास बावड़ी या तालाब का निर्माण अवश्य किया गया।

सन्दर्भ

१. पद्‌म गुप्त संदर्भ साहसोद चरित १, ६०, ८, ११४

२. एपीग्राफिया इण्डिका भाग १४ पृ. २३६, धनपाल कृत "पायलनदी" पृ १६८

३. भाटिया प्रतिमपाल दि परमाराज पृ. २८१.

४. पद्‌म गुपत, १८ पृ. २८५-८७.

५. मेरूतुंग प्रबंध चिन्तामणि (टोनी) पृ ७२ (जिन विजय) पृ. ४६.

६. अलबरूनी भाग एक पृ. १६१, २०२-३, इंदोर गजेटियर ११ पृ. २६५

७. भाटिया प्रतिमपाल दि परमाराज पृ. २८४

८. गर्ग आर. एस., धार राज्य का इतिहास पृ. ६

ग्वालियर राज्य के जल-प्रबंध विकास में माधवराव सिंधिया प्रथम का योगदान

डॉ. के. रतनम् एवं अरविन्द सिंह गौर

प्राकृतिक संरचना की दृष्टि से ग्वालियर राज्य मुख्यतः दो भागों में विभक्त था उत्तरी विभाग के अंतर्गत ग्वालियर क्षेत्र तथा दक्षिण में मालवा का भाग था। ग्वालियर राज्य प्राकृतिक सम्पदाओं से परिपूर्ण था, इसके अन्तर्गत चम्बल, बेतवा तथा नर्मदा प्रमुख नदियाँ थी। इन नदियों के अतिरिक्त पार्वती, पहूज तथा कुआरी आदि प्रमुख सहायक नदियाँ थी। राज्य में प्राकृतिक सम्पदा के रूप में ग्वालियर गिर्द, श्योपुर, नरवर, भेलसा (विदिशा), शाहजहाँपुर, अमझेरा, मंदसौर और शिवपुरी में घने वन थे।[1]

सन् १८८६ ई. में माधवराव सिंधिया ग्वालियर राज्य के शासक बने। माधवराव सिंधिया को ग्वालियर राज्य के आधुनिकीकरण एवं प्रशासनिक सुधारों के लिये जाना जाता है। उन्होंने राज्य की प्रत्येक प्रशासनिक इकाई में सुधार करने हेतु प्रशासनिक सेवाओं में अनुशासन एवं अधिकारियों को कर्तव्यों के प्रति उत्तरदायी रहने के लिये निर्देशित करते हुए अधिकारियों द्वारा दौरों के नियमों में सुधार तथा मितव्ययता पर विशेष बल दिया है।[2]

ग्वालियर राज्यान्तर्गत नवीन नगर पालिका कानून के अनुसार नगरपालिका के अधिकार क्षेत्र में स्वच्छता, जन स्वास्थ्य, प्रकाश, शिक्षा, चिकित्सा, मण्डी, उद्यान, वृक्षारोपण तथा जल प्रबंधन आदि विभाग अधिकृत किए गए।[3]

माधवराव सिंधिया के काल में जल-मल निकास के लिए सन् १६०६ ई. में एक जल निकास एवं पूर्ति योजना तैयार की गई। इस योजना के अंतर्गत गन्दे पानी की निकासी के लिए सम्पूर्ण नगर में खुली नालियों, फ्लश मूत्रालय, मल पात्र डिपों तथा कूड़ा भट्टियों की व्यवस्था की गई थी। इस योजना के क्रियान्वयन के लिए माधवराव सिंधिया के निर्देशन में राज्य द्वारा लगभग २५ लाख की राशि स्वीकृत की गई, जिससे सन् १६३६ ई. तक ग्वालियर तथा मुरार में जल निकास कार्य पूर्ण किए गए जिस पर स्वीकृत राशि से लगभग ४ गुना व्यय किया गया। मुरार जल निकास कार्य के

लिए १,६३,५६४ रूपये व्यय किया गया तथा कुल ग्वालियर में जल-मल निकास कार्य पर १,८०,००० रूपये व्यय किये गए।[४]

जल-मल निकास योजना पर माधवराव सिंधिया के काल में शिवपुरी में ३,७१,८७३ रूपये, उज्जैन में ३२,००० रूपये व्यय किए गए। इसके अतिरिक्त भेलसा, गुना, मंदसौर, बड़नगर आदि में भी जल मल निकास प्रबंधन की दृष्टि के अनुरूप कार्य किए गए।[५]

ग्वालियर राज्य में माधवराव सिंधिया के पूर्व पेय जल आपूर्ति एवं प्रबंधन के लिए कुएँ, बावड़ी तथा तालाब ही प्रमुख साधन थे। माधवराव सिंधिया के कार्यकाल में ही सर्वप्रथम पेय जल आपूर्ति एवं प्रबंधन का आधुनिकीकरण किया गया। सन् १६२६ ई. में ग्वालियर राज्य की रीजेन्सी परिषद् द्वारा जल पूर्ति ग्रह के निर्माण को स्वीकृति प्रदन की गई।[६] इस जल पूर्ति ग्रह के निर्माण के लिए तिघरा सिंचाई जलाशय को चुना गया। जल पूर्ति ग्रह के निर्माण से पूर्व यह जलाशय ग्वालियर राज्य के क्षेत्र में समूची कृषि व्यवस्था के लिए सिंचाई हेतु जल उपलब्ध कराता था।

माधवराव सिंधिया से पूर्व ग्वालियर राज्य के कृषकों को सिंचाई के लिए प्राकृतिक वर्षा पर आश्रित होना पड़ता था और कृषि के उपयोग के लिए जल प्रबंधन का राज्य की ओर से कोई व्यवस्था नहीं थी। माधवराव सिंधिया ने राज्य की नवीन कृषि नीति का निर्माण कर कृषकों को अप्राकृतिक सिंचाई संसाधनों के लिए प्रोत्साहित एवं प्रशिक्षित किया। उन्होंने राज्य में विभिन्न वावड़ियों एवं जलाशयों का निर्माण कराया जिनमें सिमरिया ताल पर निर्मित बाबड़ी तत्कालीन समय में सिंचाई एंव पेयजल की सबसे महत्वपूर्ण इकाई थी।

ग्वालियर राज्य में पेयजल प्रबंधन की दृष्टि से माधवराव सिंधिया ने अपनी रीजेन्सी परिषद् में एक अन्य पावर हाउस के निर्माण की स्वीकृति प्रदान की।[७] इस पावर हाउस का निर्माण करने के लिए मोतीझील का चयन किया गया। इस पावर हाउस के माध्यम से लश्कर, ग्वालियर तथा मुरार तीनों नगरों में जल एवं विद्युत प्रबंधन की योजना का निर्माण किया गया।

७ मार्च १६२६ ई. को तत्कालीन वायसराय लार्ड इर्विन के ग्वालियर आगमन पर माधव राव सिंधिया ने मोतीझील पर निर्मित होने वाले पावर हाउस का शिलान्यास करवाया[८] तथा इस पावर हाउस को 'इर्विन पावर हाउस' की संज्ञा दी गई। इस पावर हाउस का निर्माण कार्य सन् १६३० में पूर्ण हुआ तथा अप्रैल १६३० से इस पावर हाउस ने ग्वालियर, लश्कर तथा मुरार में जल पूर्ति आरंभ कर दी।[९]

माधवराव सिंधिया सदैव ही लोकोपयोगी सेवाओं के प्रति संवेदनशील रहे। माधव राव सिंधिया के शासनकाल में ग्वालियर राज्य में जल पूर्ति के लिए व्यक्तिगत नल कनेक्शनों को स्वीकृति प्रदान की। माधवराव सिंधिया के रीजेन्सी परिषद के निर्णय के अनुरूप ग्वालियर राज्य में नगर पालिका द्वारा जल पूर्ति हेतु व्यक्तिगत नल कनेक्शन प्रदाय किए जाने लगे। जिसके परिणामस्वरूप सन् १९३३ तक सम्पूर्ण राज्य में २५०० व्यक्तिगत नल कनेक्शन प्रदाय किए गए।[९]

७ सितम्बर १९३२ तक ग्वालियर राज्य में जल पूर्ति प्रबंधन वाणिज्य विभाग के अंतर्गत था। वाणिज्य विभाग का कार्यपालन यंत्री राज्य में सम्पूर्ण जल पूर्ति प्रबंधन को देखता था तथा सम्पूर्ण कार्य उन्हीं के तकनीकी नियंत्रण में होता था। अक्टूबर १९३२ में राज्य की जल पूर्ति हेतु जल पूर्ति ग्रहों के रख-रखाव का दायित्व विद्युत प्रदाय कम्पनी लश्कर को दे दिया गया।

इर्विन जल पूर्ति ग्रह की औसतन क्षमता ११ लाख गैलन जल की थी जो एक दिन की पूर्ति के लिए पर्याप्त थी।[१०] इस जल पूर्ति योजना मे एक वित्तीय वर्ष में २२,५०,०००, रूपये व्यय हुआ था।[११] इर्विन जल पूर्ति ग्रह का विद्युत ग्रह एवं विद्युत उत्पादन के रूप में भी प्रयोग किया गया। इस विद्युत ग्रह में प्रतिदिन औसतन ३००० बोल्ट का आल्टरनेटिव करेन्ट प्राप्त होता था।[१२] माधवराव सिंधिया के काल में शिवपुरी, उज्जैन, मंदसौर, सरदारपुर, मुरैना, श्योपुर एवं शाहजहाँपुर में जल पूर्ति के लिए योजनाएँ बनाई गई, जिनका क्रियान्वयन माधवराव सिंधिया के उत्तराधिकारी महाराजा जीवाजी राव सिंधिया के काल में प्रारंभ हुआ। १४ अक्टूबर १९३८ को जल पूर्ति ग्रह मंदसौर का उद्घाटन जीवाजीराव सिंधिया द्वारा किया गया। १ मई १९३९ को तत्कालीन महाराजा जीवाजीराव सिंधिया द्वारा शिवपुरी में जल पूर्ति ग्रह का उद्घाटन किया गया। इस जल पूर्ति ग्रह के निर्माण में राज्य का १,५२,००० रूपये व्यय हुआ। राज्य के विलयनीयकरण होने तक ग्वालियर राज्य के अंतर्गत माधवराव सिंधिया के काल में स्वीकृत विलयनीकरण होने तक ग्वालियर राज्य के अन्तर्गत माधवराव सिंधिया के काल में स्वीकृत जल पूर्ति ग्रह के निर्माण का कार्य उज्जैन, मंदसौर, शाहजहाँपुर, मुरैना, शिवपुरी तथा सरदारपुर में पूर्ण हो चुका था।

ग्वालियर राज्य में यह काल जहाँ नगरीकरण एंव आधुनिकीकरण के लिए इतिहास में जाना जाता है वही जल आपूर्ति एंव प्रबंधन की दृष्टि से माधव राव सिंधिया का शासनकाल न केवल महत्वपूर्ण था बल्कि उनके द्वारा विकसित जल पूर्ति योजनाएँ एवं संशोधन वर्तमान में भी ग्वालियर में उपयोगी है।

संदर्भ

१. ग्वालियर राज्य जनगणना रिपोर्ट १६११ आलीजाह दरबार प्रेस ग्वालियर, १६११
२. फाइल नम्बर १२६ (सन् १६२०) प्राइवेट सेक्रेटरी ऑफिस ग्वालियर, राज्य अभिलेखागार भोपाल।
३. ग्वालियर राज पत्र ३० सितम्बर १६११, अंक ३६, आलीजाह दरबार प्रेस ग्वालियर पृ. ६६
४. माइकल एच. ब्राउन, ग्वालियर, टू डे, द टाईम्स ऑफ इण्डिया प्रेस बॉम्बे १६४०, पृ. ३०
५. वही
६. माधवराव सिधिया पॉलिसी दरबार भाग १०, पृ. २८
७. कॉमर्शियल डायरेक्टरी ग्वालियर स्टेट, आलीजाह दरबार प्रेस ग्वालियर, १६३४, पृ. ८-६
८. वही
६. माइकल एच. ब्राउन, पूर्वोक्त, पृ. २६
१०. वही
११. व.सु. कृष्णन (सं.), म.प्र. गजेटियर जिला ग्वालियर, जिला गजेटियर विभाग, म.प्र. शासन भोपाल सन् १६६८
१२. माइकल एच. ब्राउन, पूर्वोक्त, पृ. २६
१३. कॉमर्शियल डायरेक्टरी ग्वालियर स्टेट, आलीजाह दरबार प्रेस ग्वालियर पृ. ८-६
१४. एडमिनिस्ट्रेटिव रिर्पोट ऑफ ग्वालियर राज्य, आलीशाह दरबार प्रेस, ग्वालियर, १६०१ पृ. २०७

कुएं एवं बावड़ियों निर्माण में महिलाओं का योगदान मेवाड़ व मारवाड़ के संदर्भ में

डॉ. सुशीला शक्तावत

मेवाड़ और मारवाड़ में कुओं और बावड़ियों झालरे, नाडे और टांको का निर्माण करना धर्म का सर्वोच्च स्वरुप समझा जाता रहा हैं। इस कार्य में आस्था रखने वाले लोग सदियों से इनका निर्माण करते आ रहें हैं, जिनमें समाजसेवी, राजा, प्रजा, रानियां, पासवानें, डावड़िया, नाजर और ओहदेदार शामिल है। जगत ग्राम के मन्दिर के शिलालेख से यह स्पष्ट होता है कि "जीणोद्धार कार्य का महत्व एवं पुण्य उतना ही है जितना कि वापी, कूप, सरोवर, उद्यान एवं भवनादि के नूतन निर्माण का।[1] यह तथ्य उल्लेखनीय है कि राजा महाराजाओं व उनके ओहदेदारो ने जितने भी तालाब, कुएं, बावड़िया, टांके और नाड़े-नाड़ी बनवाये वे सब के सब उनके निजी काम के लिए बनाये गये थे। किसी जलाशय से उनका परिवार पानी काम मे लेता था तो किसी पर उन फौजो का अधिकार होता था। इसके विपरीत रानियों, महारानियों, पड़दायतो, पासवानों और रखेलो ने जितने भी जलाशय बनाये बे आम जनता के लिए बनाये गये थे, इसके पीछे दो बाते थीं। (१) जलाशय जनता के लिये बनाना एक बहुत बड़े धर्म का काम माना जाता था। (२) दूसरा उन को यह भी ज्ञान था राजा को तो प्रजा याद रखेगी लेकिन रानियों महारानियों, पड़दायतो, पासवानों, रखेलो को कौन और क्यों याद करेगा इसलिए उन्होंने अपने नाम से, तालाबों, कुओं, बावड़ियों, झालरो, टांको और नाड़े नाड़ियो का निर्माण कराया ताकि लोग उनको पानी भरने के बहाने याद करे।

मध्यकाल में इन कुओं और बावड़ियों को सुन्दर एवम् आकर्षक बनाने के लिए उन्होंने पत्थरों को तराश कर तरह-तरह की कलाकृतियों का प्रदर्शन करते हुए इन कुओं- बावड़ियों का निर्माण कार्य आगे बढ़ाया। यह कार्य उस वक्त के समर्थ लोगों का सूचक बन गया था। बाद में उसी कड़ी में झालरों का निर्माण हुआ। कोयटा (कुएं के पानी की सतह) तक चारों तरफ से पानी तक पहुंचने के लिए पावड़ियों का निर्माण कर उन्होंने इस कार्य को एक नई दिशा दीं। उन्हें जिन स्थानों पर कुओं और

बावड़ियों का निर्माण कार्य करना उचित नहीं लगा, वहाँ पर उन्होंने वर्षा के पानी का वर्ष भर उपयोग करने के लिए टांके एवम् नाड़े-नाड़ियां बनवायें जिनमें वर्षा का पानी इकट्ठा किया जाता था।

मेवाड़ में महिलाओं द्वारा निर्मित कुएं बावड़ियां

'शिलालेख' एवं अन्य ऐतिहासिक सामग्री में उनके द्वारा निर्मित जलाशयों की जानकारी प्राप्त होती हैं।

बड़लावाली सराय तथा बावड़ीः- उदयसिंह की रानी सोनगरी ने १५५४ ई. में बड़लावाली सराय तथा पनघट की बावड़ी बनवायी थी। वहां तेलियों का निवास होने से इस सराय को तेलियों की सराय के नाम से भी पुकारा जाता है।[२] वर्तमान में पनघट की बावड़ी के स्थान पर बी.एन. स्कूल के मुख्य द्वार के सामने का पार्किंग स्थल है एवं सराय के स्थान पर अतिथि गृह बना हुआ है।[३]

देबारी के पास की बावड़ी :- महारानी झाली बीरा बाई ने अपने पीहर सादड़ी के रास्ते पर देबारी के बाहर बावडी, मंदिर तथा धर्मशाला का निर्माण करवाया था। यह सभी निर्माण कार्य १५५७ ई. से १५५९ ई. क बीच हुए थे।

सुन्दरबाव- खवासण सुंदर ने १६६० ई. में उदयपुर से ४ कि.मी. दूर उत्तर पूर्व में ग्राम पारड़ा के पास एक बावड़ी बनवायी।[५] यह बावड़ी विशाल तथा कारीगरी का नमूना हैं। पारड़ा धूलकोट से उत्तार में स्थित हैं।[६] महाराणा राजसिंह ने पारड़ा ग्राम में 'सुन्दरबाव' बनवाने के उपलक्ष्य में व्यास बलभद्र गोपाल के पुत्र गोविन्दराम व्यास को भुवाणा गांव में ७५ बीघा भूमि दान की।[७]

भुवाणा की बावड़ी- सुन्दरबाव की प्रतिष्ठा पर महराणा राजसिंह ने गोविन्दराम व्यास को ग्राम भुवाणा में ७५ बीघा जमीन दी। इस भूमि पर गोविन्दराम की मां ने बावड़ी बनाई तथा यात्रियों की सुविधा के लिए एक सराय बनवायीं।[८] यह आयड़ में गंगोदव कुण्ड के पास स्थित महासतिदा के पूर्व में स्थित है। इसके आगे सुन्दरबाव निर्मित है।[९]

त्रिमुखी बावड़ी- उदयपुर से ९ कि.मी. दूर देबारी के भीतर झरना की सराय के निकट महराणा राजसिंह की राणी रामरसदे जी अजमेर जिले के परमार रायसल की प्रपौत्री जुझारसिंह की पौत्री और पृथ्वीसिंह की पुत्री थी बनवायी। "जया" नाम की बावड़ी का निर्माण माघ शुक्ला २, गुरुवार सं. १७३२ (१६७५ ई.) में हुआ। इसको अब त्रिमुखी बावड़ी कहा जाता है। इस बावड़ी के निर्माण में २४,०००/- रुपये लगे थे।[१०]

राजवल्लभ में वापी निर्माण के निर्देशों के अनुरुप यह जयसंज्ञक बावड़ी है।[११] वह बावड़ी जो तीन मुखवाली अर्थात् जिसमें तीन तरफ सीढ़ियां हों और जिसमें नौ कूट

अर्थात् डेरियां हो, उसे जया बावड़ी कहा जाता है।[१२] त्रिमुखी बावड़ी में तीन तरफ से अन्दर उतरने की सीढ़िया हैं तथा प्रत्येक दिशा की सीढ़िया तीन खण्डों में विभक्त है। प्रत्येक खण्ड में नौ सीढ़िया हैं और नौ सीढ़ियों के समाप्त होने पर वहां लम्बी फारगती (कूट) है। उसके ऊपर स्तम्भयुक्त मण्डप निर्मित हैं। इस प्रकार एक ओर २७ सीढ़ियां और ३ कूट बने हुए हैं। तीनों तरफ ८१ सीढ़ियां तथा ६ कूट बने हुए हैं।

इस वापी के प्रत्येक तरफ की सीढ़ियों के दो कूटों के बीच दोनों तरफ एक-एक देवमूर्ति स्थापन की ताकें रखी गयी हैं और इस दृष्टि से प्रत्येक भाग की सीढ़ियों की तरफ छह-छह ताकें हैं, यह सभी मिलाकर अठारह हैं। इन ताकों के अतिरिक्त मध्य के कुण्ड भाग में भी चारों तरफ कई ताकें हैं, जिनमें पहले गंगा, सूर्य, विष्णु के दस अवतारों तथा अन्य देवी देवताओं की प्रतिमाएं प्रतिष्ठित थी।[१३]

इस बावड़ी की तीन दिशाओं में बनी सीढ़ियों के अलावा चौथी दिशा में ऊपर अर्थात् सीढियों से पूर्व के चरण में समान्तर एक स्तम्भ युक्त मण्डप बना हुआ है, जो गवाक्ष की तरह बावड़ी के जलमय भाग में आया हुआ है। इस गवाक्ष मण्डप और नीचे सीढ़ियों के बीच में बने मण्डपों के स्तम्भ, उनके ऊपर के लिये बने कर्ण उनके ऊपर लगाये गये उतरंग तथा उनके ऊपर रखी गयी आयताकार शिला-पट्टियों की छवाई इत्यादि सभी परिसज्जा से इतर भवन निर्माण अभियांत्रिकी सम्बन्धी १७ वीं शताब्दी के मेवाड़ की तकनीकी को उद्घाटित करती हैं।[१४] इसके निर्माण कार्य के देख-रेख करने वाले लाला पोरवाड़ और धाबाई सतीदास थे। इसका मुख्य शिल्पी नाथू गोड़ था।[१५] इसका शिलालेख बावड़ी में पूर्व की तरफ से उतरने वाली सीढ़ियों के बायी तरफ ताक में आज भी लगा हुआ है।[१६]

बाईजी राज का कुण्ड:- महाराणा जयसिंह ने निम्बार्क सम्प्रदाय के स्थल हेतु देहली दरवाजे के पास भूमि प्रदान की। यहां (१६८०-१६६८ई.) के समय में बाईजी राज का बनवाया हुआ एक विशाल कुण्ड है।[१७] यह कुण्ड बाईजी राज के कुण्ड के नाम से जाना जाता है जिसके कोने पर श्री नवनीत लाल जी का मन्दिर है।[१८]

घोसुण्डी की बावड़ी:- चित्तौड़-कोटा मार्ग पर चित्तौड़ से २१ किमी. दूर उत्तर-पश्चिम में एक किमी. दूर घोसुण्डी गांव स्थित है। इस गांव के नजदीक चित्तौड़- कोटा ब्रोडगेज के उत्तर में घोसुण्डी की बावड़ी स्थित है। इसके उत्तर- पूर्व में बरगद के पेड़ तथा पश्चिम में चामुण्डा माता का मन्दिर है।[१६]

जल स्त्रोत के विस्तार में इस बावड़ी का अपना विशिष्ट स्थान है। इसका निर्माण महाराणा रायमल की रानी श्रृंगार देवी मारवाड़ के राजा जोधा की पुत्री ने करवाया

था।[२०] बावड़ी में उतरने के लिए पश्चिम से पूर्व की ओर सीढ़िया बनी हुई है। बावड़ी के बाहरी सिरों के दोनों ओर दो ताकों में गणेश आदि देवताओं की मूर्तियां लगी हुई हैं। प्रथम चार सीढ़िया .३० मीटर चौड़ी तथा २२ मीटर ऊंची है। पांचवी सीढ़ी .६० मीटर चौड़ी तथा .१५ मीटर ऊंची है। सभी सीढ़ियों की लम्बाई ३.६६ मीटर है। चार- एक के क्रम में कुल २६ सीढ़िया बनी हुई हैं।[२१]

सीढ़ियों के दोनों ओर दीवारों में बड़े-बड़े पत्थरों की चिनाई से बड़ी-बड़ी ताकें बनी हुई हैं। यहां से देव-प्रतिमाएं हटा ली गयी हैं। सीढ़ियों के अन्त में २.१३ मीटर लम्बा, चौड़ा तथा ऊंचा मण्डप बना हुआ है। यह चार स्तम्भों पर स्थित है। मण्डप के ऊपरी सिरे पर काले पत्थरों को तराशकर हाथियों तथा बतखों के सुन्दर चित्र उत्कीर्ण हैं। मण्डप पर गोखड़ा बना हुआ है, जिसके पूर्व-पश्चिम में यहां बड़े-बड़े पत्थरों की बैठक व्यवस्था है। ऊपर मुख्य बावड़ी के विपरीत दिशा में मण्डप के चित्रों के ठीक ऊपर बतखों के चित्र अंकित हैं।[२२] बैठक व्यवस्था में सहारा लेने वाले पत्थरों को कलात्मक तक्षण से तराश कर बैठक वाले पत्थर में फंसाया गया है। देखने से यह पत्थर पीछे की तरफ स्वतंत्र झुके लगते हैं। जबकि यह वास्तव में कारीगरी का नमूना है।[२३]

तारा बावः- उदयपुर से लगभग ६६ किमी. दूर सादड़ी (गोडवाड) नगर में तारा बाव स्थित है। पहले यह नगर के बाहर थी, परन्तु अब नगर के अन्दर आ गयी हैं। तारा बाव एक कलात्मक विशाल बावड़ी और बरादरी है, तीर्थस्वरुप वह बावड़ी ताराचन्द का अमर स्मारक बन गया है।[२४] इसका निर्माण बहुत कुछ ताराचन्द के काल में हो चुका था, परन्तु उसके पुत्र "सुरताण" ने इसे पुरा करवाया था इसकी प्रतिष्ठा वैसाख कृष्ण २ गुरुवार सं. १६५४ (१५९७ई.) के दिन हुई थी।[२५]

यह वापी[२६] पांच मंजिल की है। इसमें दो तरफ से नीचे उतरने के लिए सीढ़िया बनी हुई हैं, जो नीचे पुनः एक हो जाती है। दोनों ओर बनी सीढ़ियों के मध्य में दो मंजिलों में दो "महामंडप" निर्मित हैं। यह बावड़ी स्थापत्य का उत्कृष्ट नमूना है, इसके ऊपर ताराचन्द की छतरी बनी हुई है। बावड़ी पर विशाल रहट बना हुआ है, जिससे समीपवर्ती बाड़ी में जल सिंचन किया जाता था। जल की नालियां अभी भी मौजूद हैं। इसके निर्माण में मटमैले लाल पत्थर का उपयोग हुआ था।[२७]

झाली बावः- चित्तौड़ के पश्चिमी तरफ पहाड़ से मिला हुआ नगर आबाद है, जिसको तलहटी कहते है। इस कस्बे में किले के पाडलपोल दरवाजे के बाहर महाराणा उदयसिंह की रानी झाली री बनवायी हुई एक बावड़ी है। जिसको झाली बाव कहते हैं।[२८]

बावड़ी महाराणा उदयसिंह री रानी भयिनी अजन कुंवर ने एक बावड़ी तथा धर्मशाला बनवायी। इसका निर्माण १५५३ से १५५७ ई. के बीच हुआ।[२९] महारानी सोलंकी सहज कुंवर ने १५५४ मे एक सराय तथा १५५५ मे एक बावड़ी बनाई।

कुण्डः- शाहपुरा महाराजा भारतसिंह जी की माता कछवारा जी ने संवत् १६९२ ई. में एक कुंड बनवाया। कुंड उत्सव मे मांजी साहब रा ४०,००० रु. व्यय हुए।[३०]

मारवाड़ में कुएं व बावड़िया

मारवाड़ में कुएं व बावड़िया के निर्माण में महिलाओं द्वारा दिये गये योगदान उल्लेखनीय है विभिन्न स्त्रोतों से इसकी जानकारी होती हैं:-

चांद बावड़ीः- राव जोधाजी की चांद कंवर नाम की सोनगरी (चौहान) रानी ने फतेहपोल के पास चांद बावडी का निर्माण कराया था। इसको चौहान बावड़ी भी कहते हैं लेकिन यह बावड़ी मुख्यतः चांद बावड़ी के नाम से ही जानी जाती है। संवत् १६४५ में इसका विकास हुआ। रेरुजी लिखित मारवाड़ का इतिहास की पृ. सं. ९३ पर दर्शाया गया है कि राव जोधा की जसमदे नामक हाडी रानी ने एक कुआं बनवाया था।[३१] मारवाड़ रा परगना री विगत पृ.सं. ५९३/३६ पर भी यह दर्ज किया गया है।[३२] कि राव जोधा की चौहान रानी ने कुओं को विकसित कर एक बावड़ी बनवाई थी जो पहले 'चौहान बावड़ी' कही जाती थी किन्तु बाद में उसे चांद बावड़ी कहा जाने लगा।

फूलेलाव तालाब की बावड़ीः- यह बावड़ी फूलेलाव में स्थित है जो पहले बड़े कुएँ के रुप में थी। महाराजा जसवन्तसिंह प्रथम की रानी जसवन्तदेशेखावत ने १७१५ में इसका विकास कर पुनः निर्माण करवाया और उसे बावड़ी का स्वरुप प्रदान किया[३३] इसके तालाब को पाटकर जब से इसको 'व्यास पार्क' बनाया गया है. तब से इस बावड़ी को विकसित कर इसको चारों तरफ से बन्द कर दिया गया है। इसमें पम्प लगाकर बगीचे को पानी दिया जाता है। कुछ वर्ष पूर्व इसका पानी जन स्वास्थ्य अभियांत्रिकी विभाग ने वितरित किया था।

गोल नाड़ी की बावड़ीः- गोळनाड़ी तो पहले से ही थी किन्तु महाराजा गजसिंह जी की रानी और महाराजा जसवन्तसिंह जी की माँ राणावत गुलाब कंवर ने उसमें यह बावड़ी बनवाई।[३४] अगर इस बावड़ी को साफ कराया जाये तो इसका पानी पुनः पीने योग्य हो सकता है।

गोराधाय की बावड़ी (गोरिन्दा बावड़ी):- इस बावड़ी का निर्माण गोराधाय ने संवत् १७१६ में कराया था।[३५] यह गोराधाय महाराजा जसवन्तसिंह की धाय थी।[३६] मारवाड़

रा परगना री विगत पृ.सं. ५६६/६६ में दर्शाया गया है कि गोरा राठौड़ किसना झंवर की पुत्री थी।[३७]

रुपाधाय की बावड़ी :- इस बावड़ी का निर्माण का कार्य रुपाधाय ने हनुमान जी की भाखरी के पास मालासर तालाब में महाराजा गजसिंह जी के समय कराया था। रुपा महाराज गजसिंह जी की धाय और गहलोत चांपा की पत्नी थी।[३८] इस बावड़ी को आज पाट दिया गया है। यह स्थान आज के मेड़तीगेट के अन्दर करीब ५० गज की दूरी पर मकानों के बीच आया हुआ है।

पड़दायत की बावड़ी:- इस बावड़ी का निर्माण रामणा के केसू की बेटी जो महाराणा मानसिंह की पड़दायत थी, ने मेड़तिया दरवाजा के बाहर कराया था। महाराजा मानसिंह राज्य कार्य से विटक होकर इस बावड़ी पर बनी साल में आकर ठहरे थे और वहीं से दूसरे दिन शेखावत जी के तालाब पर चले गये थे।[३९] यह बावड़ी नैनीजी के मंदिर के सामने स्थित है, जिसे अब कचरा डालकर पाटा जा रहा है।

मगराय की बावड़ी:- इस बावड़ी का निर्माण पड़दायत मगरायजी ने महाराजा तख्तसिंह के समय मे नागोरी गेट के बाहर कराया था।[४०] इस बावड़ी के पास उसने अपने रहने के लिए महल व बाग बनवाया था। बावड़ी में पानी हैं परन्तु बहुत गहरा हैं। यह बावड़ी मगराय जी के वंश की निजी सम्पति है। महाराजा तख्तसिंह जी ने इन महलों में होली खेली थी और कई बार गोठ गूगरी की थी।

सोड़ीसर बावड़ी:- इस बावड़ी का निर्माण महाराजा विजयसिंह जी ने अपने राज्यकाल में जोधपुर से करीब १५ कि.मी. दूर नादण गांव के पास कराया था इसके पास सोड़ीसर का तालाब भी है।[४१]

रावटी की बावड़ी:- इस बावड़ी का निर्माण महाराजा जसवन्तसिंह (द्वितीय) की पासवान ने करवाया।[४२] यह बावड़ी बड़ी सुन्दर है और इसमें पानी भी बहुत है। तालाब सूख जाने पर इस बावड़ी का पानी काम लिया जाता रहा है।

धाय बावड़ी अथवा खटूकड़ी की बावड़ी:- मारवाड़ री ख्यात में वर्णित बावड़ी- कुआं के अनुसार इस बावड़ी का निर्माण महाराजा जसवन्तसिंह की धाय ने करवाया था अतः इसका नाम "धाय की बावड़ी" रखा गया है।[४३] इसका पानी पीने योग्य है।

इन्द्र कुंवरी की बावड़ी:- राव मालदेव के समय सहदेव सोलंकी ने एक बावड़ी बनवायी उसका नाम सहदेव की बावड़ी रखा गया। इसके बाद सन् १६०५ में सवाई राजा सूरसिंह जी की राजकुमारी इन्द्रकुंवर ने बावड़ी का पुनः जीर्णोद्वार करवाया उस समय से यह बावड़ी इन्द्र कुंवर री बावड़ी कहलाई। महाराजा जसवन्तसिंह ने संवत्

१७०३ में यह बावड़ी ख्वाजा फरासत को दे दी, जिसने इस पर मीनारें एवं महल बनाये।[४४] इसके स्वर्गवास के उपरान्त यहीं पर दफनाया गया। इस कारण यह बाद में मिय्या का बाग कहलाया। इस प्रकार समय[२] पर इस बावड़ी को विभिन्न नामों से पुकारा जाता रहा हैं।

अनारा की बावड़ीः- यह बावड़ी विद्याशाला और सूरसागर की सड़क पर आई हुई है। इसका निर्माण महाराजा गजसिंह जी की पासवान अनारा बेगम ने किया था।[४५]

केसा की बावड़ीः- इस बावड़ी का निर्माण महाराजा गजसिंह जी की पासवान अनार बेगम की बहिन ने कराया था। यह बावड़ी भी ७ आकार की है।[४६] इस पर पूर्व में अरहट लगा हुआ था। इसके बाद इस बावड़ी पर जाली लगाकर इसे कुएं का आकार दिया गया। वर्तमान में यह बावड़ी विद्याशाला का कुआं कहलाती है।

पांचवे माजीसा के मन्दिर की बावड़ीः- महादेव जी के मन्दिर के साथ-साथ इस बावड़ी का निर्माण महाराजा मानसिंह जी की पांचवी रानी ने करवाया था।[४७] इस मंदिर नें प्लास्टर ऑफ पेरिस की बनी हुई बलरामजी की सुन्दर मूर्ति है। जो अब जीर्ण-शीर्ण हो रही हैं। इस बावड़ी में पानी पीने के काम नहीं आता है।

जोधपुर के झालरे

तूंवर जी का झालराः- यह झालरा महाराजा अभयसिंह जी की पटरानी तूंवर जी जो कि पाटन के बक्षीराम की पुत्री थी, ने सन् १७४८ में बनवाया था।[४८] मारवाड़ रा परगना री विगत में पेज नं. ५८४ पर दर्शाया गया है[४९] कि इस झालरे का निर्माण महाराजा अजीतसिंह जी की रानी तूंवर जी करवाया था। महाराज अजीसिंह जी का स्वर्गवास सन् १७२४ में हो गया था। सत्य की खोज अब भी जारी है।

मायलाबाग का झालराः- इस झालरे एवम् इसके पास के महलों का निर्माण महाराजा विजयसिंह जी की पासवान गुलाबराय ने सन् १७७५ में करवाया था।[५०] पहले यहां पर दो मंदिर एवं एक बावड़ी भी थी। बावड़ी को विकसित कर झालरा में परिवर्तित कर दिया गया। यह स्थान पहले राजसिंह की हवेली थी जिसके कुछ भाग में मायलाबाग के महल बनाये गये थे। बाद में हवेली भाभा मोतीसिंह को इनायत कर दी गई थी।

जाड़ेजा जी का झालराः- यह झालरा महाराजा गजसिंह की रानी जाड़ेजा जी प्रेमवती ने बनाया था। मारवाड़ री परगना री विगत के पृ.सं. ५८४ पर दर्शाया है।[५१] लेकिन उसी की पृ.सं. ५६७ पर दर्शाया गया है कि इस झालरे का निर्माण महाराजा अजीतसिंह जी की रानी जाड़ेजा जी ने चांदपोल के बाहर कराया था।[५२] हो सकता है कि उन्होंने इसका कुछ विस्तार किया हो जिन्हें निर्माण कर्त्ता बतलाया गया है।

संदर्भित सूची

१. जगत के अम्बिका मन्दिर का शिलालेख, वैसाख बदी ५ संवत् १०१७, वरदा वर्ष ६, अंक ४, पृ. ६१ (अक्टु. १९६३)।
२. चित्तौड़- उदयपुर पाटनामा, भाग ३, पृ. २१६ व तथा २२०-अ (७६८-६६)।
३. उदयपुर अतीत वर्तमान मज्झमिका ईश्वर सिंह राणावत, पृ. ४६।
४. चित्तौड़ उदयपुर पाटनामा भाग ३, पृ. २२०-अ (८००)
५. श्यामलदास- वीरविनोद, भागर पृ. ४३६
६. पूरोहित देवनाथ- उदयपुर दर्शन, पृ. १०८
७. भुवाणा गांव की बावड़ी का शिलालेख, सं.१७१७ (१६६० ई.) वीर विनोद भाग-२, पृ. ५७८।
८. उपरोक्त सं १७१७ (१६६० ई.) वीर विनोद, भाग-२, पृ.४३६।
९. वीर विनोद भाग १, पृ. १५८-५६।
१०. त्रिमुखी बावड़ी की प्रशस्ति, माघ शुक्ला २, गुरुवार सं. १७३२ (१६७५ ई.)
११. राजवल्लभ, अंक ४, श्लोक २८।
१२. राजवल्लभ, अंक ४, श्लोक २८, पंक्ति २।
१३. राजशेखर व्यास- मेवाड़ की कला और स्थापना, पृ २२३।
१४. राजशेखर व्यास- मेवाड़ की कला और स्थापना, पृ २२४।
१५. त्रिमुखी बावड़ी की प्रशस्ति, सं. १७३२ (१६७५ ई.)
१६. उदयपुर अतीत और वर्तमान- मज्झमिका, ईश्वरसिंह राणावत, आलेख पृ. ४६।
१७. बाईजीराम महाराजा जयसिंह की पुत्री जो सादड़ी ब्याही गयी थी परन्तु विधवा हो गयी, उसने अपने धन से यह कुण्ड बनवाया था।
१८. देवनाथ पुरोहित- उदयपुर दर्शन, पृ. ८०-८१।
१९. जल संसाधन पृ. १२३
२०. घोसुण्डी की बावड़ी का शिलालेख; वैसाख सुदि ३, बुधवार सं. १५६१ (१७ अप्रेल, १५०४ ई.) बंगा.ए.सो.ज; भाग ५६, पृ. ७६-८२; ओझा; जोधपुर राज्य का इतिहास; भाग १, पृ. २५१
२१. वही पृ. १२३
२२. ईश्वरसिंह राणावत- जल संसाधन पृ. १२४
२३. वही पृ. १२४
२४. तारा बावड़ी का लेख; सं. १६५४ (१५९७ ई.) पंक्ति १५
२५. उपरोक्त; पंक्ति ४-१७

२६. कुछ समय पूर्व बावड़ी का जीर्णोद्धार कराते समय बावड़ी के लेख को वहां से हटा दिया गया है। इस लेख की छाप के आधार पर रामवल्लभ सोमानी ने इसे प्रकाशित कराया था। (मरु भारती; वर्ष १५, अंक ३, पृ.६-८)
२७. राजेन्द्र प्रकाश भटनागर; भामाशाह एवं ठा. ताराचन्द; पृ. ४६
२८. गौरीशंकर हीराचन्द्र ओझा, उदयपुर राज्य का इतिहास, भाग-१, पृ.१३०
२९. वही पृ. १३०
३०. ईश्वरसिंह राणावत जल संसाधन, पृ.१२६
३१. विश्वेश्वरनाथ रेउ- मारवाड़ का इतिहास, पृ.६३
३२. मारवाड़ री परगना री विगत पृ.सं. ५३३/५३६
३३. गो.ही - ओझा- जोधपुर राज्य का इतिहास भाग- १, पृ.३११
३४. वही - पृ.२७१
३५. मारवाड़ रा परगना री विगत पृ. सं. ५६६-५६६
३६. वही, पृ. सं. ५६७
३७. मानसिंह की ख्यात, पृ. सं. १६६
३८. नेणसी की ख्यात, भाग-१, पृ.सं. १८८, वीर विनोद भाग-२, पृ.सं. २३७
३९. गो. ही. ओझा- जोधपुर राज्य का इतिहास भाग-२, पृ.सं.१६०
४०. टॉड राजस्थान का इतिहास, जिल्द २, पृ.सं.१०७६
४१. मानसिंह की ख्यात पृ.सं. १६८
४२. मारवाड़ का परगना री विगत, पृ.सं. ५३०-३१
४३. जोधपुर की ख्यात, जिल्द १, पृ.सं. २५७
४४. वही पृ. सं. २५०
४५. वही पृ.सं. १७१-१७२
४६. मारवाड़ परगना री विगत पृसं. ५६४
४७. गौरीशंकर हीराचन्द ओझा, जोधपुर राज्य का इतिहास भाग२, पृ.सं. २१६
४८. जोधपुर राज्य की ख्यात, जिल्द२, पृ.सं. १६१
४९. मारवाड़ परगना री विगत पृ.सं. ५८४
५०. श्यामलदास- वीर विनोद, भाग २, पृ.सं. ८५६
५१. मारवाड़ परगना री विगत, पृ.सं. ५८४
५२. वही पृ.सं. ५६७

बाबर द्वारा वर्णित जल-संसाधन

डॉ. कमला शंकर राठौर एवं कु. नम्रता श्रीवास्तव

मुगल बादशाह जहरुधीन मुहम्मद बाबर ने अपनी आत्मकथा 'तुजुक-ए-बाबरी' में कुँओं, सरोवरों (हौज), झीलों और अन्य साधनों के बारे में वर्णन किया है।

बाबर ने अपनी आत्मकथा 'तुजुक-ए-बाबरी' में हिन्दुस्तान के सिंचाई व्यवस्था का वर्णन करते हुए लिखता है कि हिन्दुस्तान के बहुत से जिले समतल मैदान है। परन्तु किसी में भी सिंचाई के लिए नहर (आवेराता) नहीं है। खेतों में सिंचाई केवल नदियों के माध्यम से की जाती थी। कई स्थानों पर देखने को मिलता है कि बँधा हुआ पानी प्रयोग किया जाता है। कुछ नगर ऐसे है जहाँ पर खोदकर नहर लाई जा सकती है तथापि वहाँ पानी नहीं लाया गया है। खरीफ की फसल वर्षा के जल से तैयार होती है। यह विचित्र बात है कि वर्षा के अभाव में भी रबी की फसल हो जाया करती थी। बाबर ने अपनी आत्मकथा में जल संचय के लिए सर्वाधिक हौज (सरोवर) के बारे में वर्णन करता है। २२ अगस्त १५२७ ई० को बाबर जब धौलपुर में था तो वहाँ पहाड़ी को कटवाकर एक छत्तदार अष्टाकार हौज (सरोवर) के निर्माण का आदेश दिया। अक्टूबर १५२८ ई० को वह उस छत्तदार हौज के निरीक्षण करने स्वयं पहुँचा। उसी समय उसने आदेश भी दिया कि वे हौज (सरोवर) के नीचे की सतह चिकनी करके उसमें जल दीवार के बराबर भर दे।[१] बाबर ने आगरा में अष्टभुजा हौज (सरोवर) का निर्माण करवाया था। सबसे पहले बड़ा हौज (सरोवर) तथा उसकी चहारदीवारी तैयार की गई। इसके बाद पत्थर के भवन के सामने एक हौज (सरोवर) बनवाया। जिसके किनारे एक दलान था जो खम्भों पर बनाये जाते थे और सामने से खुले होते है। इन निर्मित हौज के माध्यम से आगरा के बाग-बगीचों की सिंचाई की जाती थी।[२] वह आगे लिखता है कि खलीफा, शेख जैन, युसुफ अली तथा अन्यं लोगों ने भी यमुना नदी के पार जहाँ भी भूमि मिली वहाँ हौज (सरोवर) के साथ बड़े एवं उत्तम उद्यानों का निर्माण करवाया।[३] चंदेरी में २१ जनवरी १५२८ ई० की रात के पड़ाव में बज्जत खाँ द्वारा निर्मित तालाब के पार बने बाँध के ऊपर ठहरे थे।[४] चंदेरी के बारे में बाबर लिखता है कि वह एक विचित्र प्रदेश है। इसके चारों ओर जल धाराएँ पायी जाती

है। एक पहाड़ी के ऊपर किला स्थित है। इसके भीतर एक चट्टान को काटकर हौज (सरोवर) का निर्माण किया गया है। किले के सामने तीन बड़े-बड़े तालाब है। पिछले हाकिमों ने इनके चारों ओर बाँध बँधवा कर उन्हें बनवाया है।[५] बाबर ने लिखा है कि दौलपुर[६] एक चोंचदार पहाड़ी के ऊपर स्थित है। उसी पहाड़ी पर भवन बनाने का आदेश देता है और कहता है कि यदि वह अधिक ऊँची न हो तो उसमें छत्तदार एक अष्टाकार हौज (सरोवर) का निर्माण किया जाये। हौज (सरोवर) के चारों ओर आम-जामुन तथा अन्य प्रकार के वृक्ष बड़ी संख्या में लगवाये गये।[७] इन वृक्षों के सामने १० - १० के एक कुंए का निर्माण का आदेश दिया। लगभग कुंआ निर्माण हो चुका था और इस कुएँ के माध्यम से हौज (सरोवर) में पानी पहुँचता था। यह हौज (सरोवर) के किनारे एक ऊपर एक बाँध था जिसे सिकन्दरशाह निर्माण करवाया था। बाँध की ऊँचाई तक वर्षा ऋतु में जल एकत्रित होता है। यही जल झील के रुप में ले लेता था। इस झील के पूर्व में उद्यान है जिसकी सिंचाई की जाती थी।

बाबर अपनी आत्मकथा में लिखता है कि लाहौर, दीपालपुर, सरहिन्द, और समीपस्थ प्रदेशों में रेहट (रेंट) के द्वारा पानी निकाला जाता है। कुएँ की गहराई के अनुसार दो रस्सी लेकर उन्हें इस प्रकार ब्राँध दिया जाता है कि एक चक्कर बन जाता है और इनमें लकड़ी के डण्डे लगा दिये जाते हैं और इन डण्डों से घड़े बाँध दिये जाते हैं। इस प्रकार के रस्सों से और उनसे बँधे हुए घड़ों में रेहटँ (रेंट) चलाया जाता हैं, जो कुएँ के ऊपर लगा रहता है। इस रेहटँ की धूर के एक पर एक-दूसरा दाँतेदार पहिया रखा जाता है और फिर दूसरे के साथ तीसरा पहिया जोड़ दिया जाता है। यह एक सीधी धुरी से बनाया जाता हैं जब बैल अंतिम पहिये को मोड़ते हैं तो उसके दाँते दूसरे पहिये को घुमाते हैं और फिर तीसरा पहिया घुमता है, जिस पर घड़ों का गोल रस्सा टिका रहता है। घड़ों के चक्कर से जहाँ पानी गिरता है वहाँ एक कठौता होता है और जल नालियों से होता हुआ प्रत्येक स्थान पर पहुँच जाता है।[८]

बाबर लिखता है कि आगरा, बयाना, चन्दवार तथा उस क्षेत्र में चरसा[९] (चमड़े का थैला) से सिंचाई होती है। इसमें बड़ा परिश्रम करना पड़ता है और बड़ी भद्‌दी विधि है। कुएँ के किनारे दो शाखाओं वाली एक लकड़ी लगा दी जाती है। इन दोनों के मध्य एक गड़ारी लगा देते हैं। एक बड़ा चरसा (चमड़े का थैला) में रस्सी बाँध दी जाती थी। रस्सी गड़ारी पर रख दी जाती है। एक आदमी को बैल हाँकना पड़ता है तथा दूसरे को चरसा खाली करना पड़ता है। जब बैल चरसा खींच कर वापस होता है तो रस्सी बैल के मार्ग पर जिस पर मूत्र तथा गोबर पड़ा रहता है, लथेड़ दी जाती है और फिर वही रस्सी कुएँ में पहुँचती है जिससे कुएँ का पानी गंदा हो जाता है।[१०]

बाबर ने सिंचाई के साधन के रुप में 'डोल'[११] का भी अधिक वर्णन किया है। कुछ खेतों को जिन्हें सिंचाई की आवश्यकता होती है। स्त्री तथा पुरुष डोल भर-भर कर खींचते है।[१२] डोल के माध्यम से छोटे-छोटे तालाब या गड्ढ़ों के माध्यम से खेतों में पानी पहुँचाया जाता है। इसमें जहाँ नालियों के माध्यम से पानी नहीं पहुँच पाता है, उस स्थान को सिंचित करने के लिए डोल की सहायता लेनी पड़ती थी। उत्तर भारत में आज भी सिंचाई के रुप में डोल का प्रयोग किया जा रहा है।

हिन्दुस्तान के निवासियों के रहन-सहन के बारे में बाबर लिखता है कि "हिन्दुस्तान के गाँव और नगर क्षण भर में बस जाते हैं और क्षण भर में एकदम उजाड़ हो जाते हैं। बरसों में बसे हुए नगर एक या डेढ़ दिन में ऐसे उजाड़ हो जाते हैं कि वहाँ बस्ती का कोई चिन्ह भी नहीं छूटता।[१३] परन्तु यदि किसी स्थान पर बसना चाहते हैं तो चारों-ओर आदमी ही आदमी नजर आते हैं क्योंकि हिन्दुस्तान की आबादी बहुत है और यहाँ बिना सिंचाई के खेती होती है और यहाँ बस्ती बहुत है, ये लोग या तो कुँआ खोद लेते हैं या तालाब बना लेते हैं। क्षण भर में ही गाँव या कस्बा बस जाता है।"[१४]

बाबर अपने युद्ध काल के दौरान जब आगरा में था, उसने विचार किया कि जहाँ भी मैं ठहरने का निश्चय करूँ, वहाँ रेहटँ लगवाऊँ और कृत्रिम नदी बनाकर सुन्दर एवं सुव्यवस्थित स्थान का निर्माण करवाऊ। जब आगरा के निकट कोई सुन्दर स्थान न मिला तो मैंने विवश होकर किसी स्थान का उत्तम से उत्तम प्रयोग करने का निश्चय किया। सर्वप्रथम एक बड़ा कुआँ खुदवाना शुरु किया जिससे हमाम (स्नानागारें) में पानी आ सके। फिर उस भूमि का काम आरम्भ किया गया जिस पर आमली के वृक्ष है और जहाँ अष्टकोण तालाब है। फिर एक बड़ा तालाब और इसका अहाता बनवाना शुरु किया और एक अंत में अन्य तालाब तथा उसके चारें ओर चहारदीवारी बनवाई। फिर मैने भवनों व बागों का निर्माण पूरा करवाया।[१५]

बाबर आगे लिखता है कि आगरा के दुर्ग के अंदर इब्राहीम के महल और दुर्ग प्राचीर के मध्य में एक रिक्त स्थान था, जहाँ पर मैने १० गज - १० गज एक बड़ी वाइन (बावड़ी) का निर्माण करने का आदेश दिया। हिन्दुस्तान की भाषा में एक बड़े कुएँ को जिसमें नीचे उतरने के लिए सीढ़ियाँ बनी हुई हो जिसे वाइन (बावड़ी) कहते हैं। इसके अंदर एक इमारत बनाई गई जिसमें छोटी-छोटी तीन मंजिले थीं। सबसे नीचे की मंजिल में तीन खुले हुए बड़े कमरे जिनमें कुएँ के अंदर से मार्ग है। प्रत्येक मंजिल पर जाने के लिए इसी प्रकार का मार्ग बना हुआ है। एक मंजिल से दूसरी में तीन सीढ़ियों से बराबर पहुँचा जाता है। सबसे नीचे के कमरे में एक जीना है जो

कुएँ में पानी तक पहुँचता है। इसका उपयोग जब पानी नीचे चला जाता है तब किया जाता है। वर्षा ऋतु में जल का स्तर ऊँचा होकर सबसे ऊपर की मंजिल तक पहुँच जाता है। बीच की मंजिल में उत्कीर्ण पत्थरों का एक कमरा है और उसके समीप ही एक गुम्बद है, रेहटँ को घुमाने वाले बैल इसके चारों ओर घूमते हैं। कुएँ के ऊपर के क्षेत्र में ५-६ सीढ़ियों का एक जीना है। कुएँ के एक ओर खाई इस प्रकार खुदी हुई है इसका पेंदा कुएँ के मध्य से कुछ ऊँचा है। गुम्बद के नीचे घूमते हुए पशु पानी के रेहटँ को घुमाते है जिससे एक खाई से दूसरी खाई में पानी पहुँचता है। अंतिम खाई पर एक और रेहट लगा हुआ है जिससे पानी प्राचीर के बराबर उठ जाता है और ऊपर के बाग में बहता है।[१६]

खानवा के युद्ध[१७] के समय बाबर ने अपने मीर आखू (अश्व सेनापति) कासिम को आगे चलने वाले लोगों के साथ रवाना करते हुए आदेश दिया कि मिर्धा के परगने में कुएँ बनवाये जाये क्योंकि वह स्थान सेना के शिविर के लिए उपयुक्त है। १६ फरवरी १५२८ ई० को आगरे के पास से कूच करके बाबर उसी मार्ग पर डेरा डलवाया जहाँ कुएँ बन चुके थे।[१८] फिरोजपुर का चश्मा (झरना) और कोटिला के तालाब का वर्णन करते हुए बाबर लिखता है कि "मैने फिरोजपुर के झरने और कोटिला के तालाब के विषय में बहुत कुछ सुना था। जिस घाटी में से इस झरने का पानी निकलता है उसमें कनरी के पुष्प खूब खिले हुए थे। ये बहुत सुन्दर है, परन्तु उतने नहीं जितनी इसकी प्रशंसा की जाती है। मैने आदेश दिया कि उस स्थान पर १० गज लम्बा और उतना ही चौड़ा पत्थर काटकर एक हौज बनाया जाएँ। उस रात को हम घाटी में ही ठहरे और दूसरे दिन प्रातःकाल कोटिला के तालाब देखने गये। यह बहुत बड़ा तालाब है, परन्तु किसी ओर से भी देखों, यह अच्छा मालूम नहीं होता। तालाब के बीच में एक ऊँची जगह है और इसके चारों ओर बहुत सी नावें है। तालाब के किनारे पर बसे हुए कस्बों के लोग गड़बड़ी के समय इन नावों पर बैठकर भाग जाते हैं।[१९]

बाबर १४ अक्टूबर १५२८ ई० को सीकरी पहुँचा और वहाँ एक बाग लगाने का आदेश दिया। उस बाग के सिंचाई के लिए कुओं का निर्माण से संतुष्ट नहीं हुआ तो उस कार्य में लगे कर्मचारियों को प्रताड़ित (डाँटा) भी किया।[२०]

बाबर ने कुएँ के बराबर एक अन्य कुआँ का वर्णन करता है और लिखता है कि कुएँ का धरातल पहले कुएँ के जल-धरातल से आधा है, बैल रेहट चला कर पहले कुएँ से दूसरे कुएँ में जल पहुँचाते हैं। इस कुएँ में एक रेहट लगा हुआ है। इसके द्वारा जल किले की चहारदीवारी से होता हुआ ऊपर के उद्यान में जाता है। कुएँ के मुँह के ऊपर एक पत्थर का भवन बना हुआ है।[२१]

बसावर[२२] और चौसा[२३] के मध्य में एक पहाड़ी की शिखा पर झरने पर पड़ाव किया गया। यह एक पूर्णतया झरना है। हिन्दुस्तान में जहाँ जल-धाराएँ नहीं है, वहाँ लोग झरने की खोज में रहते हैं। यदि संयोग से कही कोई झरना मिल जाता है तो वह बूँद-बूँद करके भूमि से फूटता है। उन स्थानों के झरने के सनान भूमि से जल उबलता नहीं निकलता है। बाद में चलकर इसी झरने के पास पत्थरों का एक अष्टाकार हौज (सरोवर) बना दिया जाये।[२४] आगे चलकर इस झरने का नाम 'चश्मा-ए-बादशाही' होने की बात अब्दुल्लाह कहता है।

कचवा[२५] नामक विचित्र स्थान का वर्णन करते हुए बाबर करता है। वह लिखता है कि कचवा के चारों ओर छोटी-छोटी पहाड़ियाँ है। कचवा के उत्तर-पूर्व में पहाड़ियों में एक बाँध बना हुआ है जिसके कारण एक बहुत बड़ी झील जिसका घेरा पाँच अथवा छः करोह[२६] है, बन गई है। यह झील कचवा को तीनों ओर से घेरे हैं। इसका उपयोग नौका-विहार के लिए प्रयोग में किया जाता है। बाबर ग्वालियर से दक्षिण-पूर्व की ओर बारह मील दूर पर स्थित एक झरने का निरीक्षण करने गया। बारह मील से कम की मात्रा पर मध्यान्ह की नमाज के समय इस झरने पर पहुँचे जहाँ एक पनचक्की के योग्य जल एक ढाल से एक बीस मील की ऊँचाई से आ रहा था। झरने के नीचे एक बहुत बड़ी झील का भी वर्णन करता है। जल के तट पर चानों के बहुत बड़े-बड़े टुकड़ें हैं मानों वे बैठने के लिए बने हो, किन्तु कहा जाता है कि जल सर्वदा वहाँ तक नहीं रहता है।[२७]

बाबर लिखता है कि सैयिद रुकनी,[२८] शिराजी जिबागर[२९] को एक खिलअत पहनाई गई। उसे इनाम देकर आदेश दिया गया कि वह मेहराबदार कुएँ, जिसके विषय में वह जितना जानता हो, उसके अनुसार, पूरा करें। २३ दिसम्बर १५२८ ई० को जब धौलपुर की सैर करने निकला तो वह पत्थर का कुआँ, २६ पत्थर के फब्वारें तथा स्तम्भ और नालियाँ,[३०] जो ढलवाँ चान से निकाली गई थी और उसको तैयार भी की गई। उसी दिन तीसरे पहर में कुएँ से जल निकालने का प्रबन्ध किया गया। जल में दुर्गन्ध होने के कारण सावधानी की दृष्टि से आदेश दिया गया कि पन्द्रह दिन तक चौबीस घंटे निरन्तर रेहट चलाकर जल निकाल दिया जाये। पत्थर काटने वालों, मजदूरों एवं समस्त कारीगरों को आगरा के उस्तादकारों एवं मजदूरों की प्रथानुसार इनाम दिया गया।[३१]

बाबर जब हिन्दुस्तान में था तो उसको काबुल की अव्यवस्था के बारे में जानकारी प्राप्त होती है। वह लिखता है कि वहाँ का समाचार सुनकर मेरी आँखों में आँसू डबडबा आये। उसी के माध्यम से काबुल में सुधार करने की बात लिखता है। उसमें

जल प्रबन्धन के लिए खुद काबुल में बाँध का निर्माण, जो बूतखाक के जल को खुद काबुल के सकरे मार्ग से निकास के समय रोके गये। गजनी बाँध की मरम्मत का आदेश देता है। वह आगे लिखता है कि मै तूतूम दरा से दक्षिण-पश्चिम के ख्वाजा बस्ता नामक पुश्ते की ओर जल लाया था और वहाँ हौज (सरोवर) का निर्माण करके पौधे लगवा दिये। वह स्थान नजरगाह के नाम से प्रसिद्ध हो गया। इसका कारण कि वह नदी के घाट के समीप है और उत्तम ही दृश्य प्रस्तुत करता है।[३२]

इस प्रकार स्पष्ट है कि बाबर ने अपनी आत्मकथा में जल के संसाधनों पर व्यापक प्रकाश डाला है। उसने जहाँ-जहाँ बागों को लगवाया वहाँ-वहाँ कुँओं, झरनों तथा हौजों (सरोवर) का निर्माण किया। हिन्दुस्तान में ही नहीं काबुल, गजनी तथा अन्य जगहों पर जल संचय के उपायों पर व्यवस्थित कार्य किया। आधुनिक युग में भी बाबर द्वारा वर्णित संसाधनों का स्वरुप दिखाई देता है।

संदर्भ ग्रंथ

१. बाबर, बाबरनामा अनु० सैयद अतहर अब्बास रिजवी, मुगल कालीन भारत (बाबर) (अलीगढ़, १९६०) पृ. ५०।

२. वही, पृ. २११।

३. वही, पृ. २१२।

४. वही, पृ. २६५।

५. वही, पृ. २६८।

६. दोलपुर को आधुनिक धौलपुर के नाम उल्लेखित था। बाबरनामा (रिजवी)

७. बाबरनामा (रिजवी), पूर्वोद्धृत पृ. २७४।

८. बाबर, तुजुक-ए-बाबरी, अनु० मथुरा लाल शर्मा (ग्वालियर, तिथि रहित) पृ. ६७-६८; इब्नेबत्तूता ने सर्वप्रथम परोक्ष में रेहट का वर्णन किया है-द रेहला आफ इब्नेबत्तूता, मेहदी हुसेन (सम्पा०) (बड़ौदा, १९६३) पृ. १७२।

९. चरसा एक प्रकार के चमड़े का बना बड़ा थैला होता था जिसको लकड़ी के रिंगनुमा आकार में बाँधा जाता है तथा रस्सी को बाँधने के लिए लकड़ी का टगँना लगाया जाता है। आधुनिक युग में भी इस प्रयोग होता लेकिन इसे चरसा के नाम से नहीं बल्कि 'मोट' के नाम से उत्तर भारत में चर्चित है।

१०. बाबरनामा (रिजवी), पूर्वोद्धृत, पृ. १७१।

११. डोल को हम एक तरह बाँस से बने गहरे आकार का बड़ा बर्तन के स्वरुप में हम देखते हैं। गाँवों में इसे आज भी 'ओड़चा' या 'दौरी' के रुप में जानते हैं। इसमें चार रस्सियाँ लगी होती है। दो रस्सियाँ एक तरफ तथा दो रस्सियाँ दूसरी तरफ लगी होती है। दो व्यक्ति एक तरफ पकड़कर पानी को सिंचाई के रुप में प्रयोग करते हैं।

१२. बाबरनामा (रिजवी), पूर्वोद्धृत, पृ. १७१।

१३. इसको 'पुल्सा' या 'वल्सा' कहते हैं। कहने का तात्पर्य है कि जब शत्रु सेना आती है तो हिन्दुस्तान के हर भाग के निवासी अपने बड़े-बड़े सामान को जमीन में गाड़ देते है और आवश्यक वस्तुओं को लेकर ऐसे स्थानों पर चले जाते हैं जहाँ युद्ध की विपत्तियाँ नहीं सहनी पड़े।

१४. तुजुक-ए-बाबरी (मथुरा लाल शर्मा), पृ. ६६।

१५. वही, पृ. १०५।

१६. वही, पृ. १०७-१०८; इब्नेबत्तूता ने इसी प्रकार के वाई का उल्लेख किया है। द रेहला आफ इब्नेबत्तूता, पृ. १५५, १८७; द्रश्टव्य इस्लामिक कल्चर, भाग ६८, १६८४, पृ. ११-१२।

१७. खानवा का युद्ध राणा साँगा और बाबर के बीच लड़ा गया।

१८. तुजुक-ए-बाबरी (मथुरा लाल शर्मा), पृ. १२१।

१६. वही, पृ. १४२।

२०. बाबरनामा (रिजवी), पूर्वोद्धृत, पृ. ५०।

२१. वही, पृ. २३।

२२. बसावर को लोग भुसावर के नाम से भी जाना जाता है जो भरतपुर में है- बाबरनामा (रिजवी)।

२३. सम्भवतः आइन-ए-अकबरी में चौसा का वर्णन है।

२४. बाबरनामा (रिजवी), पूर्वोद्धृत, पृ. २५५।

२५. 'कचवा' अथवा 'कजवा' जिसे इब्नेबत्तूता ने 'कजर्रा' लिखा है। उद्धृत, सैयिद अतहर अब्बास रिजवी, तुगलुक कालीन भारत, भाग २ (अलीगढ़, १६५७) पृ. २६६।

२६. पाँच या छः करोह का अर्थ दस-बारह मील से लगाया गया है।

२७.बाबरनामा (रिजवी), पूर्वोद्धृत, पृ. २७६।

२८.इसके नाम के विषय में विभिन्न पाण्डुलिपियों में रुकनी, दकनी, तथा जकनी विभिन्न रुप में लिखा गया है।

२९.जिबनगर का अर्थ होता है हौज (सरोवर) बनाने वाला।

३०.कुँआ एक हौज को भरने के लिए बनाया गया था। २६ फव्वारें एवं रोक के स्तम्भ जल को नालियों में पहुँचाने के लिए बनाये गये थे- बाबरनामा (रिजवी)।

३१.बाबरनामा (रिजवी), पूर्वोद्धृत, पृ. २६६।

३२.वही, पृ. ३०५-३०६।

ग्राम इकलेरा स्थित भूलन बावड़ी ऐतिहासिक परिप्रेक्ष्य में

डॉ. अल्पना दुभाषे

मालवा की प्राकृतिक सीमाओं के विषय में निर्धारण इस प्रकार किया गया है मालवा के दक्षिण में नर्मदा नदी, उत्तर में चंबल नदी, पश्चिम में गुजरात और पूर्व में बुंदेलखंड तथा गोंडवाना। यह सीमा निर्धारण मध्यकाल से ही चला आ रहा है। डॉ. यदुनाथ सरकार ने अपने ग्रंथ 'हिस्ट्री ऑफ औरंगजेब' में लिखा है, कि मालवा के पूर्व तथा पश्चिम में बुंदेलखंड तथा गोंडवाना के प्रांत फैले हुए थे।[1] उत्तर भारत के समृद्ध मैदानी क्षेत्रों तथा दक्षिण में दक्खन देश के बीच स्थित होने से यह अधिक संपन्न प्रदेश रहा।[2]

मालवा क्षेत्र में एक भाग देवास है, तो उत्तरी अक्षांक्ष २२० और २४० और पूर्वी देशांश में ७५० और ७७० पर स्थित है।[3]

सतारा के साहू महाराज से देवास राज्य पर पवार शासन की स्थापना हुई। सन् १७३२ में देवास के दो भाग कर दिये गये। ई.एम.फास्टर ने लिखा है, कि दोनों भाई अपनी राजी मर्जी से खुशी-खुशी अलग हो गये।

बड़ी पाती के परगने

देवास, बागोद, सांरगपुर, गढ़गुच्या

छोटी पाती के परगने

देवास, बागोद (पाडल्या) सारंगपुर, गढगुच्या, रिंगणोद

देवास रियासत के दोनों भाग भौगोलिक दृष्टि से समान थे। बड़ी पाती ४४६ वर्गमील तथा छोटी पाती ४४० वर्गमील में फैला हुआ था। दोनों राजाओं ने देवास के परगनों का समान रूप से विभाजन किया। १५ सिंतबंर, १६४० को बड़ी पाती के विक्रमसिंह राव पवार और छोटी पाती के श्रीमंत सदाशिवरावखासे साहब ने आपसी समझौते से परगनों का पुनः विभाजन जनसुविधा के आधार पर किया।[4]

वर्तमान में समसामयिक विषय जल संसाधन है। देवास जिले के उत्तर में टोंकखुर्द तहसील के अंतर्गत ग्राम इकलेरा मुख्यालय से लगभग ३० कि.मी. दूर स्थित है। यह रियासतकाल में ग्वालियर स्टेट के अंतर्गत आता था। उपजाऊ प्रदेश होने के कारण कृषि के उत्पादन हेतु अनेकानेक कुऐं तथा बावड़ियाँ स्थित है। इसी शृंखला में 'भूलन बावड़ी' तथा कुआं विशेष आर्कषण का केन्द्र है। संभवतया यह निर्माण १५०० से १५५० के लगभग अकबर के काल में हुआ था।[५]

भूलन बावड़ी के निर्माण में प्रयुक्त सामग्री

इस बावड़ी के निर्माण में काफी समय लगा होगा। इसका निर्माण मुख्यतः चूना, कालिया लकड़ी, काला पत्थर, ईंट तथा बिल्व का गोंद आदि को पत्थर से पीसकर उपयोग किया गया था। इस बावड़ी के नीचे (तले) में कालिया लकड़ी के चौड़े पाट रखकर दीवार का निर्माण किया गया है। जिससे की इसकी मजबूती बनी रहे।

इस बावड़ी की लंबाई ५० फीट तथा चौड़ाई ४० फीट हैं तथा इसकी गहराई लगभग १०० फीट है। चारों तरफ किनारों से इस बावड़ी के अंदर जा सकते है। इस बावड़ी के अंदर दीवारों से १० फीट की दूरी पर दूसरी दीवार बनी हैं जो, कि ८ फीट चौड़ी गली चारों तरफ से बनी हुई है। इन्हीं गली में (इधर-उधर दोनों तरफ लगभग ५६ दरवाजे बने हुए है)।[६] बावड़ी के अंदर ही स्नान तथा तैयार आदि होने के लिए कमरें बने हुए हैं। मुगलकाल में मुस्लिम आक्रांताओं से तथा बाद में अंग्रेजों के अत्याचारों के भय से गाँव के लोग इस बावड़ी के अंदर सुरक्षा हेतु छिप जाया करते थे अर्थात् उन्होंने इस बावड़ी को आश्रय स्थल बना लिया था। यह भी पता चलता है कि राजपूत घराने की स्त्रियाँ (पर्दा होने के कारण) बावड़ी का पानी सुरंग के रास्ते से ले जाया करती थी।

इस बावड़ी के पानी का उपयोग गाँव के लोगों को पीने तथा आसपास की जमीन पर सिंचाई के लिए किया जाता था।

इस बावड़ी की अगर वर्तमान स्थिति को देख जाएँ तो इस बावड़ी के तीन हिस्से धंस चुके हैं तथा एक हिस्सा ही बचा हुआ है। बावड़ी का एक हिस्सा भी सुंदर लग रहा है तथा अपनी समकालीन कला को विभूषित कर रहा है। आज सरकार ने इस बावड़ी के एक हिस्से को बंद करवा दिया है।

इसी गाँव में इकलेरा माताजी की टेकरी तथा गाँव के बीच में इसी शैली में पाटीदार समाज के व्यक्तियों का एक कुआँ बना हुआ है। इस कुए की आकृति तथा भूलन बावड़ी की आकृति एक समान हैं। इस कुएँ में भी अनेक दरवाजे लगे हुए हैं।

इस कुएँ का भी निर्माण पानी पीने तथा सिंचाई के लिए किया गया था। इस कुँए के उत्तर-दक्षिण दिशा का भाग धंस चुका हैं। यह कुआँ भी १०० फीट गहराई, ६० फीट लंबाई तथा ४० फीट चौड़ाई लिये हुये हैं। इसमें भी चारों दीवारों के कोने से अंदर जाने का रास्ता हैं। इसमें भी कई दरवाजे दिखाई पड़ते हैं। इसको बनाने में चूने, पत्थर, ईंट, बील्व के गोंद को मिलाकर बनाया गया हैं। इस कुएँ में एक साथ आठ-आठ चड़स चलाई जाती थी। यह कुआँ भी एक समय पर पर्यटकों को देखने का केन्द्र बिंदु हुआ करता था।

वर्तमान में इस बावड़ी और कुएँ की जीर्णशीर्ण व्यवस्था हो गई हैं। आज गाँव के लोग तथा सरकार का इस अनमोल धरोहर की तरफ ध्यान नहीं जा रहा हैं। लगभग ५०० से ५५० वर्ष पूर्व बनी बावड़ी एवं कुएँ का पानी सिंचाई के साधन के रूप में काम में आ रहा हैं। आज भी चार-चार जल मोटरें इस कुएँ पर चलती है। आवश्यकता इस बात की है, कि ऐसी जल संसाधन की अद्भुत मिसाल पर शासन का ध्यान आकर्षित कर उसका उचित रख-रखाव किया जाना चाहिए तभी वर्तमान समय की गहन जल समस्या से निजात मिल सकेगी और इस संगोष्ठी की उपादेयता सिद्ध हो सकेगी।

सन्दर्भ सूची

१. बेवरीज एच., आईन ए अकबरी, भाग २ (अनुवाद) नई दिल्ली, सन् १९८९, पृ. २०६।

२. कुमार प्रमीला, मध्यप्रदेश का प्रादेशिक भूगोल, पृ. १७६।

३. लुआर्ड, सी. ई., देवास स्टेट गजेटियर, सन् १९०६-०७ पृ.-१

४. उदृतः गंगराडे किरण देवास के पवार राज्यों के राजनीतिक एवं सांस्कृतिक योगदान, (१८१९-१९४७) टंकित शोध प्रबंध, पृ. क्र ०६।

५. स्थान पर जाकर देखने से मालूम हुआ कि यह निर्माण लगभग ५०० वर्ष पूर्व का है। गाँव के बुजुर्गो एवं पुजारी से चर्चा पर आधारित है।

६. तस्वीरें एवं साम्मुख्य के आधार पर।

ग्वालियर में मध्य कालीन जल स्त्रोत - एक पत्थर की बावड़ी व जैन प्रतिमा समूह

रजनी श्रीवास्तव

मध्य कालीन ग्वालियर नगर मात्र राजनीति का ही केन्द्र नहीं रहा वरन् संस्कृति के विभिन्न आयामों का पोषक केन्द्र भी रहा है। इतिहास के पन्नों पर विख्यात 'ग्वालियर दुर्ग' को शीश पर सम्भाले हुए 'गोपाचल पर्वत' की दृढ़ शिलाओं पर शिल्पित 'भगवान पार्श्वनाथ' की प्रतिमा, अन्य सहस्त्रों विशाल पाषाण-प्रतिमाऐं व अनुपम जल स्त्रोत- 'एक पत्थर की बावड़ी, समय के सुंदरतम अवदानों में से एक है। यहां उपर्युक्त बावड़ी, जैन प्रतिमाऐं ही नहीं वरन् संपूर्ण पर्वत दर्शनीय है।

इस विशाल परिसर को संरक्षित करने व आगामी पीढ़ियों के लिये 'पावन चिन्ह' छोड़ने के लिये यहां के तत्कालीन शासक तोमर वंशीय राजा श्री वीरम देव, श्री डूंगरसिंह एवं श्री कीर्तिसिंह के राज्यकाल में वि.सं. १३९८ (सन् १३४१) से वि.सं. १५३६ (सन् १४७९) के मध्य करीब १३८ वर्ष तक संसार प्रसिद्ध मूर्तिशिल्प विशेषज्ञों द्वारा पर्वत तराश कर ये बावड़ी व प्रतिमाऐं शिल्पित की गई थी। जब ये बनकर तैयार हुई तो तत्कालीन महाकवि ' पं. रद्धू' जैन ने धूमधाम से इन मूर्तियों की प्रतिष्ठा कराई।[1]

गोपाचल पर्वत क्षेत्र पर सरोवरों, बावड़ीयों व कुंडो का निर्माण भी समय-समय पर होता रहा है जिससे इस क्षेत्र में जल प्रदाय व्यवस्था हमेशा सुचारू रूप से रही है। पर्वत व दुर्ग पर जहां भी किसी भवन का निर्माण करवाया जाता था तो वहीं से पहाड़ काटकर पत्थर की सामग्री की पूर्ति की जाती थी और फिर उस गढ्ढे को उचित ढंग से बनाकर सरोवर का रूप दे दिया जाता था । इस तरह से एक पंथ दो काज हो जाते थे । एक ओर पर्वत पर जल प्रदाय व्यवस्था में वृद्धि होती थी तो दूसरी ओर भवन निर्माण के लिये पत्थर सुलभ हो जाता था । इसी कारण तत्कालीन काल में विभिन्न सरोवरों, तालों, बावड़ीयों व कुंडों का नवनिर्माण एवं पुर्निर्माण किया गया।[2]

इन्हीं में से एक महत्वपूर्ण जल स्त्रोत है- 'एक पत्थर की बावड़ी' । जो कि एक महत्वपूर्ण जल स्त्रोत होने के साथ ही स्थापत्य कला की दृष्टि से भी अद्वितीय है।

एक पत्थर की बावड़ी गुफा समूह धरातल से लगभग २०० फीट की ऊंचाई पर स्थित है।

भगवान पार्श्वनाथ की बैठे हुए अवस्था में विशाल प्रतिमा यहां स्थापित है। यहां पर लगभग १२ फीट ऊंचाई लिये हुए जैन तीर्थकर 'नेमिनाथ' की खड़कासन प्रतिमा बनाई गई है। इस प्रतिमा को लगभग 10x10x15' आकार के पहाड़ी चट्टान को काटकर बनाया गया है। कक्ष की चारों ओर की दीवारों व छत पर तीर्थंकर के जन्म से लेकर निर्वाण तक के सभी कथानकों को अति सुंदर ढंग से उत्कीर्ण किया गया है। इस प्रकार यहां कुल २६ गुफायें हैं जिनमें लगभग २० प्रतिमाऐं १० फीट से ३० फीट तक ऊंची हैं इतनी ही प्रतिमायें ८ फीट से १५ फीट ऊंची है। सामान्य रूप से गज-कलश और मालाधरों का अंकन मिलता है। सभी में लांछन सिंह दृष्टव्य है।[३]

तोमर नरेश 'गणपति देव' पुत्र 'डूंगरसिंह' का ग्वालियर पर शासनकाल लगभग १४२७ से १४५६ ई. तक लगभग ३२ वर्ष तक रहा। जिनका प्रमाण ये अभिलेख हैं।[४] इसी दौरान उन्होंने संभवतयाः 'एक पत्थर की बावड़ी गुफा समूह का निर्माण करवाया होगा। डूंगरसिंह का शासन काल जैन धर्म एवं जैन साहित्य का स्वर्णयुग था। उन्होंने ग्वालियर में जल प्रदाय व्यवस्था, नहरों, सिंचाई की उत्तम व्यवस्था की।

डूंगरसिंह के राज्यकाल में जैन धर्म, जैन साहित्य की प्रगति एवं जैन मूर्तियों का निर्माण चरम-सीमा पर था। 'फजल अली' ने डूंगरसिंह के गोपाचल क्षेत्र पर जल प्रदाय व्यवस्था की प्रशंसा करते हुए लिखा है कि डूंगरसिंह ने आठ कुऐं, एक बावड़ी का निर्माण ग्वालियर दुर्ग पर कराया था।[५]

रइधू १६वीं शताब्दी के तोमरों के आश्रित कवि थे । रइधू ने उल्लेख किया है कि डूंगरसिंह को जैन धर्म पर आस्था थी।[६] इस प्रकार यह स्पष्टतया कहा जा सकता है कि तोमर शासक 'डूंगरसिंह' व उनके उत्तराधिकारी पुत्र कीर्तिसिंह के राज्यकाल के दौरान वे जैन प्रतिमाऐं बनना प्रारंभ हुई थीं जो ग्वालियर गढ़ को चारों ओर से घेरे हुए हैं। जैन ग्रंथ प्रशस्ति संग्रह में उल्लेख है कि डूंगरसिंह ने जैन मूर्तियों को उत्कीर्ण कराने में पर्याप्त धन व्यय किया।[७]

इन्हीं गुफा समूहों में गुफा नं.१ के ऊपरी भाग में बावड़ी स्थित है जिसे एक पत्थर की बावड़ी कहा जाता है। जैसे कि नाम से ही स्पष्ट है कि यह बावड़ी और यह संपूर्ण गुफा क्षेत्र एक ही पहाड़ी की चट्टान को तराश कर बनाया गया है और इनमें कहीं भी कोई अतिरिक्त पत्थर जोड़कर नहीं लगाया गया है। धरातल से इस क्षेत्र तक पहुंचने के लिये लगभग २०० सीढ़ियां बनी हुई है। सामने की तरफ लगभग

१५० सीढ़ियां सीधे चढ़ने के बाद यहां से दायीं ओर ऊपर की तरफ ५०-६० सीढ़ियां बनी हुई हैं। ये सीढ़ी चढ़ने के बाद पहाड़ी चट्टानों से काटकर बनाये गये बरामदे आते हैं। यद्यपि मध्यकाल में यह सीढ़ियां उपलब्ध नहीं थी वरन् ढलान के माध्यम से कारीगर तथा लोग यहां तक पहुंचते थे। यहां पर लगभग आधे से एक कि.मी. लम्बे क्षेत्र को पहाड़ी चट्टान को काटकर समतल स्थल बनाया गया है। गोपाचल पर्वत की सीधी सपाट चट्टान को काटकर उथली गुफाऐं बनाई गई हैं। चूंकि यह स्थल लगभग २०० फीट की ऊंचाई पर है। अतः नित्य यहां जल लाने में कठिनाई होती थी अतः उस समय यहीं एक बावड़ी बनाने का निश्चय किया गया जिसमें प्राकृतिक रूप से वर्षा के द्वारा आंतरिक तौर से चट्टानों से रिस-रिस कर जल संग्रहित होता था। इसका एक ही मुख्य द्वार है जो लगभग ६ फीट ऊंचा व ३ फीट चौड़ा है जिसे अब सुरक्षा के तौर पर शटर द्वारा बंद कर दिया गया है परन्तु शटर के बीच के रिक्त स्थानों से बावड़ी के अंदर की स्थिति को साफ देखा जा सकता है। आंतरिक रूप से यह बावड़ी चार कक्षों वाली है। मुख्य द्वार से बांयी ओर यह बावड़ी लगभग २० फीट लंबी है तथा दायीं ओर भी लगभग इतनी ही लंबी है। सामने की ओर लगभग २५ से ३० फीट लंबी है। चूंकि यह बावड़ी जल से पूर्णतः भरी हुई है अतः इसकी गहराई का आंकलन करना कठिन है। जल से लबालब भरी होने के कारण बावड़ी का जल मुख्य द्वार से चट्टानों के माध्यम से नीचे की ओर बह रहा है जिसने एक छोटे से झरने का रूप ले लिया है।

इस क्षेत्र में वर्षा जल का भंडारण इस सुंदर एवं वैज्ञानिक पद्धति से किया जाता रहा है, कि यहां कभी भी जल संकट उत्पन्न नहीं हुआ। आधुनिक युग में जहां पानी की तंगी से पूरे देश में जल संकट गहराता जा रहा है और सर्वत्र वर्षा जल संग्रहण की जानकारी दी जा रही है वहीं हमें यह जानकर गर्व अनुभव होता है कि मध्यकाल में हमारे पूर्वज वर्षा जल संग्रहण की तकनीक में हमसे कई कदम आगे थे तथा वे हमारे लिये वर्षा के जल के संग्रहण हेतु कई उदाहरण छोड़ कर गये हैं। जिसका एक उदाहरण यह 'एक पत्थर की बावड़ी' है जो वर्षा जल संग्रहण तकनीक का उत्तम प्रमाण है।

संदर्भ ग्रंथ सूची

१. गौरी, गुलाब खाँ, ग्वालियर का राजनैतिक व सांस्कृतिक इतिहास, पृ.क्रं.-२०१, प्रकाशन वर्ष-१९८६, प्रकाशक- बी.आर. पब्लिशिंग कार्पोरेशन, नई दिल्ली।

२. वही, पृ.क्रं.-२००

३. त्रिपाठी, एस.एम. एवं जैन, नवनीत कुमार एवं तेनवार, टीकम - जैन ज्ञान, शोध पत्र - ग्वालियर क्षेत्र में तीर्थंकर महावीर की प्रतिमाऐं- प्रतिमा शास्त्रीय अध्ययन (प्रारंभ से १५ वीं सदी तक), पृ.क्रं. - ३१६, वर्ष-२००५

४. डॉ. (श्रीमती) मीना श्रीवास्तव, शोध प्रबंध - तोमर राजवंश का आलोचनात्मक अध्ययन, जीवाजी वि. वि. ग्वालियर, वर्ष - १९९५, पृ.क्रं.-२९७

५. सूची क्रं. -१, पृ.क्रं.-८२

६. सूची क्रं. -४, पृ.क्रं.-२९७

७. वही।

उत्तर मध्यकालीन मारवाड़ के शासकों के जोधपुर शहर में जलाशयों के शिलालेख - एक परिचय

डॉ. तेजेन्द्र वल्लभ व्यास

सामान्यतः जलापूर्ति का प्रमुख स्त्रोत वर्षा है। जहां वर्षा प्रति पर्याप्त मात्रा में हो वहां जल की कमी नहीं होती है, परन्तु भौगोलिक कारणों से राजस्थान मे पानी का अभाव है। राजस्थान की मरूभूमि में वर्षा बहुत कम होती है तथा न ही इसके आसपास अधिक वर्षा वाले क्षेत्र अवस्थित है। यहाँ के मरूस्थलीय भू-भाग में अनियमित मानसून के कारण प्रति वर्ष जल संकट उत्पन्न होता है। प्रान्त की लगभग सभी नदियाँ मौसमी है। वर्षा में लबालब और गर्मी में तपती रेत। राजस्थान में वर्षा का औसत ५८.६४ मिली मीटर है। जोधपुर में वर्षा का औसत केवल ३१ मिली मीटर है। यहाँ एक बरसाती नदी लूनी के अतिरिक्त कोई बड़ी नदी नहीं है। जिससे यहाँ के नागरिको को कई कठिनाईयों का सामना करना पड़ता था। कुएँ खोदने पर अत्यन्त गहराई पर पानी निकलता है।

मारवाड़ में जल के प्राकृतिक स्त्रोतों की कमी, सीमित वर्षा तथा प्रायः नैसर्गिक कारणों से उत्पन्न होने वाले दुर्भिक्ष की स्थिति यहाँ की पहचान जैसी बन गई है। अनिश्चित और कम वर्षा के कारण मारवाड़ में पानी को बहुत अधिक महत्वपूर्ण समझा जाता है। जीवन के लिए जल की महत्ता को स्वीकारते हुए यहाँ के शासकों, उनकी रानियाँ तथा समाजसेवी लोगों ने नगरों, कस्बों तथा गांवों में अनेकानेक तालाब, बावड़ियों, कुएं बनवाकर अपनी उदारता का परिचय दिया।

१२ मई १४५९ को राव जोधा ने वर्तमान जोधपुर नगर और मेहरानगढ़ दुर्ग की नींव रखी। जोधपुर नगर की स्थापना के समय आबादी बहत ही कम थी। उस वक्त पानी की मांग की पूर्ति शहर में उपलब्ध पानी की विभिन्न स्त्रोत जैसे तालाब, कुओं, बावड़ियों आदि से होती थी। समय के साथ-साथ इस शहर की आबादी बढ़ती गई लेकिन जल स्त्रोत नहीं बढ़े। जोधपुर शहर के जल संकट में कुपित संत चिड़ियानाथजी के अभिशाप को भी योगदान बताया जाता है। नेणसी री ख्यात में

उल्लेख हुआ है, कि जब मेहरानगढ़ दुर्ग की नींव रखी गई यहाँ चिड़ियानाथजी की धुणी थी। दुर्ग निर्माण कार्य में वह धुणी बाधा डाल रही थी। अतः निर्माण कार्य में लगे कर्मचारियों ने चिड़ियानाथजी से अपनी धुणी हटाने का आग्रह किया राजहठ मे कुपित होकर चिड़ियानाथजी ने प्रति तीसरे वर्ष अकाल पडने का एवं यह नगरी हमेशा जल के अभाव को झेले ऐसा अभिशाप दिया।[1] संत अभिशाप से उत्पन्न जल संकट के निराकरण हेतु राव जोधा ने कई जलाशयों का निर्माण करवाया। उनकी रानियों ने रानीसर व चौखेलाव तालाब का निर्माण करवाया। जोधाजी के बाद मारवाड़ के शासकों, रानियों तथा पासवानों ने भी इस परम्परा को कायम रखा और नगर में विभिन्न जलाशयों कुओं व बावड़ियों का निर्माण करवाकर प्रजा को जल सुगमता प्रदान करने का प्रयास किया।

यहाँ के लोगों ने भी इस कार्य में महत्वपूर्ण सहयोग दिया। जल का प्रबन्ध करने, तालाब व कुएँ खुदवाने में ये लोग पुण्य प्राप्ति समझते थे। महाराजा मानसिंह ने मानसागर तथा नाथसागर का कुआ खुदवाया। उनकी राजकुमारी सिरे कँवर ने बाईजी का तालाब खुदवाया। महाराजा जसवन्तसिंह प्रथम के ृासनकाल में पुष्करणा व्यास तापोजी ने तापी बावड़ी का निर्माण करवाया।

प्रस्तुत शोध पत्र में जोधपुर शहर में विद्यमान विभिन्न जलाशयों पर उत्कीर्ण अभिलेखों का अध्ययन करने का प्रयास किया गया है।

मण्डोर रेल्वे स्टेशन के सामने पहाड़ी के नीचे स्थित बावड़ी पर एक अभिलेख[2] उत्कीर्ण है जिसका मूल पाठ इस प्रकार है –

१. ओम नमः शिवाय ।।................. रोद्र ....भ ....

सर्वम्भ समाधिपति ....प्रध

२. वो सुराणां। श्री मत्सुधा धवल हेम विनानवर्ती

देव–सदा–जयति पाशधरः

३. प्रचेता। अविहत चक्र प्रसरो विक्रमाकान्त सकल बलि राज्यो (ज्यः)। दूर

निराऔत

४. नरक स्म जयति र्म्माधू गूणिना मग्रेसरो भवति

५. बहि (:) इबर कारव्येक (य) ता ''यो यशया वित्ति निच्चेयन।।३।। अप्य ....

तनु ....

६. भव्य दिग्गामिनो (न)। अविषम दृष्टिर्ल्लोके तथा पिन्वीश्वर सिद्ध।।४।।

आयुश्चल धनम सार मिति।

७. हपूर्व मत्वा स्थिर यश पृथित्वों स्वादू प्रकीर्ण सलिला सुमनोहर

८. जय वापी निपासिव सो (स) यशसां चखनि ।।५।।

सवत्सर सप्तसुद्वात्वा।

९. ं रि स्वा (शा) धिकेषु (द्वाचत्वा)

जोधपुर शहर में स्थित विद्याशाला से मेहरानगढ़ दुर्ग की ओर जाने वाले मार्ग पर स्थित क्रिया के झालरे पर लगे एक गोवर्धन पर शिलालेख उत्कीर्ण है।[3] प्रस्तुत शिलालेख में महाराजा श्री जसवन्तसिंह और महाराज कुमार श्री अजीतसिंह की सेवा में रहने वाले शालिहोत्र शास्त्र के ज्ञाता तिरवाड़ी सुखदेव चतुर्भुजोत के वचन ने झालरा बनवाने, सुखदेवसुत उदयराम द्वारा वि.सं. १७७५ माघ सुद १ को उसे खुदवाने बंधवाने और उसके प्रपौत्र मोतीराम द्वारा झालरे की प्रतिष्ठा, वि.सं. १८८५ माघ मास, शुक्लपक्ष, १३ त्रयोदशी सामेवार पुष्य नक्षत्र में करवाने का उल्लेख हुआ है। इस दिन पुष्य नक्षत्र के अतिरिक्त चन्द्रमा वृश्चिक राशि में स्थित था। यहाँ यज्ञमंडप स्थापित करके बहुत से वेदपारग ब्राह्मणों की उपस्थिति में इसकी प्रतिष्ठा हुई थी। प्रस्तुत शिलाखेख का पाठ इस प्रकार है।

१. रामजी

२. स/१७७५ (रा) महा सु

३. द ? त्रापाड़ी (त्रिवाड़ी) सुषदे

४. व जी झालरो करायो

५. न सुषदेव सुत ३

६. दे राम झालरो ब

७. घा मो उदेराम सु (त)

८. सीवरप (सीवराम) सु

९. त मोतीराम झालरा

१०. री प्रतिष्ठा ५ वीं स ११

११. १८८५ रा माघ मासे

१२. सुकल पक्षे पुन्यत्र १३ त्रयोदसी

१३. सोमवार पुषय नक्ष

१४. त्रे चद्र (चन्द्र) वृक्षिक रामिग

१५. ह पिता प्तास्मिन भद्र पोध

१६. भस्थापतः त्रिवाडी जी

१७. सुषदेव जी कस्य प्र (पा) (प्रो)

१८. त्र मोतीराम विधि

१९. नाझालरा जलस्य (जलाशय)

२०. प्रतिठा कृताब

२१. ह भि वद पा (सु)

२२. ब्राह्मणः सह

२३. शु भवत क

२४. कल्याण म (स्तु)

नवचौकिया से फतेहपोल की ओर जाने वाले मार्ग पर चांदबावड़ी स्थित है।[४] चांदबावड़ी में प्रवेश मार्ग के बाई ओर एक अभिलेख उत्कीर्ण है। अभिलेख के अनुसार महाराजा श्री विजयसिंह के दरबारी नाजरजी के द्वारा चाँद बावड़ी के पढ़ढे (दीवार) एवं समीप एक मंदिर बनवाये जाने का उल्लेख हुआ है। शिलालेख का मूल पाठ इस प्रकार है-

१. श्री रामजी

२. महाराजा जी श्री बिजैसि

३. घजी रै नाजर दरबारी जी

४. बुहाण बावड़ी रो पढा ने

५. देवरो ब रायौ संमत

६. १८१० रा मीती वि सा

७. ब बद १३ समीसर

जोधपुर के मुख्य बाजार घण्टाघर के निकट उम्मेद उच्च माध्यमिक विद्यालय के सामने विद्यमान गुलाबसागर पर लगे एक कीर्तिस्तम्भ पर महाराजा विजयसिंह के शासनकाल का एक अभिलेख उत्कीर्ण है। यह कीर्ति स्तम्भ चतुष्कोण कमलांकित शिखर से अलंकृत है। इसके पूर्व भाग में सप्तसप्ति (सूर्य भगवान), दक्षिण भाग में तीन हाथों में क्रमशः भाला, त्रिशुल, डमरू युक्त गंगाधारी शिव है। जो चतुर्थ हस्त में बीजोरा लिए हुए है। पश्चिम दिशा में चतुर्भुज ब्रह्म हैं, जो वेद ग्रंथ माला और कमण्डल धारण किए हुए है। उत्तर में चतुर्भुज गणेशजी कमल, परशु, मोदक (लड्डू) और पुष्पमाला ग्रहण किए हुए है। वि.सं. १८४५ शुक्ल, १७१०, भाद्रपद मास, शुक्लपक्ष की पंचमी, गुरूवार को राजराजेश्वर महाराजधिराज श्री विजयसिंह जी की धर्मपत्नी महाराणीजी श्री १०८ श्री पासवान जी श्री गुलाबरायजी के द्वारा गुलाबसागर का निर्माण करवाया गया। इस समय महाराज कुमार श्री शेरसिंह जी थे। शिलालेख में श्री शेरसिंह को गुलाबराय ने अपना पुत्र (दत्तक) बतलाया है। उसका और सपुत्र तेजसिंह (तेजकरण) धा, उसकी मृत्यु आश्विन सुदि १० वि.सं. १८४२ को चेचक से हो गयी थी। प्रस्तुत शिलालेख में कुल ग्यारह पंक्तियाँ है।[५]

श्रीरामजी

१. श्री गणेशाय नमः।। स्वस्ति श्री ऋद्धिर्वृद्धिज्जयों मगंलाभ्युदयश्च।। अ.

२. थास्मिन शुभ संव (ब) त्सरे श्रीनृपति विक्रमाके समायति (ती) त संवत ।।

३. १८४५ श्री शाल (लि) वाहन शाके १७१० प्रवतमाने श्री दवौ दक्ष (क्षि) णा।

४. ....यने वर्षो (वर्ष) त्तौ मा (म) हाभगस्य प्रदमासोत्त (म)

५. पक्षे पचम्यां पुण्य लियो गुरूवासरे घटी ५५ पल २६ स्वातिन क्षत्रे, घटी ४५

६. पल ३७ व्र (ब्रा) इन नाम योगे घटी ८ पल २६ व (ब) करणे एवं पंचांग शुद्धा अ (द्वाब) त्र

७. दिने गोव्रा (ब्रा) ह्मनण-प्रतिपालक क्षात्रधर्म प्रवर्तक सर्व (र्व) सामंत मुकुट (कु) निरा

८. जितचणा(णस्य) स्मं (?) राजराजेश्वर मा (म) हा राजधिराज महाराजाजी श्री १०८ श्री श्री

९. श्री श्री श्री विजयसिंघजी कस्य स्व.... धर्मपत्नी महाराणीजी श्री १०८ श्री पासवा

१०. नजी श्री श्री श्री गुलाबराय जी कया करा.... पितं तत्पुत्र मा (म) हाराज कुंवार (कुमार)

११. श्री १०८ श्री से (शे) र सिं (सि) घ (ह) जी सागरस्य नाम गुलाबसागरः।

उपर्युक्त शिलालेखों के आधार पर यह कहा जा सकता है कि गौरवशाली मारवाड़ के शासकों तथा प्रशासकीय अधिकारी, जोधपुर शहर की जनता को पीने के पानी को उपलब्ध कराने के लिए सदैव तप्पर रहते थे। उपलब्ध शिलालेखों में विभिन्न जलाशयों के निर्माण की सूचनाओं के साथ ही साथ तत्कालीन प्रशासकीय, सामाजिक एवं धार्मिक अवस्था का भी ज्ञान होता है।

संदर्भ :-

१.. विश्वेश्वरनाथ रेऊ, मारवाड़ का इतिहास, भाग १, पृ. ६२

२. वरदा, वर्ष ६, अंक ४, पृ. ५८१

३. मांगीलाल व्यास 'मयंक', मारवाड़ के अभिलेख, पृ. १२१

४. गोविन्दलाल श्रीमाली, राजस्थान के अभिलेख, भाग २, पृ. ६०३

५. वही, भाग २, पृ. ४६०

सिवाना परगने का जल प्रबन्ध -(विगत के विशेष सन्दर्भ में)

डॉ. अनिल पुरोहित एवं श्रीमती सोनल पुरोहित

सिवाना, मारवाड़ राज्य का अत्यधिक महत्वपूर्ण किला रहा है । यह सामरिक किला, मध्यकालीन भारतीय इतिहास में महत्वपूर्ण स्थान रखता है । जोधपुर से ३० कोस दूर दक्षिण में स्थित सिवाना पंवार शक्ति का केन्द्र रहा है। नैणसी की विगत से ज्ञात होता है कि बाड़मेर के शासक धरणीवराह ने अपने भाई भोज को जालोर का क्षेत्र भाई-बंट में दिया था । उसके पुत्र वीरनारायण ने सिवाना के उस ऐतिहासिक दुर्ग का निर्माण १०२० के लगभग करवाया जहां अलाउद्दीन जैसे साम्राज्यवादी शासक को भी अधिकार करने में कठिनाई हुई थी।[1] लूनी तथा सूकड़ी नदी के प्रवाह पर स्थित होने के कारण यह इलाका जल-उपलब्धता की दृष्टि से महत्वपूर्ण था । किन्तु लूनी तथा सूकड़ी दोनों की बारहमासी नदियां नहीं हैं अतः इस परगने में जल-प्रबन्ध एक अनिवार्य आवश्यकता था । उत्तर पूर्व तथा दक्षिण में पहाड़ियां होने से पहाड़ी के तलहटी के क्षेत्रों में पानी एकत्र होता था और पानी का बहाव अधिक होने पर अच्छी मात्रा में पानी एकत्र होता था । किन्तु सिवाना के तालाबों में अधिकांश में भी ४-८ माह से अधिक नहीं टिकता था । पानी एकत्र होने पर सेंवज (गेहू-चना) की फसल होती थी । किन्तु दुसाखिया गावों की संख्या बहुत अधिक नहीं है । तालाबों के सूखने पर जनता सिंचाई तथा पीने के जल हेतु भूमिगत - जल - संसाधनों पर निर्भर रहती थी । अतः जल उपलब्धता तथा वितरण को सुनिश्चित करना आवश्यक था । मारवाड़ रा परगना री विगत में नैणसी ने तफसीलवार कस्बा सिवाना सहित अन्य गांवों में जल संसाधनों के प्रकार, प्रबन्धन पर प्रकाश डाला है । साथ ही वह जल-उपलब्धता के आधार पर गांवों को इकसाखिया (एक फसल खरीफ) तथा दुसाखिया (रबी तथा खरीफ दोनों) का विभाजन करता है । अधिकांश दुसाखियां गांवों में कोसीटा (वह कुंआ जिसका पानी ज्यादा गहराई पर ना हो और चड़स् (सूंडिया) से पानी निकाला जाता है) चांच (साधारण कच्चा कुआं) तथा अरहट प्राप्त होने है । इससे इनकी सिंचाई व्यवस्था का पता चलता है । प्रस्तुत शोध-पत्र में नैणसी की

विगत के आधार पर प्राप्त होने वाली जल-संग्रहण इकाइयों का अध्ययन किया गया है । साथ ही जल की उपलब्धता किस तरह से फसलों प्रकार को प्रभावित करती थी इसका विश्लेषण भी किया गया है।[२]

सिवाना किले के सम्बन्ध में नैणसी मात्र एक तालाब का उल्लेख करता है तथा लिखता है कि यहां पानी अटूट रहता था । सम्भवतः चूंकि यह एक सामारिक महत्व का किला अधिक था इसलिये किले में स्थाई विशाल सेना तथा शासक - प्रशासक वर्ग का आवास लम्बे समय तक नहीं रहता था । बाकी समय में सुरक्षा हेतु रखी गई सेना के लिये तालाब का पानी पर्याप्त सिद्ध होता होगा ।

नैणसी बहुत ही विस्तार से सिवाना परगने के गांवों में प्राप्त होने वाले विविध जल - संसाधनों का उल्लेख करता है । सिवाना परगने में प्राप्त होने वाले विविध जल संसाधनों (सिंचाई तथा पीने हेतु) की संख्या इस प्रकार थी - (नोट इस अध्ययन में बसते हुए ८६ गांव सम्मिलित है)[३] -

तालाब - ६५ अधिकांश में ४ से ८ माह से अधिक पानी नहीं रहता था । एक मात्र बीठीजी ऐसा गांव है जहां पानी अठारह महीने तक रहता है । ढलान वाले क्षेत्र, बहाव वाले क्षेत्र तथा भराव वाले क्षेत्रों में पानी एकत्र कर तालाब खोदे जाते थे ।

कोसीटा - २७५-२८५ तक की संख्या प्राप्त होती है । कोसीटा प्राप्त होने वाले अधिकांश क्षेत्र (गांव) उत्तर तथा पूर्व दिशा में हैं । यहां लूनी तथा सूकड़ी नदियां चलती है अतः सिंचाई हेतु जल प्राप्त करने के लिये अधिक गहराई वाले कुओं की आवश्यकता नहीं होती थी ।

चांच - ४८ नैणसी (अध्ययन के अन्तर्गत लिये गये बसते ८६ गांवों में से) केवल तीन गांवों मांगलो[४], देवली आली[५] तथा बालोतरा में चांच का उल्लेख करता है।

कुएं - अधिकांश गांवों में कुओं का उल्लेख हैं । इनकी संख्या लगभग ६६-६८ है । नैणसी कुए में प्राप्त होने वाले पानी यथा - मीठा, खारा, भलभला आदि का उल्लेख करने के साथ कुओं की गहराई ४ से लगाकर १४ पुरूष भी बतलाता है । वह पक्के बंधवा कुओं का भी उल्लेख करता है । इससे स्पष्ट है कि पीने के पानी हेतु समुचित प्रबन्ध गांव तथा राज्य की ओर से किया जाता था ।

कई स्थानों पर नैणसी, नाड़ी, बेहर तथा बेरियों का उल्लेख करता है । किसी गांव में तो बेरियां तालाब में स्थाई रूप से निर्मित की जाती थी, जब तालाब का पानी सूख जाता था तब बेरियों का पानी पीने हेतु उपयोग में लिया जाता था । पानी के

बहाव वाले क्षेत्रों में जल - सूखने पर कच्ची बेरियां खोदकर जल - प्राप्त किया जाता था - बेरियां खिण पीवै[६] -

बावड़ी - ८६ गांवों में से केवल दो गांवों में बाबड़ी का उल्लेख है जिनमें से गांव गुघरट[७] में एक बावड़ी बतलाता है जो षड़कोण आकर की है । वहीं गांव राकसी[८] में तालाब के अन्दर बन्धवाई हुई बाबड़ी का वर्णन करता है । यहां पानी बरसोदियो अर्थात् बारहों महीने रहता है ।

यहां यह बात ध्यान देने योग्य है कि जिन क्षेत्रों से लूनी तथा सूकड़ी बहकर निकलती है वहां कई गांवों में तालाब नहीं है (उदाहरण के तौर पर समदड़ी दहीबढ़ी, जणीयाणों, होठलूं, लालीया आदि) ।

नैणसी विगत में सिवाना परगने के गांवों की दिशा तथा दूरी का (सिवाना गढ से) उल्लेख करता है । अतः दिशाओं के आधार पर विभाजन कर सिवाना परगने की जल-वितरण तथा प्रबन्धन प्रणाली को अच्छी प्रकार से समझा जा सकता है ।

सिवाना परगने में जल - संसाधनों का भौगिलिक वितरण

उत्तर दिशा

गांवों की संख्या	-	२८
इकसाकिया/दुसाकिया	-	१४ / १४
कोसीटा	-	१७२-१७८
चांच	-	२५ - २८ (मात्र दो गांवों में)
अरहट	-	१३३-१३९
नाड़ी	-	नहीं
कुए	-	१३ = ३ कुएं पक्के बंधवाएं हुए ।
बावड़ी	-	१ गांव सीरांणो - बूरी हुई है ।
तालाब	-	२५

सिवाना परगने की उत्तर दिशा के गांवों में प्राप्त कोसीटा तथा अरहटों की संख्या से सहज ही अनुमान लगाया जा सकता है कि यहां सिंचाई हेतु कम गहराई वाले तथा अधिक गहराई वाले कुएं खोदे गये थे । चूंकि लूनी तथा सूकड़ी के यह बहाव क्षेत्र वाले गांव है अतः नदी के बहाव के समय यहां भूमिगत जल स्तर (अण्डरग्राउण्ड

वाटर लेवल) काफी ऊंचा रहता होगा । यहां आधे गांव (१४) दुसाखिया है जहां रबी तथा खरीफ की फसल दोनों प्राप्त की जाती है । रबी (उनाली) की पैदावार अच्छी होने का उल्लेख नैणसी देता है- उनाली खेता सखरा - अर्थात् यहां सिंचित भूमि अधिक थी तथा पैदावार अच्छी होती थी । मुख्य फसले थी - बाजरी, मूंग, मोठ ज्वार आदि।[९]

रेल (बहाव) आती है तो सेंवज - गेंहू तथा चने की अच्छी पैदावार होती है । यहां यह बात ध्यान देने योग्य है कि गांव की टणोद् में कोई अरहट अथवा कोसीटा ना होने पर भी यह दुसाकिया है।[१०] पास ही लूनी नदी बहती है अतः सिंचाई का पानी वहीं से उपयोग में लिया जाता है । इस दिशा के चार गांवों में तालाब नहीं है - किसी में कुएं नहीं है । जैसे लालीया[११] के बारे में नैणसी लिखता है कि तालाब, बेरो नहीं - नदी सूकड़ी नजीक सींधोलवाटी तठे पीवै ।

दक्षिण दिशा

गांवों की संख्या - १२

इकसाकिया/दुसाकिया - १०/२

कोसीटा - नहीं

चांच - नहीं

अरहट - नहीं

नाड़ी - नहीं

कुए/बेरे - १० अधिकांश पक्के तथा सागरी - अर्थात्

गहराई तथा अटूट पानी वाले

बावड़ी - १

तालाब - ११

परगने के दक्षिण के गांवों में यद्यपि नदी का प्रत्यक्ष प्रवाह नहीं है किन्तु भू-जल विपुल मात्रा में उपलब्ध है अतः इस क्षेत्र में कोसीटा व चांच प्राप्त नहीं होते किन्तु कुएं पक्के तथा सागरी है तथा तालाबों की संख्या समुचित है । अधिकांश गांव इकसाकिया हैं अतः यह सहज ही अनुमान लगाया जा सकता है कि सिवाना के इस क्षेत्र में अधिकांश जल स्त्रोत जन साधारण के उपयोग हेतु निर्मित किये गये थे, सिंचाई

हेतु नहीं । यहां नैणसी ने स्पष्ट लिखा है - पीयल नहीं । ज्यादातर गांव पहाड़ी की तहलटी में है अतः पैदावार अच्छी है। यहां - मूंग, मोठ, ज्वार बाजरी तथा गेहूं के पास तिल तथा कपास की पैदावार भी प्राप्त होती है । पहाड़ी से झरना बहता है (गांव तेलवाड़ा) जो पीने के उपयोग में लिया जाता है।१२

पश्चिम दिशा

गांवों की संख्या - २३

इकसाकिया/दुसाकिया - २० / ३

कोसीटा - ४० (बालोतरा)

चांच - २० (केवल बालोतरा में)

अरहट - ६२-६८ (४० बालोतरा में)

नाड़ी -

कुए /बेरे - ११/२०-२५ अधिकांश कुए सागरी

बावड़ी - ४

तालाब - १३

इस क्षेत्र में केवल बालोतरा में चांच, कोसीटा तथा अरहट प्राप्त होते है। यहां से लूनी नदी नजदीक से होकर गुजरती है अतः बालोतरा में पानी की उपलब्धता अच्छी रहती थी । यह गांव दुसाकिया था । यद्यपि इस दिशा के अन्य गांवों के नजदीक भी लूनी का बहाव था - किन्तु यह फैलाव वाला क्षेत्र अधिक है । बारिश अच्छी हो और रेल आती थी तो सेंवज होती थी । यहां अधिकांश कुएं सागरी है चूंकि सिवाना के पश्चिम की तरफ लूनी धीमी पड़ जाती है अतः यहां पानी अधिक टिकता नहीं था - लोग पीने के पानी हेतु बेरियों पर निर्भर रहते थे । आगे जाकर पानी खारा या भलभला मिलता है । पचपदरा में नमक के आगारों का उल्लेख नैणसी करता है।[१३]

ऊगोण दिशा

गांवों की संख्या - २०

इकसाकिया/दुसाकिया - १२/८

कोसीटा - ३०-३२ (गांव बांभसेण में १५

करमाबास + २ भुरड)

चांच - २० - २५ (केवल बांभसेण में)

अरहट - २ (राकसी)१० (करमावास) २ (भुरड़)

कुएं / बेरे - ३ + २५

बावड़ी - नहीं

तालाब -

नाड़ी - नहीं

बांभसेण, करमावास, राकसी तथा भुरड़ - दुसाखिया पैदावार वाले है । यहां लूनी नदी बहरकर निकलती है अतः सिंचाई साधन अरहट तथा कोसीटा भी इन्हीं क्षेत्रों में हैं । जल उपलब्धता के कारण बांभसेण में तालाब प्राप्त नहीं होता । यहां पैदावार अच्छी है - खेत निपट सखरा।[१४] यहां कुओं की संख्या कम है । पानी बहाव से प्राप्त करते है बाद में बेरिया खोदकर अथवा दूसरे गांवों के कुओं पर पीते है । तिल, कपास आदि की पैदावार प्राप्त होती है ।

इनके अतिरिक्त नैणसी में एक, बायकोण में एक तथा कूण दिशा में एक गांव का उल्लेख करता है ।

उपरोक्त अध्ययन से यह ज्ञात होता है कि लूनी - सूकड़ी के बहाव वाले क्षेत्रों में पड़ने वाले गांव समूह थे । प्राकृतिक रूप से प्राप्त जल को संग्रहित करने तथा भूमिगत जल के उपयोग हेतु परगना सिवाना में अनेक जल संसाधनों का निर्माण किया गया था । पूरे परगने में कोई कोहर (गहरा कुआँ) नहीं मिलता - यह इस बात का संकेत है कि इस पूरे क्षेत्र का भू-जल स्तर ऊँचा था तथा कम गहराई पर ही जल प्राप्त हो जाता था । सर्वाधिक समृद्ध क्षेत्र उत्तर दिशा के थे जहां लगभग आंधे गांव दुसाखिया है ।

संदर्भ

१ नैणसी , मुहणोत : मारवाड रा परगनां री विगत , भाग २, पृ. ११५ , राजस्थान प्राच्य विद्या प्रतिष्ठान , जोधपुर

२ वही , पृ. ११५ ॐ २७०

३ वही , पृ. २३२ ॐ २६२

४ वही , पृ. २३४

५ वही , पृ. २३८

६ वही , पृ. २३५

७ वही , पृ. २५५

८ वही , पृ. २३५

९ वही , पृ. २३२ ॐ २६५

१० वही , पृ. २३३

११ वही , पृ. २४०

१२ वही , पृ. २५८

१३ वही , पृ. २४७

१४ वही , पृ. २३५

सिंधिया पूर्व ग्वालियर में जल प्रबंधन

डॉ. सुनील सक्सैना

ग्वालियर की स्थापना के विषय में कहा जाता है कि इसकी स्थापना राजा सूरज सिंह जो कि एक कछवाहा सामंत था ने कुंतलपुरी अथवा कुंतलपुर के रूप में की थी।[1] राजा सूर्यसेन के समय में ही ग्वालियर में जल प्रबंधन की व्यवस्था दृष्टिगोचर होती है। राजा सूर्यसेन कुष्ठरोग से पीड़ित था और वह एक दिन गोपगिरी पहाड़ी पर शिकार खेल रहा था तो उसने प्यास लगने पर ग्वालिपा ऋषि से पानी मांगा। इस पानी को ग्रहण करते ही सूर्य सेन कुष्ठरोग से मुक्त हो गया। इस घटना के उपरान्त सूर्यसेन ने गोपगिरी पहाड़ी पर एक दुर्ग का निर्माण कराया और जिस तालाब से ऋषि ने उसे जल दिया था उस स्थान पर सूर्यसेन से एक बड़ा तालाब बनवाया जिसे ग्वालियर इतिहास में सूरज कुण्ड कहा जाता है।

राजा सूर्यसेन द्वारा निर्मित सूरज कुण्ड ग्वालियर के जल प्रबंधन इतिहास में प्रथम जल संग्रह स्त्रोत माना जा सकता है इस कुण्ड की निर्माण तिथि को बलबंत राव सिंधिया ने सन् २७५ ई. बतलाया है।[2] महेन्द्रपाल ने इस निर्माण तिथि का समर्थन किया है। इतिहासकार एम.पी.गर्दे ग्वालियर दुर्ग की निर्माण तिथि तीसरी शताब्दी में सन् २७५ ई. से सन् २८२ ई. के मध्य मानते हैं। अतः इस कुण्ड का निर्माण काल भी उसी तिथि का रहा होगा।[3] पुरातत्वविद् कनिंघम ने ग्वालियर दुर्ग की तिथि संवत् २३२ ई.[4] तथा गुलाव खां गोरी ने २७५ ई.[5] मानी है। मुख्यतः इतिहासकारों ने सूर्यसेन द्वारा निर्मित ग्वालियर दुर्ग एवं सूरज कुण्ड की तिथि सन् २७५ ई. मानी है।

प्रथम शताब्दी ई. में ग्वालियर में नागवंश शासकों के शासन के प्रमाण मिलते हैं।[6] पहली शताब्दी से लेकर चौथी शताब्दी तक ग्वालियर नाग शासकों के अधीन रहा। जिस मध्य ग्वालियर में प्राकृतिक जल स्त्रोतों का उपयोग किया जाता था। नागवंश के अंतिम शासक राजा गणपति देव ने अपने शासन काल में वर्तमान ग्वालियर डबरा के मध्य विभिन्न कुओं एवं तालाबों का निर्माण कराया था। गणपति देव को समुद्रगुप्त ने पराजित करके ग्वालियर क्षेत्रा को अपने अधीन कर लिया। सन् ४६७ ई. तक ग्वालियर क्षेत्रा में गुप्त शासकों के अधीन विभिन्न जल स्त्रोतों की दृष्टि से जलाशयों

का निर्माण कराया गया तथा मानव एवं पशुओं के लिये पृथक-पृथक तालाबों का निर्माण कराया गया।

गुप्त शासकों के पतन के बाद सन् ५१५ ई. में ग्वालियर का क्षेत्रा मिहिरकुल शासक के अन्तर्गत आ गया जिसमें ग्वालियर दुर्ग में सूर्य मंदिर का निर्माण कराया।[७] मिहिरकुल ने ग्वालियर दुर्ग में जल निकास एवं जल संचय के लिये विशिष्ट कार्य किया तथा सूर्य मंदिर में भी जल निकास के लिये विशेष कार्य किया। ग्वालियर दुर्ग के जल निकास प्रबंधन को वर्तमान स्वरूप में भी देखा जा सकता है। मिहिरकुल के बाद कुछ संक्रमण काल को छोड़कर ग्वालियर गुर्जर प्रतिहारों के अधीन रहा। इस काल के शासक मिहिर भोज ने ग्वालियर में प्राकृतिक जल स्त्रोतो को संग्रहित करने के लिये प्रयास किये।[८]

कच्छपघात वंशी शासक कीर्तिराज के समय में ग्वालियर में एक बाबड़ी के निर्माण का उल्लेख मिलता है।[९] इसी बाबड़ी का उपयोग जल प्रबंधन की दृष्टि से किया जाता था। तोमर शासकों में मानसिंह तोमर का काल ग्वालियर से स्वर्णकाल माना जाता है।[१०] मानसिंह तोमर ने इस पहाड़ी पर ग्वालियर दुर्ग को अत्यंत सुन्दर ढंग से व्यवस्थित किया इनके काल में ग्वालियर का राजनैतिक एवं सांस्कृतिक विकास तीव्र था उन्होंने सिंचाई पर विशेष ध्यान दिया।[११] मानसिंह तोमर ने ग्वालियर में सिंचाई के प्राकृतिक एवं अप्राकृतिक स्त्रोतों को विकसित कराया, जल संसाधन के लिये राज्य में विभिन्न कुओं एवं तालाबों का निर्माण कराया।[१२] सिंधिया पूर्व शासकों ने मानसिह तोमर कला संगीत के पोषक के साथ-साथ लोकोपयोगी सेवाओं के प्रति अतिसंवेदनशील रहा। उसने जहाँ अपने राज्य में संगीत कला एवं साहित्य का पोषग किया वहीं उसने कृषि के विकास के लिये सिंचाई के संसाधनों के विकास पर विशेष ध्यान दिया।[१३]

मानसिंह तोमर ने ग्वालियर दुर्ग में मानमंदिर का निर्माण कराया, यह महल स्थापत्य की दृष्टि से भव्य एवं मनोहर था ही परन्तु जल प्रबंधन की दृष्टि से वर्तमान में भी अत्यंत महत्वपूर्ण है। इस महल में जल निकास के लिये जिस प्रकार की नालियों का निर्माण किया गया है वह पूर्व के ग्वालियर के किसी स्थापत्य में देखने को नहीं मिलता है। महल में जल निकास प्रबंधन इतना उत्कृष्ट है कि कहीं भी पानी एकत्रित नहीं होता है बल्कि भूमिगत स्त्रोतो में समाहित हो जाता है। संभवता तत्कालीन निर्माताओं ने भविष्य में जल विपदाओं एवं जल संरक्षण को दृष्टिगत रखते हुए निर्माण कार्य किया होगा।

सिंधिया पूर्व ग्वालियर में जल प्रबंधन का समग्र मूल्यांकन करने के बाद हम इस निष्कर्ष पर पहुँचते है कि ग्वालियर की स्थापना के समय से ही प्रथम शासक सूर्यसेन के समय में ही ग्वालियर दुर्ग में सूरजकुण्ड का निर्माण से लेकर मानसिंह तोमर के काल तक ग्वालियर में प्राकृतिक एवं गैर प्राकृतिक जल संसाधनों का विकास एवं उचित प्रबंधन होता रहा है।

संदर्भ

१. कनिंघम, आर्कियोलौजीकल सर्वे रिपोर्ट जिल्द २.२०२७२-७३

२. बलवंतराव भैया साहब सिंधिया, हिस्ट्री ऑफ फोर्ट ऑफ दि ग्वालियर पृ. ६।

३. ग्वालियर दुर्ग पेम्पलेट नं. ६, मई १६४६।

४. कनिंघम, आर्कियोलौजीकल सर्वे रिपोर्ट, जिल्द २ पृ. ३७।

५. गुलाब खां गोरी, ग्वालियर का राजनैतिक एवं सांस्कृतिक इतिहास पृ. ७८।

६. डॉ. आनन्द मिश्रा, ग्वालियर राज्य का आर्थिक इतिहास पृ. १।

७. मिहिर कुल का ग्वालियर प्रस्तर लेख, कार्पस इंसक्रिप्शन इंडिकेरम जिल्द ३ पृ. १६१-६४।

८. के.एम. मुन्शी, ग्लोरी, डेट वाज़ गुर्जर डेज पृ. ११६-१२१।

६. कुलियाते ग्वालियरी पृ. ३६।

१०. कनिंघम, आर्कियोलौजीकल सर्वे रिपोर्ट, जिल्द २ पृ. ३८७।

११. कु. रश्मि परिहार ग्वालियर का सामाजिक एवं आर्थिक इतिहास (सांस्कृतिक धरोहर के आधार पर) अप्रकाशित शोध प्रबंध इतिहास, जीवाजी विश्वविद्यालय २००५।

१२. जलाल हिजारी, ग्वालियर नामा पृष्ठ अंकित नहीं (मूलग्रंथ अलीगढ मुस्लिम विश्वविद्यालय में सुरक्षित)।

१३. कुलियाते ग्वालियर पृ. ४१।

डूंगरपुर की ऐतिहासिक झील : गेपसागर

डॉ. मलिका बोहरा

राजस्थान के २२ रजवाड़ों में दक्षिण राजस्थानं का डूंगरपुर राज्य एक महत्वपूर्ण रजवाड़ा रहा है । यहां के महारावलों ने समय-समय पर नगर के सौन्दर्यकरण एवम् पेयजल सुविधा हेतु कुओं, बावड़ियों तथा सरोवरों का भी निर्माण किया । डूंगरपुर की स्थापना के समय पुराने किले का जीर्णोद्धार हुआ तथा यहां जलकुण्डों, बावड़ियों व सरोवरों का निर्माण हुआ । जिनमें से अनेक आज भी मौजूद है । इनमें कई प्राकृतिक है, तो कई मानव निर्मित हैं, जिनमें सन् १४२५-२७ के मध्य में यहां के तत्कालीन महारावल गेपारावल (गोपीनाथ) द्वारा बनवायी गयी गेपसागर झील प्रमुख है।

महारावल वीरसिंहदेव द्वारा कहीं सन् १२५८, कहीं १२७८ ई. कहीं १३०४ तो कहीं १३५८ ई. में डूंगरिया भील को मारकर डूंगरपुर बसाना व राजधानी स्थिर करना लिखा है,[1] मगर शिलालेखों व ताम्रपत्र में वि.सं. १४१५ (सन् १३५८) में डूंगरपुर का बसाया जाना लिखा गया है।[2] इस समय महारावल वीरसिंहदेव जीवित नहीं थे, बल्कि उनके पोते डूंगरसिंह ने अपने नाम से डूंगरपुर बसाया, जो युक्तिसंगत है । वीरसिंहदेव के मिले तीन शिलालेख जो वि.सं. १३४९ (चैत्रादि १३५०) वैशाख सुदि ३ शनिवार (११ अप्रेल सन् १२९३) का है, जो बड़ौदा के तालाब के पास उनके बनवाये शिवालय में पत्थर की कुण्डी पर खुदा हुआ था, जिसमें वीरसिंहदेव के राज्य समय का महाप्रधान (मुख्यमंत्री) वामण नामक व्यक्ति का उल्लेख था।[3] महारावल वीरसिंहदेव के बाद उनके पुत्र भचूण्ड ने तथा महारावल डूंगरसिंह व कर्मसिंह जैसे शासकों ने डूंगरपुर नगर का विस्तार किया तब पेयजल सुविधा हेतु कई बावड़ियों, कुओं व तालाबों का निर्माण करवाया, जिनमें महारावल कर्मसिंह की रानी माणिकदेवी द्वारा बनवाई डेसा गांव[4] में बनी डेसा बावड़ी प्रमुख थी। महारावल कर्मसिंह के पुत्र महारावल कान्हडदेव १३८८-१४०६ ई. के बीच डूंगरपुर पर राज्य किया । उन्होंने डूंगरपुर के ओबरी गांव के पास वैराठ गांव के निकट अपना एक महल व कानेरा तालाब बनवाया,[5] जिसमें महल नष्ट हो गया है, तालाब अभी भी है, जिसके जल का उपयोग गांव वाले कर रहे हैं।

कान्हडदेव के बाद उनके पुत्र महारावल प्रतापसिंह (पातारावल) ने (सन् १४०६-१४२६ ई.) डूंगरपुर में अपने नाम से पातेला दरवाजा, पातालपुर गांव व पातेला तालाब बनवाया,[६] जिसमें दरवाजा नष्ट हो गया है वहां नये मकान बना लिये गये है। तालाब अभी भी मौजूद है, जिसके जल का उपयोग लोग कर रहे हैं ।

महारावल पातारावल के बाद महारावल गेपारावल[७] ने सन् १४२५-१४४८ ई. तक राज्य किया । उनकी एक रानी लीलावती ने सागवाड़ा कस्बे के आंतरी गांव में 'बीलियावाव' बनवाई इस महारावल के समय में डूंगरपुर में गेपापोल दरवाजा बना, जो अब गिरा दिया गया है तथा गैपसागर तालाब बना।[८] इस तालाब के निर्माण को लेकर कई जनश्रुतियाँ है। इन जनश्रुतियों के अनुसार वर्तमान में गेपसागर तालाब बना है, वहां पहले चौबीसा ब्राह्मणों के खेत थे।[९]

श्यामलदास ने महारावल की आज्ञा से चौबिसा ब्राहमणों के खेत खरीद कर वहां तालाब निर्माण का कार्य शुरू किया । जब तालाब, पेंदें में बनी कोटड़ी और उपर की पांच सीढ़ियां जो 'दावड़ा ना पखथियां' के नाम से प्रसिद्ध है, वे बने तो यहां के नागर ब्राह्मणों को श्यामलदास से बड़ी स्पर्द्धा व जलन होने लगी, क्योंकि वे भी धन व वैभव सम्पन्न थे। उनसे श्यामलदास द्वारा सरोवर निर्माण का कार्य सहन न हो सका, इसलिए कुछ वृद्ध नागर मिलकर महारावल के पास गये व निवेदन किया कि "जो सरोवर का निर्माण हो रहा है, वह ठीक नहीं है। श्यामलदास ने उनसे कहा कि "अब तो बहुत पैसा खर्च हो चुका है । इसे बीच में अधूरा कैसे छोड़ा जाये ?" तब नागरों ने कहा कि "तुम महारावल से निवेदन करो कि तालाब का निर्माण करवाना जैन शास्त्रों के विरूद्ध है और यह कार्य करके बड़ी भारी भूल हुई है । अतः मैं तालाब न बनवाकर मंदिर बनवाना चाहता हूँ, इसलिए अब तंक जो रूपया लगा है उसकी भरपाई हेतु राज्य की तरफ से भूमि दे दी जाये ताकि मंदिर बनवा सकुं।" श्यामलदास को नागरों की यह बात अच्छी लगी । वह महारावल के पास गया। महारावल तो चाहते ही यही थे । उन्होंने तुरंत उसकी प्रार्थना स्वीकार करली तथा शहर के माणक चौक के बीच बिना मूल्य भूमि उसे दे दी व मंदिर बनवाने की स्वीकृति भी दे दी। उधर श्यामलदास ने उस स्थान पर आदिनाथ (ऋषभदेव) का सुविशाल मंदिर बनवाया तथा महारावल ने उसके आरंभ किये गये तालाब का कार्य पूर्ण करवाकर अपने नाम (गेपा, गोपीनाथ) से गेपसागर[१०] नाम रखा। उन्होंने गेपसागर तालाब के किनारों पर 'दावड़ा ना पखथियां'[११] से उपर ओर सीढ़ियां बनवाई तथा तीन गुम्बजों वाली छतरी बनवाकर उसका नाम 'चौबीसों की छतरी' रखा, क्योंकि यहां पहले चौबीसा ब्राहमणों के खेत रहे थे। सर्वेक्षण के दौरान पाया कि गैपसागर को साढे तीन कि०मी० की

परिधि जिसमें बीच में (टमततल) उतार-चढ़ाव भी है, में बांधा गया। यह पश्चिम से उत्तर दिशा में ए आकार में बंधा। पहले यह शहर के सुपर मार्केट से चौराहे तक बांधा गया। फिर चौराहे से पुराना बसस्टेण्ड व रामबोला मठ तक बांधा गया। वहां जाते-जाते मात्र ५ फीट की दीवार हो जाती है। पूर्व दिशा में पहाड़ियां आ जाती है, जो इसे बांधने में मददगार रही। इस तालाब के उत्तर व पश्चिम में बलवाड़िया पत्थर की सीढ़ियां बनाई गई है, जो मजबूती लिये हुए हैं।

रियासत काल में महारावल गेपारावल के समय १४२५-२७ ई. में बनी गेपसागर झील के निर्माण के बाद इसी महारावल ने तालाब के मध्य में सन् १४२८ में बादल महल का निर्माण करवाया।[12] यह महल दो चरणों में बना । पहले चरण में चबूतरा व उपर मंजिल बनाई गई। दूसरे चरण में उसके उपर दूसरी मंजिल महारावल पूंजराज के समय में (सन् १६०६-१६५७) बनी। इस महल में डूंगरपुर शैली के गोखड़ों के साथ सादगी तथा मजबूती की प्रतीक राजपूत शैली व अलंकरण की प्रतीकवाली मुगलशैली की स्थापत्यकला के दर्शन स्वतः ही हो जाते हैं। इनके समय के चार शिलालेख मिलते हैं, जिनमें दो पर वि.सं. १४८४ व वि.सं. १४६८ लिखा हुआ है। बाकी दो पर संवत मिट गये है, जिसका विवरण वीरविनोद के भाग-२ पर मिलता हैं। इस झील के दक्षिण तट पर महारावल उदयसिंह द्वितीय द्वारा बनवाया गया सन् (१८८३-८७ के बीच बना) उदयविलास महल[13] तथा यही पास में महारावल विजयसिंह (१८६८-१८६८ ई.) द्वारा बनवाया हुआ विजयराजराजेश्वर मंदिर मौजूद है। सन् १६१८ में इस महारावल की मृत्यु ३१ वर्श की उम्र में हो जाने से इस मंदिर का अधूरा निर्माण कार्य उनकी रानी देवेन्द्रकुंवर ने पूर्ण करवाया था।

गेपसागर की मरम्मत का कार्य समय-समय पर होता रहा। डूंगरपुर के २७वें महारावल शिवसिंह ने अपने समय में (१७३०-१७८५ ई.) व्यापक स्तर पर मरम्मत कार्य किया। इस हेतु तालाब की पाल पर छतरियों का निर्माण करवाया, जिन्हें 'शिवशाही छतरियां' कहते है। यहां एक छोटा चबूतरे में पारेवा पत्थर की प्रशस्ति गड़ी हुई है, जिसके उपर की लिखावट नष्ट हो गयी है। नीचे की लिखावट में महारावल शिवसिंह, भाई हमीरसिंह, अम्बावगांधी, रेवादास कैदारगांधी, मेहता अनूपजी, अखेचंद गांधी, तखतजी, गंगाराम गौड़, धार परमारजी, रामकृश्णजी, परमार सेठ सांचावत, नाथजी चूंडावत, चौहान भगतजी, चौहान जेतसिंह, मुणसेंध डाबी, बलवंत वैजणिया, तखतसिंह चौहान, लाभचन्द, परमार जीतूजी, कपूरचन्द गांधी, मेहता मोतीचंद के नाम लिखे हुए हैं।[14] इस पाल पर तीन अन्य छतरियों वाली ऊंचाई पर बनी बड़ी छतरी जिसे 'चौबीसों की छतरी' कहते हैं जो अत्यन्त सादी है जब कि उसीकी सीध में दो सुन्दर

शिवशाही छतरियां बनवाई गई। यहां महारावल शिवसिंह के समय गंवरीबाई नागरण ने जिसे 'वागड़ की मींरा' कहते हैं, ने भी 'गौरीश्वर की देवरी' बनवाई थी, जो आज भी मौजूद है।[१४] वर्तमान में राज्य सरकार द्वारा पाल का नवनिर्माण हो गया है, मगर छतरियों की ऐतिहासिकता अभी भी बरकरार है।

इसी पाल पर एक संत मावजी महाराज की चरण पादूकाएं वाली देवली भी बनी हुई है, कहते हैं कि महारावल शिवसिंह ने मावजी महाराज की परीक्षा लेने के लिए उनसे शर्त रखी कि वे इतने चमत्कारी संत है तो गेपसार के पानी पर चलकर दिखाएं। इस पर मावजी महाराज क्रुद्ध हुए तथा श्राप दिया कि "मैं क्या चलुंगा? यहां तो गधे चलेंगे।"[१५] ऐसा ही हुआ कुछ समय बाद यहां अकाल इतना पड़ा कि तालाब का पानी सूख गया तथा गधे-घोड़े ही चरने लगे। तब महारावल को बड़ा पश्चाताप हुआ, उसने मावजी महाराज से माफी मांगी। मावजी की इस करामत से श्रृद्धालुओं ने उनकी देवजी बनवाकर पादूकाएं रखवाई, जो आज भी मौजूद है।

डूंगरपुर राज्य में महारावल शिवसिंह के काल में (१७३०-८५ ई.) कई इमारतों पर शिवशाही छतरियां[१६] बनी, जिसमें कई टूट चुकी है, मगर यहां के गेपसागर की पाल पर आज भी वे दो शिवशाही छतरियां मौजूद है, जो अच्छी दशा में है। ये छतरियां इस तालाब की शोभा बढ़ाने के लिए बनवाई गई थी ताकि लोग इसमें बैठकर तालाब को निहार सके। ठण्डी हवाओं का आनन्द ले सके। इस पाल पर एक छतरी महारावल गेपारावल के समय में (१४३६-१४५६ ई.) बनी, जिसे चौबीसों की छतरी कहतें है, जो इन छतरियों से बड़ी है और जमीन से ज्यादा ऊंची बनी है। उस पर जाने के लिए सीढ़ियां चढ़नी होती है। चौबीसों की छतरी स्थापत्यकला की दृश्टि से सादगी लिए हुई है। यह करीब २५' ग १०' के स्थान को घेरे हुए है। इसकी ऊंचाई करीब २५ फीट है। इसे ईट-चूने व पत्थरों से बनाया गया है, जबकि शिवशाही छतरियां स्थापत्यकला की दृश्टि से अत्यन्त सुन्दर है। तालाब की पाल पर बनी हुई है, जो जमीन से डेढ़ फीट ऊंचे चबूतरे पर बनाई गई है। इन छतरियों की ऊंचाई १८ फीट है, जबकि लम्बाई व चौड़ाई ५' ग ५' की है। यह सामान्यतः पारेवा पत्थर की है। शिवशाही छतरियों में दूसरी छतरी पहले वर्तमान में जहां 'भागामहल' (पुराना विद्युत विभाग का कार्यालय) मौजूद है, वहां बनी हुई थी, मगर जब महारावल उदयसिंह द्वि तीय (१८४६-९८ ई.) में 'भागामहल' बनवाया तब इसे हटाकर पाल की सीढ़ियों की तरफ स्थापित की। इस महारावल के समय वि.सं. १९३२ (१८७५) के अश्विन मास में लगातार तीन दिन तक वर्षा होने से यह तालाब धोबियों की पाल तथा खाड़िये की पाल की ओर से टूट गया था, तब उसका सारा पानी केलाबाग (वर्तमान में महारावल

स्कूल का बागीचा) में घुस गया था। महारावल ने बडे धैर्य से काम लेते हुए तालाब व बगीचे को दुरूस्त करवाया था।[१७] केलाबाग का नाम उन्होंने अपने नाम से 'उदयबाग' रखा।

वर्तमान में डूंगरपुर शहरवासियों के पेयजल की आपूर्ति का मुख्य स्त्रोत डूँगरपुर से ५ कि.मी. दूर सिमलवाडा रोड पर कलाल घाटा के पाटडी गांव का एडवर्डसमन्द तालाब तथा ११ कि.मी. दूर सागवाड़ा रोड के लोलकपुरा ग्राम पंचायत का विजयसागर तालाब का पानी है। इसके अलावा कुछ रिसायतकालीन बावड़ियां है।

समय-समय पर यहां पेयजल स्त्रोत हेतु कई बावड़ियां व तालाब बनते रहे। इनमें महारावल पूंजराज के समय में (सन् १६०६-५७ ई.) डूंगरपुर में बनी 'नौलख बावड़ी',[१८] पूंजपुर गांव में बना पूंजेला तालाब[१९] प्रमुख है। महारावल जसवन्तसिंह प्रथम की रानी फूलकुंवरी द्वारा वीरपुर गांव में बनी (सन् १६६१-६१) दो बावड़ियां प्रमुख है।[२०] यहां सन् १७०२-३० के मध्य महारावल रामसिंह के समय में नगर के घाटी क्षेत्र में बनी 'रामवाव',[२१] महारावल शिवसिंह के समय में समीपस्थ खेड़ाकछवासा गांव में बना रणसागर तालाब,[२२] महारावल फतहसिंह के समय सन् १७६०-१८०८ में यहां के महारावल स्कूल के पास बने 'उदयविहार' बगीचे में बनी 'राणीवाव',[२३] महारावल उदयसिंह द्वितीय के समय (१८४६-६८ ई.) में डूंगरपुर के घाटी क्षेत्र में बनी 'उदयवाव'[२४] यहां के भेरवे की बाड़ी में ठाकुर अभयसिंह सूरमा द्वारा बनवायी 'गलालवाव'[२५] महारावल विजयसिंह के समय में (१८६८-१६१८ ई.) बना ब्रिटेन सम्राट एडवर्ड सप्तम्[२६] की स्मृति में बना एडवर्डसंमद तालाब प्रमुख है। ये सभी अच्छी दशा में है तथा ये किसी न किसी रूप में पेयजल आपूर्ति का स्त्रोत बने हुए है।

सन्दर्भ

१. ओझा : डूंगरपुर राज्य का इतिहास पृ-६०

२. उपरोक्त वही पृ-६०

३. उपरोक्त वही पृ-६१

४. डैसा गांव की प्रशस्ति लेख में राऊल जैयसल (जयकृश्ण) जो महारावल कर्मसिंह का पुत्र था। डूंगरपुर की गद्दी पर वि.सं. १४४१-४३(सन् १३८४-८६) के बीच राज्य करने का उल्लेख मिलता है, जिसका डूंगरपुर राज्य के अब तक के किसी भी ग्रंथों में उल्लेख नहीं मिलता है। नवीन शोध से यहां के इतिहासकार महेश पुरोहित ने इसे सिद्ध किया है।

५. डूंगरपुर राज्यपत्र : ५ जनवरी १९५५ पृ-७५

६. ओझा : डूंगरपुर राज्य का इतिहास पृ-६४

७. शिलालेखों में महारावल गेपारावल के कई नाम मिलते हैं यथा गईप, गजपाल, गोप, गोपाल व गोपीनाथ।

८. ओझा : डूंगरपुर राज्य का इतिहास पृ-६७

९. डूंगरपुर राज्यपत्र : शुक्रवार मिति प्रथम ज्येश्ठ कृश्णा सप्तमी सं. १९९८ पृ-१९२

१०.डूंगरपुर राज्यपत्र : शुक्रवार ५ जून १९४२ पृ-१९३

११.श्यामदास दावड़ा महाजन था, इसलिए उसकी स्मृति में यहां तालाब के किनारे आरंभिक सीढ़ियां बनवाई गई वे 'दावड़ा ना पखथियां' के नाम से जानी जाती है।

१२.महेश पुरोहित का लेख : राजस्थान पत्रिका २० जनवरी १९९८ 'डूंगरपुर का बादल महल'।

१३.ओझा : डूंगरपुर राज्य का इतिहास पृ-१७८

१४.डूंगरपुर राज्यपत्र : बुधवार ५ जुलाई १९४४ पृ-१९०

१५.पंड्या रवीन्द्र डी. : संत मावजी कालीन ग्रंथ महारासलीला के लघुचित्र पृ-८

१६.डूंगरपुर राज्यपत्र : रविवार मिति अश्विन पूर्णिमा सं. १९९८ पृ-१०

१७.डूंगरपुर राज्यपत्र ' मंगलवार मिति मार्ग शीर्श कृश्णा चतुर्थी वि.सं. १९९९ पृ-५०

१८.ओझा : डूंगरपुर राज्य का इतिहास पृ-१००

१९.उपरोक्त वहीं ।

२०.डूंगरपुर राज्यपत्र : रविवार मिति पोश शुक्ला अश्टमी वि.सं. १९९७ पृ-१३

२१.ओझा : डूंगरपुर राज्य का इतिहास पृ-१२८

२२.१. उपरोक्त वही पृ-१३१

२. डूंगरपुर राज्यपत्र : सोमवार मित्ति वैशाख शुक्ला नवमी वि.सं. १९२७ पृ-५

२३.डूगरपुर राज्यपत्र : मंगलवार मित्ति मार्ग शीर्श कृश्णा चतुर्दशी वि.सं. १९९९ पृ-५०

२४.ओझा : डूंगरपुर राज्य का इतिहास पृ-१७५

२५.डूंगरपुर राज्यपत्र : मंगलवार मित्ति वैशाख कृश्णा पंचमी वि.सं. १९९८ पृ-१९९

२६.ओझा : डूंगरपुर राज्य का इतिहास पृ-१८८

बुंदेलाशासकों के काल में जल प्रबंधन (मध्यप्रदेशीय बुंदेलखण्ड के विशेष संदर्भ में)

मधुलता मिश्रा

चंदेलों की सत्ता के अस्ताचलगामी हो जाने के पश्चात् बुंदेलों का अभ्युदय सूर्योदय के समान हुआ। 'छत्रप्रकाश ग्रंथ' से प्रारंभिक बुंदेला शासकों की जानकारी मिलती है।[१] बुंदेलों का अदम्य शौर्य एवं पराक्रम मध्यकालीन इतिहास में सुविख्यात है। बुंदेला शासकों ने अकबर से लेकर औरंगजेब के शासनकाल तक निरंतर मुगल सत्ता के विरुद्ध संघर्ष किया।[२] बुंदेलों की उत्पत्ति 'विंध्येला' शब्द से हुई है। 'विंध्येला' शब्द का संबंध विंध्याचल की श्रेणियों और विंध्यवासिनी देवी के मंदिर से मानी जा सकती है। विंध्यवासिनी देवी बुंदेलों की इष्ट देवी थीं। बुंदेलों की उत्पत्ति के बारे में अनेक दंतकथाएँ प्रचलित हैं। परन्तु उनकी प्रामाणिकता में संदेह है। ऐसा माना जाता है कि बुंदेला गहरवार नरेश वीरभद्र के पुत्र पंचम के वंशज थे।[३]

बुंदेलखण्ड भारत का हृदयस्थल है। मध्यकाल में बुंदेला शासकों द्वारा यहाँ शासन किया गया एवं राज्य की सीमाओं का विस्तार किया गया। महाराज छत्रसाल बुंदेला द्वारा यमुना के दक्षिण व दक्षिण-पश्चिम सीमाओं का विस्तार किया गया। उत्तर में यमुना, दक्षिण में नर्मदा, पश्चिम में राज्य की सीमा चम्बल नदी तथा पूर्व में टोंस नदो तक थी।[४]

साहित्यिक स्रोतों एवं सर्वेक्षण द्वारा विदित होता है कि मध्यकाल में प्रजा हित में जो कार्य करवाये गये उनमें यह जलप्रबंधन प्रमुख था। जल प्रबंधन का अर्थ है, 'जल के उपयोग के संसाधन बनाना' व स्रोतों का निर्माण करना। इन बुंदेला शासकों ने जलप्रबंधन के स्रोतों में प्रमुख रूप से कुओं, सरोवरों, बावड़ियों एवं चोपड़ों का निर्माण कराया।

'केशवदेव' रचित 'वीरसिंह देव' चरित्र से ज्ञात होता है कि महाराज वीरसिंह ने बुंदेलखण्ड में जल प्रबंधन के लिए अनेक जलस्रोतों का निर्माण कराया।[५] जिनमें प्रमुख रूप से वीरसागर, सिंहसागर, देवसागर, नंदनसागर, उमरा बावड़ी, सिरोल बावड़ी,

दतिया की बावड़ी, बड़ोनी की बावड़ी तथा कालीबावड़ी प्रमुख हैं। इसी प्रकार लाल कवि द्वारा रचित 'छत्रप्रकाश' से ज्ञात होता है कि छत्रसाल बुंदेला ने छत्रसाल का कुआँ, गढ़पहरा का तालाब एवं कुंडलपुर के सरोवर का निर्माण कराया। इन जलस्रोतों में प्रमुख का विवरण इस प्रकार है-

१. वीरसागर

वीरसिंह देव ने अपने नाम के प्रथम शब्द 'वीर' के ऊपर वीरसागर का निर्माण कराया। यह सरोवर प्राकृतिक सौंदर्य के साथ-साथ पहाड़ियों के मध्य प्राकृतिक सुषमा से भरपूर है। यह सरोवर एक झील के समान सुंदर है। इसके किनारे बसे हुए गाँव का नाम भी इस सरोवर के नाम पर वीरसागर पड़ गया।

२. सिंहसागर

गढ़कुड़ार के उत्तरी भाग में भी विंध्यवासिनी देवी के मंदिर की पहाड़ी से लगा हुआ यह सरोवर है जिसे सिंदूरसागर भी कहा जाता है। ये सरोवर विशाल एवं दर्शनीय है। इस सरोवर का नामकरण महाराज के नाम के द्वितीय शब्द सिंह के आधार पर किया गया।

३. देवसागर (दिनारा)

इस सरोवर का निर्माण जिला शिवपुरी के दिनारा नामक स्थान पर वीरसिंह 'देव' ने अपने नाम के तृतीय शब्द देव के आधार पर कराया गया था। इस सरोवर का निर्माण भी सार्वजनिक हित के लिए किया गया था।

४. नंदनवारा सरोवर

इस सरोवर का निर्माण वीरसिंह देव ने टीकमगढ़ में करवाया। यह वारि राशि का नंदनस्थल जल का आगार है। इस बांध का निर्माण बरगी नदी की दो पहाड़ियों के मध्य खंदक को बांधकर तैयार किया गया था। जनसाधारण के स्नान की सुविधा के लिए राजा ने इन नदियों के तटों पर पक्के घाटों का निर्माण भी कराया था।

बावड़ी

वीरसिंह देव ने जलकल्याण हेतु अनेक बावड़ियों का निर्माण कराया। इनका उद्देश्य न केवल जलप्राप्ति के स्रोत उपलब्ध करवाना था बल्कि लोगों को प्राकृतिक आपदा एवं अकाल के समय कार्य देना था। उनके द्वारा निर्मित प्रमुख बावड़िया निम्नलिखित हैं-

१. उमरा बावड़ी

ग्राम उमरा में वीरसिंह देव ने एक बावड़ी का निर्माण करवा था जो स्थापत्य कला की दृष्टि से अत्यन्त महत्वपूर्ण है।

२. सिरोल बावड़ी

सिरोल ग्राम में भी उमरा बावड़ी के समान ही एक बावड़ी राजा ने निर्मित करवायी थी।

३. कटेरा बावड़ी

कटेरा कस्बे में भी एक बावड़ी का निर्माण कराया गया था।

४. दतिया की बावड़ी

दतिया में भी वीरसिंह देव ने एक बावड़ी बनवायी जो आज भी दर्शनीय है।

५. बाड़ोनी की बावड़ी

वीरसिंह देव को बाड़ोनी से बहुत अधिक लगाव था इसलिए उन्होंने वहाँ भी एक बावड़ी निर्मित करवायी।

६. चंदेल वेर दतिया

दतिया में चंदेर वेर की बावड़ी स्थापत्य कला की दृष्टि से अनोखी है।

जलप्रबंधन के क्षेत्र में बुंदेला शासकों ने विशाल तालाबों का निर्माण व जीर्णोद्धार कराया था।

कुंडलपुर का तालाब (वर्द्धमान सागर)

इसका जीर्णोद्धार महाराज छत्रसाल द्वारा करवाया गया। उन्होंने यहाँ के वर्द्धमान के चारों ओर पक्के घाट का निर्माण करवाया व जीर्णोद्धार कार्य पूरा होने पर माघ शुक्ल १५ सोमवार विक्रम संवत् १७५७ को पंचकल्याणक प्रतिष्ठा कर विशाल समारोह किया। महाराज छत्रसाल द्वारा किये गये जीर्णोद्धार का उल्लेख यहाँ स्थापित शिलालेख में भी मिलता है जो यहाँ प्रवेश द्वार पर लगा है। इस शिलालेख में २४ पंक्तियाँ हैं।

संदर्भ

१. झा, विवेकदत्त एवं डॉ. नागेश दुबे, बुंदेलखण्ड का सांस्कृतिक तथा राजनैतिक इतिहास, सरोज प्रकाशन, सागर, २००६, पृ. ६

२. पटैरिया, शिवअनुराग, बुंदेलखण्ड, मध्यप्रदेश हिन्दी ग्रंथ अकादमी, २००५, पृ. १

३. गजेटियर, जिला छतरपुर, भोपाल

४. इत जमुना उत नर्मदा, इत चम्बल उत टोंस

छत्रसाल सो लरन् की, रही न काहू होंस। (–लालकवि छत्रप्रकाश)

५. तिवारी, गोरेलाल, बुंदेलखण्ड का संक्षिप्त इतिहास, काशीनागरी प्रचारिणी सभा, १९९०, पृ. १७६

६. त्रिपाठी, के.पी., बुंदेलखण्ड की सांस्कृतिक विरासत, समय प्रकाशन, दिल्ली, १९९४, पृ. ९

गौरी सरोवर - भिण्ड स्थित पृथ्वीराज चौहान का स्मृति अवषेश

डॉ. सुरेन्द्र कुमार विमल

भिण्ड भारत के मध्य स्थित राज्य मध्यप्रदेष के उत्तर-पश्चिम में ग्वालियर से लगभग ७४ कि०मी० की दूरी पर स्थित है। मानचित्र पर इसकी स्थिति का अक्षाषीय विस्तार २५'५५' उत्तरी अक्षांष से २६'४८' उत्तरी अक्षांष के बीच तथा देशान्तरीय विस्तार ७८'१२' पूर्वी देशान्तर से ७९'०५' पूर्वी देशान्तर के बीच स्थित है।[1]

भिण्ड जिला सामान्य रूप से भिण्ड भदावर के नाम से प्रसिद्ध है। मनु के समय में इस प्रदेश को शूरसेन के नाम से जानते थे। भदावर प्रदेश इसी शूरसेन का पूर्वी भाग था।[2] मनुस्मृति में शूरसेन की गणना में ब्रह्मावर्त के प्रमुख देशों में की गई है।[3] एक मत के अनुसार यह प्रदेश भदौरिया शासकों के अधिकार में रहा। इस कारण भदावर कहलाया।[4] भदावर से इस क्षेत्र का नाम भिण्ड कैसे हुआ यह भी हमें पुराण से ही प्राप्त होता है। ऐसा माना जाता है। कि रामायण काल में भिण्ड क्षेत्र में घोर वियावान जंगल था और जहां विभाण्डक ऋशि आश्रम बना कर घोर तपस्या करते थे। इन्ही विभाण्डक ऋशि के शिष्य श्रृंगी ऋशि थे, जिन्होंने अयोध्या नरेश दशरथ के आमंत्रण पर पुत्र काम यज्ञ किया था। तपोनिधि विभाण्डक ने यही समाधि ली थी। कालान्तर में विभाण्डक का नाम बिगड़ते-बिगड़ते भाण्डव, भाण्डी और भिण्डी हुआ और इन्ही के नाम पर बाद में नगर बसने पर इस स्थान का नाम भिण्ड हुआ।[5]

पुराणों के अनुसार इस क्षेत्र पर नंद वंश के राजाओं तथा कण्व वंष के राजाओं का शासन भी दीर्घ काल तक रहा।[6] प्रथम शताब्दी ईसापूर्व में यह क्षेत्र नागाओं के अधीन रहा। इसके पश्चात कुषाणों ने नगाओं को परास्त कर समूचे उत्तर भारत पर अधिकार कर लिया।[7] कनिष्क के उत्तरवर्ती शासकों के समय इस क्षेत्र में नागाओं ने अपनी शक्ति का पुनः विस्तार किया। समुद्रगुप्त की प्रयाग प्रशस्ति के अनुसार यह क्षेत्र नागाओं के अधीन रहा। चन्द्रगुप्त द्वितीय का विवाह नाग कन्या कुबेर नागा के साथ हुआ था तथा स्कन्दगुप्त ने इस क्षेत्र के विषयपति के रूप में सर्वनागा को

नियुक्त किया था।[८] मंदसौर प्रशस्ति ग्वालियर लेख एवं ऐरण अभिलेख के अनुसार यह क्षेत्र गुप्तों के बाद हूणों के अधिकार में रहा। हूण शासक मिहिरकुल को पराजित कर यशोधर्मन ने इस क्षेत्र पर अधिकार किया।[९]

यह क्षेत्र नौवी तथा दसवी सदी के अंत तक गुर्जर प्रतिहारों के शासनाधीन रहा। इसके पश्चात चंदेलों ने इस क्षेत्र को अपने अधीन कर लिया।[१०]

भिण्डी ऋषि की तपस्थली भिण्ड ऐतिहासिक के साथ-साथ एक धार्मिक नगरी भी है। इसने यदि राजवंषों के शौर्य और साहस को देखा है तो उनके पुण्य और प्रताप का प्रभाव भी इस क्षेत्र में रहा है। भिण्ड स्थित 'गौरी सरोवर' उसी धार्मिक आस्था का प्रतीक है। भिण्ड नगर के मध्य विशाल भू-भाग पर बने ऐतिहासिक तालाब गौरी सरोवर आने-जाने वालों को बरबस ही अपनी ओर आकर्षित करता है।

सरोवर की ऐतिहासिकता के विषय में विद्वानों का कथन है कि इस सरोवर का निर्माण मध्य काल में चौहान नरेश पृथ्वीराज चौहान के द्वारा संपन्न कराया गया। इतिहास सम्मत के अनुसार शाकम्भरी का प्रसिद्ध चौहान शासक तरायन के प्रथम युद्ध (११९१ ई०) के विजेता पृथ्वीराज चौहान महोबा के चंदेल सेनापति मलखान बनाफर पर आक्रमण करने की नियत से भिण्ड नगरी तक आ पहुचा। इस बात की पुष्टि जगनिक कृत आल्हाखण्ड से भी होती है।[११] पृथ्वीराज चौहान ने यहां पर अपने इष्ट देव शिव की प्राण प्रतिष्ठा की चूंकि उस समय यह क्षेत्र एक वियावान वनखण्ड था इसीलिये इस मंदिर का नाम वनखण्डेश्वर पड़ा।[१२]

अतिक्रमण और प्रदूषण की चपेट में आकर यह सरोवर अपना अस्तित्व खोता चला गया। आधुनिक सुख सुविधाओं की प्राप्ति में मनुष्य ने इस सरोवर का स्वरूप संकुचित कर दिया है। वर्तमान में गौरी सरोवर के अस्तित्व को बरकरार रखने के लिये कई स्थानीय एवं शासकीय प्रयास किये जा रहे है परन्तु सभी निरर्थक है। सुन्दर नीला जल आज जलकुम्भी से घिर चुका है। ऐतिहासिक महत्व के इस सरोवर को, जो भिण्ड में पृथ्वीराज चौहान के एक स्मृति अवशेष के रूप में स्थित है, आवश्यकता है स्थानीय एवं शासकीय प्रयासों की जो इसके अस्तित्व को पुनः स्थापित कर सकें।

संदर्भ

१. जिला गजेटियर, भिण्ड।

२. वाल्मिकी रामायण किष्किन्धा काण्ड-४८/१०।

३. मनु स्मृति २/१६।

४. झम्मनलाल तर्कतीर्थ, लम्बेचू समाज का इतिहास पृ० १३५।

५. डॉ० शिवशंकर कटारे, भदावर का इतिहास पृ० ८।
६. भिण्ड जिला गजेटियर पृ० १५।
७. डॉ० शिवशंकर कटारे, भदावर का इतिहास पृ० २६।
८. के०सी० श्रीवास्तव, प्राचीन भारत का इतिहास तथा संस्कृति पृ० ४२५।
६. भिण्ड गजेटियर पृ० १७।
१०. डॉ० शिवशंकर कटारे, भदावर का इतिहास पृ० २६।
११. वही पृ० ४०।
१२. डॉ० राजीव मिश्रा, भिण्ड जिले के मंदिरों का ऐतिहासिक अध्ययन, अप्रकाशित शोध-प्रबंध, जीवाजी विश्वविद्यालय, ग्वालियर, पृ० १११।

मध्यकालीन मेवाड़ में जल प्रबंधन व मुद्रा – परस्पर महत्ता

दिलीप कुमार गर्ग

जल संसाधनों का प्रबंधन एवं मुद्रा व्यवस्था आज उतनी ही प्रासंगिक है, जितनी अतीत में थी। मुद्रा व जल संसाधन एवं उनका प्रबंधन मानव जीवन की अनिवार्यता व उसका (जीवन) एक महत्वपूर्ण हिस्सा है। मध्यकालीन मेवाड़ में भी जल प्रबंधन, इसके संसाधनों के निर्माण व सरंक्षण पर समय-समय पर कार्य हुआ है। मेवाड़ में सार्वजनिक उपयोग हेतु तालाब, कुएँ, बावड़ी आदि के माध्यम से जल संसाधनों का अधिकाधिक संरक्षण और निर्माण की विकसित परम्पराएं रही हैं।[१] इसके पीछे मूल कारण यहां पर वर्षवाहिनी नदियों का अभाव[२] व इसकी भौगोलिक स्थिति है।[३] इस क्षेत्र के संदर्भ में एक महत्वपूर्ण बात यह है कि यहां वर्षा पर्याप्त मात्रा में होती थी,[४] ऐसी दशा में जल संरक्षण व जल संसाधनों के लिए झीलों, तालाबों, बाबड़ियों, कुओं आदि निर्माण कार्यों में मेवाड़ अपनी चरम अवस्था में गुजरा है। इनमें मुख्यत: पिछोला, फतहसागर, जयसंमद, राजसमुद्र (राजसमंद) जानासागर, रूप सागर, देबारी तालब, त्रिमुखी बावड़ी, राजनगर की बावड़ी इत्यादि झीलों व तालाबों का निर्माण हुआ।[५]

उपर्युक्त सभी निर्माण कार्य मुद्रा के बिना असंभव थे, क्योंकि इन निर्माण कार्यों के लिए आवश्यक सामग्री, कारीगर, मजदूर इत्यादि के लिए धन परम आवश्यक था। मेवाड़ में ये सब मुद्रा की वजह से था, क्योंकि यहां की मुद्रा व्यवस्था अर्थात् वित्तीय व्यवस्था विकसित रही थी। अतः जल संसाधन व मुद्रा परस्पर पूरक एवं महता रखते है। मुद्रा के माध्यम से ही जल प्रबंधन की ओर ध्यान दिया जा सका और जल प्रबंधन से आम जीवन को पेय जलापूर्ति तो हुई, साथ ही कृषि और व्यापार वाणिज्य बढ़ा, नगरों का विकास हुआ क्योंकि नगर निर्माण व बस्तियों की वसावट की प्राथमिक आवश्यकता पर्याप्त जल संसाधनों की उपलब्धता होती है। मेवाड़ में उदयपुर, राजसमंद, गोगुन्दा, चावण्ड आदि मध्यकालीन शहरों का विकास नदियों अथवा तालाबों से परिपूर्ण जल बाहुल्यता वाले स्थानों पर हुआ। अतः जब कृषि, व्यापार, उद्योग द नगरों का विकास हुआ ऐसे में मेवाड़ क्षेत्र की आर्थिक समृद्धि स्वयं बढ़ी व मुद्रा का विकास हुआ।

(अ) जल संसाधनों के प्रबंधन व निर्माण में मुद्रा का महत्व -

मध्यकालीन मेंवाड़ में जल संसाधनों के निर्माण व संरक्षण में मुद्रा ने निर्णायक भूमिका रही है। मुद्रा के बिना ये सभी निर्माण कार्य शून्य थे। मेवाड़ महाराणाओं (राजा) ने व्यक्तिगत रूचि लेकर जलाशय निर्माण करवाये। शिलालेख व अन्य ऐतिहासिक सामग्रियों[७] में यहां के शासकों, जागीरदारों, अधिकारियों, तथा जन सामान्य द्वारा जलाशय निर्माण की जानकारी प्राप्त होती है।[८] मुद्रा के माध्यम प्रमुखतः निम्नलिखित जलाशयों का निर्माण हुआ -

(१) पिछोला - महाराणा लाखा[९] के काल में छीतर नाम धनाढ़य बनजारे ने १३८७ ई. में इसका निर्माण करवाया।[१०] निकट में पिछोला गांव होने से यह तालाब पिछोला कहलाया। यह लगभग २.५ मील लम्बाई एवं १.५ मील चौड़ाई में निर्मित है। इसके अंतर्गत लगभग ५६ मील भूमि का जल शामिल होता है।[११] इसको व्यवस्थित करने, संरक्षण व निर्माण और मरम्मत के लिए काफी मात्रा में धन खर्च हुआ और समय समय पर महाराणाओं ने इस ओर ध्यान दिया। १५२५ ई. में जब यह बांध फूट गया, उस समय महाराणा सांगा[१२] ने इसकी मरम्मत करवाई[१३]। इसके बाद समय-समय पर मेवाड़ महाराणाओं उदयसिंह व अमरसिंह ने इस बांध की पाल को ऊँचा व पक्का बनवाया[१४]। वि.सं. १९०४ (१८४७ई.) में इस टूट जाने पर महाराणा स्वरूप सिंह ने पूर्वी भाग में स्वरूप सागर बनवाया। महाराणा सज्जन सिंह ने भी इसकी मरम्मत करवाई।[१५]

(२) उदयसागर - उदयपुर से ५ कि.मी. पूर्व दिशा में स्थित यह तालाब २.५ मील लम्बा एंव २ मील चौड़ा है। इसमें १८५ वर्ग मील भूमि क्षेत्र का जल संग्रहण होता है। महाराणा उदयसिंह ने १५५९ से १५६४ में इसका निर्माण करवाया[१६]। जब महाराणा उदयसिंह ने उदयपुर को राजधानी बनाया, ऐसी दशा में यहां आधारभूत सुविधाएं पर्याप्त जल, प्रचुर मात्रा में खाद्य सामग्री आदि की उपलब्धता निश्चित करना अनिवार्य था इसलिए उदयसागर का निर्माण करवाया गया[१७]। इस बांध की भराव क्षमता ११०० मी.क्यू. फीट है[१८]।

उदयसागर के निर्माण में मजदूरी, कारीगरी, भार वहन इत्यादि में कुल १७४७८१रु. (एक लाख चौहतर हजार सात सौ इक्यासी) खर्च हुआ था और १३६३१६ रु. (एक लाख छतीस हजार तीन सौ सोलह) रु. दान-पुन्य, ब्राह्मण भोज अन्य कपड़ा मोती घोड़े इत्यादि पर व्यय हुए। इस प्रकार कुल मिलाकर ३११०९७ रु. (तीन लाख ग्यारह हजार सन्तान्वे) रुपये खर्च करके यह उदयसागर नामक तालाब निर्मित हुआ[१९]।

(३) जनासागार - १५ नवम्बर १६६४ ई. को महाराणा राजसिंह ने अपनी माता जनादे बाई जी के नाम पर बड़ी नामक ग्राम के निकट तालाब का निर्माण करवाया। ३१ जनवरी १६६६ ई. को तालाब की प्रतिष्ठा पर इसका नाम जनासागर रखा[२०]। उदयपुर से पश्चिम दिशा में १० किमी. दूर स्थित यह बांध ६७.३ मीटर लम्बा है। ३.२३किमी भू क्षेत्र वाला यह जलाशय ११.२ मिलियन क्यूबिक मीटर भराव क्षमता वाला है।[२१]

इस तालाब के निर्माण पर कुल व्यय ६,८८,०००रु. (छः लाख अठासी हजार रु.) हुआ[२२]। जबकि राजप्रशस्ति के अनुसार इस पर लगभग छः लाख अस्सी हजार रुपया खर्च हुआ[२३]। जनासागर प्रशस्ति के अनुसार इसकी प्रतिष्ठा पर भी लगभग दो लाख इकसठ हजार रु. दान पुण्य में खर्च हुआ[२४]। महाराणा फतहसिंह[२५] ने जनासागर की मरम्मत एवं नहर निर्माण हेतु बाइस हजार एक सौ छः रु. आठ आने व्यय किये[२६]।

(४) राजसमुद्र - यह झील उदयपुर से ६६ कि.मी. उत्तर दिशा में राजस्थान के राजसमंद जिले में स्थित है[२७]। यह ४८ कि.मी. लम्बी व २.४ कि.मी. चौड़ा है तथा ४६६.२ कि.मी. भूमि क्षेत्र से जल आवक होती है[२८]। जब वि. सं. १७०८ में मेवाड़ में अकाल पड़ा। लगातार चार पांच वर्षों तक इस क्षेत्र में पानी की भारी कमी हो गई। ऐसी हालत को देखते हुए मेवाड़ महाराणा राजसिंह[२९] ने कृषकों तथा जनसाधारण के कष्टों के निवारण हेतु इस तालाब का निर्माण करना निश्चय किय[३०]।

१ जनवरी १६६२ ई.(माघ औष्ण सप्तमी वि.सं. १७१८) को मुहूर्त कर नींव की खुदाई[३१] से २० जनवरी १६७६ ई. (माघ शुक्ल १५. वि सं. १७३२) तक तालाब के संपूर्ण निर्माण व प्रतिष्ठा[३२] तक प्रथम चरण में ४६६४६२५.२५ (छियालीस लाख चौसठ हजार छह सौ सवा पच्चीस रु.)[३३] द्वितीय चरण में १०५०७६०८ (एक करोड़ पांच लाख सात हजार छह सौ आठ रु.) खर्च हुआ।

राज समुद्र निर्माण कार्य के वर्षवार (१६६१-१६७७) व्यय का ब्यौरा एक अन्य समकालीन रचना में मिलता है, जिसमें निर्माण कार्य पर कुल व्यय ४४२५८३८ रु. उल्लिखित है[३४]। इस प्रकार राजसमुद के निर्माण पर ४६६४६२५.२५ रु. तथा दान इनाम आदि पर १०५०७६०८ रु. थी। अतः कुल राशि १५१७२२३३.२५ रु. थी[३५]।

इस प्रकार इतनी विशाल धनराशि खर्च करके मेवाड़ महाराणा राजसिंह ने इस क्षेत्र के लोगों की जलापूर्ति हेतु इस जलाशय का निर्माण करवाय।

(५) देवाली का तालाब अथवा फतहसागर -

उदयपुर में स्थित फतहसागर पूर्व में देवाली तालाब के नाम से प्रसिद्ध था। १६८७ ई. में मेवाड़ महाराणा जयसिंह ने इस तालाब का निर्माण करवाया[३६]। इस बांध के समीप ही देवाली गांव होने से यह देवाली का तालाब नाम से भी प्रसिद्ध हुआ[३७]। इस तालाब के वर्तमान स्वरूप का निर्माण महाराणा फतहसिंह[३८] ने ६१४१८६ (छः लाख चौदह हजार एक सौ नवासी) रु. लगाकर इस बांध को ऊंचा, चौड़ा और मजबूत बनाया। यह २.४१ कि.मी. लम्बा १.६० कि.मी. चौड़ा व १०.६६ मीटर गहरा है इसकी भराव क्षमता १५.६२ मिलियन क्यूबिक मीटर है[३६]।

(६) जय समुद्र - यह झील उदयपुर से ५२ कि.मी. दक्षिण पूर्व में स्थित है। झील की लम्बाई १४.४८ कि.मी. तथा चौड़ाई १.६ से ८ कि.मी. तक है। इस झील में ७२.५ कि.मी. क्षेत्र का पानी आता है[४०]।

गोमती, झामरी, रूपारेला और बागार नामक चार छोटी-छोटी नदियों का जल एकत्रित होकर दो पहाड़ों के बीच के ढेबर नामक नाके में होकर निकलता था। इस जगह पर मेवाड़ के महाराणा जयसिंह ने १६८७ से १६९१ ई. तक इस पानी को रोककर तालाब बनाया[४१]। १६९८ ई. में जय समुद्र का निर्माण पूर्ण हुआ, इस पर कुल १८ लाख रुपये खर्च हुए [४२]।

(७) त्रिमुखी बावड़ी - माघशुक्ल द्वितीया गुरूवार वि.सं. १७३२ (१६७५ ई.) को मेवाड़ महाराणा राजसिंह की रानी रामरसदे[४३] ने देबारी के घाटे में जया नाम की वापिका का निर्माण करवाया, इसे त्रिमुखी बावड़ी भी कहते हैं[४४]। इस बावड़ी के निर्माण में २४००० रु. व्यय हुए [४५]।

(८) राजनगर की बावड़ी - उदयपुर से उत्तर पूर्व दिशा में ६६ कि.मी. राजस्थान के राजसमंद जिले में स्थित है। मेवाड़ महाराणा राजसिंह की पटरानी चारूमति ने माघ शुक्ल सप्तमी वि.स.: १७३२ (१२ जनवरी १६७६) को ३०००० रु. (तीस हजार) व्यय करके बनवाया[४६]।

इसके अलावा मेवाड़ क्षेत्र में कई अन्य जलाशयों का निर्माण किया गया जिन पर काफी धन खर्च हुआ। डॉ. गोपाल व्यास ने अपने लेख में महाराणा राजसिंह कालीन १० बावड़ियों का विवरण दिया है। व्यास के अनुसार इन बावड़ियो के निर्माण में औसत व्यय ३० हजार रुपये प्रति बावड़ी आया, इस प्रकर कुल तीन लाख रुपये व्यय करके जल को संरक्षित किया गया। साथ ही रंगसागर में जल संरक्षण में १५०००० रुपये खर्च होने का उल्लेख भी डॉ. व्यास करते हैं[४७]।

उपर्युक्त विवरण से स्पष्ट है कि मुद्रा ने मेवाड़ में जल संरक्षप के लिए किए गये निर्माण कार्यों में निर्णायक भूमिका अदा की है।

संदर्भ एवं पाद टिप्पणी

१. स्मारिका - महाराणा राजसिंह व्यक्तित्व एवं कृतित्व (सं.) - प्रो. के.एस. गुप्ता, वीर शिरोमणि महाराणा प्रताप समिति उदयपुर में प्रकाशित डॉ. मीना गौड़ का लेख ''महाराणा राजसिंह के लोक कल्याण कारी कार्य '' पृ. २६-३०.

२. राणावत, डॉ. मनोहर सिंह (सं.) - ''मुहणोत नैणसी की ख्यात' श्री नटनागर शोध संस्थान, सीतामऊ, १६८७ ई. भाग १, पृ. ३ - १७वीं सदी के मेवाड़ क्षेत्र में बेड़च नदी में थोड़ा बहुत जल वर्ष भर बहता रहता था।

३. राणावत, डॉ. ईश्वर सिंह - ''राजस्थान के जल संसाधन मेवाड़ के संदर्भ में १६वीं व १७वीं शताब्दी'', चिराग प्रकाशन उदयपुर, प्रथम संस्करण २००४, पृ. १५.

४. उपर्युक्त - पृ. ३० - १६वीं, १७वीं शती के ऐतिहासिक ग्रंथों के विवरण तथा सघन वनों से निश्चित ही उस समय वर्ष का औसत अधिक रहा होगा।

५. (अ) ओझा, गौरीशंकर हीराचंद - ''उदयपुर राज्य का इतिहास'' प्रथम खण्ड, राजस्थानी ग्रंथागार, जोधपुर द्वितीय संस्करण १६६, पृ. ६-७. (ब) संदर्भिका राजस्थान सुजस - (प्रधान सं.) रोहित कुमार, सूचना एवं जनसंपर्क विभाग, राजस्थान, जयपुर संस्करण २००८ में पृ. ४०६ पर डॉ. जे.के. ओझा का शोध आलेख ''मेवाड़ के महत्वपूर्ण सागर व संमद''।

६. राणावत, डॉ. ईश्वर सिंह - पूर्वोक्त पृ. २४१

७. प्रमुखतः राजप्रशस्ति, जयसमुद्र प्रशस्ति, जनासागर प्रशस्ति, त्रिमुखी बावड़ी प्रशस्ति (१६७५), वीर विनोद, ओझा, कर्नल टॉड के ग्रंथ, मुहणोत नैणसी की रचना।

८. राणावत, डॉ. ईश्वर सिंह - पूर्वोक्त पृ. ६३-६४

६. पिन्हे, ए.एफ. - 'हिस्ट्री ऑफ मेवाड़'' बुक्स ट्रेजर जोधपुर संस्करण २००७ पृ. १३ - महाराणा लाखा ने मेवाड़ में १३८३ से १४१८ ई. तक शासन किया।

१०. मुहणोत नैणसी ख्यात - पूर्वोक्त पृ. ५७.

११. महामहोपाध्याय कविराजा श्यामलदास-''वीर विनोद - मेवाड़ का इतिहास'', मोतीलाल बनारसीदास, दिल्ली १६८६ पृ. ७.

१२. पिन्हे- पूर्वोक्त पृ. १६-२० - महाराणा सांगा - १५०६ ई. से १५२७ ई.तक मेवाड़ का शासक।

१३. भाटी, डॉ. हुकमसिंह (सं.) ''सीसोदा वंशावली एवं राजस्थान के रजवाड़ों की वंशावलियां'' प्रताप शोध प्रतिष्ठान उदयपुर १६६५, पृ. ५३-५४.

१४. राणावत, डॉ. ईश्वर सिंह - पूर्वोक्त - पृ. ६६.

१५. राजस्थान सुजस - डॉ. जे.के. ओझा ' पूर्वोक्त पृ: ४०६.

१६. ओझा, गोरीशंकर - पूर्वोक्त - पृ. ७.

१७. राणावत, डॉ. ईश्वरसिंह - पूर्वोक्त - पृ.६७

१८. राजस्थान सुजस- डॉ. जे. के. ओझा पूर्वोक्त - पृ. ४०६- ४०७.

१६. राणावत, डॉ. ईश्वरसिंह पूर्वोक्त पृ. ६६.

२०. (अ) उपर्युक्त- पृ. २६३ -परिशिष्ट संख्या ५ जनासागर की प्रशस्ति। (ब) राज प्रशस्ति महाकाव्य रणछोडदास कृत संस्कृत ग्रंथ मोतीलाल मेनारिया (सं.), साहित्य संस्थान, उदयपुर प्र.सं. १६७३ अष्टमः सर्गः लोक ४६-४६ पृ. ८७-८८.

२१. राणावत पूर्वोक्त - पृ.१०१.

२२. ओझा, गौरीशंकर - पूर्वोक्त खण्ड २ पृ. ५७५.

२३. राजप्रशस्ति महाकाव्य - रणछोड़दास कृत संस्कृत ग्रंथ- (सं.) मोतीलाल मेनारिया - साहित्य संस्थान उदयपुर प्र.सं. १६७३ अष्टमः सर्गः लोक ४६ पृ. ८८.

२४. राणावत, डॉ. ईश्वर सिंह पूर्वोक्त पृ. २६३ व १०२.

२५. पिन्हे- पूर्वोक्त पृ. ७२-७३.

२६. राणावत, डॉ. ईश्वर सिंह - पूर्वोक्त १०२.

२७. (अ) गुप्ता, मोहनलाल - राजस्थान जिलेवार सांस्कृतिक एवं ऐतिहासिक अध्ययन, राजस्थानी ग्रंथागार जोधपुर २००७, खण्ड प्रथम उदयपुर संभाग- पृ.१६७. (ब) राजस्थान सुजस जिला दर्शन पृ. १२२४.

२८. राणावत, डॉ. ईश्वर सिंह पूर्वोक्त पृ. १०३.

२६. ओझा, गौरीशंकर - पूर्वोक्त पृ. ५३१-५३२ महाराणा राजसिंह १० अक्टूबर १६५२ से २२ अक्टूबर १६८० तक मेवाड़ शासक।

३०. स्मारिका - महाराणा राजसिंह व्यक्तित्व एवं कृतित्व में डॉ. मीना गौड़ का लेख पूर्वोक्त पृ. ३०.

३१. राज प्रशस्ति महाकाव्य - पूर्वोक्त नवं सर्गः, ्लोक १४, पृ. ६२.

३२. पूर्वोक्त - अष्टादसः सर्गः ्लोक ४० पृ. १६५.

३३. (अ) पूर्वोक्त एकविशः सर्गः श्लोक २२ पृ. १६५.
(ब) वीर विनोद - पूर्वोक्त भाग द्वितीय खण्ड प्रथम पृ. ४४८ - कुल खर्च एक करोड़ पांच लाख सैंतालीस हजार पांच सौ चौरासी रु. हुआ।
(स) ओझा, गौरीशंकर - पूर्वोक्त खण्ड २ पृ. ५७४ व पृ. ६ पर यही राशि उल्लिखित है।

३४. (अ) राणावत, डॉ. ईश्वर सिंह पूर्वोक्त पृ. ११३ व पृ. २६७, पर वि.सं. १७१८ से १७३४ तक व्यय विवरण दिया हुआ है।
(ब) स्मारिका - महाराणा राजसिंह पूर्वोक्त डॉ. गोपाल व्यास का लेख महाराणा राजसिंह की राजनीतिक, सामाजिक और आर्थिक दृष्टि -पृ. ६ व पृ.१५.

३५. (अ) राणावत - पूर्वोक्त पृ. ११२
(ब) राज प्रशस्ति - पूर्वोक्त भूमिका पृ. ३५ पर मोतीलाल मैनारिया ने राजप्रशस्ति के आधार पर कुल व्यय १५१७२२३३.२५ रु. सही माना है।

३६. (अ) ओझा, गौरीशंकर - पूर्वोक्त भाग दो - पृ. ५८३.

(ब) राजस्थान सुजस - पूर्वोक्त डॉ. जे.के ओझा का लेख, पृ. ४०६.

३७. राणावत, डॉ. ईश्वर सिंह पूर्वोक्त पृ. ११५.

३८. पिन्हे, पूर्वोक्त पृ. ७२-७३ - १८८६ में इस तालाब का निर्माण कार्य आरम्भ हुआ।

३९. राणावत, डॉ. ईश्वर सिंह पूर्वोक्त पृ. ११६.

४०. राणावत, डॉ. ईश्वर सिंह - पूर्वोक्त पृ. ११७ जयसमुद्र प्रशस्ति सर्ग १२- इस तालाब का निर्माण मुहूर्त माघ शुरू दशमी वि.सं. १७४३.

४१. (अ)ओझा, गौरीशंकर - पूर्वोक्त भाग २ पृ. ५८३.

(ब) वीर विनोद - मेवाड़ का इतिहास, द्वितीय भाग, खण्ड १, पृ. ६६७.

४२. राणावत - पूर्वोक्त १२०, व पृ. २६८ परिशिष्ट संख्या १० जयसमुद्र प्रशस्ति

४३. ओझा, गौरीशंकर – पूर्वोक्त पृ. ५७५-५७६ अजमेर के परमार रायसल की प्रपोत्री, जुझारसिंह की पौत्री व पृथ्वी सिंह की पुत्री।

४४. (अ) राज प्रशस्ति महाकाव्य – पूर्वोक्त त्रयोदशः सर्गः लोक २७-२६, पृ. १३८-१३६

(ब) ओझा, गौरीशंकर – पूर्वोक्त भाग २ पृ. ५७५.

४५. राणावत- पूर्वोक्त पृ. १३०, व पृ.२६२ परिशिष्ट संख्या ४ त्रिमुखी बावड़ी की प्रशस्ति वि.सं. १७३२.

४६. (अ) राज प्रशस्ति – पूर्वोक्त चतुर्दशः सर्गः लोक ११-१२ पृ. १४६-१४७.

(ब) राणावत, डॉ. ईश्वर सिंह – पूर्वोक्त पृ. १३२.

(स) ओझा, गौरीशंकर पूर्वोक्त पृ. ५७६.

४७. स्मारिका – महाराणा राजसिंह – डॉ. गोपाल व्यास का लेख – पूर्वोक्त पृ. १०-११.

मुगलकालीन भारत के उद्यानों में जल प्रबंधन

कु. रूचि भारद्वाज एवं डॉ. एन. बी. लाल

बाबर के द्वारा स्थापित साम्राज्य हुमायूँ के समय को छोड़कर औरंगजेब के काल तक निरंतर विकासोन्मुख रहा और इसी क्रम में मुगलकालीन कला संस्कृति का विकास हुआ। मुगलकालीन कला संस्कृति में उद्यान कला का विशिष्ट स्थान है। बाबर के समय से ही भारत में उद्यान कला का विकास प्रारंभ हुआ जो शाहजहां के काल में अपने चरमोत्कर्ष पर पहुँच गया। अकबर कालीन उद्यानों में काबुल के समीप बाग-ए-वुफा और बाग-ए-किलान सबसे अधिक प्रारंभिक उद्यान हैं।[१] बाग-ए-वुफा में जल निकास एंव जल सिंचाई के लिए समान रूप से व्यवस्था की गई तथा बाग-ए-किलान के मध्य में एक चौकोर बाबड़ी का भी निर्माण कराया गया जिससे संपूर्ण बाग की सिंचाई की जाती थी।[२]

बाबर ने उद्यान कला की दृष्टि से आगरा में जौहर बाग तथा रामबाग का निर्माण करवाया। रामबाग का मूल नाम हस्तवाहिश्त अथवा नूर-ए-अफशां था।[३] रामबाग आगरा में जमुना नदी के समीप है तथा जमुना के जल का उपयोग रामबाग में सिंचाई के लिए किया जाता था। बाबर स्वयं लिखता है कि 'भारत में तीन मौसम देखने को मिलते हैं, यहां पर केवल नदियों, कुँओं और बांधों से सिंचाई होती है।[४] बाबर का उक्त कथन उसकी भारत के जल प्रबंधन के प्रति अर्ध जानकारी का द्योतक है, क्योंकि भारत के विभिन्न भागों में प्राचीन काल से ही नहरें तालाबों तथा बांधों के द्वारा सिंचाई के प्रमाण मिलते हैं।[५] भारत में जल को अस्तित्व के पांच तत्वें में सबसे अधिक महत्वपूर्ण माना गया है।[६] विभिन्न प्राचीन ग्रंथों एवं महाकाव्यों में जल के महत्व को केवल रेखांकित ही नहीं किया जात है, बल्कि उसकी स्तुति भी की गई है।

मुगल साम्राज्य की स्थापना के साथ भारत में एक नवीन फारस एवं भारतीय शैली का मिश्रित कलारूप विकसित हुआ इसका प्रभाव स्थापत्य कला के अंतर्गत उद्यानों में देखने को मिलता है। बाबर कालीन रामबाग उद्यान मुगल-इस्लामिक स्थापत्य की मिश्रित शैली का प्रथम उदाहरण है।[७] बाबर के कात में धौलपुर में कमल

उद्यान विकसित किया गया। इस उद्यान में चारों ओर पत्थर की बड़ी-बड़ी नालियाँ जल निकासी के लिए बनायी गयीं। वर्षाकाल में अथवा बाग को सिंचित करते समय जल का अवरोध न हो इसका विशेष ध्यान रखा गया है। बाबर के काल में जिन उद्यानों को विकसित किया गया उसमें जल प्रबंधन का विशिष्ट स्थान रखा गया।[८] जल प्रबंधन की दृष्टि से बाबरकालीन उद्यान अत्यंत व्यवस्थित प्रतीत होते है। बाबर ने आगरा में पुराने लोधी फोर्ट में एक तीन मंजिला सीढ़ी कुँआ का निर्माण कराया। बाबर का उदाहरण उसके बाद होने वाले बादशाहों ने अपनाया। जिन्होंने अपने किलों में सीढ़ी कुँआ और अनेक उद्यान गर्म क्षेत्रों में बनवाये थे।[९]

बाबर के बाद मुगल सल्तनत का उत्तराधिकारी हुमायूँ बना और उसने काबुल और आगरा में उद्यानों का निर्माण कराया हुमायूँ बहुत सफल शासक नहीं रहा परंतु उसने अपने शासनकाल में दिल्ली में दीनपनाह नामक एक नये शहर की स्थापना की जो सम्भवतः पौराणिक शहर इन्द्रप्रस्थ का भू-भाग था। हुमायूँ कालीन उद्यान चौकोर तथा ज्यामितीय आकार के थे भारत की जलवायु के अनुरूप इन उद्यानों में प्राकृतिक वर्षा से एकत्रित जल एवं नदियों के जल से सिंचाई की जाती थी। मुगलकाल में कब्रिस्तान में भी उद्यान विकसित किये जाते थे। आगरा स्थित हुमायूँकालीन उद्यान ३० एकड़ में बना हुआ है और ३६० मी. लम्बी पत्थर की दीवारों से बंद है। प्रत्येक केन्द्र में प्लास्टर किये हुए द्वार है। इन द्वारों से उद्यान चार भागों कंकड़ीय मार्ग द्वारा जो ४० फीट चौड़ा है, विभाजित किया गया है, ये कब्र तक जाते हैं। उद्यान में एक विशाल तालाब है। अब तक कुँए से भरा जाता है। लेकिन यह पहले यमुना से स्वतः ही भर जाता था। नदी के श्रोत बदल गये है और यह अब उद्यान से कुछ दूरी पर है। तंग वाटरकोस चूने पत्थर के १४ इंच चौड़े और कुछ इंच गहरे मुख्य द्वारों के केन्द्र में बहते हैं। आयताकार तालाब मध्य रास्ते पर बना है।[१०]

हुमायूँ के मकबरे का चारबाग ३० एकड़ जमीन में स्थापित है। ३६० मी. लंबी दीवार से घिरा हुआ है। उद्यान में पानी का प्रवेश उत्तरी द्वार में से होकर किया गया है। द्वार के पीछे एक बड़ा जलाशय है, जो यमुना नदी से भर जाता है। संपूर्ण उद्यान के लिए मिट्टी के पाये से होकर केन्द्रीय जल प्रवाह की व्यवस्था बनायी गयी है। जो बहुत ही अद्‌भुत है और बाबर ने धौलपुर के उद्यान में इसी तकनीक और कला का प्रयोग किया था।[११]

अकबरकालीन उद्यान सामान्यतः चौकोर अथवा आयताकार है जिनमें चारों ओर जल निकास और जल संचय की समुचित व्यवस्था की गई है। उद्यानों की आहतों की चारों दीवारों के बीच-बीच में सामान्यतः चार प्रवेश द्वार है जिसके अंदर स्थित

कमरों में सुंदर पक्की ईंटों के फर्श तथा जल संचय के लिए उचित व्यवस्था है। इन उद्यानों के समीप कुछ दूरी पर बड़े तालाब का निर्माण कराया गया था जिन तालाबों में वर्षा का पानी एकत्रित कर उद्यानों की सिंचाई की जाती थी।[९२] अकबर ने अपनी प्रशासनिक व्यवस्था में जल एवं मल निष्कासन के लिए आवश्यकतानुसार व्यवस्थाऐं की थी। जल एकत्रीकरण एवं वितरण का दायित्व सूबों को दिया गया था।[९३]

जहाँगीर कालीन उद्यानों की यह प्रमुख विशेषता है कि उद्यानों के मध्य में बैठने के लिए ऊँचा प्लेटफार्म बनाया जाता था। जिसके चारों तरफ आकर्षक किनारों से जल प्रवाह किया जाता था। जहांगीर कालीन परी महल में जहाँगीर ने सन् १६४० ई. में एक विशिष्ट प्रकार के उद्यान का निर्माण कराया था जिसका क्षेत्रफल लगभग ४०० वर्ग गज था। इस उद्यान को चार बाग के नाम से भी जाना जाता है। इस उद्यान में जल प्रबंधन की दृष्टि से महल के पृष्ठ भाग में एक बड़ा टैंक निर्मित किया गया था जिसमें प्राकृतिक संसाधनों से जल एकत्रित किया जाता था तथा साथ ही महल में उपयोग के उपरांत प्रयोग किये गये जल को विशिष्ट प्रकार की नालियों के माध्यम से पुनः इस टैंक में एकत्रित किया जाता था। जहाँगीर कालीन परीमहल का जल प्रबंधन वर्तमान जल संग्रहण (वाटर हार्वेस्टिंग) से भी अधिक उत्कृष्ट था। क्योंकि प्राकृतिक अथवा गैर प्राकृतिक जल की एक बूंद का भी दुरूपयोग इस महल में नहीं होता था।[९४]

जहाँगीरकालीन उद्यानों में गुजरात का ज्यात बाग जल प्रबंधन की दृष्टि से अत्यंत महत्वपूर्ण है। सन् १६३८ ई. में जर्मन यात्री डी. मैनडेल्क्लों ने ज्यात बाग को देखकर कहा था कि भारतीय उद्यानों में जल प्रबंधन की इतनी सुंदर व्यवस्था भी हो सकती है कि जो सभी के लिये अनुकरणीय हो।[९५]

शाहजहाँ का काल स्थापत्य की दृष्टि से स्वर्ण काल माना जाता है शाहजहां कालीन उद्यानों में कश्मीर का शालीमार बाग, आगरा में एत्मात्उद्दौला के मकबरे का बाग, सिकंदरा का दिलखुश बाग, उदयपुर में वैरीनग बाग एवं अचीवल बाग अत्यंत महत्वपूर्ण है।[९६] उसने आगरा, दिल्ली, लाहौर में समानांतर रूप से स्थापत्य कार्य को कराया, इन सभी स्थानों पर उसने उद्यानों का भी निर्माण कराया। इन उद्यानों में जल निकास एवं सिंचाई के लिए समुचित प्रबंध था। आगरा में अंगूरी बाग, दिल्ली में तालकटोरा बाग उद्यानकला की दृष्टि से अनुपम उदाहरण है। दिल्ली के लाल किले और आगरा के ताजमहल के उद्यानों में सफेद संगमरमर की जितनी खूबसूरत नालियों का निर्माण किया गया है वह मुगलकालीन किसी भी शासक के काल में देखने को नहीं मिलता है। प्रत्येक नाली को गोलाकार रूप प्रदान करते हुए जल विसर्जन के मुख पर

विशेष प्रकार का चतुर्भुजीय आकार प्रदान किया गया है। दोनों ही ऐतिहासिक स्थलों में अग्र तथा पृष्ठ भाग में उद्यान है तथा उद्यानों की सिंचाई के लिए, जमुना के जल स्त्रोतों की व्यवस्था का बोध होता है। शाहजहाँ कालीन उद्यानों में प्राकृतिक जल स्त्रोतों के अतिरिक्त गैर प्राकृतिक जल स्त्रोतों के उपयोग का भी प्रारंभ हुआ था। सिंचाईके लिए कौल्हू के द्वारा जमीन से जल निकालने की व्यवस्था की थी।

मुगल सल्तनत का अंतिम प्रमुख शासक औरंगजेब था। जिसे कलाओं में किसी प्रकार की अभिरूचि नहीं थी। यद्यपि औरंगजेब का सिंहासनारोहण शालीमार बाग में हुआ था, लेकिन उसे उद्यानों में कोई अभिरूचि नहीं थी। औरंगजेब के समय उसकी पुत्री जैवन्निसा ने दिल्ली में चारबुर्जी बाग का निर्माण करवाया था। इस उद्यान में सिंचाई के लिये एक विशिष्ट प्रकार की बाबड़ी का निर्माण कराया था। इस बाबड़ी में नीचे उतरने के लिए १०० से अधिक सीढ़ियां प्रतीत होती है। संभवतः ग्रीष्मकाल में वर्षा से पूर्व जलस्तर कम रह जाने पर इन सीढ़ियों का उपयोग किया जाता होगा अथवा बाबड़ी की सफाई के लिए भी इन सीढ़ियों का उपयोग किया जाता होगा।

संदर्भ

१. एस.एम. जाफर, समकल्चरल आस्पैक्ट्स ऑफ मुस्लिम इन इंडिया, पृ. ११६

२. लक्ष्मीरानी, मुगलकालीन उद्यानकला की ऐतिहासिक समीक्षा पृ. १७१

३. बाबर, बाबरनामा, अनुवाद बेवरीज पृ. ३६

४. वही।

५. डॉ. जगदीश शर्मा, भारतीय संस्कृति का इतिहास, पृ. २६६।

६. यजुर्वेद ११/७/३०१।

७. डॉ. जगदीश शर्मा, पूर्वोक्त, पृ. ३००।

८. ऐलिजाबेथ बी. मोयनाहन, पैराडाइज एज ए गार्डन इन पर्शिया एण्ड मुगल इंडिया, पृ. ६८

६. वही। पृ. १०२।

१०. वही। पृ. ११२।

११. लक्ष्मी रानी, पूर्वोक्त।

१२. वही।

१३. वही।

१४. जरनल ऑफ रॉयल सोसायटी ऑफ एशिया वाल्यूम १०, जनवरी १६३६, पृ. ३७

१५. डॉ. डी. मैनडेलक्लों का यात्रा विवरण उद्धरित एस.एम. जाफर, पूर्वोक्त, पृ. २१७।

१६. जहाँगीर, तुजुक-ए-जहाँगीरी (हिन्दी अनुवाद)।

चितौड़गढ़ दुर्ग के तालाब, बावड़ियाँ व कुण्ड

आमिर खान

चित्तौड़गढ और बाकी सब गढ़ैया चित्तौड़गढ राजस्थान के दक्षिण-पूर्वी पठारी भाग में अरावली की पहाड़ियों के दक्षिण-पूर्व में स्थित है। इसकी समुद्रतल से ऊँचाई लगभग 600 फीट की औसत ऊँचाई पर स्थित है तथा इस स्थान से 74-12 एवं 75-49 पूर्वी देशान्तर तथा 23° 32 एवं 25° 13 डिग्री अक्षांश के मध्य स्थित है।

चित्तौड़गढ –अजमेर-खण्डवा ब्राड-गेज रेलवे लाइन पर पश्चिमी रेलवे का जंक्शन है।[१]

ऐतिहासिक परिचय - चित्तौड़ प्राचीनकाल से राजा -महाराजाओं, सम्राटों एवं शक्तिशाली योद्धाओं का लक्ष्य रहा है। जिसके कारण यहॉं का इतिहास विचित्र एवं पेचीदा रहा है। प्रारम्भ से ही राजस्थान के अलग-अलग क्षेत्रों में राजपूतों के विभिन्न राजवंशों ने अपने-अपने राज्य स्थापित कर रखे थे। जिनमें मेवाड़ के गुहिलों का महत्वपूर्ण स्थान है। गुहिल वंश की उत्पत्ति एवं उनके आदि निवास के बारे में विद्वानों में मतभेद है।[२] जैन धर्म ग्रन्थों में गुहिलों के वल्लभी के राजा शिलादित्य का वंशज बताया है तो अबुल-फजल गुहिलों को ईरान के बादशाह नौर शेर खाँ आदिल के वंशज बताया है[३] तो कर्नल टॉड[४] ने भी इन्हें वल्लभी नरेश शिलादित्य का वंशज बताया है उनके अनुसार ५२४ ई. में विदेशियों ने शिलादित्य के राज्य पर आक्रमण किया उस संघर्ष में शिलादित्य अपने परिवार सहित मारा गया. केवल उसकी पत्नी पुष्पावती, जो उस समय तीर्थ यात्रा पर गई हुई थी, बच गई। रानी पुष्पावती गर्भवती थी, जिसने 'गोह' (गुहदत्त) नामक पुत्र को जन्म दिया जो आगे चलकर मेवाड़ का शासक बना।

जनश्रुति के अनुसार आठवी सदी में बापा रावल ने मेवाड़ के क्षेत्र में एक स्वतन्त्र राजवंश की नींव रखी जो गुहिल के नाम से विख्यात हुआ।

बापा के बाद गुहिल शासक - भट्ट ग्रन्थों में बापा रावल के उत्तराधिकारियों के बारे में विशेष जानकारी नही मिलती। डॉ. गोपीनाथ शर्मा ने बापा के उत्तराधिकारियों के

नाम क्रमशः इस प्रकार दिये है - भोज, महेन्द्र, नाग, शिलादित्य, अपराजित, कालभोज, खुमाण प्रथम, भृतभट्ट सिंह, खुमाण द्वितीय, महायक खुमान तृतीय भर्तुभट्ट द्वितीय, अल्लट, नरवाहन शक्तिकुमार, अम्बाप्रसाद और उसके बाद लगभग १० शासक ऐसे हुए है जिनके बारे में विशेष जानकारी नही मिलती।

उसके पश्चात जैत्रसिंह (१२१३-१२५२ ई.) मेवाड़ के सिंहासन पर बेठा।[५] उसने अपनी सैनिक विजयों से मेवाड़ को ही सुदृढ़ नहीं बनाया अपितु उसकी सीमाओं का विस्तार करके राजनैतिक प्रभाव को भी बढ़ाया। जैत्रसिंह के पश्चात तेजसिंह, समरसिंह, व रतनसिंह गुहिलों के सिंहासन पर बैठ। रतनसिंह के शासन के समय राज्य को दिल्ली के सुलतान अलाउद्दीन खिलजी के आक्रमण का सामना करना पड़ा[६] और अलाउधीन ने मेवाड़ की स्वतंत्र सत्ता का अंत कर दिया। रतनसिंह अन्तिम गुहिल शासक हुआ। तत्पश्चात राणा हम्मीर ने मेवाड़ में सिसोदिया राजवंश की नीवं रखी। राणा हम्मीर के पश्चात क्षेत्रसिंह, महाराणा लाखा, मोकल, महाराणा कुम्भा, महाराणा रायमल, महाराणा सांगा, महाराणा रतनसिंह द्वितिय, महाराणा उदयसिंह, व महाराणा प्रतान आदि ने मेवाड़ पर शासन किया। महाराणा प्रताप के समय १८ जून १५७६ ई. को हल्दीघाटी नामक स्थान पर अकबर की सेना से युद्ध हुआ[७] एवं अकबर की विजय हुई। परन्तु मेवाड़ को अधीन करने की उसकी चिर अभिलाषा कभी पूरी नहीं हुई।

चितौड़गढ दुर्ग के तालाब, बावड़ियाँ व कुण्ड

ऐसे असंख्य बावड़ियाँ, तालाब व कुण्ड चितौड़गढ़ दुर्ग पर स्थित है जो मध्यकाल में चितौड़गढ़ दुर्गवासियों के पानी के लिए महत्वपूर्ण स्त्रोत है जिनमें वर्ष भर पानी रहता है। जिनकी संरक्षण की आवश्यकता है। यहां के महत्वपूर्ण जलाशय इस प्रकार है-

१. भीम गौड़ी :- चितौड़गढ़ दुर्ग पर चारभुजा नाम का एक विशाल मंदिर है, इस मंदिर से एक पगड़ंडी दक्षिण में जाती है, वहां पर भीम गौड़ी नामक एक पानी की बावड़ी है, जिसके बारें में माना जाता है कि महाभारत काल में पाण्डवों के वनवास के दौरान भीम ने माता कुंती की प्यास भुजाने के लिए जमीन में गोड़ी मारकर इस बावड़ी का निर्माण किया था।[८] इस बावड़ी में वर्ष भर पानी भरा रहता है।

२. घी, तेल की बावड़ी:- दुर्ग पर विजय स्तम्भ के उत्तर में यह कुण्ड विद्यमान है। कहा जाता है कि महाराणा रायमल की पुत्री का विवाह गागरोन के खिंची राजा के साथ हुआ था।[९] कहा जाता है कि उस विवाह में घी, तेल इकठटा किया गया कि

उसे रखने हेतु भूमि खोदकर पक्के कुण्ड बनाये गये थे, इसी कारण इन्हें घी, तेल की बावड़ियों के नाम से जाना जाता है।

३. गौमुख कुण्डः- विजय स्तम्भ के समीप ही गौमुख कुण्ड है यहां भू-गर्भित जल चान में लगे गौमुख से शिवलिंग पर निरन्तर झरने के रूप में गिरता है। यह स्थल तीर्थ स्थल माना जाता है तथा लोग इस कुण्ड में प्रायः स्नान करने आते हैं।[१०] इस कुण्ड का पानी स्वच्छ रहता है। कहा जाता है यह कुण्ड आज तक भीषण अकाल के समय में भी नहीं सुखा है।

४. हाथी कुण्डः- गौमुख कुण्ड के बाहर आने पर कुछ दूर दक्षिण की ओर जाने पर सड़के दोनों ओर दो जलाशय बने हुए है। पश्चिम की ओर का जलाशय हाथी कुण्ड कहलाता है। जहां पहले हाथी पानी पिया करते थे।

५. खातण बावड़ीः- हाथी कुण्ड के सामने की तरफ का जलाशय खातण बावड़ी[११] के नाम से जाना जाता है। जनश्रुति के अनुसार इस बावडी का निर्माण जेतू नामक वैश्य महिला ने अपने चरखे की कताई से अर्जित धन से इस बवड़ी का निर्माण करवाया था।[१२] इसमें कुमदुनी छाई रहने से इसका जल स्वच्छ रहता है।

६. जयमल पत्ता तलाबः- जयमल पत्ता के महलों के पूर्व में एक जलाशय है जो जयमल पत्ता के तालाब कहलाता है।[१३] इसमें भी वर्ष भर जल एकत्रित रहता है।

७. सुर्य कुण्डः- कालिका माता के मंदिर के सामने उत्तर-पूर्व दिशा की ओर एक शीतल जल कुण्ड है। जो सुर्य कुण्ड कहलाता है।[१४] जिसका निर्माण बापा ने करवाया।[१५] उसके पश्चाता राणा सांगा ने इस कुण्ड को विस्तार देकर मरम्मत की।[१६] वर्तमान में यह जर्जर अवस्था में है।

८. पद्मिनी सरोवरः- कालिका मंदिर से कुछ आगे सड़क की पूर्व दिशा में तालाब की पाल पर पद्मनी महल बनें हुए हैं। पद्मिनी महल के चारों ओर पानी भरा रहता है, पद्मिनी रावल रतन सिंह की रानी थी। पद्मिनी महल के कमरें में बड़े-बड़े कांच लगे हैं। जिसमें से पानी के बीच में बने जनाना महल में खड़े व्यक्ति का प्रतिबिम्ब दिखाई देता है। कहा जाता है कि सुल्तान अलाउधीन खिलजी ने रानी पद्मिनी का प्रतिबिम्ब इसी स्थान पर खड़े होकर कांच में से जनाना महल की निचली सीढ़ी पर खड़े हुए देखा था।[१७] इस तालाब में भी वंर्ष भर पानी भरा रहता है।

९. चतरंग मोरी तालाबः- पद्मिनी महल के आगे चौगानियाँ नामक चौडा मैदान है। इसी मैदान से आगे सड़के के पूर्व दिशा में तालाब आता है जो चतरंग मोरी तालाब के नाम से प्रसिद्ध है। जिसका निर्माण चितौड़गढ़ के संस्थापक चित्रांगद मौर्य

ने करवाया था।[१८] यह तालाब काफी बड़ा है जिससे भी वर्ष भर पीने का पानी प्राप्त किया जा सकता है।

१०. रक्त तलाईः- चतंरग मोरी तालाब से सड़के पूर्व दिशा की ओर मुड़कर राजटीला नामक स्थान की तरफ जाती है। राजटीला से कुछ ही दूरी पर एक गहरा गर्त है। जो रक्त तलाई कहलाता है कहा जाता है कि चितौड़ के विभिन्न साकों को दौरान इस भूमि पर इतना खून बहा कि बड़े-बड़े गड्डे खून से भर गये। यह गड्डे ही रक्त-तलाई कहलाते हैं।[१६] इस तलाइयों में बरसात के दिनों में काफी जल एकत्रित हो जाता है जो कई महीनों तक भरा रहता है।

११. भीमलत कुण्डः- दुर्ग पर राव रणमल की हवेली के आगे भीमलत कुण्ड आता है। इसका पानी पीने, नहाने व सिंचाई के काम आता है। वेसे भीमलत कुण्ड वैज्ञानिक रूप से एक भू-गर्भित गर्त है जो पृथ्वी के आंतरिक हलचल से निर्मित है जिसे बाद में कुण्ड का रूप दे दिया गया।[२०] महाराणा कुम्भा ने चितौड़[२१] में रामकुण्ड[२२] जलयंत्र (रहट) सहित कई बावड़ियो और तालाब का निर्माण करवाया।

१२. रत्नेश्वर तालाबः- महाराणा सांगा के पुत्र रतनसिंह द्वितीय ने अपने महलों जिनमें वे रहते थे जिन्हें रतन सिंह के महल भी कहा जाता है के सामने एक सुन्दर तालाब बनवाया जिसे रत्नेश्वर तालाब कहा जाता है।[२३] इस तलाब से महल में जरूरत के पानी कि व्यवस्था की जाती थी। इस तालाब से वर्ष भर पीने के पानी की पूर्ति की जा सकती है, लेकिन देख-रेख के अभाव में इस तालाब में काफी गंदगी जमा हो गई है।

१३. कुकड़ेश्वर कुण्डः- चितौड़गढ़ दुर्ग पर हिगँलू-आहड़ा के महल स्थित है। इन महलों के नीचे सड़क पूर्वी किनारे पर एक गहरा जलाशय कुकड़ेश्वर कुण्ड कहलाता है।[२४] ऐसा कहा जाता है कि सन् ७५५ ई. में राजा कुकड़ेश्वर ने इसका निर्माण करवाया था। इस कुण्ड का दृश्य बहुत ही सुन्दर है। इस कुण्ड में भी वर्ष भर जल एकत्रित रहता है।

चितौड़गढ़ दुर्ग पर स्थित इन विभिन्न जलाशयों, बावड़ियों व कुण्ड के अध्ययन से हम अनुमान लगा सकते हैं कि मध्यकाल में यह सब जल स्त्रोत ही दुर्ग पर पानी की आवश्यकता की पूर्ती में सहायक थे। जो वर्तमान में भी वर्ष पर्यन्त भरे रहते हैं, यदि इनकों पर्याप्त संरक्षण मिले तो यह जल स्त्रोत वर्तमान में भी चितौड़गढ़ की पानी समस्या को कुछ हद तक हल करने में सहायक होंगें।

सन्दर्भ ग्रन्थ सूची

१. ओझा, गौरीशंकर हीराचन्द : उदयपुर राज्य का इतिहास, भाग-१, पृ. ४५

२. वाजपेयी, विभिन्न बिहारी : मेवाड़ परिचय, पृ. ४५

३. अबुल फजल : आइने अकबरी पृ. ७६

४. टॉड, कर्नल : एनाल्स एण्ड एन्टीक्वीटिज ऑफ राजस्थान, भाग-१ पृ.२५

५. ओझा, गौरीशंकर हीराचन्द : उदयपुर राज्य का इतिहास, भाग-१, पृ. ४५

६. उपरोक्त पृ. १७६

७. उपरोक्त पृ. ४३३

८. गोपाल सिंह चुण्डावत - ऐतिहासिक गढ़ चितौड़गढ़ पृ. ६६

६. उपरोक्त पृ. ७३,

१०. ओझा, गौरीशंकर हिराचन्द : उदयपुर राज्य का इतिहास भाग-१ पृ. ५०

११. श्यामलदास : वीर विनोद, भाग-१ पृ.१६१-१६२

१२. गोपाल सिंह चुण्डावत : ऐतिहासिक गढ़ चितौड़गढ़ पृ.७६

१३. ओझा, गौरीशंकर हिराचन्द : उदयपुर राज्य का इतिहास भाग-१ पृ. ५०

१४. ठाकुर लाल सिंह शक्तावत : द फोर्ट ऑफ चितौड़गढ़ पृ. ६०, डॉ. ईश्वर सिंह राणावत : राजस्थान के जल संसाधन पृ.५८

१५. डॉ. ईश्वर सिंह राणावत : राजस्थान के जल-संसाधन, पृ. ५८

१६. उपरोक्त पृ.५८

१७. श्यामलदास : वीर विनोद भाग-१ पृ.-१६५

१८. एन्टीक्वीटीज ऑफ चितौड़गढ़ (जयपुर -१६८४) पृ. २१

१६. गोपाल सिंह चुण्डावत - ऐतिहासिक गढ़ चितौड़गढ़ पृ. १००

२०. उपरोक्त पृ.१०३

२१. औझा उदयपुर राज्य का इतिहास भाग-१ पृष्ठ ४८, ईश्वरसिंह राणावतः राजस्थान के जलसंसाधन पृ. ६० (कीर्तिस्तम्भ प्रशस्तिः श्लोक ३३, औझा के मातानुसार उनमें से एक भीमलत कुण्ड होना चाहिए)

२२. अमरकाव्य : सर्ग १०, श्लोक ३३, पृ.१६५

२३. औझा उदयपुर राज्य का इतिहास भाग-१, पृ. ४८

२४. श्यामलदास वीर विनोद भाग-१, पृ.१६१-१६२, डॉ. जी.एन शर्माः सोशियल पृ. ७०

16. डॉ. मीना श्रीवास्तव
विभागाध्यक्ष एवं प्राध्यापक, इतिहास,
शासकीय कमला राजा कन्या
स्नातकोत्तर स्वशासी महाविद्यालय,
ग्वालियर, मध्य प्रदेश

17. डॉ. अनुराधा माथुर
प्रवक्ता, इतिहास,
राजकीय कला महाविद्यालय,
अलवर, राजस्थान

18. डॉ. जे.के. ओझा
सेवानिवृत्त प्राचार्य एवं प्राध्यापक,
इतिहास, कानोड़, राजस्थान

19. डॉ प्रियदर्शी ओझा
अतिथि व्याख्याता,
मोहनलाल सुखाड़िया विश्वविघालय,
उदयपुर, राजस्थान

20. डॉ. एस. पी. व्यास
प्राध्यापक एवं विभागाध्यक्ष, इतिहास,
जोधपुर विश्वविद्यालय,
जोधपुर, राजस्थान

21. डॉ. मनोरमा उपाध्याय
सहायक प्राध्यापक, इतिहास,
जोधपुर, राजस्थान

22. डॉ. दिग्विजय भटनागर
सह आचार्य, इतिहास,
मोहनलाल सुखाड़िया विश्वविद्यालय,
उदयपुर, राजस्थान

23. डॉ. अन्नपूर्णा शाह
विभागाध्यक्ष, भारतीय संस्कृति,
एम.वी.एम. कला महाविद्यालय,
राजकोट, गुजरात

24. डॉ. प्रद्युम्न कुमार भट्ट
प्राचार्य, आप्रा, महाविद्यायलय मार्ग,
भानपुरा, जि. मंदसौर, मध्य प्रदेश

25. डॉ. मम्ता चंसोरिय
प्राध्यापक, इतिहास,
सरोजिनी नायडू शासकीय
कन्या स्नातकोत्तर महाविद्यालय,
भोपाल, मध्य प्रदेश

26. डॉ. उष पुरोहित
व्याख्याता, इतिहास विभाग,
महिला पी.जी. महाविद्यालय,
जोधपुर, राजस्थान

27. डॉ. बी.के. श्रीवास्तव
सहायक प्राध्यापक, इतिहास विभाग,
डॉ. हरीसिंह गौर विश्वविद्यालय,
सागर, मध्य प्रदेश

28. डॉ. मधुबाला कुलश्रेष्ठ
प्राध्यापक एवं विभागाध्यक्ष, (इतिहास),
महारानी लक्ष्मीबाई शासकीय उत्कृष्ट
महाविद्यालय, ग्वालियर, मध्य प्रदेश

29. डॉ. विशाल कुमार शर्मा
अध्यक्ष, इतिहास विभाग,
हिन्दू कॉलिज, सोनीपत
हरियाणा

30. डॉ. रमेशचन्द्र यादव
वरिष्ठ मार्गदर्शक,
पुरातत्वीय संग्रहालय, गुजरी महल,
ग्वालियर, मध्य प्रदेश

31. डॉ. के. रतनम्
सहायक प्राध्यापक (इतिहास),
महारानी लक्ष्मी बाई शासकीय
उत्कृष्ट महाविद्यालय,
ग्वालियर, मध्य प्रदेश

32. अरविन्द सिंह गौर
शोध छात्र (इतिहास),
ग्वालियर, मध्य प्रदेश

33. डॉ. सुशीला शक्तावत
विभागाध्यक्ष (इतिहास),
गुरूनानक कन्या स्नातकोत्तर
महाविद्यालय, उदयपुर, राजस्थान

34. डॉ. कमला शंकर राठौर
प्रवक्ता, इतिहास विभाग,
जगतपुर पी.जी. कालेज, जगतपुर,
वाराणसी, उत्तर प्रदेश

35. कु. नम्रता श्रीवास्तव
शोध छात्रा, इतिहास विभाग,
वाराणसी, उत्तर प्रदेश

36. डॉ. अल्पना दुभाषे
प्राधयापक एवं विभागाध्यक्ष,
इतिहास विभाग, श्री कृ.प. शा.
स्नातकोत्तर महाविघालय,
देवास, मध्य प्रदेश

37. रजनी श्रीवास्तव
शोधार्थी, ग्वालियर, मध्य प्रदेश

38. डॉ. तेजेन्द्र वल्लभ व्यास
व्याख्याता (इतिहास),
श्री पुष्टिकर श्री पुरोहित सूरजराज
रूपादेवी स्मृति महाविद्यालय,
जोधपुर, राजस्थान

39. डॉ. अनिल पुरोहित
व्याख्याता, इतिहास,
जोधपुर, राजस्थान

40. श्रीमती सोनल पुरोहित
शोधार्थी, इतिहास,
जोधपुर, राजस्थान

41. डॉ. सुनील सक्सैना
सहायक प्राध्यापक, इतिहास
शासकीय के.आर.जी. महाविघालय,
ग्वालियर, मध्य प्रदेश

42. डॉ. मलिका बोहरा
व्याख्याता, इतिहास,
श्री भोगीलाल पंड्या राजकीय
महाविद्यालय, डूंगरपुर, राजस्थान

43. मधुलता मिश्रा
शोधछात्रा, प्राचीन भारतीय इतिहास,
संस्कृति एवं पुरातत्त्व विभाग,
डॉ. हरीसिंह गौर विश्वविद्यालय,
सागर, मध्य प्रदेश

44. डॉ. सुरेन्द्र कुमार विमल
अतिथि व्याख्याता,
शासकीय कमलाराजा कन्या स्वशासी
महाविद्यालय, ग्वालियर, मध्य प्रदेश

45. दिलीप कुमार गर्ग
शोध छात्र, इतिहास,
उदयपुर, राजस्थान

46. कु. रूचि भारद्वाज
शोध छात्रा (इतिहास),
ग्वालियर, मध्य प्रदेश

47. डॉ. एन. बी. लाल
प्रवक्ता (इतिहास),
राजकीय महाविद्यालय माठ,
मथुरा, उत्तर प्रदेश

48. आमिर खान
शोधार्थी, इतिहास,
उदयपुर, राजस्थान

List of Contributors

1. K.P. Singh
   J. R. F., I.C.H.R., New Delhi
   Mohanlal Sukhadia University,
   Udaipur, Rajasthan
2. Ritu Sharma
   J. R. F., I.C.H.R., New Delhi
   Mohanlal Sukhadia University,
   Udaipur, Rajasthan
3. Dr. Asha Shrivastava
   J.R.F., I.C.H.R., New Delhi
4. Dr. Pushpa Dullar
   Professor and Head,
   Visual Art Department,
   Banasthali University, Rajasthan
5. Dr. Gayatri Tandon
   Assistant Professor,
   Visual Art Department,
   Banasthali University, Rajasthan
6. Dr. Vinay Shrivastava
   Department of History,
   Chhatrasal Govt. P.G. College,
   Panna, Madhya Pradesh
7. Dr. Meghna Sharma
   Assistant Professor, History,
   Bikaner University,
   Bikaner, Rajasthan
8. Dr. Aman Kumar Singh
   Faculty, Conservation,
   Delhi Institute of Heritage
   Research and Management,
   New Delhi
9. डॉ. श्याम सुंदर निगम
   निदेशक, कावेरी शोध संस्थान,
   उज्जैन, मध्य प्रदेश
10. डॉ. गिरीश नाथ माथुर
    सेवानिवृत्त प्राध्यापक, इतिहास,
    श्रमजीवी महाविद्यालय,
    उदयपुर, राजस्थान
11. डॉ. पूरन सहगल
    निदेशक, मालव लोक संस्कृति
    अनुष्ठान, मनासा,
    जिला नीमच, मध्य प्रदेश
12. डॉ. संजय स्वर्णकार
    सहायक प्राध्यापक (इतिहास),
    महारानी लक्ष्मीबाई शासकीय उत्कृष्ट
    महाविद्यालय, ग्वालियर, मध्य प्रदेश
13. डॉ. ईश्वरसिंह राणावत
    निदेशक, प्रताप शोध प्रतिष्ठान,
    भूपाल नोबल्स संस्थान,
    उदयपुर, राजस्थान
14. डॉ. अशोक कुमार सिंह
    प्राध्यापक, इतिहास,
    महात्मा गांधी काशी विद्यापीठ,
    वाराणसी, उत्तर प्रदेश
15. अविनाश कुमार दुबे
    शोधार्थी, वाराणसी, उत्तर प्रदेश